, Anonymous

Catalogue, Catholic educational exhibit : with supplementary list of errors and omissions, also list of awards decreed by the World's fair, World's Columbian exposition, Chicago, 1893

, Anonymous

Catalogue, Catholic educational exhibit : with supplementary list of errors and omissions, also list of awards decreed by the World's fair, World's Columbian exposition, Chicago, 1893

ISBN/EAN: 9783742861467

Manufactured in Europe, USA, Canada, Australia, Japa

Cover: Foto ©Lupo / pixelio.de

Manufactured and distributed by brebook publishing software (www.brebook.com)

, Anonymous

Catalogue, Catholic educational exhibit : with supplementary list of errors and omissions, also list of awards decreed by the World's fair, World's Columbian exposition, Chicago, 1893

CATALOGUE

CATHOLIC EDUCATIONAL EXHIBIT

WORLD'S COLUMBIAN EXPOSITION,

CHICAGO, 1893.

Southeast Gallery, Section I, Manufactures and Liberal Arts Building.

CHICAGO:
LA MONTE-O'DONNELL CO., PRINTERS
1893.

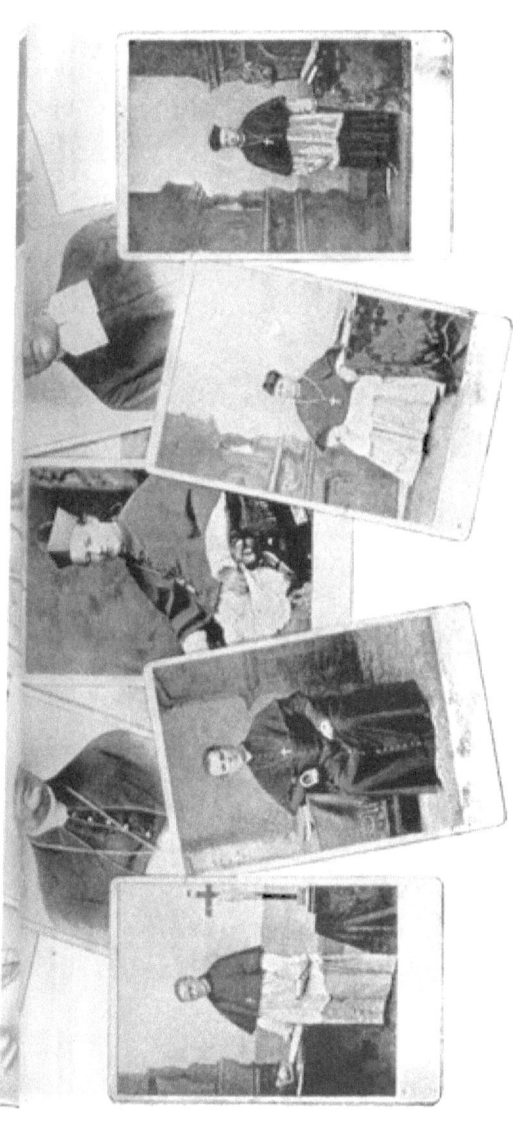

WORLD'S COLUMBIAN EXPOSITION.—THE COMMITTEE ON THE CATHOLIC EDUCATIONAL EXHIBIT.

ARCHBISHOP GROSS, Oregon City.
ARCHBISHOP ELDER, Cincinnati.
CARDINAL GIBBONS, Baltimore.
ARCHBISHOP RYAN, Philadelphia.
ARCHBISHOP KENRICK, St. Louis.
ARCHBISHOP RIORDAN, San Francisco.

ARCHBISHOP KATZER, Milwaukee.
HIS HOLINESS POPE LEO XIII.
ARCHBISHOP CORRIGAN, New York.
ARCHBISHOP IRELAND, St. Paul.

ARCHBISHOP WILLIAMS, Boston.
ARCHBISHOP FEEHAN, Chicago.
ARCHBISHOP JANSSENS, New Orleans.
BISHOP SPALDING, Peoria (Pres't).
BROTHER MAURELIAN, Sec'y and Manager.
ARCHBISHOP SALPOINTE, Santa Fe.

CATALOGUE

Catholic Educational Exhibit

World's Columbian Exposition,

CHICAGO, 1893.

Southeast Gallery, Section I, Manufactures and Liberal Arts Building.

CHICAGO:
LA MONTE-O'DONNELL CO., PRINTERS.
1893.

302716

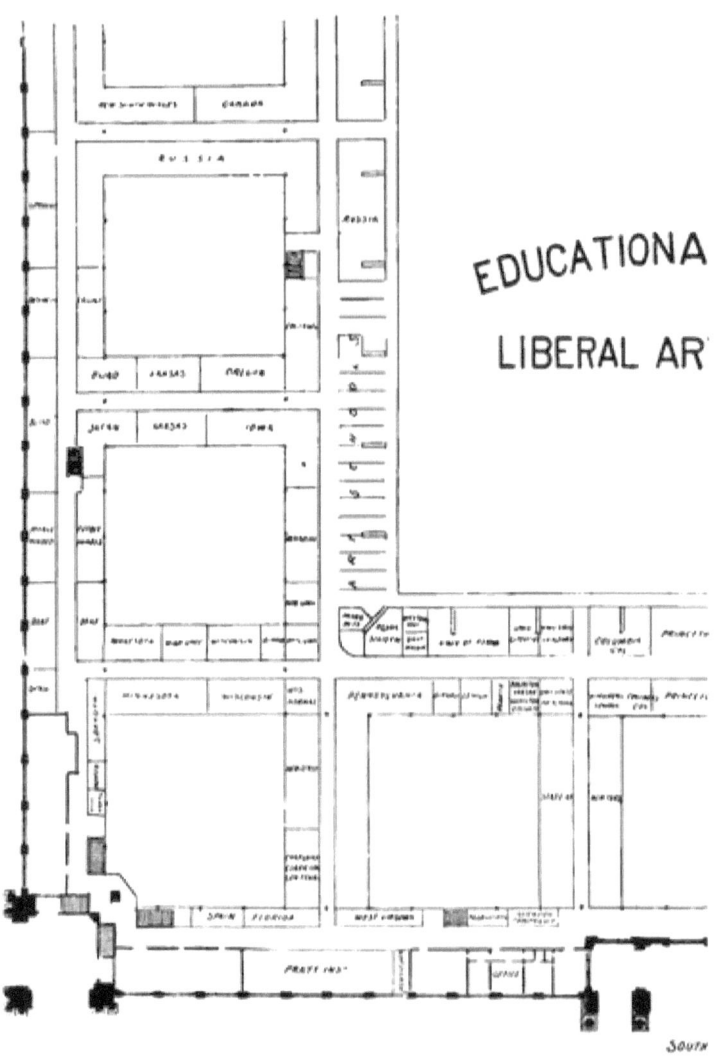

Diagram of allotment of space in the "Manufactures and Lib[eral Arts]"

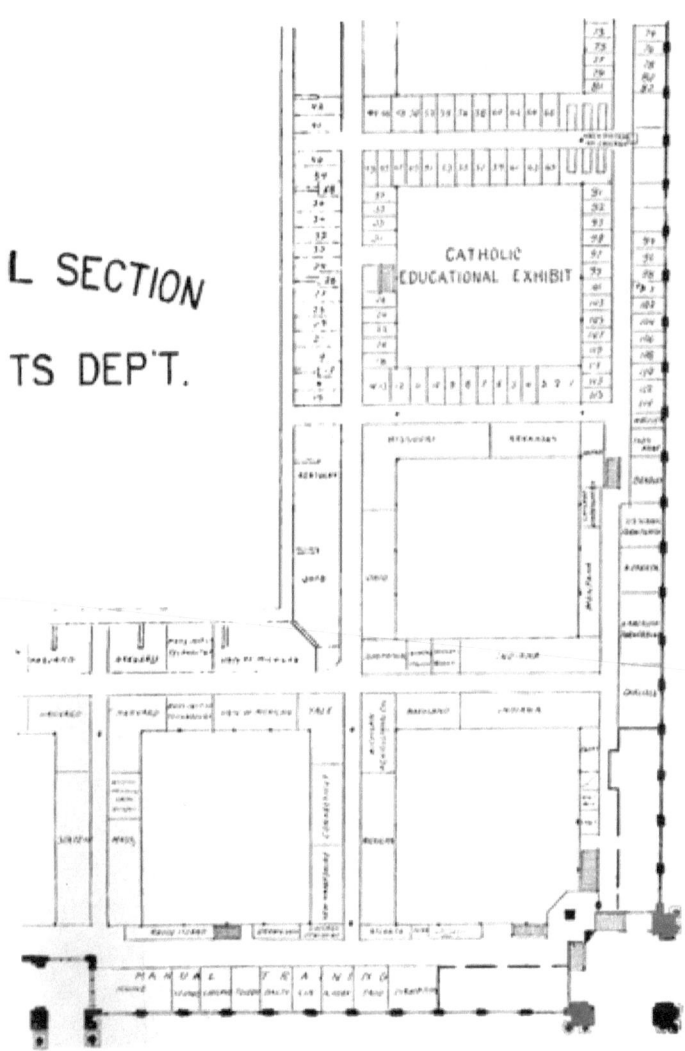

"Educational Section, South Gallery ral Arts Building."

Catholic Educational Exhibit

WORLD'S COLUMBIAN EXPOSITION.

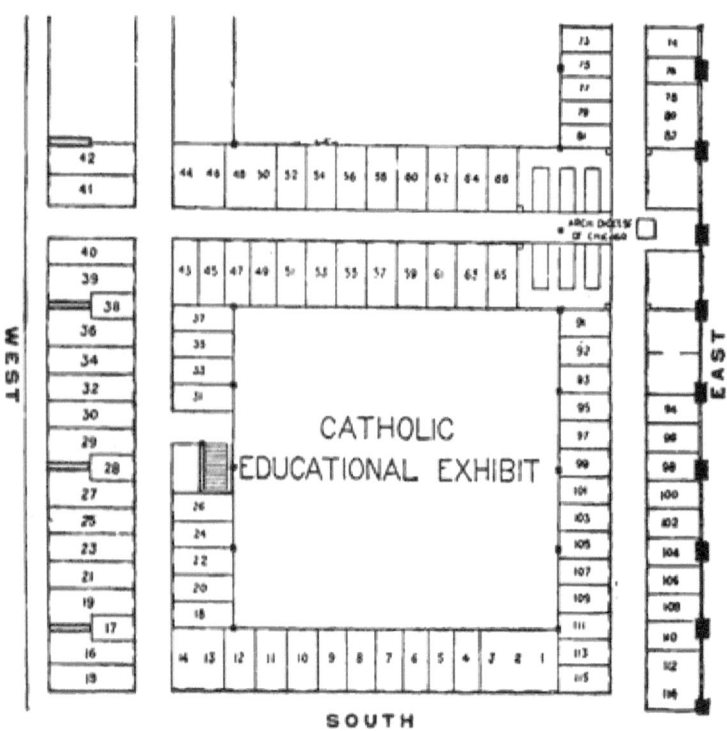

Allotment of space to Catholic Educational Exhibits, Southeast Gallery, Section I, Liberal Arts Department, 29,214 square feet floor space, or 60,000 square feet of wall surface and desk-room.

Location of Diocesan Exhibits.

	ALCOVE
BROOKLYN,	Nos. 18, 20
BUFFALO,	Nos. 29, 30, 32, 34
CHICAGO,	Nos. 67, 68, 69, 70, 71, 72, 73, 74, 86, 87, 88
CLEVELAND,	Nos. 31, 33
COVINGTON,	No. 36
DENVER,	No. 45
DETROIT,	No. 39
DUBUQUE,	Nos. 35, 37
FORT WAYNE,	No. 38
GREEN BAY,	Nos. 24, 26
LA CROSSE,	No. 43
MANCHESTER,	No. 53
MILWAUKEE,	Nos. 1, 2, 3, 4
NATCHEZ,	No. 45
NEW YORK,	Nos. 5, 6, 7, 8, 9, 10, 11, 12, 13, 14, 76, 78
NEW ORLEANS,	No. 22
PHILADELPHIA,	Nos. 15, 16, 40, 75, 99, 103
PITTSBURGH,	Nos. 47, 49, 51
SAN FRANCISCO,	Nos. 17, 19, 21, 23, 25, 27, 28
SIOUX FALLS,	No. 53

RELIGIOUS TEACHING ORDER EXHIBITS.

	ALCOVE
BENEDICTINE FATHERS,	No. 53
BROTHERS OF MARY,	Nos. 89, 91, 93, 95, 55
BROTHERS OF THE SACRED HEART,	Nos. 81, 83
BROTHERS OF THE CHRISTIAN SCHOOLS,	Nos. 75, 77, 79, 95, 96, 97, 98, 99, 100, 101, 102, 103, 104
BROTHERS OF THE CHRISTIAN SCHOOLS (Spain, France, England and Belgium),	Nos. 105, 106, 107, 108, 109, 110, 111, 112, 113, 114, 115
BENEDICTINE SISTERS,	No. 53
CONGREGATION DE NOTRE DAME (Diocese of Boston),	No. 4
CONGREGATION DE NOTRE DAME (Diocese of Sacramento),	No. 66
GRAY NUNS,	No. 5
SCHOOL SISTERS OF NOTRE DAME,	Nos. 1, 2, 3, 4, 58, 60
SISTERS OF CHARITY (B. V. M.),	No. 59
SISTERS OF CHARITY (Emmittsburg),	No. 52
SISTERS OF CHARITY (Nazareth),	Nos. 54, 56
SISTERS OF DIVINE PROVIDENCE,	No. 66
SISTERS OF LORETTO,	Nos. 62, 64
SISTERS OF MERCY,	Nos. 56, 57, 59
SISTERS OF PROVIDENCE (Vigo Co.),	No. 65
SISTERS OF ST. DOMINIC,	No. 4
SISTERS OF ST. FRANCIS,	No. 66
SISTERS OF ST. JOSEPH,	No. 63
SISTERS OF THE PRECIOUS BLOOD,	No. 57
URSULINE NUNS,	No. 62
VISITATION NUNS,	No. 38

INDIVIDUAL EXHIBITS.

	ALCOVE
CATHOLIC UNIVERSITY OF AMERICA, Washington, D. C.,	No. 92
CATHOLIC ARCHIVES OF AMERICA, From Notre Dame University,	No. 44
AMERICAN CATHOLIC HISTORICAL SOCIETY, Philadelphia, Pa.,	No. 40
CATHOLIC TEXT BOOKS,	No. 42
COLUMBIAN LIBRARY OF CATHOLIC AUTHORS,	No. 41

...PREFACE...

Beneath the smoke of recent controversy, like the incantation of a magician, was the Catholic Educational Exhibit fashioned. Just as the wand of peace was waved and away past the clouds of battle, lo! to the gaping world it stood revealed a marvel, a glory and a boast. The Parochial School is apotheosized. The Catholic philosophy of education is vindicated, and thousands of falsehoods have been stigmatized and coffined to be resurrected—never!

The World's Columbian Exposition simply dwarfs all previous attempts at similar displays.

It has been the giant mother of giants. Comparatively speaking, one of its largest offsprings is the Catholic Educational Exhibit. History has no record to show even a meagre approach to its immense showing. 29,214 square feet of floor space, affording over 60,000 square feet of wall and desk surface for the purpose of display, 1,000 linear feet of aisles—these are the official figures that bespeak its magnitude.

The preparation of this Catalogue has been no easy task. Doubtless, many errors and omissions will be noted. The main cause of these will be known when the facts in the case are recalled. Although nearly 1,200 establishments sent exhibits, less than one-fourth the number forwarded lists or catalogues of their work.

Again, the irregularity and tardiness in the arrival of many of the displays rendered the preparation of this Catalogue a very long-drawn, difficult and unsatisfactory labor.

But it is all over now and we rejoice in the triumphant success.

The ardent expectations of the most sanguine have been distanced. From all lips, partisan and non-partisan, have dropped words of praise and exclamations of astonished delight.

All honor to the Most Reverend Prelates, whose positive confidence in Catholic Institutions prompted this magnificent output of intelligent and true education. Praised be the Right Reverend Prelates, Pastors, Superiors of Religious Teaching Orders, and Institutes, and the busy-bee Teachers in the honey-combed hives of the school-houses for the zeal that produced the glorious tribute to education, epitomized in the following pages.

Preface.

The range of the work shown is as limitless as the subject permits. We appeal to these pages to bear out the statement. It is needless to say that the Catholic Educational Exhibit would not have been possible without financial aid. This important element, like the schools that produced the work shown, was supplied by the Most Reverend and Right Reverend Prelates, the Reverend Clergy, Catholic Institutions and many of the Laity. There are obligations still existing; there are expenses yet to be incurred. We sincerely hope that generously disposed persons will give substantial expression of their appreciation.

Several unique features of the display deserve special mention in this preface. The first of these is the wondrous variety and consummate skill of the needle and fancy work, that, in response to our circular of instruction, was so generously forwarded from the convents in our land. The second is the portrait in oil of the Right Reverend John Lancaster Spalding, D. D., Bishop of Peoria, and President of the Catholic Educational Exhibit. The portrait, to be seen at headquarters, is a gift to the exhibit from the Reverend Clergy of the Diocese of Peoria. It is a tribute of affection to their learned and zealous Bishop.

For the purpose of giving due credit and proper recognition to all classes of exhibits, the Catalogue is divided as follows:

PART I.
Diocesan Exhibits.
Collective Exhibits of Religious Teaching Orders.
Individual Exhibits.

PART II.
Classification of Exhibits by Dioceses.

PART III.
Classification of Exhibits by Religious Teaching Orders.

We beg leave to express thanks personally for the warm-hearted and wondrous willingness with which all have responded to our invitations and instructions. We can not fail to set down here an acknowledgment of the courtesy with which we have ever been treated by the Officers of the Exposition, and to call the attention of all to the fair-minded and unprejudiced course they have pursued in all our relations with them in the World's Columbian Exposition.

We shall be happy to supply the deficiencies of this Catalogue, and to correct any errors that may exist, by the publication of a supplementary list. Information on this subject is respectfully invited.

Brother Maurelian,

Secretary and Manager.

RESOLUTIONS

Adopted by the Archbishops at Their Meeting in Chicago, September 14, 1893.

The Archbishops of the United States of America, assembled in Chicago, September 14, 1893, hereby express their appreciation of the zeal of those who have responded to their invitation of July, 1890, to unite in the National Catholic Educational Exhibit at the World's Columbian Exposition.

They cheerfully indorse the sentiment universally expressed as to the high merit of all kinds of work from institutions of every grade, ranging from the kindergarten to the university and ecclesiastical seminary.

In recognition of the services rendered the great cause of Catholic Education by those who have in any way contributed to this magnificent exhibit,

Resolved, That we acknowledge the services of our beloved brother, Right Reverend John Lancaster Spalding, to the Catholic Church in the United States, in having consented to assume the responsibility of President of the Catholic Educational Exhibit, and in having guided this undertaking to a successful issue by his wisdom, prudence and skill.

Resolved, That we express our sense of the value of the labors of Brother Maurelian, secretary and manager, in the difficult work of directing the preparation and installation of the exhibits, and that we tender him our sincere thanks for his services in behalf of Catholic Education.

Resolved, That we express our heartfelt pleasure and high appreciation of the earnest efforts of our prelates, clergy, the religious of the various brotherhoods and sisterhoods, secular educators, Catholic authors and publishers and the laity in general, who have made this exhibit possible by their co-operation.

Resolved, That graded certificates of award be issued to institutions having exhibits according to the extent and merit of each, and that fac-similes of the signatures of His Holiness Pope Leo XIII., of His Eminence Cardinal Gibbons, and of Bishop Spalding be engraved on the certificates, and that they be countersigned by the secretary.

Resolved, That Right Reverend Bishop Spalding, president, be requested to appoint a committee on awards to carry out the intent of the foregoing resolution.

Resolved, That we offer our grateful acknowledgments to the World's Fair Officials for their uniform kindness and courtesy to our representatives at the World's Columbian Exposition.

Resolved, That these resolutions be spread on the minutes, and that they be duly made known to all interested.

THE ARCHBISHOPS OF THE UNITED STATES OF AMERICA.

P. W. RIORDAN, *Archbishop of San Francisco*,
Chairman Committee on Resolutions, Catholic Educational Exhibit.

CHICAGO, September 14, 1893.

PART I.

DIOCESAN EXHIBITS.

ARCHDIOCESE OF CHICAGO.

MOST REV. P. A. FEEHAN, D. D.

Diocesan Committee.

Rev. H. MAGUIRE, *Chairman.*
Rev. T. J. BUTLER.
Rev. M. W. BARTH.
Rev. M. J. FITZSIMONS.
Rev. T. P. HODNETT.
Rev. A. J. TEELY.
Rev. P. J. MULDOON, *Secretary.*

The beautiful statue in Carara Marble, which adorns the exhibit, is a gift of the Clergy of the Archdiocese to Most Rev. P. A. Feehan, D. D., who has accomplished so much for education, and who so well merits the title lovingly bestowed upon him, "The Protector of Our Schools."

Printed Catalogue of the Catholic Educational Exhibit, describing schools and giving full details of the exhibits of sixty (60) Parochial Schools, one College, nine Academies, two Houses of the Good Shepherd, two Orphan Asylums, one Training School, one Ephpheta School, and one Infant Asylum.

There is a splendid exhibit of Miss Eliza Allen Starr's Art School.

PARISH SCHOOLS.

CHICAGO, ILL.

Holy Name School.

MALE DEPT.—*Brothers of St. Viateur.*

3 Volumes Class-Work. Primary and Grammar Departments.

FEMALE DEPT.—*Religious of the Sacred Heart.*

9 Volumes: Class-Work, Needle-Work, Embroidery, Crochet-Work and Photographs.

St. Agnes' School.—*Sisters of Mercy.*

12 Volumes: Bible History, Catechism, United States History, Language, Geography, Compositions, Physiology, Spelling, Writing, Arithmetic, Map Drawing, Ornamental Writing. 9 Framed Maps. 1 Volume Work by Katie Forbes, a cripple born without hands.

All Saints' School.—*Sisters of Mercy.*

13 Volumes: Bible History, Christian Doctrine, History, Mensuration, Compositions, Language, Geography, Maps, History Maps, Pen Sketches, Photographs, Theory of Music. 25 Copy Books, 4 Portfolios of Drawing, 3 Framed Maps and 2 Pen Portraits.

St. Aloysius' School.—*Sisters of Christian Charity.*

7 Volumes: Map Drawing, German, Intermediate Work, Grammar, Needle-Work and 17 Pieces of Needle-Work.

Annunciation School.—*Sisters of Charity, B. V. M.*

16 Volumes: Class-Work, Framed Maps and Samples of Needle-Work. 7 Volumes Examination Papers.

St. Bridget's School.—*Sisters of Charity, B. V. M.*

15 Volumes: Class-Work, Framed Maps and Samples of Needle-Work.

St. Charles' School.—*Sisters of Charity, B. V. M.*

7 Volumes Class-Work and 4 Volumes Map Drawing.

St. Columbkille's School.

MALE DEPT.—*Brothers of the Holy Cross.*

1 Volume each: Language, Arithmetic, Catechism, Geography, History, Orthography and Book-Keeping.

FEMALE DEPT.—*Sisters of Charity (Emmittsburg).*

16 Volumes: Kindergarten, Class-Work, Mathematics, Language, Science, English and Church History, Map Drawing, Photographs, 4 Pastel Paintings, 4 Pen Sketches and 7 Paintings from Object.

St. Elizabeth's School.—*Sisters of Mercy.*

31 Volumes: Christian Doctrine, Writing, Latin, Essay, Ancient History, Physical Geography, Algebra, Compositions, Language, Arithmetic, Physiology, Spelling, United States History, Physiology, Bible History, Drawing, 19 Maps and Photographs.

CHICAGO, ILL.—Continued.

St. Francis of Assissi's School.

Male Dept.—*Brothers of Mary.*

27 Volumes: Christian Doctrine, Sacred History, German Language Dictations, Compositions, English Language Dictations, Translations, English Compositions, Letter Writing, Arithmetic, Book-Keeping, Commercial Law, Music, English and German Penmanship, Pen-Work, United States History, Geography, Geometrical and Mechanical Drawing, Freehand Drawing and Photographs.

Female Dept.—*Franciscan Sisters.*

22 Volumes: Writing, Compositions, Arithmetic, Language, Spelling, Geography, Dictations, Grammar, Letters, Bible History, Translations, United States History, Business Forms, Map Drawing, Drawing, Fancy Pen-Work and 17 Pieces of Fancy Work.

St. Gabriel's School.—*Sisters of Mercy.*

32 Volumes: Arithmetic, Language, Compositions, Catechism, Spelling, Geography, Physiology, History, Drawing, Map Drawing, Music, Map of the United States, Crayon Portrait and Map of War Campaign.

St. George's School.—*Sisters of Notre Dame.*

2 Volumes: Penmanship, Grammar, Compositions, Arithmetic, United States History, Spelling, Christian Doctrine, Bible History, German and Geography.

Holy Angels' School.—*Sisters of Mercy.*

17 Volumes: Arithmetic, United States and Bible History, Language, Spelling, Writing, Geography, Christian Doctrine and 1 Map of Illinois.

Holy Family School.

11 Volumes Catechism, 6 Volumes History, 9 Volumes Arithmetic, 10 Volumes Penmanship, 9 Volumes Geography, 7 Volumes Grammar, 1 Volume Language, 9 Volumes Orthography, 1 Volume Current Topics, 2 Volumes Commercial Law, 1 Volume Civil Government, 1 Volume Mensuration, 10 Volumes Map Drawing, 3 Volumes Book-Keeping, 1 Volume Natural Philosophy, 2 Volumes Physiology, 1 Volume Phonography, 1 Volume Typewriting, 1 Volume Typesetting and 1 Volume Printing.

Sacred Heart School.—*Religious of the Sacred Heart.*

6 Volumes Christian Doctrine, 5 Volumes Language, 4 Volumes Geography, 6 Volumes Arithmetic, 4 Volumes United States History, 3 Volumes Physiology, 1 Volume Algebra, 2 Volumes Book-Keeping, 1 Volume Special Maps and Fancy Work.

St. Aloysius' School.—*Sisters of Charity, B. V. M.*

11 Volumes Class-Work, 3 Volumes Music, Map Drawing and Needle-Work.

St. Agnes' School.—*Sisters of Charity, B. V. M.*

5 Volumes Class-Work and 1 Volume Drawing.

St. Joseph's School.—*Sisters of Charity, B. V. M.*

6 Volumes Class-Work and 1 Volume Drawing.

Guardian Angel School.—*Sisters of Charity, B. V. M.*

2 Volumes Class-Work and 1 Volume Drawing.

CHICAGO, ILL.,—Continued

Immaculate Conception School.—*Dominican Sisters.*

5 Volumes Class-Work, 13 Framed Maps, 20 Specimens Various Kinds of Sewing, 2 Portfolios of Music, 1 Ship (Boys' Handiwork) and Photographs of School (Framed).

St. James' School.—*Sisters of Mercy.*

20 Drawing Books, 5 Copy Books Writing, 14 Volumes Language Lessons, 4 Volumes Christian Doctrine, 6 Volumes Geography, 3 Volumes History, 9 Volumes Compositions, 1 Volume Map Drawing, 1 Relief Map, 6 Volumes Daily Work, 2 Volumes Mensuration, 1 Volume Bible History and Christian Doctrine, 1 Volume United States History, 1 Volume History Tests, 1 Volume Geometry, 2 Volumes Essays, 1 Volume Book Reviews, Poems and Themes, 1 Volume Physics and Zoology, 1 Volume Doctrinal Essays, 2 Volumes Algebra, 2 Volumes Latin, 1 Volume Zoology and Botany, 4 Portfolios of Maps, 6 Volumes History and Latin, 1 Volume Physiology, 2 Volumes United States History, 1 Volume Bible History, 24 Pen Sketches, 4 Charcoal Sketches, 8 Pastel Studies, 2 Charts English Literature, Relief Maps, Crayon, Sepia and Water-Color Drawings, Kindergarten.

St. Jarlath's School.—*Dominican Sisters.*

8 Volumes: Catechism, Orthography, Language, Arithmetic, Letters, Penmanship, Geography, Map and Freehand Drawing, Bible History, Grammar, Compositions, Physiology, American Literature, Maps and Framed Drawing.

St. John Nepomucene's School.—*Benedictine Sisters.*

3 Volumes English Studies, 2 Volumes Bohemian Studies.

St. Joseph's School.—*Benedictine Sisters:*

12 Volumes Class-Work, 2 Volumes Drawings, Specimens of Crocheting, Plain Sewing, and Drawn-Work, 5 Crayon Drawings and 2 Pastel Drawings.

St. Malachy's School.—*Sisters of Mercy.*

9 Volumes Class-Work, 4 Volumes Drawing, 1 Volume Photographs, 2 Volumes Maps, 8 Pieces Framed Work.

St. Michael's School.

MALE DEPT.—*Brothers of Mary.*

1 Volume Catechism and Church History, 1 Volume German Dictations, 1 Volume German Grammar, 1 Volume German Compositions, 1 Volume German Penmanship, 1 Volume German Translations, 1 Volume English Dictations, 1 Volume English Grammar, 2 Volumes English Compositions, 2 Volumes English Penmanship, 1 Volume History, 2 Volumes Arithmetic, 1 Volume Pen-Work, Civics, Commercial Law, Music, 1 Volume Book-Keeping, 1 Volume Geography, 1 Volume Writing and Drawing, 7 Volumes Drawing, 1 Volume Geometrical and Crayon Drawings, 1 Volume General Class-Work, 1 Volume Home-Work, 1 Volume Photographs.

FEMALE DEPT.—*School Sisters of Notre Dame.*

12 Volumes English Class-Work, 7 Volumes German Class-Work, 3 Volumes English and German Class-Work, 1 Volume Ornamental Pen-Work, 14 Volumes Drawing, Samples of Plain and Fancy Sewing and Knitting, Samples of Crocheting, Tapestry and Art Embroidery, 10 Fancy Articles Painted on Celluloid and Silk, 1 Oil Painting on Celluloid.

CHICAGO, ILL.—CONTINUED.

Nativity School—BOYS AND GIRLS.—*Sisters of St. Joseph.*

20 Volumes Class-Work from First to Eighth Grade, 2 Volumes Drawing, 1 Volume Penmanship, 2 Volumes Map Drawing Third to Eighth Grade, 1 Album Photographs, 18 Volumes Theoretical and Practical Music, Photograph of School (Framed.)

Our Lady of Sorrows.—*Sisters of Providence.*

5 Volumes Class-Work from First to Twelfth Grade, Series of Penmanship, Copy Books, Series of Drawing Copy Books.

St. Patrick's School—GIRLS.—*Sisters of Charity.*

7 Volumes Graded Class-Work from Second to Eighth Grade, 1 Volume Work from First and Second Academic, 1 Volume Leaves from "Our Alma Mater," 1 Volume Freehand Drawing, 1 Album Photographs, 1 Volume Miscellaneous Items, 1 Volume Kindergarten, 5 Paintings, 2 Drawings, 7 Maps, Fancy Work and Plain Sewing.

St. Patrick's School (South Chicago).—*Sisters of Mercy.*

21 Volumes: Catechism, Spelling, Grammar, Arithmetic, Grammar, Compositions, Language, Geography, History, Drawing, Physiology, Map Drawing and Pen-Work.

St. Paul's School.—*Sisters of Notre Dame.*

17 Volumes: English and German Class-Work, Physiology, United States History, Book-Keeping, Penmanship, Geography, Hygiene, Arithmetic, Language, Grammar, Penmanship, Spelling, Compositions, Letter Writing, Translations. 9 Volumes Drawing—Map, Linear, and Freehand. Specimens of Needle-Work, Kindergarten.

Notre Dame de Chicago School.—*Sisters of Notre Dame.*

1 Volume Superior French Course, 1 Volume Elementary French Course, 4 Volumes Formes, Superior English Course, 1 Volume French and English Course. 6 Volumes: Catechism, Bible History, Grammar, Spelling, Arithmetic, 7 Astronomical Charts, 7 Geographical Charts, 1 Chronological Chart, Series of Drawing Books, Series of Penmanship, Specimens of Plain and Fancy Sewing, Embroidery, Specimens of Mending and Darning.

Mt. Carmel Academy.—*Sisters of Mercy.*

14 Volumes: Catechism, Spelling, Language, Composition, Physiology, United States History, Bible History, Map Drawing, Physical Geography, Essays, Algebra, Literature, English History, Civil Government, Rhetoric, Zoology, French, Latin, German, Music and Drawing.

St. Phillip's School.—*Sisters of Providence.*

3 Volumes: Corrected Reviews in Miscellaneous Grammar-School Studies. (Boys' Dept.), Corrected Reviews of Grammar-School Studies (Girls' Dept.); Miscellaneous Work (Girls' Dept.): Map Drawing, Needle-Work, Literature, Specimens of Penmanship and Drawing.

St. Pius' School.—*Sisters of Charity, B. V. M.*

MALE DEPT.

15 Volumes: Miscellaneous School-Work, Map Drawing, Freehand and Object Drawing.

FEMALE DEPT.

50 Volumes Graded School-Work and 29 Specimens of Map Drawing.

CHICAGO, ILL.—Continued.

St. Procopius' School.—*Franciscan Sisters.*

English—1 Volume Each: Grammar, Spelling and Arithmetic. Bohemian—1 Volume Each: Catechism, Bible History, Grammar; 2 Volumes Class-Work; 3 Volumes Drawing, 7 Framed Drawings.

Sacred Heart School.—*Sisters of Charity.*

19 Volumes Class-Work, 2 Volumes Music, 3 Volumes Map Drawing, 9 Pieces Framed Work, 1 Piece Modeling.

St. Stanislaus Kostka's School.—*Sisters of Notre Dame.*

73 Volumes Class-Work, 5 Volumes Drawing, 1 Volume Photographs, Pastel Pictures, Specimens of Various Kinds of Needle-Work.

St. Stephen's School.—*Sisters of St. Joseph.*

8 Volumes Class-Work, 1 Volume Map Drawing, 2 Volumes Drawing.

St. Teresa's School.—*Sisters of Christian Charity.*

5 Volumes Class-Work—Catechism, Bible History, German, Dictations, Language, Arithmetic, Grammar, Compositions, Spelling, Geography, Translations, United States History, Map and Pencil Drawing. 1 Volume Darning and Mending, 1 Volume Knitting, Crocheting, 1 Volume Plain Sewing, 1 Volume Articles cut and made ready for the Machine, Fancy Articles of Embroidery.

St. Thomas' School.—*Sisters of St. Dominic.*

6 Volumes Class-Work, 1 Volume Drawing, 1 Volume Map Drawing, 1 Volume Paper-Work, Framed Maps and Drawing.

St. Vincent's Academy.—*Sisters of Charity, B. V. M.*

15 Volumes Class-Work, 1 Volume Map Drawing, 2 Volumes Drawing, 2 Volumes Music, and Framed Maps.

St. Winceslaus' School.—*Franciscan Sisters.*

9 Volumes Class-Work, 2 Volumes Drawing, 1 Volume Knitting and Stitching, 1 Volume Crocheting, 1 Volume Fancy Penmanship, 27 Pieces Fancy Needle-Work.

AURORA, ILL.

St. Nicholas' School.—*Sisters of St. Francis.*

2 Writing Books, 1 Drawing Book, 2 Banners, Sewing and Kindergarten Work.

Sacred Heart School.—*Sisters of the Congregation de Notre Dame.*

2 Volumes Class-Work and 2 Maps.

FREEPORT, ILL.

St. Joseph's School.—*Sisters of St. Francis.*

8 Volumes Class-Work and 1 Volume Needle-Work.

JOLIET, ILL.

St. John Baptist School.—*Sisters of St. Francis.*

6 Volumes Class-Work, 2 Volumes Pencil Drawings, 1 Volume Fancy Pen-Work, Map Drawing, 43 Specimens Needle-Work.

LOCKPORT, ILL.

Sacred Heart School.—*Sisters of Providence.*
1 Volume Class-Work.

MORRIS, ILL.

Immaculate Conception School.—*Sisters of the Holy Cross.*
1 Volume Maps and Examination Papers.

ROCKFORD, ILL.

St. James' School.—*Sisters of St. Dominic.*
6 Volumes Class-Work, 2 Volumes Map Drawing, 2 Volumes Object Drawing and 1 Volume Penmanship.

ST. ANNE, ILL.

St. Anne's School.—*Congregation de Notre Dame.*
2 Volumes Class-Work, 13 Copy Books of Writing, Needle-Work.

WILLMETTE, ILL.

St. Joseph's School.
6 Volumes Class-Work, 1 Volume Drawing, 1 Volume Maps and Needle-Work.

ACADEMIES.

CHICAGO, ILL.

Sts. Benedict and Scholastica's Academy.—*Benedictine Sisters.*
6 Volumes Class-Work, 12 Oil Paintings, 4 Water Colors, 5 Drawings from the Antique, Bullion and Silk Embroidery.

St. Francis Xavier's Academy.—*Sisters of Mercy.*
17 Volumes Examination Papers, 15 Volumes Ornamental Penmanship, 2 Volumes Essays, 2 Volumes Photographs, 1 Volume "The Echo," 4 Volumes Music, 44 Paintings, 1 Portfolio Drawings from Still Life, 1 Portfolio Drawings from Cast, 2 Volumes Perspective Drawings and 1 Book from Medallions.

Josephinum Academy.—*Sisters of Christian Charity.*
8 Volumes Class-Work, 27 Pieces Needle-Work, 8 Oil Paintings, 7 Crayons.

St. Patrick's Commercial Academy.—*Christian Brothers.*
3 Volumes Christian Doctrine, 2 Volumes Grammar, 1 Volume Natural Philosophy, 3 Volumes Compositions, 7 Volumes Book-Keeping, 1 Volume Commercial Law, 3 Volumes Arithmetic, 1 Volume Mensuration, 3 Volumes Monthly Examinations, 4 Volumes General Class-Work, 1 Volume Phonographic Exercises, 3 Volumes Specimens of Penmanship, 8 Volumes Showing System of Penmanship.

St. Patrick's Academy.—*Sisters of Mercy.*
1 Volume each: Christian Doctrine, Algebra, History, Rhetoric, Science, Church History, Geometry, Trigonometry, Chemistry, Physics, Philosophy, Essays, French, German, Catalogues, Photographs, Academia, Maps, Poems, Gems from Geology, Literature, Herbarium. 3 Volumes Drawings, 2 Volumes Latin, 5 Volumes Thorough Bass, 2 Volumes Original Music, 4 Volumes Kindergarten Work, 21 Paintings, 11 Pieces Needle-Work, Decorated China.

BOURBONNAIS, ILL.

Notre Dame Academy.—*Sisters of Congregation de Notre Dame, Montreal.*

7 Volumes Class-Work, 1 Volume Photographs, 47 Drawings, 30 Pieces Needle-Work.

JOLIET, ILL.

St. Francis' Academy.—*Sisters of St. Francis.*

9 Volumes Class-Work, 2 Volumes Drawing, 1 Volume Pen Drawing, 1 Volume Etiquette, 1 Volume Catalogues, Essays, Studies in Water Colors, 20 Drawings, 5 Photographs, 2 Pieces Tapestry Needle-Work, 41 Articles Decorative and Fancy Needle-Work.

KANKAKEE, ILL.

St. Joseph's Seminary.—*Sisters of Congregation de Notre Dame, Montreal.*

8 Volumes Class-Work, 1 Volume Music, 11 Drawings, 15 Paintings, 2 Pieces Hair-Work, 28 Pieces Needle-Work, Kindergarten, and Photographs.

St. Rose's School.—*Sisters of Congregation de Notre Dame, Montreal.*

2 Volumes Class-Work, 4 Volumes Drawing, 1 Volume Kindergarten Work, 1 Volume Map Drawing, 1 Volume Photographs.

St. Viateur's College.—*Priests and Brothers of the Community of St. Viateur.*

1 Volume Class-Work (Preparatory Dept.), 2 Volumes Penmanship, 1 Volume Book-Keeping, 1 Volume Arithmetic, 1 Volume Spelling, Compositions, 1 Volume English Grammar, 1 Volume Rhetoric, Compositions, 1 Volume History, Compositions and Geography, 1 Volume Literary and Military Societies, 2 Volumes Latin and Greek, 1 Volume French and German, 1 Volume Mathematics and Science, 1 Volume Evidences of Religion, 1 Volume Intellectual Philosophy, 1 Volume Philosophy of History, 1 Volume—Ode "The Cross and Columbus," 1 Volume "Epines et Fleurs," 1 Volume "Liola-Legende Indienne," 6 Volumes St. Viateur's College Journal. Photographs: Faculty, Students, Associations, and College Buildings; Mineralogical, Entomological, Botanical, and Conchological Specimens from College Museum.

LONGWOOD, ILL.

Institute of Our Lady of the Sacred Heart.—*Sisters de Notre Dame.*

1 Volume Spelling, Etymology, Language, 1 Volume Grammar, Rhetoric, 2 Volumes Geography, Civil Government, 1 Volume Physiology, Natural History, 1 Volume Arithmetic, 1 Volume Algebra, Geometry, Orthography, Typewriting, 2 Volumes Compositions, 2 Volumes Literature, 1 Volume Astronomy, History, Physics, 1 Volume Harmonic Exercises, 1 Volume Book-Keeping, 1 Folio Freehand Drawing, 1 Folio Maps, 2 Folios Charts, 1 Folio Ornamental Pen-Work, 1 Cabinet of Insects, 1 Chart of Currents and Rain Fall, 16 Paintings, 7 Crayon Drawings, 1 Photograph of the Institute.

SPECIAL SCHOOLS.

CHICAGO, ILL.

Ephpheta School.—*Religious of the Sacred Heart.*

2 Volumes Class-Work, 2 Volumes Ephpheta Paper, 1 Volume Photographs, Specimens of Drawing, Carving, Modeling, and Needle-Work.

CHICAGO, ILL.—CONTINUED.

House of the Good Shepherd.—*Sisters of the Good Shepherd.*
Specimens of Needle-Work, Embroidery, Drawn-Work, and Fancy Stitching.

Chicago Industrial School—Girls.—*Sisters of the Good Shepherd.*
Specimens of Needle-Work.

St. Joseph's Orphan Asylum.—*Sisters of St. Joseph.*
5 Volumes Class-Work, 1 Album Drawing, 1 Album Lace and Crochet Work, 1 Folio Kindergarten Work, Specimens Needle-Work, Embroidery, Knitting, Painting in Oil, Photographs.

St. Joseph's Providence Asylum.—*Sisters of St. Joseph.*
1 Volume Class-Work, 2 Volumes Map Drawing, Framed Photographs.

St. Vincent's Infant Asylum.—*Sisters of Charity.*
1 Volume Kindergarten Work.

Miss Eliza Allan Starr's Art Exhibit.
Studies in Oil, Crayon and Charcoal Drawing.

FEEHANVILLE, ILL.

St. Mary's Training School.—*Christian Brothers.*
1 Album Photographs, 2 Volumes Specimens of Painting, 12 Pairs Shoes, 6 Suits of Clothes, 6 Volumes Class-Work and 1 Volume Reports.

ARCHDIOCESE OF DUBUQUE.

Most Rev. John Hennessy, D. D.

Diocesan Committee.

Rev. M. A. Cooney.   Rev. R. Slattery.

ALCOVES 35 AND 37.

Portrait of His Grace Archbishop Hennessy.

COLLEGES, ACADEMIES and SELECT SCHOOLS.

DUBUQUE, IOWA.

St. Joseph's College.—*Secular Priests.*
3 Volumes: Trigonometry, Algebra, Book-Keeping, Arithmetic, Mental and Moral Philosophy, Shakespeare and English Literature, English Grammar, Ancient and Modern History.

St. Joseph's Academy.—*Sisters of Charity, B. V. M.*
4 Volumes: Christian Doctrine, Map Drawing, Geography, Geology, Drawing, Relief Exercises, Word Building, Orthography.

DUBUQUE, IOWA.—Continued.

Visitation Academy.—*Sisters of the Visitation.*

14 Pictures, 6 Pieces of Plain Sewing, 10 Maps. 4 Volumes: Christian Doctrine, Arithmetic, Literature, Physiology and Rhetoric.

Sacred Heart School.—*Nuns of the Presentation, B. V. M.*

2 Volumes: Drawing, History, Book-Keeping, Christian Doctrine, Map Drawing and Grammar.

Presentation Convent.—*Presentation Sisters.*

3 Volumes: Christian Doctrine, Grammar, Map Drawing, Letter Writing, Spelling, Arithmetic, Kindergarten Work, Natural Science, Book-Keeping, Stenography and Typewriting.

ACKLEY, IOWA.

Sacred Heart Academy.—*Sisters of Charity, B. V. M.*

7 Volumes: Map Drawing, Mechanical Drawing, Christian Doctrine, Arithmetic, Spelling, Recitations, Modern History, Physiology, Geometry, History and Kindergarten Work.

CEDAR RAPIDS, IOWA.

St. Joseph's Academy.—*Sisters of Charity.*

7 Volumes: Drawing, Christian Doctrine, Geography, United States History, Catechism, Language, Arithmetic and Kindergarten Work.

DECORAH, IOWA.

Immaculate Conception Academy.—*Sisters of Mercy.*

1 Volume: Map Drawing, Spelling, Mechanical Drawing, Kindergarten Work, Geography, Map Drawing, Book-Keeping, Christian Doctrine and Arithmetic.

DE WITT, IOWA.

St. Joseph's Academy.—*Sisters of Mercy.*

1 Volume: Astronomy, Geography, Geometry, Physical Geography, Grammar and Church History.

LYONS, IOWA.

Our Lady of Angels' Seminary.—*Sisters of St. Francis.*

2 Volumes: Christian Doctrine, Astronomy, Geometry, Chemistry, Geology, Algebra, Physiology, Botany, Music, Philosophy, Peacock Worked on Silk, and Celluloid Painting.

MASON CITY, IOWA.

St. Francis Academy.—*Franciscan Sisters.*

2 Maps of the United States.

WAUKON, IOWA.

PARISH SCHOOLS.

DUBUQUE, IOWA.

Sacred Heart School.—*Sisters of St. Francis.*

10 Volumes: Christian Doctrine, Arithmetic, Geography, United States History, Composition, Penmanship, Grammar and Catechism.

St. Mary's School.—*Sisters of Charity, B. V. M.*

3 Volumes: Arithmetic, Spelling, Geography, Letter Writing, Map Drawing and Language.

St. Mary's German School.—*Sisters of Charity, B. V. M.*

12 Volumes: Kindergarten Work, Geography, Grammar, Christian Doctrine, Orthography, Compositions, Map-Drawing, Mechanical Drawing, Translations, Letter Writing.

St. Raphael's School.—*Sisters of Charity, B. V. M.*

4 Volumes: Compositions, Geography, Christian Doctrine, Music, Drawing, Catechism and Geography.

ALTON, IOWA.

St. Mary's School.—*Franciscan Sisters.*

1 Volume: Drawing, Spelling, German, Christian Doctrine, Compositions and Map Drawing.

BALLTOWN, IOWA.

St. Francis' School.—*Franciscan Sisters of P. A.*

2 Volumes: Christian Doctrine, Geography, Language, German, Grammar, Arithmetic and Drawing.

BELLEVUE, IOWA.

St. Joseph's School.—*Franciscan Sisters of P. A.*

2 Volumes: Christian Doctrine, Arithmetic, United States History, Compositions, Letter Writing, Grammar, Hygiene, Business Forms and Physiology.

BREDA, IOWA.

St. Bernard's School.—*Franciscan Sisters of P. A.*

1 Volume Map Drawing; 2 Volumes: Christian Doctrine, Bible History, Arithmetic, Language, Grammar, Dictation, Translations, Phonography, Compositions, Physiology, United States History, Geography and Business Forms.

CARROLL, IOWA.

St. Anthony's School.—*Franciscan Sisters of P. A.*

2 Volumes: Christian Doctrine, Arithmetic, Geography, Commercial Exercises, Letter Writing, Mechanical Drawing and United States History.

St. Joseph's School.—*Franciscan Sisters of P. A.*

2 Volumes: Mechanical Drawing, Arithmetic, Christian Doctrine, Phonography, Geography, United States History and Epistolary Correspondence.

Sts. Peter and Paul's School.—*Franciscan Sisters of P. A.*

2 Volumes: Catechism, Christian Doctrine, Bible History, Grammar, Physiology, Compositions and Geography.

CASCADE, IOWA.

St. Mary's School.—*Franciscan Sisters.*

5 Volumes: History, Christian Doctrine, Compositions, Grammar, Book-Keeping, Penmanship, Arithmetic, United States History, Physiology. Crochet Lace, Drawn-Work on Handkerchief, 2 Splashers, 2 Wreaths of Paper Flowers, 1 Fascinator, 2 Lamp Mats, 8 Tidies, Patch-Work, Child's Apron, Crochet Hood, Table Cover, Sachet Bag, 2 Wall Pockets, Child's Cape, Crochet Tidy, Child's Dress, Baby Dress, Splasher and Quilt.

St. Martin's School.—*Sisters of Charity, B. V. M.*

2 Volumes: Christian Doctrine, Arithmetic, Geography, Epistolary Correspondence, Physiology, Christian Doctrine, Arithmetic, Geography, United States History, Language and Penmanship.

CEDAR RAPIDS, IOWA.

St. Joseph's School.—*Sisters of Mercy.*

1 Table Cover Worked in White Silk and Gilt Spangles and Kindergarten Work.

CLINTON, IOWA.

St. Mary's School.—*Sisters of Charity, B. V. M.*

6 Volumes: Geometry, Rhetoric, Ancient History, Chemistry, Arithmetic, Map Drawing, Christian Doctrine, Compositions, Mechanical Drawing and Kindergarten Work. 1 Album Map Drawing, 3 Albums Paper Folding and 1 Volume Book-Keeping.

St. Patrick's School.—*Franciscan Sisters.*

1 Volume: Photographs, Letter Writing, Arithmetic, Geography, Dictations, Compositions and Christian Doctrine. 1 Volume Drawing.

DYERSVILLE, IOWA.

St. Francis' Xavier's School.—*Sisters of St. Francis.*

4 Volumes: Kindergarten Work, Christian Doctrine, Geography, United States History, and Map Drawing. 1 Knitted Scarf, 1 Paper Map and 1 Crochet Tidy.

FARLEY, IOWA.

St. Joseph's School.—*Presentation Sisters.*

1 Volume Algebra, Arithmetic, Book-Keeping, History, Geography, Physiology, Civil Government, United States History, Spelling.

FESTINA, IOWA.

St. Mary's School.—*Franciscan Sisters of B. V. M.*

2 Volumes: Christian Doctrine, German, Geography, History, Arithmetic, Paraphrasing, Compositions, Translations, United States History, Epistolary Correspondence, Book-Keeping and Grammar.

FT. DODGE, IOWA.

Our Lady of Lourdes' School.—*Sisters of Mercy.*

2 Volumes: Arithmetic, Grammar, Christian Doctrine, Astronomy, Geography and Map Drawing.

GRANVILLE, IOWA.

Parochial School.—*Franciscan Sisters.*

2 Charts Kindergarten Work, Orthography, Christian Doctrine, Geography and Map Drawing.

HAVERHILL, IOWA.

Immaculate Conception School.—*Franciscan Sisters of P. A.*

1 Volume: German Exercise, Geography, Catechism, Mechanical Drawing, Arithmetic and Christian Doctrine.

KEY WEST, IOWA.

St. Joseph's School.—*Franciscan Sisters of P. A.*

1 Volume: Arithmetic, Geography, Grammar, Physiology, History and Christian Doctrine.

LANSING, IOWA.

Immaculate Conception School.—*Franciscan Sisters of P. A.*

3 Volumes: Christian Doctrine, Arithmetic, Geography, Sacred History, Essays, Phonography, Language, Paraphrasing, Epistolary Correspondence, Penmanship, Business Forms, Civil Government, Book-Keeping, United States History, Physiology, Map and Mechanical Drawing.

LE MARS, IOWA.

St. James' School.—*Sisters of Charity, B. V. M.*

1 Volume: Christian Doctrine, Arithmetic, Geography, Grammar, Spelling, Reading and Map Drawing.

St. Joseph's School.—*Sisters of Christian Charity.*

3 Volumes: German Exercises, Geography, Christian Doctrine, Arithmetic, United States History, Map Drawings and 4 Plush Banners.

LUXEMBURG, IOWA.

Holy Trinity School.—*Franciscan Sisters of P. A.*

2 Volumes: Christian Doctrine, Arithmetic, German Exercises, United States History and Church History.

MANCHESTER, IOWA.

St. Xavier's School.—*Sisters of Mercy.*

1 Volume: Christian Doctrine, Arithmetic, Geography, Map and Mechanical Drawing and Letter Writing.

McGREGOR, IOWA.

St. Mary's School.—*Sisters of Charity, B. V. M.*

2 Mounted Charts, Grammar, Geography, Map Drawing, Physiology, History and Drawing.

MT. CARMEL, IOWA.

Sacred Heart School.—*Franciscan Sisters of P. A.*

2 Volumes: German Exercises, Christian Doctrine, Arithmetic, Geography, Grammar, Compositions, Paraphrasing, Penmanship and Drawing.

NEW VIENNA, IOWA.

St. Boniface's School.—*Franciscan Sisters of P. A.*

4 Volumes: Christian Doctrine, Grammar, Spelling, Arithmetic, Language, Geography, Book Keeping, Penmanship, German, Bible History, United States History, Civil Government, Composition and Drawing, 1 Fascinator, 1 White Apron, 1 Suit of Boy's Clothes, 2 Pairs Mittens and 3 Pairs Socks

REMSEN, IOWA.

St. Mary's School.—*Sisters of St. Francis.*

1 Volume: Bible History, Christian Doctrine, Arithmetic, Kindergarten Work and German Exercises.

ROCK VALLEY, IOWA.

Parochial School.—*Franciscan Sisters of P. A.*

25 Albums: Arithmetic, Geography, History, Physiology and Composition.

ST. DONATUS, IOWA.

St. Donatus' School.—*School Sisters of Notre Dame.*

6 Volumes: Christian Doctrine, Arithmetic, Composition, Physiology, Map Drawing, Geography and Language.

ST. LUCAS, IOWA.

St. Lucas' School.—*Franciscan Sisters of P. A.*

1 Volume: German Exercises, Compositions, Translations, Dictations and Geography.

SHERRILL, IOWA.

Sts. Peter and Paul's School.—*Franciscan Sisters of P. A.*

3 Volumes: Letters, Christian Doctrine, Arithmetic, Geography, History, German Translations, Business Forms, Civil Government and Botany.

SIOUX CITY, IOWA.

St. Mary's School.—*Sisters of Charity, B. V. M.*

Photographs of Building, Class-Rooms, Pupils, Chemical Apparatus and Art Studio.

STACYVILLE, IOWA.

Sacred Heart School.—*Sisters of St. Francis.*

1 Volume: Compositions, Arithmetic, Grammar, Hygiene, Geography.

SUGAR CREEK, IOWA.

St. Mary's School.—*Miss Anna Kloth, Teacher.*

1 Volume: Catechism, Geography, German, Spelling, Composition, Arithmetic and Drawing.

TEMPLETON, IOWA.

Sacred Heart School.—*Franciscan Sisters of P. A.*

1 Volume: German Exercises, Drawing and Arithmetic.

WILLY, IOWA.

Immaculate Conception School.—*Franciscan Sisters of P. A.*

1 Volume: Christian Doctrine, Arithmetic, Geography, Essays, Translations, Paraphrasing, Penmanship and Mechanical Drawing.

ARCHDIOCESE OF MILWAUKEE.

Most Rev. E. X. KATZER, D. D.

ALCOVES 1, 2, 3 AND 4.

Portrait of His Grace Archbishop Katzer.

ACADEMIES AND SELECT SCHOOLS.

MILWAUKEE, WIS.

Notre Dame Convent.—*School Sisters of Notre Dame.*

21 Oil Paintings, by Pupils of the Studio. 1 Volume Music, Normal Course, by Pupils of Classes '91, '92, and '93; 1 Volume "Responses," Compiled and Arranged by School Sisters of Notre Dame. 1 Globe of Wild Flowers (Wax), 1 Globe of Vegetables (Wax), 1 Plate of Confectionery (Wax), 1 Painted and Embroidered Souvenir Album, ½ Yard Knitted Lace, 1 Embroidered Lace Easel and 14 Medium-Sized Oil Paintings.

Design indicating city, name of school, year of foundation and number of pupils in each school; 73,703 pupils attending the classes of the School Sisters of Notre Dame in America.

St. Mary's Day and High School.—*School Sisters of Notre Dame.*

9 Volumes: Natural Science, Language, United States History, Bible History, Mensuration, Mathematics, Grammar, Christian Doctrine, Civil Government, Geography, Spelling. 2 Volumes Freehand Drawing, 1 Volume Kindergarten, 2 Volumes Music, 1 Volume Book-Keeping. 20 Card-Board Prisms. 2 Volumes Mechanical Drawings and 1 Volume General History.

RACINE, WIS.

St. Catharine's Academy.—*Sisters of St. Dominic.*

45 Volumes: English and German Reading, Arithmetic, Geography, Spelling, Grammar, History, Algebra, Botany, Physiology, Compositions, Language, Book-Keeping, Christian Doctrine. 1 Volume Normal Work. Essays from Sisters, 2 Lace Curtains, 1 Crayon (Infant Redeemer), 1 Painting and 1 Crayon.

PARISH SCHOOLS.

MILWAUKEE, WIS.

St. Anthony's School.—*School Sisters of Notre Dame.*

1 Volume: Language, Compositions, Spelling, Arithmetic, Penmanship, Geography, German, Grammar, Compositions and Christian Doctrine.

MILWAUKEE, WIS.—Continued.

St. Francis' School.—*School Sisters of Notre Dame.*

1 Volume: Penmanship, Spelling, Arithmetic, Grammar, History, Language, German and Compositions.

Holy Trinity School.—*School Sisters of Notre Dame.*

2 Volumes Drawing, 1 Volume: Penmanship, Arithmetic, Christian Doctrine, Geography, Natural Science, German, United States History, Grammar, Book-Keeping and Compositions.

St. Josaphat's School.—*School Sisters of Notre Dame.*

1 Volume: Penmanship, Geography, Arithmetic, Grammar, Christian Doctrine, Polish History, Compositions, Catechism and 1 Volume Free-hand Drawing.

St. Joseph's School.—*School Sisters of Notre Dame.*

2 Volumes: Penmanship, Language, Arithmetic, Book-Keeping, Geography, History, Natural Science, Grammar, German and 1 Volume Drawing.

St. Michael's School.—*School Sisters of Notre Dame.*

1 Volume Drawing; 1 Volume: Penmanship, Language, Spelling, Arithmetic, German, Christian Doctrine, Grammar, History and Compositions.

BARTON, WIS.

St. Mary's School.—*School Sisters of Notre Dame.*

1 Volume: Language, Penmanship, Geography, Arithmetic, Christian Doctrine, Geography, Grammar, United States History and Compositions.

BELGIUM, WIS.

St. Mary's School.—*Sisters of St. Dominic.*

1 Volume: History, Geography, Spelling, Language, Catechism, Reading and Physiology.

CALEDONIA, WIS.

St. Louis' School.—*Sisters of St. Dominic.*

1 Volume: German and English Reading, Penmanship, Arithmetic, Spelling, Grammar, United States History, Geography and Christian Doctrine.

KENOSHA, WIS.

St. George's School.—*School Sisters of Notre Dame.*

1 Volume: Language, Spelling, Arithmetic, Christian Doctrine, Geography, United States History, Penmanship and Grammar.

MINERAL POINT, WIS.

St. Mary's School.—*Sisters of St. Dominic.*

1 Volume German and English Compositions, 1 Crochet Cape, 1 Pair Knitted Hose, 2 Knitted Sacques, 1 Drawn Tidy, 1 Crochet Tidy, 3 Pairs Knitted Boots, 2 Satin Cushions, 1 Crochet Cushion, 1 Linen Apron, 3 Linen Handkerchiefs, 2 Samples Bead-Work and 2 Samples Lace-Work.

MOZOMANIE, WIS.

St. Barnabas' School.—*Sisters of St. Dominic.*

1 Volume: Drawing, Catechism, Arithmetic, Geography, Language, Penmanship, Reading and Spelling.

MT. CALVARY, WIS.

Our Lady of Mt. Carmel.—*School Sisters of Notre Dame.*

1 Large Volume Needle-Work.

RACINE, WIS.

Holy Name School.—*Sisters of St. Dominic.*

1 Volume: Grammar, Catechism, Language, Reading, Spelling, Arithmetic, Biography and Mensuration.

St. Mary's School.—*Sisters of St. Dominic.*

1 Volume: English and German Illustrated—Catechism, Spelling, Arithmetic, Writing and Geography.

St. Joseph's School.—*Sisters of St. Dominic.*

2 Volumes: Reading, Geography, Grammar, Catechism, Arithmetic, Language, Numbers in German and English Illustrated.

St. Patrick's School.—*Sisters of St. Dominic.*

2 Volumes: Reading, Writing, Language, Spelling, Arithmetic, Grammar, Geography, United States History, Compositions, Christian Doctrine and 1 Volume Drawing.

ROXBURY, WIS.

St. Nobert's School.

2 Volumes: Stencil Drawing, English and German, Arithmetic, Geography, Catechism, Christian Doctrine, Compositions, Reading, Spelling and Writing.

ARCHDIOCESE OF NEW ORLEANS.

MOST REV. F. JANSSENS, D. D.

COLLEGES, ACADEMIES AND SELECT SCHOOLS.

NEW ORLEANS, LA.

College of the Immaculate Conception.—*Jesuit Fathers.*

1 Volume: Philosophy, Electricity, Greek, Latin, Letters, Geometry and Algebra.

Dominican Academy (Dryades St.).—*Dominican Sisters.*

7 Volumes Book-Keeping; 1 Volume Each Arithmetic, Geometry, Trigonometry, Compositions, Letter Writing.

NEW ORLEANS, LA.—CONTINUED.

Dominican Academy (St. Charles Ave.).—*Dominican Sisters.*

13 Volumes Book-Keeping; 3 Volumes Arithmetic, 1 Volume Each: Trigonometry, Algebra, French Translations, Questions and Annotations; 2 Volumes Essays; 5 Volumes Drawing; 15 Crayons; 7 Paintings; 4 Framed Photographs and 1 Volume Magazine Published by the Pupils.

St. Aloysius' Institute.—*Brothers of the Sacred Heart.*

9 Volumes: Penmanship, Letters, Rhetoric, Algebra, Arithmetic, Grammar, Book-Keeping, History, Geometry, French, Analysis, Dictations, United States History, Geography, Map Drawing, Bible History and Spanish.

St. Alphonsus' Convent.—*Sisters of Mercy.*

10 Volumes: Christian Doctrine, Church History, Philosophy, Astronomy, Rhetoric, Physical Geography, Physiology, Grammar, United States History, General History, Arithmetic, Algebra, Sacred History, Compositions, Geography, Reading, Astronomy, Calligraphy, English and Roman History, Map Drawing, 3 Framed Maps and Framed Photographs.

St. Joseph's Academy.—*Sisters of St. Joseph.*

40 Albums: Language, Analysis, Punctuation, Correspondence, Essays, Compositions, Arithmetic, Epistolary Correspondence, Grammar, Synonyms, Bills, Dictations, United States History. In French—Grammar, Essays, Letters, Compositions; Photographs and 17 Copy Books.

St. Simeon's School.—*Sisters of Charity.*

13 Volumes: Penmanship, Geography, Arithmetic, Literature, Botany, Rhetoric, Physiology, History, Compositions, Music and 1 Volume Drawing and Photographs.

Ursuline Academy.—*Ursuline Sisters.*

20 Volumes: English, Character Sketches, French Translations, Compositions, Penmanship, Practical Arithmetic, Algebra, Miscellaneous Lessons. 1 Volume Book-Keeping, 2 Volumes Drawing, 1 Framed Needle-Work, 3 Hand-Painted Plates, 1 Frame Wax-Work, 2 Framed Photographs and 1 Crayon.

BATON ROUGE, LA.

St. Joseph's Academy.—*Sisters of St. Joseph.*

34 Volumes: Geography, Grammar, Geometry, French Translations, Physics, Map Drawing, Compositions, History, Letters, Algebra, Astronomy, Book-Keeping, Arithmetic, Copy Books and 2 Books of Maps.

CHARENTON, LA.

St. Joseph's Convent.—*Sisters of St. Joseph.*

16 Volumes: Compositions, Analyses, Letters, Poetry, Arithmetic, French, Grammar, Dictations, Parsing, Notes, Geography, Zoology, Botany, Penmanship, Rhetoric and 6 Copy Books.

DONALDSONVILLE, LA.

St. Joseph's Institute.—*Brothers of the Sacred Heart.*

6 Volumes: Penmanship, Compositions, Algebra, Trigonometry, Arithmetic, Grammar and Photographs.

JEANNERETTE, LA.

St. Joseph's Academy.—*Sisters of Mercy.*

2 Volumes: Catechism, Reading, Spelling, Geography, United States History, Bible History, Grammar, Rhetoric, Astronomy, Philosophy, Literature, Algebra, Mythology, Physiology; 1 Volume Charcoal Drawings.

THIBODEAUX, LA.

Thibodeaux College.—*Brothers of the Sacred Heart.*

5 Volumes: Compositions, Physics, Algebra, Phonography, Book-Keeping, French Exercises, Penmanship, Arithmetic, Orthography, G ography, Map Drawing, Trigonometry, Surveying, Linear Drawing, Freehand Drawing and Photographs.

PARISH SCHOOLS.

NEW ORLEANS, LA.

St. Joseph's Commercial School.—*Christian Brothers.*

21 Volumes: Mensuration, Composition, Arithmetic, Book-Keeping, Catechism, Typewriting, Notes, Drawing, Penmanship and Monthly Examination Papers.

St. Mary's Assumption School.—*School Sisters of Notre Dame.*

2 Volumes: Penmanship, Compositions, Arithmetic, Book-Keeping, Catechism, Typewriting, Notes, Drawing, Penmanship, Spelling. 1 Plush Drapery and 1 Box Needle-Work.

Notre Dame de Bon Secours School.—*Sisters of Mercy.*

3 Volumes: Christian Doctrine, Philosophy, Orthography, Reading, Geography, Grammar, United States History, Written Exercises, Penmanship, Drawing, Arithmetic, Reading, Translations, Astronomy, Rhetoric, Literature, Civil Government, Physical Geography, Compositions, Algebra, Ancient History, Modern History, Physiology, Etiquette. 1 Volume Drawing and 1 Frame of Photographs.

St. Alphonsus' School.

1 Volume: Arithmetic, Catechism, Spelling, Geography, Dictations, Grammar. 1 Volume Drawing and 4 Framed Maps.

St. Michael's School.—*Sisters of Mercy.*

1 Volume: Catechism, Christian Doctrine, Geography, United States History, Bible History, Compositions, Grammar, Book-Keeping, General History, Astronomy, Algebra, Philosophy, Rhetoric and 1 Volume Drawing.

St. Philips' School.—*Sisters of Mercy.*

MALE DEPT.

1 Volume: Christian Doctrine, Arithmetic, History, Philosophy, Physiology, Geography and Dictations.

FEMALE DEPT.

1 Volume: Christian Doctrine, Grammar, History, Physiology, Philosophy and Geography.

ST. MARTINSVILLE, LA.

St. Martin's School.—*Sisters of Mercy.*

2 Volumes: Christian Doctrine, History, Etymology, Mythology, French, United States History, Rhetoric, Grammar, Book-Keeping, Arithmetic, Algebra, Astronomy, Physical Geography, Mythology, History, Botany, Literature and Fancy Work.

ORPHANAGE.

NEW ORLEANS, LA.

St. Joseph's Orphanage.—*Sisters of Notre Dame.*

1 Volume: Language, Penmanship, Arithmetic, Catechism and Grammar.

ARCHDIOCESE OF NEW YORK.

MOST REV. MICHAEL AUGUSTINE CORRIGAN, D. D.

Diocesan Committee.

Rt. Rev. Mgr. JOHN FARLEY.
Rev. C. H. COLTON.

Rev. M. J. LAVELLE.
Rev. JOHN J. KEAN, *Secretary.*

ALCOVES 5, 6, 7, 8, 9, 10, 11, 12, 13, 14, 74 AND 76.

Portrait of His Grace Archbishop Corrigan.

COLLEGES AND ACADEMIES.

NEW YORK CITY.

Manhattan College.—*Christian Brothers.*

Natural Theology: Synoptic Analysis and Examination Papers; Evidences of Religion: Notes, Developments, and Examination Papers; Apologetic: Notes, Doctrinal Notes, Sacraments, Decalogue, Hierarchy, etc., in Synoptic Form; Philosophy: Synoptic Outline and Examination Papers; Logic: Summaries of Lessons with Illustrations; Philosophy of Literature: Essays and Examination Papers; Philosophy of History: Essays and Examination Papers; Political Economy and Civil Government: Essays; Literature: English and American, Notes and Biographical Sketches of Authors with Extracts (Illustrated); Criticism: Essays on Subject of the Hour, Topical Analysis of Ancient and Modern History, Examination Papers; Latin Translation—Grover Cleveland's Inaugural Address, '93, History of England, Extracts from Lingard, Most Rev. Archbishop Corrigan's Pastoral Letter, 1889, Aristotle and the Christian Church, (Bro. Azarias); Meters of Horace. Translation—Extracts from Quintilian, Horace, Mark Antony's Oration and DeBello Gallico. Prose Composition: Exercises. Scansion, Virgil. Latin Syntax, Synopsis with Examples. Prize Examination Papers. Greek Translations—Extracts from Plato; Extracts from Homer's Iliad; Extracts from Lucian, with Exercises in Syntax; Extracts from Homer, Scanned and Translated with Notes; Extracts from Anabasis. Prose Composition: Exercises, Examination Papers. French Translations—Grover Cleveland's Inaugural Address, '93; Life of Firmin Suc, Extracts with Critical Notes; Sentences Illustrating Rules of Grammar; French-English and English-French Exercises, Notes on Grammar with Exercises.

NEW YORK CITY.—Continued.

Manhattan College.—*Christian Brothers.*

NATURAL SCIENCES AND MATHEMATICS.

Geology: Notes and Illustrations, Examination Papers; Astronomy: Notes and Illustrations, Examination Papers; Chemistry: Chart Containing Specimens Prepared by Students, Notes, and Photographic Illustrations; Physics: Notes, and Pen Illustrations; Physiology: Synopsis of Lectures, and Pen and Crayon Illustrations by the Students; Analytical Geometry: Examination Papers, and Class-Work; Conic Sections: Examination Papers and Class-Work; Surveying and Navigation: Problems with Diagrams, Notes, and Illustrations; Trigonometry: Class-Work, Problems with Diagrams; Geometry: Problems with Demonstrations; Algebra: Class-Work, Problems; Drawing: Crayon-Work, Landscape and Figure Drawing, Applications of Projections, Specimens of Work from Croton Aqueduct, Models and Plans of Cottages.

BUSINESS DEPARTMENT.

Religion: Notes and Analysis of Lessons, Lectures. English: Essays on Business, Commerce, Historical Subjects, and Letters. Penmanship (Class-Work); English, Plain and Round-Hand. Business Calculations: Exercises in Counting-House Work, Class Exercises. Book-Keeping: Double-Entry Sets, Law (Commercial and Constitutional); Notes of Lectures Given by Professor. Phonography: Exercises in Elementary Study, Correspondence, and Amanuensis Work. Typewriting: Elementary Exercises, Business Letters, Transcription of Phonographic Notes, Office Work.

PREPARATORY DEPARTMENT.

Religion: Essays on Doctrinal Subjects. Penmanship: Class-Work, Business Letters, etc. English Grammar: Analysis and Parsing, Syntax, Common Errors Corrected, Extracts from Standard Authors, Examination Papers. History: Ancient and Modern, Synopsis of Lessons, Developments and Illustrations by Pupils. Geography: United States of America, Reproduction of Maps, Pen and Crayon Work, Notes. Geometry: Demonstrations of Theorems in Plane Geometry. Civil Government: Forms of Government, Rights of Citizens, etc. Latin: Elementary Studies, Translations from Cæsar and Ovid, Scansion, Examination Papers. Greek: Elementary Studies, Translations in English. Arithmetic: Solutions of Problems, Decimal System. Business Operations: Book-Keeping, Double Entry. Algebra: Solution of Problems, etc. Photographs of Buildings, Classes, Study Hall, Museum, Campus, Clubs, etc.

De LaSalle Institute.—*Christian Brothers.*

14 Volumes Evidences of Religion, 11 Volumes Latin Translation Exercises, 1 Volume Latin Examination Papers, 5 Volumes Greek, 6 Volumes English Grammar, 2 Volumes American Literature, 2 Volumes American Literature Examination Papers, 1 Volume Compositions, 39 Essays on Various Subjects, 4 Volumes Rhetoric, 1 Volume Rhetoric Examination Papers, 6 Volumes Arithmetic, 4 Volumes Algebra, 5 Volumes Geometry, 2 Volumes Geometry Examination Papers, 2 Volumes Mensuration, 3 Volumes Analytical Geometry, 5 Volumes Trigonometry, 2 Volumes Geography, 2 Volumes Surveying, 1 Volume Engineering, 1 Volume Engineering Examination Papers, 3 Volumes Chemistry, 2 Volumes Mechanics, 1 Volume Astronomy, 3 Volumes Natural Philosophy, 2 Volumes Physics, a Collection of Original Drawings of Surveying and Engineering. 1 Volume Developments of Solids, by One of the Professors. 2 Volumes Business Forms and Book-Keeping, 2 Volumes Phonography, 15 Volumes Typewriting, 7 Volumes French, 3 Volumes German, 7 Volumes Penmanship, 3 Volumes Letters, 9 Volumes Linear and Freehand Drawing, 7 Volumes Dictation Exercises, 3 Volumes Business Letters, Photographs of Graduates, Building, Classes, Lecture Hall, Cadets, Museum, Pupils, etc.

NEW YORK CITY.—Continued.

La Salle Academy.—*Christian Brothers.*

3 Volumes Christian Doctrine, 11 Volumes Drawing, 13 Volumes Class-Work, 7 Volumes Book-Keeping, 3 Volumes Compositions, 2 Volumes Penmanship, 4 Volumes Graded Lessons in Stenography, 4 Volumes Graded Lessons in Typewriting, 4 Volumes Business Forms, Stenography and Typewriting, 4 Volumes Lessons in Letter Writing, 4 Volumes Civil Government, 4 Volumes Stenographic Notes and Transcripts of Addresses and Lectures, 2 Volumes Debates and 1 Volume Typewriting Recreations.

Mt. St. Vincent on the Hudson.—*Sisters of Charity.*

82 Volumes: Bible History, Algebra, Arithmetic, Geography, Astronomy, Latin, Greek, German, Logic, Essays, Physics, Rhetoric. 2 Copy Books Domestic Economy, History. 27 Copy Books Music, Christian Doctrine and Geography. 28 Copy Books Book-Keeping, 40 Charts Natural Science, Illustrated, 12 Articles Honiton and Point Lace, 10 Oil Paintings, 5 Crayon Pictures, 2 Paintings in Moist Colors, 9 Panel Photographic Views of Mt. St. Vincent and Pupils, 4 Unframed Crayons, 1 Case 12 Pieces Hand-Made Undergarments.

St. Brigid's Academy.—*Sisters of Charity.*

12 Volumes: Christian Doctrine, Penmanship, Arithmetic, Grammar, History, Drawing, Dictation, Compositions, Physics, Astronomy, Physiology, Algebra, German, Geometry, 2 Framed Maps, 1 Portfolio Large Drawings, 5 Framed Crayon Pictures, 3 Large Porcelain Paintings and 1 Painted Velvet Banner.

St. Gabriel's Academy.—*Sisters of Charity.*

24 Volumes: Grammar, Geography, Orthography, United States History, Natural Philosophy, Geometry, Algebra, Physiology, Catechism, Astronomy, French, English History, Penmanship, Rhetoric, Drawing and Book-Keeping.

St. Jerome's Academy.—*Ursuline Nuns.*

2 Volumes: Arithmetic, Grammar, Spelling, Christian Doctrine, Reading, Penmanship and Map Drawing.

St. Mary's Academy.—*Sisters of Charity.*

SENIOR DIVISION.

5 Volumes: Essays, Mathematics, Church History, Literature, Rhetoric, United States History, Geography, Astronomy, Physics, Physiology.

MIDDLE AND JUNIOR DIVISIONS.

5 Volumes: Christian Doctrine, Bible History, Arithmetic, Geography, Grammar and Drawing.

St. Paul's Academy.—*Sisters of Charity.*

3 Volumes: Christian Doctrine, Arithmetic, Geography, Civil Government, English History, Astronomy, Philosophy, Grammar, Orthography, Compositions, Literature and Drawing.

Academy of the Holy Rosary.—*Sisters of St. Dominic.*

37 Volumes: Arithmetic, Algebra, Book-Keeping, Geometry, Diagrams, Catechism, Dictation, Grammar, English Compositions, Map Drawing, German Composition, Geography, German Penmanship, Music, Book-Keeping. 5 Framed Photographs, 2 Paintings on Glass, 2 Pictures. Kindergarten Work, Stenography and Typewriting. 3 Knitted Capes, 1 Knitted Sacque, 2 Pair Slippers, 1 Velvet Photograph Case, 1 Silk and Wool Hood, 1 Silk Neck-Tie, 1 Crochet Cap, 1 Pair Crochet Leggins, 2 Lace Tidies, 1 Linen Handkerchief, 2 Celluloid Calendars, 2 Celluloid Cases.

NEW YORK CITY.—Continued.

Convent of Holy Rosary.—*Sisters of St. Dominic.*

18 Volumes: Christian Doctrine, History, Arithmetic, Reading, Compositions, Book-Keeping, Grammar, Geography, Spelling, Language, Kindergarten Work, 16 Photographs of Grades, 2 Felt Table-Scarfs, 9 Undergarments, 9 Gingham Dresses, 1 Child's Dress (Drawn-Work), 6 Throws, 3 Worked Splashers, 35 Needle-Books, Cushions, Toys, etc., 1 Pair Crochet Slippers, 4 Hemstitched Handkerchiefs.

AMAWALK, N. Y.

St. Joseph's Normal College.—*Christian Brothers.*

Collection of Drawings Illustrating Christian Brothers' System. 38 Volumes of Drawing by the Students. Display of Text Books: Grammar (2), Spelling (3), Commercial Law and Book-Keeping (3), Reading (7), Arithmetic (5). Mensuration, Hints on Teaching, Notes on Teaching, Hymn Books, a Series of Copy Books, Blank Books, Roll Books, Monthly Examination Register, Normal Manual and Many Volumes of Other Publications; a Series of Drawing Books (Linear and Freehand), 14 Books, Including 2 for the Teacher. 6 Boxes of Botanical Specimens, a Collection of Woods, a Chart on Grammar, a Chart on Geography, Testimonials for Satisfactory School-Work, Phonographic Charts for Simultaneous Teaching. Relief Maps of New York, Washington, Niagara Falls and Philadelphia. 1 Volume for the Development of Solids.

WESTCHESTER, N. Y.

Sacred Heart Academy.—*Christian Brothers.*

48 Albums Linear Drawing, 3 Albums Freehand Drawing, 10 Volumes Map Drawing, 3 Small Volumes Freehand Drawing, 4 Volumes Plane Geometry, 8 Volumes Solid Geometry, 11 Volumes Physics, 11 Volumes Latin, 8 Volumes Algebra, 3 Volumes Book-Keeping, 2 Volumes Trigonometry, 5 Volumes Exercises. Specimens of Christian Doctrine, English Grammar, French, Trigonometry, German, Arithmetic, Mensuration, Phonography and Natural Philosophy. 1 Volume Phonography, 1 Volume Typewriting, 1 Volume Arithmetic, 1 Volume Dictation, 1 Album Photographs. 44 Large Drawings—Geographical, Mechanical and Ornamental. 1 Scrap Book.

PARISH SCHOOLS.

NEW YORK CITY.

Cathedral School.

Male Dept.—*Christian Brothers.*

6 Volumes Penmanship, 17 Volumes Book-Keeping. 43 Volumes "Home Work" and "Class-Work," English Grammar, Mensuration, Arithmetic, Geometry, Algebra, History, Christian Doctrine, Geography, English Composition, and Bible History. 4 Volumes Monthly Examination Papers, 4 Volumes Contrast-Pages of Penmanship, 6 Relief Maps (Plaster), a Collection of Large Drawings, 7 Large Maps (Mounted), Crayon Portrait of Archbishop Corrigan, 26 Volumes Drawing, Map of New York and Vicinity (Papier Maché), 1 Volume Fancy Pen-Work, 1 Volume Gray's Elegy (Illustrated), Photographs of School, Cadets and Drum Corps.

Female Dept.—*Sisters of Charity.*

17 Volumes: Sewing and Weaving, Drawing and Weaving, Interlacing, Piece-Work and Pasting, Map Drawing, Mechanical Drawing, Bible History, Christian Doctrine, Arithmetic, Geography, Astronomy, Grammar, Language, Penmanship, 15 Doll Dresses, 5 Sacques and 34 Specimens Embroidery, Photographs of Pupils.

NEW YORK CITY.—Continued.

St. Agnes' School,
Framed Photographs of School Building.

Assumption School.—*School Sisters of Notre Dame*
5 Volumes: Composition, History, Geography, Arithmetic, German, Orthography, Grammar and Christian Doctrine.

St. Alphonsus' School—Male Dept.—*Christian Brothers.*
2 Volumes Book-Keeping, 1 Volume Mechanical Drawing, 1 Volume Christian Doctrine, 3 Volumes Penmanship, 1 Volume Spelling, 17 Volumes Exercise Work, Geography, Letter Writing, Grammar, Arithmetic and History.

St. Augustine's School.—*Sisters of Charity.*
2 Volumes: Language, Arithmetic, Spelling, Grammar, Composition, Geography, Penmanship, Drawing and Reading.

St. Brigid's School.
Male Dept.—*Christian Brothers.*
31 Volumes Book-Keeping. 52 Volumes Home Exercises—Grammar, Invention, Punctuation, Arithmetic, Algebra, Mensuration and Composition. 47 Volumes Penmanship. 19 Volumes Penmanship and Business Forms, 32 Volumes Freehand Drawing, 8 Volumes Linear Drawing, 4 Volumes Map Drawing, 1 Volume Pen-Work, 27 Volumes Printing—Old English, Marking, French and Round-Hand. 1 Album Showing Improvement in Writing. Photographs of School, Pupils, Cadet Corps, Sanctuary Boys, Gymnastic Classes, etc.

Female Dept.—*Sisters of Charity.*
5 Volumes Drawing, 4 Volumes Specimens Sewing, 18 Volumes Spelling, Penmanship, Language, Grammar, Compositions, Arithmetic, Christian Doctrine, Geography, United States History and Dictations.

St. Francis of Assissi's.—*Franciscan Sisters.*
1 Volume: Christian Doctrine, Penmanship, Geography, Spelling, Arithmetic, History, Grammar, Map-Drawing and German.

St. Gabriel's School.
Male Dept.—*Christian Brothers.*
17 Volumes Book-Keeping, 4 Volumes English Grammar, 10 Volumes Home Work, 4 Volumes Geometry, 3 Volumes Mensuration, 2 Volumes Geography, 4 Volumes Arithmetic, 5 Volumes Compositions, 5 Volumes History, 4 Volumes Algebra, 2 Volumes Christian Doctrine, 8 Volumes Drawing, 9 Large Mounted Maps and Crayon Portrait of Rt. Rev. Mgr. Farley.

Female Dept.—*Sisters of Charity.*
11 Volumes: Grammar, Geography, United States History, Penmanship, Spelling, Drawing and Book-Keeping.

Holy Cross School.—*Sisters of Charity.*
3 Volumes: Reading, Language, Arithmetic, Penmanship, Composition and Music.

Holy Innocents' School—Male Dept.—*Christian Brothers.*
12 Copy Books Geography, 13 Copy Books Arithmetic, 11 Copy Books Grammar, 8 Copy Books Catechism, 10 Copy Books History, 11 Copy Books Spelling and Dictation, 22 Copy Books Penmanship and 3 Copy Books Class-Work.

NEW YORK CITY.—Continued.

Immaculate Conception School.

Male Dept.—*Christian Brothers.*

1 Volume Each of Maps, Penmanship (Contrast Pages), Ornamental Drawing, Dictation Exercises, United States History, Practical Geometry, Orthography; 2 Volumes of Explanation of Christian Doctrine; 4 Volumes Each of Ornamental Drawing, Arithmetic, Grammar and Penmanship Copies; 5 Volumes of Business Letters; 5 Wall Maps; 19 Volumes Exercises in Catechism, Arithmetic, Algebra and Mensuration; 33 Volumes Geography; 17 Book-Keeping; 2 Framed Pictures and 2 Charts of Geometrical Figures; 2 Large Drawings of Ships.

Female Dept.—*Sisters of Charity.*

24 Volumes: Algebra, Grammar, Arithmetic, Christian Doctrine, Geography, United States History, Catechism, English History, Composition and Penmanship.

Immaculate Conception School (E. 151st Street).—*Christian Brothers.*

1 Volume Graphic Scrap Book, 1 Volume Pictorial Scrap Book, 1 Volume Specimen Penmanship, 1 Set of Elevated Maps, 1 Chart of Monthly Lessons, 1 Souvenir Album, 1 Volume "Deutsche Sprachlehre," 1 Volume Specimen Pages of Book-Keeping, 1 Copy of Business Forms, 2 Volumes Botanical Specimens, 5 Volumes Penmanship Copies, 5 Volumes Writing Competitions, 44 Volumes Freehand Drawing, 100 Writing Copies and 5 Sets "Home Work" Copy Books.

St. James' School.

Male Dept.—*Christian Brothers.*

1 Volume Each of Colored Maps, Drawing, Plane and Spherical Geometry, Lessons in English. 2 Volumes Each of Stone and Iron Work; Solid, Plane, and Spherical Geometry; Literature and Composition and Business Forms. 4 Volumes Each of Mensuration and Geometry, Commercial Correspondence, Analysis, Business Forms, Arithmetic and Algebra. 9 Volumes Penmanship.

Female Dept.—*Sisters of Charity.*

4 Volumes: Penmanship, Arithmetic, Drawing, Sewing, Grammar, Geography, Christian Doctrine, Algebra, Music, Composition and Book-Keeping. Framed Flag of United States Made by Pupils.

St. Jerome's School.—*Ursuline Nuns.*

8 Volumes: Spelling, Reading, Writing, Arithmetic, Geography, United States History and Christian Doctrine.

St. John the Baptist School.

Male Dept.—*Brothers of Mary.*

4 Volumes: German and English Grammar and Translation, German and English Dictation and Composition, German and English Writing.

Female Dept.—*Dominican Sisters.*

4 Volumes: Arithmetic, Geography, Catechism, Language Lessons, History, Bible History, Composition and Grammar.

St. Joseph's School—**Male Dept.**—*Christian Brothers.*

1 Volume Each of Christian Doctrine and Geography, 2 Volumes Each of Grammar, Map Drawing and Linear Drawing, 5 Mounted Maps, 6 Volumes Each Mathematics and Book-Keeping, 14 Volumes Freehand Drawing, 16 Volumes Penmanship and 1 Album Photographs of Pupils.

NEW YORK CITY.—Continued.

St. Joseph's School (87th Street).—*School Sisters of Notre Dame.*
4 Volumes: Specimens of Arithmetic, Book-Keeping, Geography, History, Christian Doctrine and Bible History.

St. Joseph's School (127th Street).—*School Sisters of Notre Dame.*
8 Volumes: Grammar, Composition, Geography, United States History, Christian Doctrine, Spelling, Arithmetic, Book-Keeping.

St. Lawrence's School.—*Sisters of Charity.*
6 Volumes: Reading, Writing, Spelling, Geography, Grammar, United States History, Christian Doctrine and Composition.

St. Mary's School.

MALE DEPT.—*Christian Brothers.*
1 Volume Each of Linear Drawing, Phonography, Geometry and Algebra. 2 Volumes of Christian Doctrine and History. 4 Volumes Each of Class-Work and Geography. 9 Volumes Each of Book-Keeping and Grammar. 18 Volumes Each of Freehand Drawing and Arithmetic.

FEMALE DEPT.—*Sisters of Charity.*
11 Volumes: Weaving, Catechism, Grammar, Arithmetic, Spelling, Dictations, Compositions.

St. Monica's School.—*Sisters of Charity.*
15 Volumes: Map Drawings, Christian Doctrine, History, Grammar, Civil Government, Geography, Book-Keeping and United States History.

St. Nicholas' School.

MALE DEPT.—*Christian Brothers.*
6 Volumes: Grammar, Religious Instructions, Bible History, Arithmetic, Algebra, Penmanship and Geography. 2 Volumes Each of Class-Work and Book-Keeping, 3 Volumes Each of Linear and Freehand Drawing, 4 Volumes of Arithmetic, 8 Volumes Each of German and English Penmanship and Freehand Drawing, 3 Large Framed Drawings.

FEMALE DEPT.—*Dominican Sisters.*
12 Volumes: German and English Grammar, Compositions, United States History, Geography, German and English Penmanship, German Dictation, Catechism, Map Drawing, Mechanical Drawings, Book of Kindergarten Work. 2 Framed Photographs, 1 Apron, 1 Knitted Cape, Lace Throw, 1 Satin Cushion, 1 Satin Hand-Bag, 1 Lace Tidy, 1 Crochet Tidy, 1 Pair Shoes, 1 Pair Boots, 1 Pair Satin Slippers, 1 Drawn Throw, 1 Gingham Apron.

Our Lady of Mt. Carmel.—*Secular Teachers.*
6 Portfolios: Spelling, Geography, Grammar, Catechism, Arithmetic and Kindergarten Work.

Our Lady of Sorrows' School.—*Brothers of Mary.*
4 Volumes: Arithmetic, English and German Grammar and Composition, English and German Dictation, Translations, Writing.

St. Patrick's School.

MALE DEPT.—*Christian Brothers.*
1 Volume Each of Book-Keeping, Grammar, Catechism and Mensuration; 2 Volumes Each of Grammar, Arithmetic, Linear Drawing and Ornamental Drawing; 4 Volumes Penmanship.

FEMALE DEPT.—*Sisters of Charity.*
6 Volumes: History, Composition, Grammar, Arithmetic, Penmanship, Geometry and Book-Keeping.

NEW YORK CITY.—Continued.

St. Paul's School.

2 Volumes: Penmanship, Arithmetic, Language, Geography, Grammar, Catechism, Bible History and United States History.

St. Peter's School.

MALE DEPT.—*Christian Brothers.*

10 Volumes Book-Keeping, 12 Volumes Penmanship, 17 Volumes Ornamental Drawing, 5 Volumes Geography, 2 Volumes Christian Doctrine, 12 Pieces Linear Drawing, 8 Pieces Ornamental Drawing, 7 Volumes Arithmetic, 21 Copy Books Grammar, 18 Volumes Compositions, 24 Volumes Mathematics, 4 Large Wall Maps, 1 Volume Linear Drawing (from Object), Photographs of School Band, Senior Drawing-Class and Distinguished Pupils.

FEMALE DEPT.—*Sisters of Charity.*

6 Volumes: Music, Christian Doctrine, Catechism, Geometry, Algebra, Arithmetic, Dictation, United States History.

St. Stephen's School.—*Sisters of Charity.*

8 Volumes: Book-Keeping, Drawing, Algebra, Arithmetic, Geography, Geometry, Grammar, Composition, United States History, Christian Doctrine and Spelling.

St. Teresa's School.

MALE DEPT.—*Christian Brothers.*

28 Volumes Grammar, 27 Volumes Arithmetic, 17 Volumes Algebra, 16 Volumes Christian Doctrine, 10 Volumes Orthography, 17 Volumes Penmanship, 4 Volumes Geography, 5 Volumes Map Drawing, 3 Volumes Drawing and 1 Volume History.

FEMALE DEPT.—*Ursuline Sisters.*

23 Volumes: Language, Arithmetic, Numbers, Catechism, Geography, United States History, Christian Doctrine, English History, Grammar, Algebra and Map Drawing.

St. Vincent Ferrer's School.—*Dominican Sisters.*

18 Volumes: Christian Doctrine, Arithmetic, Geography, Grammar, United States History, Mechanical Drawing, Freehand Drawing, Language, Composition, Dictations.

HAVERSTRAW, N. Y.

St. Peter's School.—*Sisters of Charity.*

1 Volume: Composition, Grammar, Arithmetic, Christian Doctrine and Sewing.

KINGSTON, N. Y.

St. Joseph's School.—*Sisters of Charity.*

1 Volume: Arithmetic, Geography, Grammar, Physiology, Spelling, United States History, Catechism.

NEW BRIGHTON, N. Y.

St. Peter's School.—*Sisters of Charity.*

1 Volume: Arithmetic, Christian Doctrine, Spelling, Geography and Grammar.

NEWBURGH, N. Y.

St. Patrick's School.

MALE DEPT.—*Christian Brothers.*

13 Cabinets for Object Lessons, 5 Books Linear Drawing, 19 Books Ornamental Drawing, 22 Compositions on Object Lessons, 14 Bound Copy Books Miscellaneous Subjects, 54 Sets Book-Keeping (Single and Double Entry), 213 Writing Copy Books, 5 Copy Books Mensuration, 7 Copy Books Grammar, 6 Copy Books Algebra, 20 Copy Books Arithmetic, 40 "Home Exercise" Copy Books, 17 Class Copy Books, 1 Album Photographs.

FEMALE DEPT.—*Sisters of Charity.*

24 Copy Books: Book-Keeping, Penmanship, Elocution, Composition, Christian Doctrine, Geography, United States History, Grammar, Civil Government, Geometry, Literature and Specimens Sewing.

St. Mary's School.—*Dominican Sisters.*

1 Volume: Compositions, Grammar, Arithmetic, Christian Doctrine, Geography, Spelling and Penmanship.

NYACK, N. Y.

St. Ann's School.—*Sisters of Charity.*

7 Copy Books: Arithmetic, Geography, Grammar, Catechism, Dictations, History, Spelling, Numbers, Writing, Compositions and Drawing.

POUGHKEEPSIE, N. Y.

St. Mary's School.—*Sisters of Charity.*

1 Volume: Arithmetic, Geography, Grammar, 17 Maps, 4 Cards Drawing, 2 Cards Kindergarten.

RONDOUT, N. Y.

St. Mary's School.—*Sisters of Charity.*

3 Volumes: Catechism, Language, Arithmetic, Geography, Spelling, United States History, Grammar, Christian Doctrine.

ROSENDALE, N. Y.

St. Peter's School.—*Sisters of Charity.*

2 Volumes: Christian Doctrine, Church History, United States History, Geography, Spelling, Grammar, Arithmetic, Penmanship, Map Drawing.

SAUGERTIES, N. Y.

St. Mary's School.—*Sisters of Charity.*

2 Volumes: Christian Doctrine, Spelling, Grammar, History, Arithmetic, Language, Drawing and Numbers.

SING SING, N. Y.

St. Augustine's School.—*Sisters of Charity.*

5 Volumes: Church History, Christian Doctrine, Dictation, Arithmetic, Grammar, United States History, Penmanship, Reading, Composition, Maps and Drawing.

VERPLANCK, N. Y.

St. Patrick's School.—*Franciscan Sisters.*

1 Volume: Penmanship, Geography, Arithmetic, Grammar, Language, United States History and Spelling.

YONKERS, N. Y.

St. Mary's School.

Male Dept.—*Christian Brothers.*

4 Volumes Drawing, 34 Copy Books: Specimens of Penmanship, Arithmetic, Christian Doctrine, Grammar and Geography.

NEW YORK CATHOLIC PROTECTORY.

WESTCHESTER, N. Y.

Male Dept.—*Christian Brothers.*

499 Copy Books: Penmanship, Daily Exercises, Weekly and Monthly Competition. 29 Copy Books Christian Doctrine, 138 Copy Books Arithmetic, 28 Copy Books Compositions, 148 Copy Books English Grammar, 30 Copy Books Synopsis of History of the State of New York, 20 Copy Books United States History, 129 Copy Books: Compositions, Dictation, Arithmetic, Grammar, History, Civil Government and Examination Papers. 22 Exercise Copy Books Phonography, 19 Copy Books Typewriting, 23 Large Volumes Freehand Drawing. 8 Exercise Copy Books on "Holy Land": The Israelites—Their History. 28 Medium Volumes Drawing, 2 Large Volumes Freehand Drawing, 3 Volumes Mechanical Drawing, 1 Large Volume Projections; 192 Large Drawings: Figure, Ornamental and Mechanical. 9 Geographical Plaster Casts, 4 Suits of Boys' Clothes, 1 Dozen Pairs Shoes, 1 Wax Figure, 1 Dozen Pairs Stockings, 4 Specimens Chair Caning. 6 Electrotype Plates, Books, Pamphlets, etc., from the Printing Office. 1 Picture of the Building and Grounds. 50 Copies of "Sketch of the Protectory, 1863-1893." 2 Large Framed Pictures Giving Views of Buildings, Class-Rooms, Boys at Work in Shops, Brass Band, Cadets at Drill, Dormitory, Power House, etc.

Female Dept.—*Sisters of Charity.*

3 Embroidered Glove Cushions, 11 Pairs Kid Gloves, 3 Boards Sample Lace, 5 Linen Embroidered Tray Covers, 4 Children's Bonnets, 3 Silk Neckties, 5 Ladies' Waists, 1 Ladies' Morning Gown, 8 Shirts, 1 Book Stenography, 1 Embroidered Coverlet Patch-Work, 1 Wax Figure Dressed, 1 Night Dress, 3 Children's White Aprons, 4 Bonnet Stands, 1 Kid (Figure), 7 Muslin Covers, 3 Sets Underclothes, 19 Pictures, 1 Basket Flowers (Glass Globe), 6 Kindergarten Mats and 4 Glass Cases.

Institution of Mercy.—*Sisters of Mercy.*

2 Pairs Crochet Lace Curtains, 1 Cotton Crochet Curtain, 1 Satin Cushion Cover (Crochet), 2 Satin Table Covers and 1 Bolster Cover.

Roman Catholic Male Orphan Asylum.—*Sisters of Charity.*

Collection of Photographs: Asylum, Cadet Corps and New Trade-School.

Photograph of the New Seminary of St. Joseph for the Archdiocese of New York.

Picture in Colors of the Catholic Educational Exhibit of the Archdiocese of New York, devised by Hon. John Mullaly, Editor of *The Seminary*, showing an increase in School Buildings, from three (3) in number to one hundred and sixty-eight (168) during the past fifty years.

A list of all the Schools in the Archdiocese is given, and each one of the one hundred and sixty-eight School Buildings is clearly shown in the Picture, with a number referring to the list.

Around the border of the Picture are Quotations from Doctors of the Church, the Holy Father, and our most eminent Prelates, on the importance and value of Christian Education.

Printed Statistics showing the value of Parochial School Property belonging to the Archdiocese ($4,515,400), the number of Parochial Schools, cost of their maintenance, session 1892-93 ($298,227.38), and the number of Pupils.

DIOCESE OF PHILADELPHIA.

MOST REV. PATRICK J. RYAN.

Diocesan Committee.

Rev. R. KINAHAN.	Rev. H. LANE.	Rev. THOS. MULLEN.
Rev. J. J. ELCOCK.	Rev. G. BORNEMANN.	Rev. P. F. SULLIVAN.
Rev. JNO. W. SHANAHAN.	Rev. E. O. HILTERMANN.	Rev. P. J. DAILEY.
Rev. THOS. BARRY.	Rev. H. STROMMEL.	Rev. J. F. LAUGHLIN, D.D.

ALCOVES 15, 16, 40, 74, 99 AND 103.

Portrait of His Grace Archbishop Ryan.

PHILADELPHIA, PA.

American Catholic Historical Society.

Autographic Letter of Thomas Burke of North Carolina. Autographic Letter of Aedanus Burke of South Carolina. Manuscript Documents of Charles Carroll, 1st and 2d. Bishop Carroll's Funeral Oration on Washington (with Autograph Letters of Both). Autograph Letter of Charles Carroll. Autograph Letter of Bishop F. P. Kenrick. American Museum, Volume 1, 1787. De La Porterie's Boston Pastoral, 1799. M. Carey's History of Yellow Fever, 1793. Carroll's Address to Catholics, 1784. United States Catholic Miscellany, Volume 2, 1824. Pious Guide, Georgetown, 1792. Huby's Spiritual Retreat, Philadelphia, 1792. Houdet's Morality, Philadelphia, 1796. Unerring Authority, Lloyd, Philadelphia, 1789. England's Conversion and Reformation, Antwerp, 1725. England's Conversion and Reformation, Lancaster, Pa., 1813. Lingard's England, 1st American Edition, Volume 1, 1827. Butler's Lives, 1st American Edition, Volume 1, 1822. Lloyd's System of Shorthand, 1819. Silhouette and Home of Thomas Lloyd. Original Seal of Maryland. Prayer-Book Owned by Captain Maguire, 1790. Cross made from first Altar erected in Pennsylvania. 3 Medals on Board. Pectoral Cross of Archbishop Hughes. Pectoral Cross of Bishop Chanche. Pectoral Cross of Bishop Gartland. Pectoral Cross of Bishop Van de Velde. Seal and Chain of Bishop M. O'Connor. Thomas à Kempis (in German), Germantown, 1795. Pise's History of Church, Volume 1, Baltimore, 1827. Alexandria Controversy, Georgetown, 1817. O'Gallagher on Penance, New York, 1815. Brosius' Answer (German), Lancaster, 1796. Bishop Fenwick's Webbe's Masses. Sacred Concert at St. Augustine's, 1810. Devotions for Catholic Blind, Philadelphia. Pastorine's History of Church, 1st American Edition, 1807. Laity's Directory, New York, 1822. United States Catholic

PHILADELPHIA, PA.—Continued.

American Catholic Historical Society.

Directory for 1833. Two Church Music Books, 1787 and 1791. The Metropolitan, Baltimore, 1830. Catholic Christian Instructed, Philadelphia, 1786. Carey's Douay Bible, 1790. Prospectus announcing same. Carey's New Testament, 1805. The Jesuit, Volume 1, Boston, 1829. Catholic Herald, Volume 1, Philadelphia, 1833. Ring of Bishop M. O'Connor. Book Plate of Charles Carroll, Sr. Signature of Lionel Brittin. Father Farmer's Reliquary. Miniature of Rev. S. S. Cooper. Father Mathew's Autograph. Archbishop Wood's Catechism and Ordination. Autograph of Judge Gaston of North Carolina. Catalogue of Bishop Conwell's Library (Manuscript). Goshenhoppen Register. Bishop McGill's Faith the Victory, Richmond, 1865.

Box No. 2.

Bishops Egan and Conwell's Mitre, Bishop Neuman's Mitre, Gallitzin Letter (Framed), Loretto Mission (Kentucky), Picture of Archbishop Carroll, 1812, Old Panel from St. Inigo's, Md.

COLLEGES AND ACADEMIES.

PHILADELPHIA, PA.

La Salle College.—*Christian Brothers.*

COLLEGE DEPT.—SENIOR CLASS.

1 Volume Quarterly Examination Papers: Evidences of Religion, Metaphysics, Philosophy of History, English Literature, Civics, Latin, Greek, French and German.

JUNIOR CLASS.

1 Volume Quarterly Examination Papers: Evidences of Religion, Logic, English Literature, History, Mathematics, Latin, Greek, French, German, Chemistry and Essays.

SOPHOMORE CLASS.

1 Volume Quarterly Examination Papers: Christian Doctrine, History, Rhetoric, English Literature, Mathematics, Physics, Latin, Greek, French and German.

FRESHMAN CLASS.

1 Volume Quarterly Examination Papers: Christian Doctrine, History, English History, Rhetoric, Mathematics, Physics, Book-Keeping, Latin, German, Greek, French and Essays.

PREPARATORY DEPT.—FIRST CLASS.

1 Volume Quarterly Examination Papers: Catechism, Spelling, Arithmetic, Algebra, Mensuration, Geometry, English Grammar, Compositions, Geography, Book-Keeping, Writing, German and Latin.

SECOND CLASS.

1 Volume Quarterly Examination Papers: Catechism, Spelling, Arithmetic, Grammar, Compositions, History, Geography, Writing, Latin and German.

THIRD CLASS.

1 Volume Quarterly Examination Papers: Catechism, Spelling, Arithmetic, English Grammar, Compositions, Geography, United States History and Writing.

FOURTH CLASS.

1 Volume: Catechism, Spelling, Arithmetic, English Grammar, Geography, United States History, Compositions and Writing.

PHILADELPHIA, PA.—Continued.

La Salle College.—*Christian Brothers.*

DRAWING.

3 Oil Paintings (Framed), 6 Pastel Drawings (Framed), 5 Water-Color Drawings (Framed), 5 Volumes Pen-and-Ink Object Drawing, 1 Album Problems in Straight Lines and Applications, 1 Album Problems on Curved Lines and Applications, 1 Album Principles of Projections, 1 Album Projection of Solids on Auxiliary Planes, 1 Album Penetrations and Developments, 1 Album Principles of Perspective, 2 Albums (42) Water-Color Drawings.

VILLANOVA, PA., Diocese Philadelphia.

Villanova College.—*Augustinian Fathers.*

6 Photographs of Students and Class-Rooms.

PHILADELPHIA, PA.

Roman Catholic High School.—*Secular Teachers.*

24 Original Designs, 20 Mechanical Drawings, 35 Pieces Modeling in Clay 76 Wood Carvings, 72 Pieces Carpentry, 25 Wood-Work (Pattern-Making) and 52 Sets Book-Keeping.

St. Joseph's Academy.—*Sisters of St. Joseph.*

13 Volumes: Christian Doctrine, Latin, German, French Essays, English Literature, Church History, Astronomy, Zoology, Botany, Logic, Book-Keeping, Natural Philosophy, Rhetoric, History, Civics, Arithmetic, Mythology, Stenography, Grammar, Geography, United States History, Bible History, Compositions. 1 Volume Prospectuses of Academy, 1 Volume Photographs and 2 Volumes Music, 11 Copy Books Examination Papers, 10 Copy Books Compositions, 1 Album Original Designs for Oil Cloth, 1 Etching, 1 Pastel, 7 Albums Drawing, 2 Original Designs (Water Color) for Borders, 1 Crayon Portrait (Most Rev. Archbishop Ryan), 1 Crayon St. Joseph with List of Schools, Specimens of Sewing, Embroidery and Lace-Work.

Academy of Notre Dame.—*Sisters of Notre Dame.*

3 Volumes Theory of Music, 1 Volume Musical Compositions by Pupils 1 Volume Music Compiled and Arranged by Sisters of Notre Dame.

SHARON HILL, PA.

Academy of the Holy Child Jesus.—*Sisters of the Holy Child Jesus.*

7 Oil Paintings, 7 Pastel Drawings, 2 Pen Sketches, 7 Water Colors, 1 Volume Scenes from Shakespeare, 1 Volume Drawing, 1 Volume Illuminated Work on Silk, 4 Illuminated Altar Cards, Embroidery, 1 Cape, 1 Burse, 1 Stole, 1 Embroidered Throw, 3 Altar Veils, 1 Fish Dinner Set Hand-Painted Porcelain.

WEST CHESTER, PA.

Academy of the Immaculate Heart.—*Sisters of the Immaculate Heart.*

1 Embroidered Quilt and 1 Embroidered Throw.

PARISH SCHOOLS.

PHILADELPHIA, PA.

The class-work, consisting of a series of written examinations of 73 Parish Schools (counting male and female schools separately) is contained in 89 large

PHILADELPHIA, PA.—Continued.

bound Volumes, and includes work from the 12 established grades. There are 47 Volumes of Grammar-Grade Work, 31 Volumes of Secondary-Grade Work and 11 Volumes of Primary Grade Work.

The pupils' examinations represent the following branches: Christian Doctrine, Church History, Spelling, Penmanship, Grammar, Letter Writing, Etymology, Homonyms, Bible History, Ancient and United States History, Geography, Compositions, Globe Studies, Mensuration, Arithmetic, Freehand, Crayon and Map Drawing, Algebra, Book-Keeping, Chemistry, Geometry and Trigonometry (Plane and Spherical).

As the work of the different schools was bound in the same Volumes and according to grade, it was found impossible to catalogue the work of each school in detail, and, for this reason, merely the names of the City's Schools and Teachers can be given.

Cathedral School.
MALE DEPT.—*Christian Brothers.*
FEMALE DEPT.—*Sisters of St. Joseph.*

St. Agatha's School.
MALE DEPT.—*Christian Brothers.*
FEMALE DEPT.—*Sisters of the Holy Child.*

All Saints' School.—*Franciscan Sisters.*

St. Alphonsus' School.—*Franciscan Sisters.*

St. Ann's School.
MALE DEPT.—*Christian Brothers.*
FEMALE DEPT.—*Sisters of St. Joseph.*

Annunciation School.—*Sisters of the Immaculate Heart.*

Assumption School.
MALE DEPT.—*Christian Brothers.*
FEMALE DEPT.—*Sisters of the Holy Child.*

St. Bonaventure's School.—*Sisters of St. Francis.*

St. Bonifacius' School.
MALE DEPT.—*Secular Teachers.*
FEMALE DEPT.—*School Sisters of Notre Dame.*

St. Bridget's School.—*Sisters of St. Joseph.*

St. Charles Borromeo's School.
MALE DEPT.—*Christian Brothers.*
FEMALE DEPT.—*Sisters of St. Joseph.*

St. Dominic's School.— { *Ladies of the Sacred Heart*
Sisters of the Immaculate Heart.

St. Edward's School.—*Sisters of the Holy Child.*

St. Elizabeth's School.—*Sisters of St. Francis.*

St. Francis Xavier's School.—*Sisters of the Immaculate Heart.*

Gesu School.—*Sisters of the Immaculate Heart.*

Holy Trinity School.—*School Sisters of Notre Dame.*

Immaculate Conception School.—*Sisters of St. Joseph.*

PHILADELPHIA, PA.—Continued.

St. James' School.
MALE DEPT.—*Secular Teachers.*
FEMALE DEPT.—*Sisters of the Holy Child.*

St. Joachim's School.—*Sisters of the Immaculate Heart.*

St. John the Baptist's School.—*Sisters of the Immaculate Heart.*

St. John the Evangelist's School.—*Secular Teachers.*

St. Joseph's School.—*Sisters of St. Joseph.*

St. Malachy's School.—*Sisters of Mercy.*

St. Mary's School.—*Sisters of St. Joseph.*

St. Mary of the Assumption School.—*Sisters of St. Francis.*

St. Mary Magdalen de Pazzi School.—*Sisters of St. Francis.*

St. Michael's School.
MALE DEPT.—*Christian Brothers.*
FEMALE DEPT.—*Sisters of St. Joseph.*

Nativity School.—*Sisters of St. Joseph.*

Our Lady Help of Christian Schools.—*Sisters of Christian Charity.*

Our Mother of Consolation School.—*Sisters of St. Joseph.*

Our Mother of Sorrows' School.
MALE DEPT.—*Christian Brothers.*
FEMALE DEPT.—*Sisters of St. Joseph.*

St. Patrick's School.
MALE DEPT.—*Christian Brothers.*
FEMALE DEPT.—*Sisters of St. Joseph.*

St. Paul's School.
MALE DEPT.—*Christian Brothers.*
FEMALE DEPT.—*School Sisters of Notre Dame.*

St. Philip De Neri's School.
MALE DEPT.—*Secular Teachers.*
FEMALE DEPT.—*Sisters of St. Joseph.*

St. Stephen's School.—*Sisters of St. Joseph.*

St. Teresa's School.—*Sisters of the Immaculate Heart.*

St. Vincent de Paul's School.
MALE DEPT.—*Franciscan Brothers.*
FEMALE DEPT.—*Sisters of St. Joseph.*

St. Vincent's School.—*School Sisters of Notre Dame.*

Visitation School.
MALE DEPT.—*Secular Teachers.*
FEMALE DEPT.—*Sisters of the Holy Child.*

WORLD'S COLUMBIAN EXPOSITION, 1893.

ASHLAND, PA.
    St. Mauritius' School.—*Sisters of St. Francis.*

BALLY, PA.
    Blessed Sacrament School.—*Sisters of St. Francis.*

BRISTOL, PA.
    St. Mark's School.—*Sisters of the Immaculate Heart.*

BRYN MAWR, PA.
    Our Lady of Good Counsel School.—*Sisters of Mercy.*

CHESTER, PA.
    St. Michael's School.—*Sisters of the Holy Child.*
    Immaculate Heart of Mary.—*Sisters of the Immaculate Heart.*

CONSHOHOCKEN, PA.
    St. Mathew's School.—*Secular Teachers.*

WEST CONSHOHOCKEN, PA.
    St. Gertrude's School.—*Sisters of the Immaculate Heart.*

DOYLESTOWN, PA.
    Our Lady of Mt. Carmel School.—*Sisters of St. Francis.*

EAST MAUCH CHUNK, PA.
    St. Joseph's School.—*Sisters of Christian Charity.*

KELLYVILLE, PA.
    St. Charles Borromeo's School.—*Sisters of the Immaculate Heart.*

MAUCH CHUNK, PA.
    Immaculate Conception School.—*Sisters of the Immaculate Heart.*

MORRISTOWN, PA.
    St. Patrick's School.—*Sisters of the Immaculate Heart.*

PHOENIXVILLE, PA.
    St. Mary's School.—*Sisters of the Immaculate Heart.*

PORT CARBON, PA.
    St. Stephen's School.—*Sisters of the Immaculate Heart.*

POTTSVILLE, PA.
    St. Patrick's School.—*Sisters of St. Joseph.*
    St. John the Baptist's School.—*Sisters of Christian Charity.*

READING, PA.
    St. Paul's School.—*Sisters of Christian Charity.*

WEST CHESTER, PA.
    St. Agnes' School.—*Sisters of the Immaculate Heart.*

SPECIAL EXHIBITS.

CONSHOHOCKEN, PA.

St. Mathew's School.

7 Geometrical Diagrams, 1 Map Showing Lieut. Peary's Explorations, 1 Map of the Diocese of Philadelphia, Showing Industries of the Districts and Growth of the Parochial Schools, 1 Volume Describing the Above Map, 14 Problems in Spherical Trigonometry (Framed), 1 Volume Plane Trigonometry, 1 Volume Photographs, 1 Volume Class-Work.

PHILADELPHIA, PA.

St. Agatha's School.—*Christian Brothers.*

1 Album Each: Algebra and Mensuration; 2 Albums Each: Catechism, History, Arithmetic, Geography and Grammar.

St. Ann's School.—*Christian Brothers.*

1 Album Architectural Drawing and Maps, 1 Volume Lettering and Elements of Drawing, 6 Volumes Botanical Specimens, 2 Class Registers, Specimens of Monthly and Weekly Reports, 1 Photograph Album, Specimens of Class-Work, Christian Doctrine, Church and Bible History, Orthography, Grammar, Profane History, Mathematics, Mathematical, Political and Physical Geography, Arithmetic, Algebra, Mensuration, Geometry, Phonography, Compositions, Botany, Book-Keeping and Penmanship.

St. Bonifacius' School.—*School Sisters of Notre Dame.*

1 Volume Drawing.

Cathedral School.—*Christian Brothers.*

19 Volumes: Linear and Ornamental Drawing, Book-Keeping, Catechism, Penmanship, Grammar, Compositions, Mensuration, History, Arithmetic, Geography, Algebra, Dictations, Business Forms, Phonography, Typewriting, Spelling and Botany.

St. Charles' School.—*Christian Brothers.*

1 Album Each: Compositions, Penmanship, Dictations, Definitions in Arithmetic, Sacred History, Letter Writing, Spelling, Bills, Receipts, Book-Keeping, 2 Volumes United States History, 3 Albums Each: Geography, Mensuration, Christian Doctrine and Arithmetic, 4 Volumes Grammar, 2 Volumes Penmanship and 60 Sheets of Drawing.

St. Michael's School.—*Christian Brothers.*

1 Album Each: Catechism, United States History, Bible History, Algebra, Mensuration, Arithmetic, Geography, Spelling, Book-Keeping, Bills, Receipts, Phonography, Drawing, 50 Home Exercises, 50 Copy Books and 1 Pastel Drawing.

Our Mother of Sorrows' School.—*Christian Brothers*

1 Album Each: Writing, Dictations, Algebra, Arithmetic, Book-Keeping, History, Grammar, Catechism.

St. Patrick's School.—*Christian Brothers.*

1 Volume Each: Mensuration, Algebra, Arithmetic, Book-Keeping, History, Grammar, Dictation and Catechism.

St. Paul's School.—*Christian Brothers.*

1 Album Each: Spelling, Geography and History. 2 Albums Each: Grammar, Mensuration and Specimens of Penmanship. 3 Albums: Arithmetic and Bound Volumes Penmanship Specimens, 20 Miscellaneous Exercise Copy Books and 38 Copy Books Writing.

PHILADELPHIA, PA.—Continued.

St. Peter's School.

MALE DEPT.—*Christian Brothers.*
1 Volume Mensuration, 2 Volumes Arithmetic and Book-Keeping, 1 Volume Geography, 1 Volume Bills of Sale, 1 Volume Translations, 1 Volume Linear Drawing, 3 Volumes Architectural Drawing, 3 Volumes Ornamental Drawing, 1 Volume Map Drawing, 33 Mounted Maps, 2 Albums Water Colors and Pastel Painting. 1 Volume Pen-and-Ink Sketches, 1 Volume Specimens of Writing (English and German), 6 Class Registers, 1 Collection of Minerals, 1 Collection of Woods, 1 Collection of Leather, 1 Collection of Grain and Spices.

FEMALE DEPT.—*School Sisters of Notre Dame.*
1 Volume Map Drawing.

INDUSTRIAL SCHOOL AND ORPHANAGE.

EDDINGTON, PA.

St. Francis' Industrial School.

Specimens of Plumbing, Carpentry, Forging and Stone Cutting, 1 Album Each: Compositions, Language Lessons, Algebra, Geography, History. 2 Albums Each: Ornamental Drawing, Spelling, Grammar, Catechism. 3 Albums Each: Penmanship, Arithmetic and 7 Albums Linear Drawing.

PHILADELPHIA, PA.

Catholic Home.—*Sisters of St. Joseph.*

Photographs of Classes and Children, Specimens of Sewing and 2 Albums Compositions.

ARCHDIOCESE OF SAN FRANCISCO.

MOST REV. PATRICK W. RIORDAN, D. D.

Diocesan Committee.

Rev. P. SCANLAN.
Rev. J. B. MCNALLY.
Bro. MICHAEL, F. S. C.
Rev. M. D. CONNELLY, *Manager.*

Rev. P. CASEY.
Rev. J. SASIA, S. J.
Bro. GEORGE ALBERT, F. M.
Rev. P. C. YORK, *Secretary.*

ALCOVES 17, 19, 21, 23, 25, 27 AND 29.

Portrait of His Grace Archbishop Riordan.

Album of 58 Photographic Views of Preliminary Exhibit held in San Francisco, and visited by 45,000 persons.

Printed list of Schools exhibiting, and noting work from 16 Colleges and Academies, 34 Parish Schools, 11 Kindergartens and 3 Technical Institutions.

COLLEGES AND ACADEMIES.

SAN FRANCISCO, CAL.

St. Ignatius' College.—*Jesuit Fathers.*

NORMAL DEPT.

Photographs of Students, Church, College, Museum, Library, Chemical and Physical Laboratories. 14 Albums: Essays, Translations, Examinations in Greek, Latin and English; Moral and Natural Philosophy, Mathematics, Book-Keeping. 1 Volume Lecture on the Atmosphere.

Sacred Heart College.—*Christian Brothers.*

Albums and Frame of Photographs, 10 Rolls of Honor, 15 Surveys, 9 Specimens of Penmanship, 53 Albums Class-Work in Geometry, Trigonometry, Surveying, Chemistry Language, Religion, etc. 26 Volumes Corrected and Uncorrected Essays. 204 Volumes of Examinations, Penmanship and Book-Keeping.

OAKLAND CAL.

St. Mary's College.—*Christian Brothers.*

NORMAL DEPT.

Model of College Building Accompanied by Architect's Plans in 7 Frames and Photograph of College. 27 Mounted Charts, by Brother Hyacinth, Explaining Principles of Phonography, Photographs of Graduates.

COLLEGE DEPT.

413 Volumes of Essays in Greek and Latin, Examinations and Studies in Mental and Natural Philosophy, Religion, Mathematics, Hygiene, etc. 7 Surveys of St. Mary's College.

BUSINESS DEPT.

53 Volumes of Book-Keeping, Mathematics, Essays, Religion. 186 Volumes of Phonographic Exercises. 23 Volumes of Typewriting.

ART DEPT.

4 Volumes of Linear and Mechanical Drawings. 55 Studies in Crayon, Lead Pencil and Water Colors. 18 Pieces of Pen-Work.

SANTA CLARA, CAL.

Santa Clara College.—*Jesuit Fathers.*

NORMAL DEPT.

5 Text Books in Mathematics by Rev. Jos. Bayma, S. J., Pen-Work by Professor of Penmanship, Descriptive Catalogues, Photographs of Students and Graduates, Apparatus Used in Commercial Department.

STUDENTS' WORK.

14 Studies in Crayon, India Ink and Water Color; 21 Albums of Essays; Compositions in Prose and Poetry in Latin, Greek and English; Moral and Natural Philosophy, Mathematics, Book-Keeping.

SAN JOSE, CAL.

St. Joseph's College.—*Jesuit Fathers.*

Photographs of Students, Church and College. 4 Volumes: Latin, Greek and English Exercises, Mathematics, Book-Keeping.

STOCKTON, CAL.

St. Mary's College.—*Brothers of Mary.*

1 Mechanical Drawing by the Brothers, 8 Drawings by Students. 23 Volumes Class-Work: Arithmetic, Composition, Dictation, Sketches, Maps, Examinations and Penmanship.

SAN FRANCISCO, CAL.

Academy of the Sacred Heart.—*Ladies of the Sacred Heart.*

NORMAL DEPT.

12 Original Designs in Illumination of Magnificat. 1 Altar Card. 1 Illuminated Card Signed M. Henggler. Photographs.

STUDENTS' WORK.

145 Volumes of Religion, Mental and Physical Science, Architecture, French, German and English Literature and Language, Mathematics, Religion, History, etc. 14 Historical and Geographical Charts. 16 Volumes Herbaria. 18 Portfolios. Bands and Specimens of Needle-Work, Embroidery, Crochet, Lace, etc. 1 Volume of Pen-and-Ink Drawings. 11 Illuminated Cards, 3 Miniatures.

College Notre Dame.—*Sisters of Notre Dame de Namur.*

Photographs of College and Students. 1 Volume of Essays Composed and Printed by Pupils. 17 Volumes of Class-Work Embracing History, Literature, Mathematics, Book-Keeping, Religion.

St. Rose's Academy.—*Sisters of St. Dominic.*

NORMAL DEPT.

Album of California Wild Flowers. 1 Album of Photographs of Students

STUDENTS' WORK.

14 Volumes of Class-Work: Grammar, Literature, Rhetoric, Letter Writing, Historical Essays, Logic, Physical Geography, United States and French History, Astronomy, Physiology, Natural Philosophy, Etymology, Algebra, Geometry, Book-Keeping, Music and Christian Doctrine. 12 Volumes of Sketches of Old Mission, 1 Volume Columbus.

Academy of the Immaculate Conception.—*Sisters of St. Dominic,* (2d Order).

14 Volumes School Work: Grammar, Language, Composition, Rhetoric, Arithmetic, Algebra, Geometry, United States History, Geography, Astronomy, Physics, Chemistry, Stories of California Missions, Christian Doctrine. 1 Album Photographs, Maps.

ALAMEDA, CAL.

Academy of Notre Dame.—*Sisters of Notre Dame de Namur.*

7 Volumes: Sacred Science, Mathematics, Philosophy, Language, History, Geography.

BERKELEY, CAL.

Presentation Normal School.—*Presentation Nuns.*

Display Work, Drawing, Penmanship. 2 Volumes Class-Work: Including Grammar, Composition, English, Ancient and Bible History, Arithmetic, Geography, Algebra, Physics, Music and Christian Doctrine.

MARTINEZ, CAL.

Normal Institute.—*Christian Brothers.*

11 Volumes: Geometry, Trigonometry, Mensuration and Linear Drawing.

OAKLAND, CAL.

St. Joseph's Academy.—*Christian Brothers.*

5 Mechanical Drawings and Plans. 24 Volumes: Penmanship, Arithmetic, Religion. 19 Albums: Maps, Sketches, Mensuration, Geography, History, Orthography, Language, English, Mathematics, Book-Keeping and Religion.

Convent of Our Lady of the Sacred Heart.—*Sisters of the Most Holy Names.*

NORMAL DEPT.

2 Albums of Photographs Collected by Sisters and Used in Teaching Art and History. Circular. Photographs of Students.

STUDENTS' WORK.

13 Volumes Class-Work: Arithmetic, Algebra, Geometry, Physics, Physiology, Astronomy, Botany, Composition, Rhetoric, Literature, Mapping, Ancient History, History of Art, Christian Doctrine. 7 Booklets Penmanship, Juvenile Sewing Album, Painted Cushion, Table-Scarf, Glove-Case.

RIO VISTA, CAL.

St. Gertrude's Academy.—*Sisters of Mercy.*

NORMAL DEPT.

Illuminated History of Academy, Photographs.

STUDENTS' WORK.

25 Volumes Class-Work: Arithmetic, Algebra, Geometry, Spelling, Grammar, Composition, English Literature, Geography, Maps, Physical Geography, Ancient and United States History, Rhetoric, Word Analysis, Astronomy, Natural Philosophy, Physiology, Music, Penmanship, Stenography, Typewriting, Christian Doctrine. Studies in Crayon and Oil.

SANTA CLARA, CAL.

Academy of Our Lady of Angels.—*Sisters of Notre Dame de Namur.*

5 Photographs, 16 Volumes Class-Work: Arithmetic, Geography, Drawing, Composition, Christian Doctrine and Miscellaneous. Box of Needle-Work.

SAN JOSE, CAL.

College Notre Dame.—*Sisters of Notre Dame de Namur.*

NORMAL DEPT.

Photographs, Chenille Work, Irish Point Lace. Catalogues, Books Published by Former Students, Programmes and Addresses. Some Frontispieces. Selections from Herbaria, Cabinets, etc., Mounted on Transparent Celluloid. Diplomas of College. History of College.

STUDENTS' WORK.

Wild Flowers of California, Water Color; Specimens of Needle-Work and Embroidery. 115 Volumes History of Botany, Religion, Literature, Maps, Philology, Natural and Mental Science.

SANTA ROSA, CAL.

Sacred Heart Academy.—*Ursuline Nuns.*

NORMAL DEPT.

1 Embroidered Benediction Veil. Photographs.

STUDENTS' WORK.

18 Volumes of School-Work: Grammar, Composition, Rhetoric, Arithmetic Algebra, Geometry, Physics, Astronomy, Book-Keeping, Mythology, Word Analysis, Catechism, Music (Original Arrangements). 6 Charts.

SAN RAFAEL, CAL.

College San Rafael.—*Sisters of St. Dominic.*

NORMAL DEPT.

5 Studies in Life of St. Agnes. Water Color of College. 1 Album of Photographs.

STUDENTS' WORK.

14 Volumes of Class-Work: Grammar, Literature, Rhetoric, Letter Writing, Historical Essays, Physical Geography, United States and French History, Astronomy, Physiology, Natural Philosophy, Algebra, Geometry, Christian Doctrine, Historical Charts, English and Ancient History, Civil Government, French, Arithmetic, Trigonometry, Chemistry, Geology, Mythology, Class Notes, Penmanship, Stenography. 1 Volume of Water-Color Sketches of California Missions.

PARISH SCHOOLS.

SAN FRANCISCO, CAL.

Sacred Heart Presentation Convent.—*Presentation Nuns.*

STUDENTS' WORK.

7 Volumes Copy Books, 3 Volumes Drawing, 7 Volumes Exercises, 6 Volumes Compositions, 5 Volumes Examination Lessons, 2 Volumes Algebra, 1 Painted Banner, 1 Set (24) Object Charts, 1 Photo Album, 1 Album Painting Specimens, 1 Album Needle-Work, 2 Albums Writing, 1 Album Crochet Work, 1 Crayon Drawing of Most Rev. Archbishop Riordon, 1 Pastel Drawing, 1 Framed Piece of Needle-Work, 1 Map of California and 1 Fire Screen.

St. Francis' School.

MALE DEPT.—*Miss Latham, Principal.*

3 Volumes Class Exercises in Spelling, Arithmetic, Geography. 1 Volume Compositions and Drawings. 3 Volumes Daily Work in Catechism, Grammar. 1 Volume Maps. 1 Volume Mathematical Geography. 1 Volume Photographs.

FEMALE DEPT.—*Sisters of Notre Dame.*

6 Volumes of Work of Primary and Grammar Classes, Catechism, Composition, Arithmetic, Spelling, Dictation, Christian Doctrine, Grammar, United States History, Civil Government, Physiology, Penmanship, Maps and Designs. 1 Volume Photographs.

St. Boniface's School.—*Sisters of St. Dominic (2d Order).*

2 Volumes Catechism and Bible History, 2 Volumes Language and Compositions, 2 Volumes Geography and United States History, 3 Volumes Arithmetic, 1 Volume Products of California, 2 Volumes Penmanship, 2 Volumes English Compositions, 3 Volumes German Compositions, 1 Album Photo-

SAN FRANCISCO, CAL.—Continued.

St. Brigid's School.—*Sisters of Charity, B. V. M.*

STUDENTS' WORK.

1 Volume Miscellaneous Exercises, First and Second Grades. 1 Volume Miscellaneous Exercises, Third Grade. 2 Volumes Miscellaneous Exercises, Fourth Grade. 2 Volumes Miscellaneous Exercises, Fifth Grade. 2 Volumes Miscellaneous Exercises, Sixth Grade, 1 Volume Miscellaneous Exercises, Seventh Grade, 4 Volumes Miscellaneous Exercises, Eighth Grade, 1 Volume Book-Keeping, Eighth Grade. 2 Volumes Drawing from All Grades.

ACADEMIC DEPARTMENT.

1 Volume: Astronomy, Literature, Philosophy and Chemistry. 1 Volume: Christian Doctrine, Rhetoric, Composition and Modern History. 1 Volume: Botany, Zoology, Algebra and Geometry.

NORMAL WORK.

1 Herbarium of Flowers from the Pacific Coast. 1 Album Containing Photographs of Church, School and Pupils.

Presentation Convent.—ST. FRANCIS PARISH.—*Presentation Nuns.*

10 Volumes Class-Work: Grammar, Geography, United States History, Arithmetic, Composition, Algebra, Astronomy, Christian Doctrine. 1 Photograph Album. 1 Album of Drawings. 1 Album of Paintings. 2 Albums Needle-Work. 1 Album Penmanship. Display-Work: Drawings and Designs.

St. Joseph's Grammar School.—MALE DEPT.—*Brothers of Mary.*

NORMAL WORK.

3 Large Relief Maps: 1 of California, 1 of San Joaquin County, 1 of Vicinity of San Francisco, 1 Catalogue.

STUDENTS' WORK.

13 Relief Maps Various Countries, 9 Relief Figures, 1 Framed Picture of Course of Studies, 73 Volumes Class-Work, Christian Doctrine, Reading, Grammar, Ancient and Modern History, United States History, Geography, Penmanship, Composition, Rhetoric, Literature, Freehand and Linear Drawing, Elocution, Algebra, Geometry, Trigonometry, Natural Philosophy, Chemistry, Book-Keeping, Arithmetic, Commercial Calculations, Commercial Law and Shorthand. 1 Album Photographs of Boys' Classes, 21 Sets of Book-Keeping Blanks, 170 Large Drawings.

FEMALE DEPARTMENT.—*Sisters of the Holy Names.*

23 Volumes Class-Work: Grammar, Orthography, Dictation, Arithmetic, Geometry, Algebra, Compositions, United States and Church History, Literature, Physics, Astronomy, Mapping, Geography, Drawings in Pencil and Colored Crayon, Christian Doctrine, 54 Booklets of Class-Work, Maps, French and United States History, Grecian History and Literature, Grammar, Spelling, Dictations, Object Lessons, Bible History, Botany, Compositions, 1 Volume Drawing 1st, 2d and 3d Grades, 1 Volume California Wild Flowers, 35 Exercise Books of Primary Grades, 1 Photograph Album.

St. Patrick's School.—*Sisters of Charity.*

5 Volumes Class-Work of 3d, 4th and 5th Grades: Spelling, Grammar, Language, Composition, Word Analysis, Geography, United States History, Physiology, Catechism. 1 Album of Specimens of Display Work.

SAN FRANCISCO, CAL.—Continued.

St. Vincent's School.—*Sisters of Charity.*

1 Crayon Sacred Heart, 3 Crayon Studies from Models done by the Drawing Class, 3 Oil Paintings. 21 Volumes Class-Work by Pupils of Rhetoric Class, 1st, 2d, 3d, 4th, 5th and 6th Grades: Grammar, Spelling, Word Analysis, Composition, Letter Writing, Literature, Geography, United States, Bible and Church History, Arithmetic, Algebra, Geometry, Astronomy, Physiology, Physics, Drawing, Catechism. 1 Volume Maps, 1 Volume Charts.

St. Peter's School.—*Christian Brothers.*

3 Volumes Algebra, 6 Volumes Arithmetic, 1 Volume Bible History, 28 Volumes Book-Keeping, 3 Volumes Christian Doctrine, 6 Volumes Composition, 4 Volumes Dictation, 4 Volumes Drawing, 1 Volume Examination Papers, 1 Volume Geography, 1 Volume Geometrical Drawing, 1 Volume Grammar, 3 Volumes Home Work, 2 Volumes Language, 1 Volume Map Drawing, 3 Volumes Mensurations, 8 Volumes Penmanship, 2 Volumes Series Copy Books, 1 Volume United States History, 1 Photograph Album, Framed Pen-Work, Framed Drawings.

St. Peter's School.—*Sisters of Mercy.*

7 Volumes of Language, 4 Volumes Arithmetic, 3 Volumes Science, 2 Volumes Geography, 2 Volumes History, 2 Volumes Christian Doctrine, 1 Volume Penmanship, 4 Volumes Drawing, 1 Album of Photographs.

St. Rose's School.—*Sisters of Most Holy Names.*

11 Volumes Class-Work: Arithmetic, Spelling, Grammar, Word Analysis, Composition, Dictation, Geography, United States History, Penmanship, Language, Letter Writing and Catechism. 3 Booklets of Drawings, 1 Booklet Doll's Outfit, 1 Booklet Picture Stories, 1 Album Photographs.

Our Lady of Mercy's Academy.—St. Brendan's Parish.—*Sisters of Mercy.*

4 Volumes Christian Doctrine, 4 Volumes Language, 4 Volumes Composition, 6 Volumes Arithmetic, 1 Volume Book-Keeping, 4 Volumes Geography, 2 Volumes Spelling, 4 Volumes History, 1 Volume Literature, 1 Volume, Science, 3 Volumes Oral Instruction, 6 Volumes Music, 6 Volumes Drawing, 1 School Album.

BERKELEY, CAL.

St. Joseph's School.—*Presentation Nuns.*

4 Volumes Class-Work: Penmanship, Spelling, Grammar, Composition, Geography, Bible History, Catechism, Book-Keeping, Drawing, Physics and Astronomy.

OAKLAND, CAL.

Academy of Our Lady of Lourdes.—*Sisters of Mercy.*

1 Volume Christian Doctrine, 2 Volumes Mathematics, 2 Volumes Composition, 1 Volume Grammar, Rhetoric, Word Analysis and Penmanship, 1 Volume History, 1 Volume Geography, 1 Volume Astronomy and Philosophy, Botany and Physiology, 1 Volume Drawing, 1 Volume Music, 1 Photograph Album. Catalogue.

St. Anthony's School.—*Christian Brothers.*

14 Volumes Class-Work: Grammar, Spelling, Composition, Language, History, Geography, Arithmetic, Book-Keeping, Mensuration, Dictation, Catechism.

OAKLAND, CAL.—Continued.

St. Francis de Sales' School.

MALE DEPT.—*Christian Brothers.*

9 Volumes Penmanship, 2 Volumes Algebra, 3 Volumes Business Forms, 4 Volumes Spelling and Dictation, 8 Volumes Practical Arithmetic, 3 Volumes Christian Doctrine, 4 Volumes Geography, 3 Volumes Miscellaneous Work, 1 Volume Book-Keeping, 1 Volume Plane Trigonometry, 1 Volume Grammar and Parsing, 1 Volume Photographs, 1 Volume Spelling, Dictation and Letters, 1 Volume Mensuration of Solids and Algebra, 1 Volume Examinations in History and Biography, 1 Volume Compositions, Latin Exercises, Letters and Orders for Merchandise, 1 Volume Receipted Bills and Mensuration of Surfaces.

FEMALE DEPT.—*Sisters of the Holy Names.*

2 Volumes Christian Doctrine, 3 Volumes Composition, 2 Volumes Arithmetic, 1 Volume Algebra, 1 Volume Geometry, 1 Volume Astronomy, 1 Volume Physiology, 1 Volume Language, 1 Volume Spelling, 4 Volumes Miscellaneous Exercises, 5 Volumes Specimens of Every-Day Work.

St. Lawrence's School.—*Sisters of the Most Holy Names.*

10 Albums of Class-Work.

Sacred Heart School.—*Christian Brothers.*

79 Booklets Class-Work: Arithmetic, Grammar, History, Language, Geography, Penmanship, Book-Keeping, Mensuration, Algebra and Catechism. 1 Volume of Photographs.

St. Mary's School.—*Christian Brothers.*

96 Booklets Class-Work: Arithmetic, Spelling, Language, Geography, United States History, Grammar, Drawing, Penmanship, Mensuration, Book-Keeping, Christian Doctrine. 1 Volume of Photographs

St. Mary's Girls' School.—*Sisters of the Most Holy Names.*

4 Volumes Class-Work: Catechism, Geography, Grammar, Arithmetic, History, Analysis, Composition, Algebra, Practical Philosophy, Geometry, Astronomy, Literary Analysis. 1 Volume Map and Other Drawings. 1 Volume of Photographs.

St. Joseph's Institute.—*Christian Brothers.*

50 Volumes Class-Work: Arithmetic, Language, Penmanship, Geography, History, Mensuration, Christian Doctrine, Book-Keeping. 33 Albums of History, Geography, Christian Doctrine, Monthly Reports and Rolls of Honor.

St. Joseph's School.—*Sisters of St. Joseph.*

15 Volumes Daily Work and Quarterly Examinations, Language and Mathematics. 1 Volume of Photographs.

REDWOOD CITY, CAL.

Notre Dame Parish School.—*Sisters of Notre Dame.*

12 Volumes Class-Work: Orthography, Grammar, Rhetoric, Composition, Literature, History, Arithmetic, Algebra, Geography, Maps, Object Lessons, Book-Keeping and Christian Doctrine.

SAN JOSE, CAL.

St. Joseph's School.—*Sisters of Notre Dame.*
26 Volumes Class-Work, Arithmetic, Grammar, Language, English, Geography, United States History, Dictations, Botany, Hygiene, Ancient History, Composition, Book-Keeping, Catechism and Bible History.

St. Aloysius' School.—*Sisters of Notre Dame.*
1 Volume Drawing.

SAN LEANDRO, CAL.

Parish School.—*Sisters of St. Domini.*
1 Volume of Photographs.

SAN RAFAEL, CAL.

St. Rafael's School.—*Sisters of St. Dominic.*
3 Volumes Class-Work: Arithmetic, Grammar, History, Penmanship, Rhetoric, Composition, French, German, Italian, French History and Catechism. 1 Volume of Photographs.

St. Agnes' Academy.—*Dominican Sisters.*
8 Volumes Class-Work: Literature, Geography, Geology, Astronomy, Algebra, Geometry and Christian Doctrine. 1 Volume of Photographs.

St. Joseph's Primary School.—*Dominican Sisters.*
2 Volumes of Work, Including Arithmetic, Spelling, Language, Geography and Christian Doctrine.

VALLEJO, CAL.

St. Vincent's School.—*Dominican Sisters.*
17 Sets Written Examinations, 7 Charts Grammar, Pen-Work, Colors and Tints; 1 Album of Photographs.

KINDERGARTENS.

SAN FRANCISCO.

Children's Day Home.—*Sisters of Holy Family.*
Framed Pictures of Specimens of Kindergarten Work, 1 Framed Picture of Pope Leo XIII., Specimens of Kindergarten Work.

Mt. St. Joseph's Kindergarten.—*Sisters of Charity.*
3 Albums.

Sacred Heart Kindergarten.—*Presentation Nuns.*
Specimens of Sewing, Drawing, Weaving, etc.

St. Francis' Kindergarten.—*Presentation Nuns.*
1 Album Kindergarten Work.

St. Brendan's Kindergarten.—*Sisters of Mercy.*
Sewing, Embossing, Weaving, etc.

OAKLAND, CAL.
 Our Lady of Lourdes' Kindergarten.—*Sisters of Mercy.*
  3 Charts of Kindergarten Work.

VALLEJO, CAL.
 St. Vincent's Kindergarten.—*Dominican Sisters.*
  Charts of Kindergarten Work

SAN FRANCISCO, CAL.
 St. Rose's Kindergarten.—*Dominican Sisters.*
  Gifts and Occupations Illustrated.

SAN RAFAEL, CAL.
 San Rafael Kindergarten.—*Dominican Sisters.*
  Specimens of Work.

STOCKTON, CAL.
 St. Agnes' Kindergarten.—*Dominican Sisters.*
  1 Album.

 St. Joseph's Kindergarten.—*Dominican Sisters.*
  1 Album.

INDUSTRIAL INSTITUTIONS.

SAN FRANCISCO, CAL.
 St. Francis' Technical School.—*Sisters of Charity.*
  DRESSMAKING DEPT.
   Fancy Waist of White Crepe, Yoke and Cuffs of Fine Tucks and Drawn-Work. Child's Dress of White India Silk, Full Skirt, Shirred Yoke, Finished with Rosettes of Baby Ribbon. Gentleman's Dressing-Gown of Garnet Cloth, Lined with Quilted Tan Satin, Collar and Cuffs Embroidered in Forget-Me-Nots.
  EMBROIDERY DEPT.
   Address of Institution. Specimens of Darning and Embroidery. Tea Cloth, Linen Damask embroidered. Banneret embroidered.
  EMBROIDERY.
   "Flowers of the Pacific Coast," representing a Basket of California's Choicest Blossoms, embroidered in 108 Shades of Twist. White Satin Slippers embroidered in Gold Bullion, Pair Suspenders embroidered in Chenille. 1 Volume Specimens of Embroidery. Fancy Scarf (pale blue). Fancy Scarf (orange).
  FINE SEWING DEPARTMENT.
   Tea-Cloth, Specimens of Letters in Drawn-Work, 2 Volumes Specimens of Needle-Work, Infant's Cloak (India Silk), Inserting in Darning. Infant's Cloak (Bengaline Silk). French Pattern in Fancy Stitching. Child's Dress (Bengaline Silk). Fine Drawn-Work, having one thread of material between pattern.

 Mt. St. Joseph's Infant Orphan Asylum.—*Sisters of Charity.*
  7 Volumes: Arithmetic, Spelling, Grammar, Geography, United States History, 1 Volume by Children seven and eight years old. 1 Album of Photographs.

SAN FRANCISCO, CAL.—Continued.

Roman Catholic Orphan Asylum.—*Sisters of Charity.*

10 Volumes Class-Work: Arithmetic, Grammar, Geography, United States History, Literature, Dictation, Letter Writing, Book-Keeping, Physiology, Astronomy, Physics and Christian Doctrine. 11 Volumes of Penmanship. 4 Charts of Drawing. 2 Specimens of Embroidery in Cross-Stitch.

DIOCESE OF BROOKLYN.

RT. REV. CHAS. McDONNELL, D.D.

Diocesan Committee.

Rev. Thos. Taaffe.　　Rev. Jos. O'Connell, D.D.　　Rev. J. A. Hartnett, C.M.

ALCOVES 18-20.

Portrait of Rt. Rev. Bishop McDonnell.

COLLEGES, ACADEMIES AND SELECT SCHOOLS.

BROOKLYN, N. Y.

St. John's College.—*Lazarist Fathers.*

1 Volume: Christian Doctrine, French Translations, Latin, Greek, Astronomy, Geometry, Rhetoric and Compositions.

St. Francis' College.—*Franciscan Brothers.*

8 Volumes: Geography, Christian Doctrine, Grammar, Arithmetic, Physiology, Rhetoric, Algebra, Greek, Geometry, Latin, History, Philosophy and Astronomy.

Academy of the Sacred Heart.—*Sisters of the Sacred Heart.*

1 Volume: Arithmetic, Grammar, United States History, French History, Sacred History and Etymology.

Nativity Academy.—*Sisters of St. Joseph.*

Male Dept.

1 Volume: Catechism, Arithmetic, Book-Keeping, History, Drawing, Typewriting and Map Drawing.

Female Dept.

2 Volumes: Grammar, Catechism, Map Drawing, Arithmetic, Book-Keeping, Drawing, Dictation, Algebra, Geometry, Compositions, Physiology, Typewriting and Geography.

Nativity Institute.—*Sisters of St. Joseph.*

2 Volumes: Map Drawing, Algebra, Mechanical Drawing, Compositions.

Sacred Heart Institute.

Male Dept.—*Franciscan Brothers.*

7 Volumes: Catechism, Geography, Writing, Spelling, Arithmetic, United States History, Typewriting, Phonography, Grammar, Physiology, Mensuration, Compositions, Civics, Algebra, History, Book-Keeping and English Literature.

BROOKLYN, N. Y.—CONTINUED.

Sacred Heart Institute.

FEMALE DEPT.—*Sisters of St. Joseph.*
3 Volumes: Geography, Catechism, United States History, Grammar, Spelling, Arithmetic, Language, Writing, Geography, Algebra and Civics.

St. Agnes' Seminary.—*Sisters of St. Joseph.*

2 Volumes: Geography, Map-Drawing, Letter Writing, Grammar, Language, Arithmetic, Book-Keeping, General History, Autographs, Business Forms, French, Physiology, Christian Doctrine, United States History, 13 Examination Papers, 6 Paintings, 15 Specimens of Needle-Work and Crocheting.

St. Joseph's Academy.—*Sisters of Mercy.*

2 Volumes: Christian Doctrine, Mechanical Drawing, Fancy Work, Arithmetic, Physiology, Music, French Compositions, English Literature and Needle-Work.

St. Leonard's Academy.—*Franciscan Brothers.*

3 Volumes: Christian Doctrine, Arithmetic, Geography, Grammar, German, Mensuration, Algebra, Orthography, Compositions, Stenography, Penmanship, Book-Keeping and Typewriting.

St. Patrick's Academy.

MALE DEPT.—*Franciscan Brothers.*
10 Volumes: Grammar, Mechanical Drawing, Algebra, United States History, Church History, Arithmetic, Spelling, Compositions, Geography, Penmanship, Geometry, Dictations, Shorthand, Catechism, Book-Keeping, Civil Government, Typewriting, Mensuration and Commercial Law.

FEMALE DEPT.—*Sisters of St. Joseph.*
2 Volumes: Arithmetic, Dictations, Geography, Grammar, United States History, Spelling, Church History, Language, Algebra, Christian Doctrine, Map Drawing, Writing and Compositions.

St. Teresa's Academy.—*Sisters of St. Joseph.*

MALE DEPT.
1 Volume: Book-Keeping, Map Drawing, Compositions, Geography, Spelling, Algebra, Arithmetic, History, Christian Doctrine, Grammar.

FEMALE DEPT.
2 Volumes: Composition, Grammar, Geography, Spelling, Arithmetic, Mechanical Drawing, Christian Doctrine, Book-Keeping, United States History and Algebra.

St. Thomas Aquinas' Academy.—*Sisters of St. Joseph.*

2 Volumes: Christian Doctrine, Map Drawing, Spelling, Definitions, Compositions, Grammar, Geography, Civil Government, Natural Philosophy, Literature, Physiology, Arithmetic, Algebra, German and French Translation.

St. Vincent de Paul's Academy.

MALE DEPT.—*Franciscan Brothers.*
2 Volumes: Language, Grammar, Spelling, Christian Doctrine, Mechanical Drawing, Typewriting, Penmanship, Phonography, Book-Keeping, Letter Writing, Map Drawing, Arithmetic and Geography.

FEMALE DEPT.—*Sisters of St. Joseph.*
2 Volumes: Compositions, Grammar, Christian Doctrine, Arithmetic, Civics, United States History, Algebra, Geography, Spelling, Photographs.

BROOKLYN, N. Y.—CONTINUED.

Visitation Convent.—*Sisters of the Visitation.*

4 Paintings.

Visitation Academy.—*Sisters of the Visitation.*

4 Volumes and 2 Albums: Christian Doctrine, Rhetoric, Chemistry, Composition, Letters, Penmanship, Physiology, French, German, Latin, Music, Astronomy, Algebra, Physics, Literature, and Large Album of Paintings and Drawings.

St. Joseph's Academy (Flushing).—*Sisters of St. Joseph.*

46 Mechanical Drawings, 12 Paintings, 6 Essays, 1 Volume Class-Work, 1 Volume Photographs.

St. Joseph's Novitiate (Flushing).—*Sisters of St. Joseph.*

1 Volume Centennial Dramas.

PARISH SCHOOLS.

BROOKLYN, N. Y.

All Saints' School.—*Dominican Sisters.*

MALE DEPT.

1 Volume: Catechism, Arithmetic, Compositions and German Penmanship.

FEMALE DEPT.

2 Volumes: Catechism, Arithmetic, Geography, Compositions (German and English), United States History, Grammar and Penmanship.

Assumption School.

MALE DEPT.—*Franciscan Brothers.*

1 Volume: Christian Doctrine, United States History, Spelling, Grammar, Typewriting, Arithmetic, Book-Keeping, Compositions and Geography.

FEMALE DEPT.—*Sisters of Charity.*

1 Volume: Grammar, Christian Doctrine, Church History, Orthography, Questions on Reading, Geography, Grammar, United States History, Letter Writing, Civics, Compositions, Astronomy, Book-Keeping, Algebra, Geometry and Physiology.

Holy Family School.—*Sisters of St. Dominic.*

1 Volume: Penmanship, Bible History, United States History, Arithmetic, Compositions, Geography, Translations, Letter Writing, Book-Keeping, Grammar and Drawing.

Holy Trinity School.

MALE DEPT.—*Secular Teachers.*

3 Volumes: Christian Doctrine, Writing, Compositions (German and English), Grammar (German and English), Arithmetic, United States History, Typewriting, Geography, Arithmetic, Natural History, Drawing and Translations.

FEMALE DEPT.—*Sisters of St. Dominic.*

3 Volumes: Christian Doctrine, Bible History, English and German Grammar, Translations, Compositions (English and German), United States History, Geography, Natural History, Maps, Writing, Drawing, Mensuration, Spelling and 1 Volume Kindergarten.

BROOKLYN, N. Y.—Continued.

Holy Cross School.—*Sisters of St. Joseph.*

1 Volume: Christian Doctrine, Map Drawing, Arithmetic, Writing, Grammar, United States History, Geography and Letter Writing.

Our Lady of Good Counsel School.—*Sisters of St. Joseph.*

MALE DEPT.

1 Volume: Business Forms, Catechism, Arithmetic, United States History, Algebra, Map Drawing, Civics, Grammar, Geography and Spelling.

FEMALE DEPT.

2 Volumes: Christian Doctrine, Arithmetic, History, Algebra, Geography, Grammar, Civics, Spelling and Drawing.

Our Lady of Mercy School.

MALE DEPT.—*Franciscan Brothers.*

3 Volumes: Typewriting, Spelling, Catechism, Geography, Arithmetic, Writing, Grammar, United States History, Map Drawing.

FEMALE DEPT.—*Sisters of St. Joseph.*

2 Volumes: Catechism, Spelling, Grammar, Composition, Algebra, United States History, Arithmetic, Geography, Map Drawing.

Our Lady Star of the Sea.—*Sisters of St. Joseph.*

1 Volume: Catechism, Spelling, Geography, Grammar, United States History, Arithmetic and Letter Writing.

St. Ann's School.

MALE DEPT.—*Franciscan Brothers.*

3 Volumes: Writing, Arithmetic, Catechism, Geography, Spelling, Map Drawing, United States History, Book-Keeping, Algebra, Business Forms and Grammar.

FEMALE DEPT.—*Sisters of St. Joseph.*

4 Volumes: Arithmetic, Civil Government, Geography, Spelling, Map Drawing, United States History, Compositions, Grammar, Critical Reading, Algebra, History, Catechism and Business Forms.

St. Anthony's School.

MALE DEPT.—*Franciscan Brothers.*

2 Volumes: Geography, Grammar, Civics, Catechism, Spelling, Compositions, Language, Arithmetic, Phonography, Typewriting, History, Civics, Physiology, Algebra and Physical Geography.

FEMALE DEPT.—*Sisters of St. Joseph.*

5 Volumes: Catechism, History, Arithmetic, Spelling, Grammar, Geography, United States History, Literature, Hygiene, Geometry, Algebra and Compositions.

St. Benedict's School.—*Sisters of Christian Charity.*

1 Volume: Translations, Geography, Arithmetic and Catechism.

St. Bernard's School.—*Dominican Sisters.*

2 Volumes: Geography, Grammar, Spelling, Arithmetic, United States History, Bible History, Grammar, Composition, Spelling and Drawing.

BROOKLYN, N. Y.—Continued.

St. Charles' School.

MALE DEPT.—*Franciscan Brothers.*

2 Volumes: Geography, Grammar, Spelling, Arithmetic, Catechism, Penmanship, United States History, Civics, Book-Keeping, Algebra, Mensuration, Typewriting and Map Drawing.

FEMALE DEPT.—*Sisters of Charity.*

1 Volume: Christian Doctrine, Algebra, Arithmetic, History, Grammar, Civics, Geography, Compositions and Business Forms.

St. Fidelis' School.—*Dominican Sisters.*

1 Volume: Language, Grammar, Arithmetic, Spelling, Geography, United States History and Compositions.

St. Francis de Sales' School.

MALE DEPT.—*Franciscan Brothers.*

1 Volume: Spelling, Grammar, United States History, Catechism and Geography.

FEMALE DEPT.—*Sisters of St. Joseph.*

2 Volumes: Spelling, Catechism, Arithmetic, Grammar, United States History, Geography, Civics, Algebra and Composition.

St. James' Commercial School.

MALE DEPT.—*Christian Brothers.*

28 Volumes Examination Papers, 19 Volumes Typewriting, 6 Volumes Shorthand, 3 Volumes Business Letters. 4 Volumes Penmanship and Drawing, 1 Volume Shorthand, Arithmetic, Literature, 11 Volumes: Algebra, Arithmetic, Geometry, Catechism, Grammar (Shorthand), 4 Volumes Arithmetic (Shorthand), 3 Volumes Geometry, 3 Volumes Algebra, Arithmetic and Mensuration (Shorthand and Transcription), 1 Volume Photographs.

FEMALE DEPT.—*Sisters of St. Joseph.*

8 Volumes: Christian Doctrine, Definitions, Spelling, Geography, Arithmetic, Language, Drawing, Writing, Business Forms, Grammar, United States History, Algebra, Map Drawing, Sacred History, Civics, English Literature, Compositions and Natural Philosophy.

St. John's School.

MALE DEPT.—*Franciscan Brothers.*

2 Volumes: Christian Doctrine, Arithmetic, Geography, Grammar and United States History.

FEMALE DEPT.—*Sisters of St. Joseph.*

2 Volumes: Christian Doctrine, Geography, United States History, Church History, Map Drawing, Civics, Physiology, Literature and Compositions.

St. John the Evangelist's School.

MALE DEPT.—*Franciscan Brothers.*

2 Volumes: Spelling, Penmanship, Arithmetic, Language, Catechism, Geography, Typewriting, Civics, Phonography, Geometry, Algebra, Book-Keeping, Compositions, Grammar, United States History and Map Drawing.

FEMALE DEPT.—*Sisters of St. Joseph.*

9 Volumes: Arithmetic, Geography, Grammar, United States History, Dictation, Map Drawing, Bible History, Music, Language and Business Forms.

BROOKLYN, N. Y.—Continued.

St. Joseph's School.

MALE DEPT.—*Franciscan Brothers.*

3 Volumes: Geography, Map Drawing, United States History, Catechism, Spelling, Grammar, Algebra, Civics, Arithmetic, Compositions, Typewriting, Physiology, Book-Keeping, Bible History and Natural History.

FEMALE DEPT.—*Sisters of St. Joseph.*

2 Volumes: Catechism, Spelling, Algebra, Arithmetic, Geography, Grammar, United States History, Literature, Geometry, Rhetoric, Philosophy, Physiology, Writing, Compositions, Business Forms, Drawing and Needle-Work.

St. Leonards of Pt. Maurice School.

MALE DEPT.—*Sisters of St. Dominic.*

2 Volumes: Geography, Grammar, Arithmetic, German, United States History, Letter Writing, Catechism, Bible History and Kindergarten.

FEMALE DEPT.

2 Volumes: Catechism, Arithmetic, United States History, Grammar, Geography, Bible History, Compositions, Translations and Letter Writing.

St. Malachy's School.—*Secular Teachers.*

MALE DEPT.

1 Volume: Business Forms, Arithmetic, Algebra, Bible History, Spelling, Geography, United States History, Grammar, Compositions and Catechism.

FEMALE DEPT.

1 Volume: Catechism, Bible History, Spelling, Geography, United States History, Grammar, Algebra, Compositions and Bible History.

St. Mary Star of the Sea School.

MALE DEPT.—*Franciscan Brothers.*

2 Volumes: United States History, Arithmetic, Catechism, Grammar, Geography, Book-Keeping, Dictations, Spelling, Business Forms and Compositions.

FEMALE DEPT.—*Sisters of Charity.*

4 Volumes: Arithmetic, Catechism, Geography, Spelling, Physiology, Astronomy, Book-Keeping, French, Algebra, Mensuration and Civics.

St. Michael's School.—*Sisters of St. Dominic.*

MALE DEPT.

2 Volumes: Catechism, Geometry, Arithmetic, Geography, United States History, Spelling, Language and Compositions.

FEMALE DEPT.

2 Volumes: Catechism, Geography, Grammar, Spelling, Physiology, Arithmetic, Paraphrasing, United States History, Map Drawing and Kindergarten.

St. Nicholas' School.—*Sisters of St. Dominic.*

MALE DEPT.

1 Volume: Letter Writing, Compositions, Catechism, Arithmetic, Bible History, Spelling and Compositions.

FEMALE DEPT.

1 Volume: Arithmetic, Catechism, Bible History, Grammar and Geography.

BROOKLYN, N. Y.—Continued.

St. Paul's School.

MALE DEPT.—*Franciscan Brothers.*
2 Volumes: Catechism, Geography, Arithmetic, United States History and Grammar.

FEMALE DEPT.—*Sisters of Charity.*
1 Volume: Christian Doctrine, Bible and Church History, Geography, Grammar, Civics, Map Drawing and Physiology.

St. Peter's School.

MALE DEPT.—*Franciscan Brothers.*
2 Volumes: Christian Doctrine, Geography, Grammar, Civics, Geometry, Book-Keeping, Arithmetic, Compositions, United States History and Drawing.

FEMALE DEPT.—*Sisters of Charity.*
1 Volume: Rhetoric, Evangeline, Algebra, Mensuration, Arithmetic, Grammar, United States History, Civics, Map Drawing, Geography and Catechism.

Sts. Peter and Paul's School.—*Sisters of St. Joseph.*

MALE DEPT.
2 Volumes: Christian Doctrine, Geography, Grammar, United States History, Arithmetic, Spelling, Bible History.

FEMALE DEPT.
2 Volumes: Compositions, History, Spelling, Book-Keeping, Grammar, Geography, Christian Doctrine, Business Forms, Map Drawing, Bible History and Algebra.

St. Stephen's School.—*Sisters of Charity.*

MALE DEPT.
2 Volumes: Christian Doctrine, Geography, Grammar, Arithmetic, United States History, Civics, Compositions, Physiology, Algebra, Astronomy and Natural Philosophy.

FEMALE DEPT.
1 Volume: Business Forms, Catechism, Civics, United States History, Geography, Physiology, Algebra, Geometry, Arithmetic, Astronomy, Grammar and Crocheting.

Sorrowful Mother School.—*Dominican Sisters.*

1 Volume: Catechism, Bible History, Writing, Compositions, History, Letter Writing, Natural History, United States History, Geography, Map Drawing, Grammar, Translations and Kindergarten.

Visitation School.

MALE DEPT.—*Franciscan Brothers.*
2 Volumes: Grammar, United States History, Geography, Arithmetic, Spelling, Catechism and Bible History.

FEMALE DEPT.—*Sisters of St. Joseph.*
4 Volumes: Catechism, Spelling, Arithmetic, Geography, Compositions, Grammar, United States History, Algebra, Civics, Business Forms and Drawing.

ORPHANAGES AND INDUSTRIAL SCHOOLS.

BROOKLYN, N. Y.

Holy Trinity Orphan Asylum.—*Dominican Sisters.*
1 Volume; Christian Doctrine, Arithmetic, English Grammar, Geography, United States History, Bible History, German Penmanship, Compositions and Translations.

Industrial School.—*Sisters of Mercy.*
Lace-Work, Drawn-Work and Crochet-Work.

St. John's Home.—*Sisters of St. Joseph.*
3 Volumes: Arithmetic, Catechism, Language, Spelling, Compositions, Drawing and 2 Volumes Kindergarten.

St. Malachy's Home.—*Sisters of St. Joseph.*
1 Volume: Catechism, United States History, Geography, Grammar, Dictations, Arithmetic, Business Forms, Letter Writing, Bible History and Compositions.

St. Paul's Industrial School.—*Sisters of Charity.*
5 Volumes: Catechism, Bible History, Arithmetic, Algebra, United States History, Civics, Grammar, Geography and Map Drawing. Samples of Lace-Work, Needle-Work, Crochet Jacket, 1 Pair Shoes, 13 Samples on Card Embroidery, Crocheting, Muslin Button-Hole Making, 1 Dressing Gown, 2 Baby Dresses (Embroidered), 2 Dressing Sacques (Embroidered), 3 Doilies, 2 Handkerchiefs, 1 Peacock Embroidered, 2 Oil Paintings on Plaques and 1 Volume Photographs.

DIOCESE OF BUFFALO, N. Y.

RT. REV. S. V. RYAN, D. D.

Diocesan Committee.

Rev. Geo. Weber, *Chairman.*   Rev. J. Daly, *Secretary.*   Rev. P. J. Colonel.
Brother Aelred, *Manager.*   Rev. J. Mooney, *Treasurer.*

ALCOVES 29, 30, 32 AND 34.

Portrait of Rt. Rev. Bishop Ryan.

UNIVERSITY.

NIAGARA UNIVERSITY P. O., N. Y.

Niagara University.—*Lazarist Fathers.*
Oil Paintings of the College and Seminary, Most Rev. Archbishop Lynch and Rt. Rev. Bishop Timon; Crayon Portraits of Rt. Rev. Bishop Ryan, D.D., Very Rev. R. E. V. Rice, C. M., and Very Rev. P.V. Kavanagh, C.M.; 4 Seminary O. L. A. and C. Literary Association Scrolls; 4 Basilian L. A. Scrolls; 3 R. E. V. R. L. A. Scrolls; 4 B. L. A. Banners; 2 R. E. V. R. Banners; 1 N. U. G. C. Banner; 2 Souvenir Volumes; 10 Volumes Niagara Index; 3 Volumes of "Index Niagarensis"; a Number of Loose Copies of the "Index"; 11 Small Pictures of the Different Societies; 19 Mounted Photographs.

COLLEGES AND ACADEMIES.

BUFFALO, N. Y.

Canisius College.—*Jesuit Fathers.*

7 Albums: Christian Doctrine, Geography, Bible History, Letter Writing, Analysis, Essays, Latin, German, Mathematics, History, Compositions, Geography, Greek, Algebra, Greek Translations, Philosophy; 1 Album of drama "Columbus;" 1 Album Photographs, 10 Drawings.

Holy Angels' Academy.—*Gray Nuns.*

18 Volumes: Typewriting, Stenography, Catechism, Physical Geography, Analysis, Ancient History, Lessons in English, Arithmetic, Book-Keeping, Physics and Astronomy; 150 Specimens of Botany; 33 Pieces of Embroidery; 1 Eagle Embroidered in Gold, Photographs.

Mt. St. Joseph's Academy.—*Sisters of St. Joseph.*

2 Volumes: History Notes, Catechism, Geography, Dictation, Arithmetic, Orthography, German, Drawing, Fancy Work, Photographic Views and 1 Volume Maps.

St. Mary's Academy.—*Ladies of the Sacred Heart of Mary.*

10 Oil Paintings, 77 Volumes and 5 Albums: Grammar, Book-Keeping, History, Geography, Physiology, Essays, Maps and Illustrated Stories.

Sacred Heart High School.—*Sisters of St. Francis.*

4 Volumes Fancy Work, 11 Samples of Drawing, 17 Paintings, 38 Volumes: Rhetoric, Literature, History, Book-Keeping, Church History, Maps, Arithmetic, Harmony, German Grammar, German Compositions, Elementary Drawing, Spelling and Kindergarten Work. Needle-Work: 1 Altar Lace in Filet, 1 Tidy, 1 Canvas Tidy, 1 Tray Cloth, 1 Night Gown, 1 Baby Dress, 1 Green Table-Cover, 1 Neutral Tint (in Oak Frame), 1 Large Oil Painting, 1 Large Oil Painting (Landscape), 1 Map of New York, 1 Pair Silk Mittens, 1 Japanese Basket, 1 Lamp Shade, 1 Photograph Bag, 2 Fancy Wheels, 1 Fancy Toaster, 3 Watch Pockets and 2 Needle-Cases.

ALLEGANY, N. Y.

St. Elizabeth's Academy.—*Sisters of St. Francis.*

6 Volumes: Stenography, Mathematics, Drawing, Book-Keeping, Penmanship, English Literature, 3 Oil Paintings, 1 Water-Color Painting, 1 Series of Object and Ornamental Drawing, 2 Needle-Work Pictures, 1 Veil embroidered in Gold, 1 Preaching Stole, 1 Alb (Lace).

ELMIRA, N. Y.

Academy of Our Lady of Angels.—*Sisters of St. Mary.*

1 Book of Essays, 2 Volumes Class-Work, 1 Volume Drawings, 1 Pen Painting (Lyre Bird), 5 Framed Drawings.

LOCKPORT, N. Y.

St. Joseph's Academy.—*Sisters of St. Mary.*

1 Book of Essays, 1 Book Needle-Work, 1 Hand-Painted Fire Screen, 1 Oil Painting, 1 Photograph (St. Joseph's Academy) Framed; 2 Pieces Hand-Made Lace, 2 Cushions (Raised Painting) and Specimens of Needle-Work.

PARISH SCHOOLS.

BUFFALO, N. Y.

St. Joseph's Cathedral School.

MALE DEPT.—*Christian Brothers.*
53 Volumes: Mensuration, Arithmetic, Penmanship, Christian Doctrine, Orthography, Grammar, Geography, Composition, Business Forms, Bills, Book-Keeping, Letters, Home Exercise, Typewriting and Phonography. 5 Volumes: Ornamental, Linear and Map Drawing. 10 Drawings (Framed).

FEMALE DEPT.—*Ladies of the Sacred Heart of Mary.*
52 Albums: Spelling, Map Drawing, Arithmetic, History, Grammar, Geography and Catechism.

St. Agnes' School.—*Sisters of St. Francis.*
2 Volumes: Arithmetic, Grammar, Geography, Map Drawing, Penmanship and 1 Album Examination Papers.

St. Ann's School.—*Sisters of St. Francis.*
14 Volumes: Business Letters, Grammar, Geography, German, Verse Changed to Prose, Spelling, History, Language, Arithmetic, Christian Doctrine, Analysis, Parsing and Map Drawing.

St. Anthony's School (Italian).—*Ladies of the Sacred Heart of Mary*
21 Albums: Christian Doctrine, Arithmetic, Spelling, Letter Writing, Geography, Sacred History, Drawing and Penmanship.

St. Boniface's School.—*Sisters of St. Joseph.*
1 Volume: Grammar, Geography, German, Arithmetic and Drawing.

St. Bridget's School.

MALE DEPT.—*Christian Brothers.*
33 Albums: Book-Keeping, Arithmetic, Mensuration, Penmanship, Drawing, Business Forms, Typewriting, Letter Writing, History, Reports and 4 Photographs.

FEMALE DEPT.—*Sisters of Mercy.*
3 Volumes: Penmanship, Grammar, Geography, Arithmetic and Compositions.

St. Francis Xavier's School.—*Sisters of St. Joseph.*
2 Volumes: German Compositions, Map Drawing, Geography, Grammar and Arithmetic.

Holy Angels' School.—*Gray Nuns.*
11 Volumes: Penmanship, Grammar, United States History, Map Drawing and Compositions.

Immaculate Conception School.—*Sisters of St. Joseph.*
5 Volumes: Penmanship, Arithmetic, Spelling, Catechism, Geography, Analysis, Map Drawing, History, Music, Physics, Algebra and Physiology.

St. John the Baptist's School.—*Sisters of St. Joseph.*
1 Volume: Spelling, Map Drawing, Arithmetic and Geography.

BUFFALO, N. Y.—Continued.

St. Louis' School.

MALE DEPT.—*Christian Brothers.*

31 Volumes: Christian Doctrine, Bible History, German, English and German Grammar, Translations, Arithmetic, Geography, United States History, Physiology and Penmanship.

FEMALE DEPT.—*Sisters of St. Joseph.*

6 Volumes: Examination Papers, Penmanship, Drawing, Music, Arithmetic, Geography and Compositions.

St. Mary's School.—*School Sisters of Notre Dame.*

7 Volumes: Grammar, Penmanship, United States History, Mechanical Drawing, Arithmetic, Christian Doctrine, Compositions, Dictations, Geography, Spelling, Grammar and Book-Keeping; 4 Pictures in Needle-Work, 1 Bracket of Leather Flowers, 1 Wax Cross and Roses.

St. Michael's School.—*Sisters of St. Francis.*

9 Volumes: Map Drawing, Arithmetic, Compositions, Grammar, Spelling and Penmanship.

St. Nicholas' School.—*Ladies of the Sacred Heart of Mary.*

2 Volumes: Analysis, Map Drawing, Grammar, Geography and United States History.

St. Patrick's School.—*Sisters of St. Francis.*

7 Volumes: Geography, Spelling, Grammar, Physiology, Arithmetic, Letter Writing, United States History, Compositions and Penmanship.

School of Our Lady of Mercy.—*Ladies of the Sacred Heart of Mary.*

10 Volumes: Christian Doctrine, History, Arithmetic and Analysis.

Sacred Heart School (Seneca St.)—*Sisters of St. Francis.*

6 Volumes: Penmanship, Business Forms, Drawings, Compositions, Geography, Map Drawing, 1 Picture Reward of Merit, 1 Carved Ivory Cross and 3 Albums Examination Papers.

Seven Dolors' School.—*Sisters of St. Francis.*

2 Specimens Penmanship, 6 Volumes: Grammar, Arithmetic, Translation, Drawing, Geography, Map Drawing, Commercial and Business Forms, and 3 Albums Examination Papers, 1 Oil Painting(Peacock), 4 Crayon Drawings, 4 Silk Throws, 1 Silk Toilet, 2 Bobbinet Tidies, 22 Other Tidies, 3 Aprons, 2 Worsted Jackets, 1 Pair Worsted Boots, 1 Plush Box, 1 Glass Box, 1 Pair Silk Mittens, 1 Chatelaine Bag, 1 Japanese Basket, 1 Photograph Bag, 2 Fancy Bags, 4 Fancy Wheels, 1 Fancy Toaster, 1 Fancy Basket, 3 Watch Pockets and 2 Needle-Cases.

St. Stephen's School.—*Sisters of Mercy.*

1 Volume: Catechism, Arithmetic, Geography, Grammar, Letter Writing and Spelling.

St. Vincent's School.—*Sisters of St. Joseph.*

1 Volume: Geography, Map Drawing, Grammar, Arithmetic, Spelling, United States History, Mechanical Drawing and German.

ALDEN, N. Y.

St. John Baptist School.—*Sisters of St. Joseph.*

1 Volume: Arithmetic, Geography, Letters, Grammar, German and German Letters.

BUFFALO PLAINS, N. Y.

St. Joseph's School.—*Sisters of St. Joseph.*

1 Volume: American History, Arithmetic, Catechism, Grammar, Geography, Spelling and Compositions.

DUNKIRK, N. Y.

St. Mary's School.—*Sisters of St. Joseph.*

3 Volumes: German, Penmanship, Map Drawing, United States History, Christian Doctrine, Linear Drawing, Dictation and Language.

St. George's School.—*Sisters of St. Joseph.*

1 Volume: Map Drawing, Grammar, Geography, Penmanship, Grammar and Translations.

EAST BUFFALO, N. Y.

St. Agnes' School.—*Sisters of St. Francis.*

2 Volumes: Penmanship, Grammar, Geography, Arithmetic, Map Drawing and 1 Album Examination Papers.

ELMIRA, N. Y.

St. John's School.—*Sisters of St. Mary.*

1 Volume: Spelling, Business Letters, Christian Doctrine, Geography and Arithmetic.

Sts. Peter and Paul's School.—*Sisters of St. Mary.*

3 Volumes: Arithmetic, History, Geography, Map Drawing, Analysis, Grammar and Letters.

St. Mary's School.—*Sisters of St. Mary.*

1 Volume: Arithmetic, Christian Doctrine, Map Drawing, Compositions, Geography and Analysis.

GARDENVILLE, N. Y.

14 Holy Helpers' School.—*Sisters of St. Francis.*

2 Volumes: Letters, Arithmetic, Grammar, Map Drawing and Geography.

HAMBURG, N. Y.

Sts. Peter and Paul's School.—*Sisters of St. Francis.*

15 Volumes: Map Drawing, Christian Doctrine, Painting, Geography, Grammar, Arithmetic, Caligraphy, German Exercises, Mechanical Drawing, German Translations and 1 Album Examination Papers.

JAMESTOWN, N. Y.

Sts. Peter and Paul's School.—*Sisters of Mercy.*

1 Volume: Grammar, Arithmetic, Geography and Language.

LANCASTER, N. Y.

St. Mary's School.—*Ladies of the Sacred Heart of Mary.*

9 Volumes: Arithmetic, Geography, Map Drawing, Analysis, Christian Doctrine and United States History.

LOCKPORT, N. Y.

St. John's School.—*Sisters of Mercy.*

1 Volume: Christian Doctrine, Geography, Arithmetic, Grammar, Spelling, Mensuration and Drawing.

St. Patrick's School.—*Sisters of Mercy.*

1 Volume: History, Arithmetic, Algebra, History of Columbus, Grammar, Analysis, Christian Doctrine, Drawing and Kindergarten Work.

St. Mary's School.—*Sisters of St. Mary.*

1 Volume: Catechism, Arithmetic, Geography, Grammar, Spelling and Business Forms.

NEW OREGON, N. Y.

St. Mary's School.—*Sisters of St. Joseph.*

1 Volume: Spelling, Grammar, Letters, Arithmetic, Geography, Compositions, Drawing and Music.

NIAGARA FALLS, N. Y.

St. Mary's School.—*Sisters of Mercy.*

3 Volumes: Church History, Compositions, Rhetoric, Algebra, Physiology, Physical Geography, United States History, Book-Keeping, Civil Government, History of New York, Christian Doctrine and Drawing.

OLEAN, N. Y.

St. Mary's School.—*Sisters of Mercy.*

1 Volume: Christian Doctrine, Sacred History, Algebra, Geometry, Physiology, Geography, Grammar, Map Drawing, Natural Philosophy, Book-Keeping and Kindergarten Work.

OWEGO, N. Y.

Sacred Heart School.—*Sisters of Charity.*

1 Volume: Christian Doctrine, Grammar, Arithmetic, etc.

SALAMANCA, N. Y.

St. Patrick's School.—*Sisters of St. Joseph.*

1 Volume: Photographs, Geography, Algebra, Notes, Book-Keeping, Geometry, Arithmetic, Grammar, History, Spelling, Music, Drawing, Catechism.

SUSPENSION BRIDGE, N. Y.

Sacred Heart School.—*Sisters of St. Joseph.*

1 Volume: Map Drawing, Geography, Physiology, Catechism.

WEST SENECA, N. Y.

Our Lady of Victory.—*Sisters of St. Joseph.*

1 Volume: Arithmetic, Grammar, Maps, Linear Drawing and Spelling.

St. Joseph's Orphan Asylum.—*Sisters of St. Joseph.*

1 Volume: Arithmetic, Spelling, Geography, Catechism, Grammar, History and Drawing.

INDUSTRIAL SCHOOLS AND ORPHANAGES.

BUFFALO, N. Y.

St. Vincent's Orphanage and Industrial School.—*Sisters of Charity.*
1 Isabella Gown, 1 Empire Night Gown, 1 Child's Linen Lawn Dress (Made by Hand), 1 Child's Emb. Silk Dress, 2 Child's Aprons (Crochet Tops, Trimmed with Gold and Pink Ribbon), 1 Velvet Emb. Card-Case, 1 Velvet Emb. Broom-Case, 1 Dining-Room Table Center-Piece (Emb. in Silk Class), 1 Center Piece (Emb. Violets), 1 Set Doilies, Photographs of Building, School-Room, Bake-Room and Kitchen. 6 Volumes: Arithmetic, Geography, Grammar, Christian Doctrine, History and Physiology.

Le Couteulx St. Mary's Deaf Mute Institution.—*Sisters of St. Joseph.*
7 Volumes: "Le Couteulx Leader." 2 Volumes: Arithmetic, Geography, Grammar, History, Map Drawing. 3 Photographic Views, 1 Oil Painting, 10 Water Colors, 1 Specimen Wood Carving, 1 Specimen Chair Caning.

German Roman Catholic Orphan Asylum.—*Sisters of St. Francis.*
5 Volumes: Arithmetic, Geography, Map Drawing, Grammar, Translations, Drawing and Compositions. 3 Celluloid Whisk Holders, 2 Aprons, 1 Each of the Following: Picture, Painting on Doe Skin, Oil Painting, Celluloid Paper Holder, Lavender Silk Throw, Bolting-Silk Cushion, Handkerchief Case, Silk Bonnet, Work Basket, Embroidered Shawl, Spider Duster, Paper Holder, Shopping Bag, Velvet Handkerchief Case, Bobbinet Throw, Pair of Mittens, Pink Dress, Towel Rack and Silk Throw.

DUNKIRK, N. Y.

St. Mary's Orphan Asylum.—*Sisters of St. Joseph.*
1 Volume: Grammar, Arithmetic, Geography, Needle-Work, Music, Map and Linear Drawing.

WEST SENECA, N. Y.

St. John's Protectory and Orphan Asylum.
Boys' Dept.—*Brothers of the Holy Cross.*
Girls' Dept.—*Sisters of St. Joseph.*
4 Books Typesetting and Electrotyping, by the Boys. 2 Large Electrotype Plates. 4 Volumes: History, Arithmetic, Christian Doctrine, Essays, Grammar, Spelling, Geography and 4 Specimens of Quilts and Rugs.

DIOCESE OF CLEVELAND.

RT. REV. F. HORSTMANN, D. D.

ALCOVES 31 AND 33.

Portrait of Rt. Rev. Bishop Horstmann.

COLLEGES, ACADEMIES AND SELECT SCHOOLS.

CLEVELAND, OHIO.

St. Ignatius' College.—*Society of Jesus.*
12 Volumes: Drawing, French, Phonography, Grammar, Geography, Arithmetic, Penmanship, English Compositions, Sacred History, German, Spelling, Map Drawing, Christian Doctrine, Latin, Algebra, Book-Keeping, Polyglot, Mathematics, History, French, Physics and Greek.

CLEVELAND, OHIO.—Continued.

Ursuline College.—*Ursuline Sisters.*

3 Volumes: Drawing, Christian Doctrine, Spelling, Language, Bible History, Grammar, Arithmetic, Geography and United States History.

Notre Dame Academy.—*Sisters of Notre Dame.*

3 Volumes: Christian Doctrine, Church History, Geography, Bible History, Spelling, Language, United States History, Definitions, Grammar, Compositions, Rhetoric, Literature, Algebra, Geometry, Trigonometry, Astronomy, Ancient History, Zoology, Physiology, Theory of Music, Book-Keeping and Drawing.

TIFFIN, OHIO.

Ursuline Convent.—*Ursuline Sisters.*

6 Volumes: Christian Doctrine, Drawing, Rhetoric, Philosophy, Book-Keeping, Mythology, Elocution, Trigonometry, Astronomy, Arithmetic, Chemistry, Drawing and Compositions.

TOLEDO, OHIO.

Ursuline Convent of the Sacred Heart.—*Ursuline Sisters.*

9 Volumes: Bible History, Catechism, Arithmetic, Grammar, Map and Mechanical Drawing, Essays, Astronomy, Book-Keeping, Rhetoric, Algebra and 1 Volume Photographs. 1 Oil Painting, 5 Kindergarten Charts, 2 Vases and 6 Pieces of Needle-Work.

VILLA ANGELA (Nottingham, P. O.), OHIO.

Ursuline Academy.—*Ursuline Sisters.*

8 Volumes: Christian Doctrine, Bible History, Botany, Scientific Papers, Arithmetic, Mathematics, Literature, Drawings, Paintings and Etchings, and 1 Portfolio Drawings and Botanical Specimens.

PARISH SCHOOLS.

CLEVELAND, OHIO.

Holy Name School.—*Sisters of the S. H. of Mary.*

4 Volumes: Book-Keeping, Sacred History, United States History, Language, Grammar, Geography, Christian Doctrine, Drawing, Spelling, Music and Penmanship.

Immaculate Conception School.—*Ursuline Sisters.*

1 Volume: Christian Doctrine, Compositions, Physiology, Natural History, Geography, United States History, Music, Map and Mechanical Drawing.

Our Lady of Lourdes' School.—*Sisters of Notre Dame.*

1 Volume: Christian Doctrine, German, Grammar, United States History and Theory of Music.

St. Adalbert's School.—*Sisters of Notre Dame.*

1 Volume: Christian Doctrine, Compositions, Bible History, Penmanship and Letter Writing.

CLEVELAND, OHIO.—Continued.

St. Augustine's School.—*Sisters of St. Joseph.*

4 Volumes: Physiology, Arithmetic, Christian Doctrine, Book-Keeping, Rhetoric, Map Drawing, History and Literature.

St. Colman's School.—*Sisters of St. Joseph.*

1 Volume: Drawing, Language, Arithmetic, Dictations, Christian Doctrine, Orthography, United States History and Bible History.

St. Francis' School.—*Sisters of Notre Dame.*

1 Volume: German, Grammar, Dictations, Compositions and Geography.

St. John's Cathedral School.

MALE DEPT.—*Brothers of Mary.*
13 Volumes: Christian Doctrine, Mechanical Drawing, Geography, Map Drawing, Orthography, Dictations, Letter Writing and Compositions.

FEMALE DEPT.—*Ursuline Sisters.*
3 Volumes: Christian Doctrine, Map Drawing, Arithmetic, Algebra, United States History, Literature, Physiology, General History and Church History.

St. Joseph's School.—*Ursuline Sisters.*

2 Volumes: Christian Doctrine, Catechism, Grammar, German Translations, Letters, Language, Spelling, Dictations and United States History.

St. Malachy's School.—*Ursuline Sisters.*

Language, Arithmetic, Geography, Grammar, United States History, Book-Keeping, Catechism, Algebra, Physics, Drawing.

St. Mary's Annunciation School.—*Sisters of the Humility of Mary.*

1 Volume: Drawing, Composition, Dictation and Spelling.

St. Mary's Assumption School.

MALE DEPT.—*Brothers of Mary.*
3 Volumes: Drawing, Arithmetic, Grammar, Geography, United States History and Letter Writing.

FEMALE DEPT.—*Ursuline Sisters.*
1 Volume: Grammar, Spelling, Arithmetic, German and United States History.

St. Michael's School.—*Sisters of Notre Dame.*

1 Volume: German, Arithmetic, Grammar, United States History and Geography.

St. Patrick's School.—*Brothers of Mary.*

62 Volumes: Drawing, Dictations, Algebra, Book-Keeping, United States History, Grammar, Language, Business Forms, Christian Doctrine, Commercial Arithmetic, Mechanical Problems, Bible History and Drawing.

St. Peter's School.—*Sisters of Notre Dame.*

2 Volumes: Bible History, Arithmetic, Spelling, Definitions, Grammar, Compositions, German Language, German Compositions, Geography, United States History, Theory of Music, Penmanship, Christian Doctrine, Mental Arithmetic, Dictations, English Compositions, Mechanical Drawing, Photographs School and Church.

CLEVELAND, OHIO.—CONTINUED.

St. Procopius' School.—*Sisters of St. Joseph.*
1 Volume: Christian Doctrine, Arithmetic, Geography and History.

St. Stanislaus' School.—*Sisters of St. Francis.*
1 Volume: Christian Doctrine, Bible History, Arithmetic, Bible History, Grammar, Geography and Compositions.

St. Stephen's School.—*Sisters of Notre Dame.*
1 Volume: German Composition, Grammar, Spelling, Dictation, Compositions, Letters, Map Drawing and Penmanship.

St. Wenceslaus' School.—*Sisters of St. Joseph.*
1 Volume: Arithmetic, Algebra, Christian Doctrine, United States History, Bible History, Geography, Book-Keeping, Compositions, Letter Writing, Grammar, Music, Drawing.

AKRON, OHIO.

St. Mary's School.—*Sisters of Notre Dame.*
1 Volume: Arithmetic, Bible History, Spelling, Grammar, United States History, Geography and Penmanship.

St. Vincent's School.—*Sisters of Notre Dame.*
1 Volume: Arithmetic, Christian Doctrine, Grammar, United States History, Geography and Penmanship.

AVON, OHIO.

Holy Trinity School.—*Sisters of St. Francis.*
2 Volumes: Drawing, Christian Doctrine, Arithmetic, German Exercises and Map Drawing.

ASHTABULA, OHIO.

St. Joseph's School.—*Secular Teachers.*
2 Volumes: Arithmetic, Penmanship, Christian Doctrine, Spelling, Grammar, United States History and Geography.

ASHTABULA HARBOR, OHIO.

Our Mother of Sorrows' School.—*Secular Teachers.*
1 Volume: Geography, Christian Doctrine, Map Drawing, Spelling, Grammar and Arithmetic.

BELLEVUE, OHIO.

St. Mary's School.—*Sisters of St. Francis.*
1 Volume: Arithmetic, Map Drawing, Grammar, Algebra, Astronomy, United States Constitution, Letters, Diagrams and Compositions.

CANTON, OHIO.

St. John's School.—*Sisters of Notre Dame.*
1 Volume: Christian Doctrine, Compositions, Geography, Grammar, Dictations, Catechism and Spelling.

CANTON, OHIO.—Continued.

St. Peter's School.—*Sisters of Notre Dame.*

1 Volume: Christian Doctrine, Grammar, Arithmetic, Compositions, Letter Writing, Penmanship, Theory of Music, Astronomy, Physics and Book-Keeping. The Following Exercises in German: Christian Doctrine, Bible History, Grammar, Letter Writing, Compositions and Penmanship.

DEFIANCE, OHIO.

Our Lady of Perpetual Help.—*Sisters of Notre Dame.*

6 Volumes: Dictations, Spelling, Language, Arithmetic, Christian Doctrine, Compositions, Letter Writing, Geography, Drawings, Physics, Physiology and Christian Doctrine.

DELPHOS, OHIO.

St. James' School.—*Sisters of Notre Dame.*

3 Volumes: Drawing, Christian Doctrine, Arithmetic, Grammar, Composition, Spelling, Catechism and Photographs.

ELYRIA, OHIO.

St. Mary's School.—*Sisters of St. Joseph.*

1 Volume: Catechism, Arithmetic, Christian Doctrine, History, Spelling, Grammar, Music, Compositions, Geography, Map Drawing, Arithmetic and Book-Keeping.

FINDLAY, OHIO.

St. Michael's School.—*Secular Teachers.*

1 Volume: Christian Doctrine, Arithmetic, Spelling and Geography.

FOSTORIA, OHIO.

St. Wendelin's School.—*Secular Teachers.*

1 Volume: Christian Doctrine, Arithmetic, Composition, Grammar, Spelling, Definitions and Book-Keeping.

FREMONT, OHIO.

St. Joseph's School.—*Sisters of Notre Dame.*

1 Volume: Grammar, Drawing, Spelling, Christian Doctrine.

FULTON CANAL, OHIO.

Sts. Philip and James' School.—*Secular Teachers.*

Map Drawing, Algebra, Arithmetic, Spelling, Christian Doctrine, Mechanical Drawing and Penmanship.

GALION, OHIO.

St. Joseph's School.—*Sisters of St. Francis.*

2 Volumes: Bible History, Geography, German Exercises, Arithmetic, Penmanship, Orthography and Map Drawing.

GLANDORF, OHIO.

Catholic District School.—*Sisters of the Most Precious Blood.*

1 Volume: Christian Doctrine, German, Arithmetic, Spelling and Definitions.

LIMA, OHIO.

St. Rose of Lima School.—*Sisters of Charity (Mt. St. Joseph).*

1 Volume: Christian Doctrine, Drawing, Philosophy, History, Geometry, Arithmetic, Penmanship, United States History and Mechanical Drawing.

MASSILLON, OHIO.

St. Mary's School.—*Secular Teachers.*

8 Volumes: Christian Doctrine, Arithmetic, Geography, United States History, Penmanship, Drawing, Spelling, Grammar and Natural History.

MT. ST. JOSEPH, OHIO.

St. Bridget's School.—*Sisters of Charity.*

3 Volumes: Christian Doctrine, Language, Geography, Penmanship, Drawing, Music, Astronomy, History, Geology, Physical Geography, Penmanship, Botany, Physics.

NAPOLEON, OHIO.

St. Augustine's School.—*Sisters of Notre Dame.*

1 Volume: Christian Doctrine, Grammar, Catechism, United States History, Geography and Compositions.

NORTH RIDGEFIELD, OHIO.

St. Peter's School.—*Sisters of St. Francis.*

1 Volume: Bible History, Catechism, Grammar, United States History, Arithmetic, Geography, Grammar, Dictations and Spelling.

NILES, OHIO.

St. Stephen's School.—*Sisters of the Humility of Mary.*

Arithmetic, Grammar, Catechism, Compositions, Map Drawing, Letter Writing, Christian Doctrine and Mechanical Drawing.

NORWALK, OHIO.

St. Mary's School.—*Sisters of St. Joseph.*

1 Volume: Christian Doctrine, Geography, Bible History, Spelling, Letter Writing, Arithmetic and Grammar.

St. Paul's School.—*Sisters of Notre Dame.*

German Exercises, Christian Doctrine, History, Grammar, Arithmetic, Geography, Dictations, Compositions, United States History and Penmanship.

OTTAWA, OHIO.

Sts. Peter and Paul's School.—*Sisters of the Precious Blood.*

1 Volume: Christian Doctrine, Compositions, Arithmetic and Spelling.

SANDUSKY, OHIO.

Holy Angels' School.—*Ladies of the Sacred Heart.*

1 Volume: Grammar, Christian Doctrine, Arithmetic, Orthography, Geography and United States History.

Sts. Peter and Paul's School.—*Ladies of the Sacred Heart.*

1 Volume: Compositions, Catechism, Algebra, Book-Keeping, Arithmetic, Grammar, History and Map Drawing.

TIFFIN, OHIO.

St. Mary's School.—*Ursuline Sisters.*

1 Volume: Grammar, Christian Doctrine, Arithmetic, Orthography, United States History, Map and Mechanical Drawing.

St. Joseph's School.—*Ursuline Sisters.*

2 Volumes: Grammar, Spelling, Geography, Bible History, Penmanship, Arithmetic and Book-Keeping.

TOLEDO, OHIO.

St. Francis de Sales' School.

MALE DEPT.—*Christian Brothers.*

45 Albums History; 15 Albums Book-Keeping; 80 Albums Arithmetic; 102 Albums Penmanship; 27 Albums Compositions; 16 Albums Mensuration; 4 Volumes Penmanship (Contrast Pages); Collection of Large Maps; 156 Small Maps; 54 Albums Christian Doctrine; 40 Albums Spelling; 35 Albums Geography; 20 Albums Abbreviations.

FEMALE DEPT.—*Ursuline Sisters.*

71 Albums Christian Doctrine; 39 Albums Modern History; 3 Albums Physical Geography; 27 Albums English Literature; 2 Albums Rhetoric; 2 Albums Natural History; 11 Albums Physiology; 71 Albums Arithmetic; 14 Albums Algebra; 14 Albums Geography; 15 Albums Spelling; 14 Albums Penmanship; 27 Albums Map Drawing; 56 Small Maps; 2 Large Maps; 31 Albums Grammar; 43 Albums Geography; 31 Albums Music; 29 Specimens of Letter Writing; 12 Albums Natural History; 2 Albums Letters and Addresses; 1 Volume Surface Forms; 1 Volume Language Stories; 1 Volume "Story of Toledo"; Kindergarten Work; Paper Cutting and Folding.

St. Mary's School.—*Sisters of Notre Dame.*

1 Volume: Christian Doctrine, Music, Drawing and Arts.

WELLSVILLE, OHIO.

Immaculate Conception School.—*Sisters of St. Joseph.*

1 Volume: Drawing, Catechism, United States History, Mental Arithmetic, Practical Arithmetic, Music and Grammar.

YOUNGSTOWN, OHIO.

Immaculate Conception School.—*Ursuline Sisters.*

2 Volumes: Christian Doctrine, Arithmetic, Geography, Language, Penmanship and United States History.

St. Columba's School.—*Ursuline Sisters.*

3 Volumes: Christian Doctrine, Algebra, Arithmetic, Drawing and United States History.

St. Joseph's School.—*Ursuline Sisters.*

Arithmetic, Maps, Catechism, Spelling, Grammar, Music, Geography, Compositions and Rhetoric.

DIOCESE OF COVINGTON, KY.

RT. REV. CAMILLUS P. MAES, D.D.

Diocesan Committee.

Very Rev. F. Brossart, V.G., *Chairman.*   Rev. W. Gorey, *Secretary.*
Very Rev. L. Haas, O.S.B.

ALCOVE 36.

ACADEMIES AND SELECT SCHOOLS.

COVINGTON, KY.

Academy of St. Walburg.—*Benedictine Sisters.*

    3 Volumes: Spelling, Grammar, Literature, Geography, Map Drawing, History and Music.

La Salette Academy.—*Sisters of Charity of Nazareth.*

    6 Volumes: Map Drawing, Christian Doctrine, Spelling, Latin, Geometry, Algebra, Philosophy, Practical Science, Arithmetic, Letter Writing, Bible History, Music and Book-Keeping.

Notre Dame Academy.—*Sisters of Notre Dame.*

    2 Volumes: Christian Doctrine, Bible History, Arithmetic, Spelling, Dictations, Definitions, Language, Compositions, Penmanship, Theory of Vocal Music, Geography, Hints on Letter Writing, United States History, Roman History, Literature, Astronomy, Rhetoric, Botany and Physics.

LEXINGTON, KY.

St. Catharine's Academy.—*Sisters of Charity of Nazareth.*

    5 Volumes: Map Drawing, Arithmetic, Compositions, Grammar, Christian Doctrine and Spelling.

MAYSVILLE, KY.

Visitation Academy.—*Visitation Nuns.*

    4 Volumes: History, Grammar, Analysis, Map Drawing and Physiology.

NEWPORT, KY.

Immaculate Conception Academy.—*Sisters of Charity of Nazareth.*

    5 Volumes: Church History, Christian Doctrine, Map Drawing, Arithmetic, Grammar, Geography, Mental Arithmetic, Compositions, Remembered Reading, Spelling, Natural Philosophy, Zoology, Physiology, Drawing and Music.

St. Martin's Academy.—*Sisters of Providence of Kentucky.*

    1 Volume: Grammar, Compositions, History, Arithmetic. 1 Volume: Specimens of Fancy Needle-Work.

PARISH SCHOOLS.

COVINGTON, KY.

Cathedral School of St. Mary's.—*Sisters of Charity of Nazareth.*

2 Volumes: Christian Doctrine, United States History, Grammar, Arithmetic, Letter Writing and Map Drawing.

St. Aloysius' School.—*Sisters of St. Francis.*

6 Volumes: Arithmetic, Spelling, Geography, Bible History, Penmanship, Compositions, German, United States History and Christian Doctrine.

St. Augustine's School.—*Sisters of Notre Dame.*

3 Volumes: German, Arithmetic, Letter Writing, Map Drawing, Music, Composition, Geography and History.

St. John's School.—*Sisters of Notre Dame.*

2 Volumes: Letter Writing, Compositions, Dictations, German Exercises and Map Drawing.

St. Joseph's School.

MALE DEPT.—*Brothers of Mary.*

12 Volumes; Arithmetic, Grammar, Geography, Book-Keeping, Map Drawing, Analysis, Composition and Drawing. 1 Large Relief Map of United States.

FEMALE DEPT.—*Benedictine Sisters.*

2 Volumes: Arithmetic, Map Drawing, Letters, Geography, Compositions, Christian Doctrine, Spelling and History.

St. Patrick's School.—*Sisters of Charity of Nazareth.*

3 Volumes: Map Drawing, Letter Writing, Geography, Compositions, Christian Doctrine, Penmanship and Map Drawing.

Mother of God School.—*Sisters of Notre Dame.*

3 Volumes: Arithmetic, Christian Doctrine, Spelling, German Exercises, Music, Penmanship and Map Drawing.

ALEXANDRIA, KY.

St. Mary's School.—*Sisters of Notre Dame.*

1 Volume: Arithmetic, German Exercises, Composition, Penmanship and Spelling.

ASHLAND, KY.

Holy Family School.—*Sisters of St. Francis.*

2 Volumes: Geography, Penmanship, Spelling, Language, Arithmetic, Bible History, Grammar, Compositions, Physiology, Map and Linear Drawing.

BELLEVUE, KY.

Sacred Heart School.—*Sisters of Notre Dame.*

1 Volume: Arithmetic, German Exercises, Compositions, Spelling, Penmanship and Grammar.

BIRMINGHAM, ALA.

St. Paul's School.—*Benedictine Sisters.*

1 Volume: Sacred History, Compositions, Astronomy, Catechism, Dictation, Letters, Geography, Arithmetic, Language and Spelling.

COLD SPRINGS, KY.

St. Joseph's School.—*Sisters of Notre Dame.*

1 Volume: German Exercises, Catechism, Penmanship and Compositions.

CARROLLTON, KY.

St. John's School.—*Sisters of Notre Dame.*

1 Volume: Bible History, Catechism, Arithmetic, Geography, United States History and Compositions.

DAYTON, KY.

St. Francis' School.—*Ursuline Nuns.*

1 Volume: Arithmetic, German Exercises, Christian Doctrine and Compositions.

FRANKFORT, KY.

St. Joseph's and St. Aloysius' School.—*Sisters of Charity of Nazareth.*

14 Volumes: Christian Doctrine, Geography, Map Drawing, Grammar, Language, Reading, History, Bible History, Mathematics, Algebra, Physical Geography, Astronomy, Latin and Rhetoric.

LEXINGTON, KY.

St. Paul's School.—*Sisters of Charity of Nazareth.*

1 Volume Class-Work: Christian Doctrine, Mensuration, Arithmetic, Etymology, Grammar, Physiology, Algebra, Political Science, Synonyms, Spelling and United States History.

St. Peter Claver's (Colored) School.—*Sisters of Charity of Nazareth.*

2 Volumes: Map Drawing, Arithmetic, Grammar, Catechism, Spelling and Letters.

NEWPORT, KY.

Immaculate Conception School.—*Sisters of Charity of Nazareth.*

4 Volumes: Christian Doctrine, Church History, Catechism, Definitions, Spelling and Arithmetic.

Corpus Christi School.—*Ursuline Nuns.*

3 Volumes: Drawing, History, Arithmetic, German and Grammar.

St. Stephen's School.—*Sisters of Notre Dame.*

3 Volumes: Penmanship, Letter Writing, Compositions, Dictations, German Exercises, Map Drawing, Phonography and Arithmetic.

PARIS, KY.

St. Mary's School.—*Sisters of Charity of Nazareth.*

2 Volumes: Catechism, Spelling, Dictation, Grammar, Arithmetic, Geography and Map Drawing.

ORPHANAGE.

COLD SPRINGS, KY.

St. Joseph's Orphanage.—*Sisters of Notre Dame.*

1 Volume: Christian Doctrine, Composition, Bible History, Arithmetic, Grammar, Spelling, Dictation and German Exercises.

DIOCESE OF DENVER.

RT. REV. NICHOLAS P. MATZ, D. D.

Diocesan Committee.

Rev. J. P. CARRIGAN.   Rev. J. T. MURPHY, O. P., *Secretary.*   Rev. W. O'RYAN.

ALCOVE 45.

COLLEGES AND ACADEMIES.

DENVER, COL.

College of the Sacred Heart.—*Jesuit Fathers.*

1 Volume: Mental Philosophy, Mathematics, United States History, Chemistry, Physics, Ancient History, Compositions, Christian Doctrine, Latin Grammatical Analysis, Book-Keeping, Arithmetic, Orthography, Geography, Penmanship and 1 Volume of "The Highlander," Published Monthly.

Loretto Academy.—*Sisters of Loretto.*

1 Volume: Grammar, Geography, Physical Geography, Literature, Physiology, History, Arithmetic and Orthography.

St. Mary's Academy.—*Sisters of Loretto.*

1 Volume: Christian Doctrine, Arithmetic, Geography, Orthography, Letter Writing, Grammar, Book-Keeping, Algebra and Logic.

CANNON CITY, COL.

Mt. St. Scholastica's Academy.—*Benedictine Sisters.*

2 Volumes: Christian Doctrine, Arithmetic, Geography, Grammar, Algebra, Geometry, Compositions, Physiology, Orthography, Literature, Phonography, Book-Keeping, Freehand Drawing and Physics.

PARISH SCHOOLS.

DENVER, COL.

Annunciation School.—*Sisters of Charity.*

1 Volume: Arithmetic, Geography, Christian Doctrine, Orthography, United States History, Bible History, Penmanship and Photographs.

DENVER, COL.—Continued.

Immaculate Conception School.—*Sisters of Charity.*

3 Volumes: Christian Doctrine, Arithmetic, Geography, History, Orthography, Grammar, Physiology, Book-Keeping, Letter Writing, Penmanship, Freehand Drawing, Map Drawing and Music.

Sacred Heart School.—*Sisters of Charity.*

3 Volumes: Grammar, Letter Writing, Business Forms, Freehand Drawing, Penmanship, Geography, Arithmetic, United States History, Physiology, General History, Bible History, Geometry and Algebra.

St. Catherine's School.—*Sisters of Mercy.*

1 Volume: Specimens Kindergarten Work.

St. Joseph's School.—*Sisters of Mercy.*

1 Volume: Bible History, Grammar, Orthography, Arithmetic, United States History, Freehand Drawing and Photographs.

St. Leo's School.—*Sisters of St. Joseph.*

1 Volume: Christian Doctrine, Freehand Drawing, Object Lessons, Orthography, Penmanship, Arithmetic, Language Lessons, Geography, Map Drawing, Bible History, Grammar, United States History and Natural History.

St. Patrick's School.—*Sisters of St. Joseph.*

1 Volume: Christian Doctrine, Freehand Drawing, Object Lessons, Language Lessons, Arithmetic, Grammar, Geography, Map Drawing, Letter Writing, United States History, Bible History, Photographs of Teachers and Pupils.

DURANGO, COL.

St. Columba's School.—*Sisters of Mercy.*

1 Volume: Christian Doctrine, Book-Keeping, Algebra, Arithmetic, Geography, Grammar, History, Orthography, Penmanship, Physiology, Botany, Natural Philosophy, Music and Photographs.

HIGHLANDS, COL.

St. Dominic's School.—*Dominican Sisters.*

1 Volume: Christian Doctrine, Grammar, Orthography, Geography, Object Lessons, Map Drawing, Language, Vocal Music and Bible History.

LEADVILLE, COL.

St. Mary's School.—*Sisters of Charity.*

1 Volume: Christian Doctrine, History, Arithmetic, Geography, Grammar, Algebra, Book-Keeping, Church History, Literature and Physics.

PUEBLO, COL.

St. Patrick's School.—*Sisters of Charity.*

1 Volume: Christian Doctrine, Arithmetic, Penmanship, United States History, Orthography, Pen Drawing, Freehand Drawing, Vocal Music, Object Drawing and Map Drawing.

GEORGETOWN, COL.

School of Our Lady of Lourdes.—*Sisters of St. Joseph.*

1 Volume: Arithmetic, Christian Doctrine, Object Lessons, Geography, Grammar, United States History, History of the Church, Letter Writing, Algebra, Book Keeping, Compositions and Physiology.

ORPHANAGE.

DENVER, COL.

Mt. St. Vincent's Orphan Asylum.—*Sisters of Charity.*

1 Volume: Christian Doctrine, Geography, Arithmetic, Orthography, United States History, Object Lessons, Map Drawing and Freehand Drawing.

DIOCESE OF DETROIT.

RT. REV. JOHN S. FOLEY, D.D.

ALCOVE 39.

Portrait of Rt. Rev. Bishop Foley.

ACADEMIES AND SELECT SCHOOLS.

DETROIT, MICH.

St. Mary's Institute.—*Polish Felician Sisters.*

6 Volumes: Penmanship, Drawing, Book-Keeping, Grammar, Geography, Christian Doctrine, Compositions, History, Science, United States History, Polish History, Bible History, Polish Language, Twenty Pieces of Fancy Work, 1 Large Embroidered (Gold) Picture (Madonna, with Seal of Detroit and Poland Affixed).

St. Joseph's Commercial School.—*Christian Brothers.*

1 Large Volume Linear Drawing, 2 Volumes Freehand Drawing, 1 Volume Business Practice, 65 Volumes Book-Keeping, 2 Volumes Arithmetic, 7 Volumes Grammar, 2 Volumes Civics, 8 Volumes Spelling, Geography, Correspondence, Christian Doctrine, Compositions and Commercial Law, 5 Cases "Aids to Object Lessons," 15 Specimens Marble, 10 Framed Drawings and 1 Large Crayon.

MONROE, MICH.

St. Mary's Academy.—*Sisters of the Immaculate Heart of Mary.*

12 Volumes: Christian Doctrine, Essays, Poems, Mathematics, History, Grammar, Geography, Language, Mental Science, Stenography, Typewriting, 2 Herbariums; 1 Volume "History of St. Mary's Academy," 1 Volume Specimens of Needle-Work, 4 Photographs and 1 Folio of 150 Art Studies.

PORT HURON, MICH.

Sacred Heart Academy.—*Sisters of Providence.*

1 Volume: Examination Papers, Christian Doctrine, Bible History, Arithmetic, Geography, Algebra, Ancient and Modern History, United States History, Literature, Rhetoric, Astronomy, Physics, Geology, Logic and Table Etiquette.

PARISH SCHOOL.

YPSILANTI, MICH.

St. John's School.—*Sisters of Providence.*

2 Volumes: Catechism, Arithmetic, Penmanship, Bible and United States History, Rhetoric, Phonography, Typewriting, Church History and Algebra.

DIOCESE OF FORT WAYNE, IND.

RT. REV. JOSEPH RADEMACHER.

Diocesan Committee.

Very Rev. J. H. Brammer.   Very Rev. T. C. Walsh, C. S. C.   Rev. J. H. Oechtering.
Rev. August Seifert, C. B. P. S.   Very Rev. M. E. Campion, *Secretary.*

ALCOVES 36, 44, 46, 48 AND 50.

NOTRE DAME, IND.

University of Notre Dame du Lac.

Full length Life-Size Portrait in Oil of Very Rev. E. Sorin, C. S. C., Founder of the University. Ten Portraits in Oil Work by Professor Gregori and his Pupils of the Art School, Notre Dame. Topographical Survey of the University Precincts Scale 1:792, drawn by Class of 1893. Samples of Work done in Iron by Students First Year's Course Practical Mechanics. Samples of Work done in Wood by Students of the Institute of Technology, Notre Dame. Crayons from Life and Casts by Students of Professor Ackerman's Class. Blue Prints and Examples of Linear Drawing from Institute of Technology. Photographs made by Class of Photo-Micrography. Twenty-Six Bound Volumes of the Notre Dame Scholastic, Illustrating Work of the Students in Classes of English Composition, Rhetoric, English Literature and Belle Letters. Specimens of Books Printed and Published at Notre Dame. Bound Volumes of the Ave Maria Printed and Published, Notre Dame. Paintings and Lithographs Illustrating the Growth of Notre Dame. A Few Photographs and Souvenirs of Persons Connected with the University of Notre Dame du Lac. 120 Photographs of the Department of Experimental Bacteriology, Photo-Micrography, Electrical Engineering, Art Schools, Libraries, Physical Cabinets, Lecture Rooms and Laboratory, Department of Natural History, Law School, College of Music, Gymnasium, Institute of Technology, School of Manual Labor, Normal School, Theological Seminary of the Holy Cross, Literary, Athletic and Aquatic Associations, Chemical Department, Observatory, and the Various Colleges, Halls and Dormitories of the University made by the Members of Father Alexander Keroch's Photograph Class. Twelve Photographs of Gregori's Famous Mural Frescoes in the Columbian Gallery, Notre Dame.

CATHOLIC HISTORICAL COLLECTIONS OF AMERICA.

Dept. A.

The Bishop's Memorial Hall.

Life-Sized Portraits in Oil of Bishop Carroll; Bishop Egan; Bishop Concannen; Bishop Flaget; Archbishop Hughes; Bishop Luers, by Gregori; Bishop Persico; Cardinal Manning, by Carnivale; Bishop England, by Irish Arbit; Abbott Smith, by Healy; Bishop Fenwick, by P. Wood; Bishop Chabrat, by Du Bois; Cardinal Franchi, by Carnivale; Cardinal McCloskey, Archbishop Kenrick and Archbishop Spalding, by Gregori; Archbishop Conwell, by Nagle; Archbishop Purcell, by Wood; Bishop Kelly, by Wood; Cardinal Ledochowski, by Carnivale; Cardinal Simeoni, by Carnivale; Father Badin, by Clement; Father Junipero Serra, by Wood; John Gilmary Shea and Orestes A. Brownson, by Gregori; Bishop Rosati, by Gregori; Life-Sized Portrait in Crayon of Bishop Cretin, by Gregori; Photographs and Engravings of Deceased Bishops; Original Manuscripts of Sermons Preached by Various American Bishops.

Case 1.

Gold-embroidered and jeweled Mitres used by the first Bishops of Baltimore. Precious Mitre worn by Most Rev. Archbishop Spalding. Gothic Mitre, designed by Pugin, used by Archbishop Bayley when he imposed the Biretta Rosa on Cardinal McCloskey. Gold-embroidered red velvet Mitre used by Archbishop Kenrick of Baltimore. Gold-plated Crosier used by the early Archbishops of Baltimore. Mitten of White Wool worn by Pope Pius IX. when he gave his last blessing to the attendants surrounding his deathbed. Red Silk Zuchetto worn by Pius IX. when elected Pope. Lock of the Hair of Pius IX. and pieces of his Cassock, Mantle and Surplice enshrined in a Gold Casket. Gold Chalice used by several Popes and Cardinals. White Silk Zuchetto worn by Pope Leo XIII. Gold Chalice, made 1524, owned and used by Archbishop Carroll, gift of Bishop Borgess. Crosier of Olive Wood from Garden of Gethsemene, inlaid with Silver, Mother-of-Pearl, Ebony and Ivory, supposed to have been given to the first American Bishop by the Bishop who Consecrated him—Rt. Rev. Dr. Wormesley of England. Pen and Holder used to sign the Decrees of the Third Plenary Council of Baltimore. Original Miniature of Pope Leo XIII. Gold Pen and Holder used by Bishop Keane when Writing the Statutes of the Catholic University of America. Several Miniatures and Photographs of Baltimore Dignitaries. Gold Cross and Chain worn by Archbishop Eccleston when Consecrated, also worn by Archbishop Elder when consecrated Bishop of Natchez. German Bible, in 2 Volumes, printed in German at Nuremberg, 1470. Catholic Bible printed 1473, five months before birth of Martin Luther.

Case 2.

Gold-emoroidered Mitre used by Bishop Penalvery Cardenas, first Bishop of Louisiana and the Floridas, gift of Archbishop Janssens. Gold-embroidered Mitre worn by Rt. Rev. Bishop Dubourg and successor in Diocese of New Orleans. Gold mitre worn by Archbishop Odin when first Bishop of Galveston. Pectoral Cross and Chain worn by Bishop Dubourg. Gold Episcopal Ring worn by Archbishop Blanc. Episcopal Ring worn by Archbishop Odin. Silver Mission Chalice used by Archbishop Odin and Archbishop Perché. Pallium with jeweled clasps, worn by Archbishop Leray. White linen Mitre used by Archbishop Perché. Mozetta of purple moire antique worn by Archbishop Leray. Gold Mitre worn by Bishop Verot, first Bishop of St. Augustine. Decoration and Cross of the Holy Sepulchre, presented to Archbishop Perche. Holy Bible, first Catholic Bible published in the United States, 1790. Bible printed in 1805, owned and used by Mother Seton, first Sister of Charity in the United States. Catholic New Testament published in English in 1682. Silver cruets and salver used in the Cathedral of New Orleans. Rare Engravings and Photographs of Personages connected with Archdiocese of New Orleans.

CATHOLIC HISTORICAL COLLECTIONS OF AMERICA.

Dept. A.—CONTINUED.

CASE 3.

Curious old Mitre used by first Bishop of Louisville. Wooden Crosier used by Bishop Flaget. Gold Pectoral Cross used by Bishop Flaget. Gold-embroidered Sandals used by Bishop Flaget. Silver and Gold Mission Chalice used by Bishop Bruté. Gold-embroidered Red Mitre used by Bishop Bruté. Jeweled Mitre worn by Bishops De la Hailandiere and Bazin. Richly embroidered Mitre used by Bishop de St. Palais. Silver Crosier given to Bishop Bruté by the Archbishop of Vienna. Gold-plated Crosier used by the Second Bishop of Vincennes and his Successors. Lock of Bishop Bazin's Hair. Pocket Missal, 1647, used by Bishop Bruté. Gold Lined Silver Ciborium used by the early Missionaries of Southern Indiana. Gold Lined Pyx used on early Missions of Vincennes. Gold-embroidered Mitre used by Bishop Luers. Gold Episcopal Ring used by Bishop Luers. Gold-embroidered Mitre used by Bishop Miles and his Successors. Silver and Gold Chalice used by early Missionaries of Northern Indiana. Mitre worn by Bishop Rappe. Gold Episcopal Cross and Chain used by Bishops Rappe and de Goesbriand. Seal of Bishop Gilmoure. Daguerreotypes and Photographs of Dignitaries of Indiana and Kentucky.

CASE 4.

Beautiful English Mitre of exquisite Needle-Work used by Bishop Fenwick of Cincinnati. Embroidered Mitre used by Bishop Rosecrans. Precious Mitre used by Archbishop Purcell. Flemish Mitre used by Bishop Lefevere. Jeweled Mitre used by Bishop Baraga and successors. Gold-embroidered Silver-Cloth Mitre used by Bishop Borgess. Pewter Chalice used by early Jesuit Missionaries of Michigan, also by Father Richard. Silver and Gold Crosier given to Archbishop Purcell by the Germans of Cincinnati. Cane containing Relic of a Saint used by Bishop Baraga. Curious Semi-Circular Mitre used by Bishop Young. Exquisitely chiseled Crosier of Silver and Ebony given to Bishop Lefevere, of Detroit, by Bishop Mallou, of Bruges. Quaint old Pyx in the form of a Silver Cross used by the early Missionaries of Ohio. Silver Pax used by Deacons at Solemn High Mass. Sub-Deacon's Pax. Lock of Archbishop McHale's Hair. Bishop Reze's Seal. Gold-embroidered Gauntlets used by Bishop Lefevere.

CASE 5.

Jeweled Mitre used by Bishop Connell, gift of Archbishop Ryan. Precious Mitre used by Bishop Neumann. Gold-plated Silver Cross worn by Bishop Egan. Gold-embroidered white Gauntlets used by Bishop Egan. Silver Chalice used by Prince Gallitzin. Episcopal Ring worn by Bishop Conwell. Gold-embroidered and jeweled Mitre worn by Bishop Hendricken. Jeweled Mitre used by Bishop Shannahan. Cane used by Prince Gallitzin. Silver and Bronze Medals of Cathedral, Philadelphia. Writing of St. Ligouri, attested by Bishop Neumann. Bronze Medals of Archbishop Wood and St. Charles' Seminary. Photographs of Philadelphia Dignitaries.

CASE 6.

Gold-embroidered Roman Mitre used by the first Bishops of New York. Precious Mitre used by Archbishop Hughes. Gold Pectoral Cross used by Archbishop Hughes and Bishop de Goesbriand. Cardinal's Biretta, Zuchetto and Mozetta worn by Cardinal McCloskey. Lock of Cardinal McCloskey's hair in a Jeweled Locket. Jeweled Mitre worn by Bishop Bacon. Lock of Cardinal de Cheverus' hair. Cross blessed by Bishop de Cheverus, first Bishop of Boston. Precious Mitre worn by Bishop Fitzpatrick. Lock of Bishop Tyler's hair. Embroidered Mitre used by Bishop Galberry. Mitre worn by Bishop O'Reilly, who was drowned at sea. Mitre used by Bishop McFarland. Jeweled Crosier used by Bishop Timon of Buffalo. Cardinal's Hat used by Cardinal Jacobini. Several rare old Daguerreotypes and Books owned by Eastern Bishops. Pen and Holder used by John Gilmary Shea, LL. D., when writing the last pages of his History. Pencil used by Father Lambert, LL. D., when writing his famous Book "Notes on Ingersoll."

CATHOLIC HISTORICAL COLLECTIONS OF AMERICA.

Dept. A.—Continued.

Case 7.

Gold-Embroidered Silk Mitre used by Bishop Quarter. Pectoral Cross and Chain worn by Bishop Van de Velde. Pectoral Cross worn by Bishop O'Regan. Gold Cross and Chain used by the Fourth Bishop of Chicago. Gold-embroidered Mitre used by Bishop Foley. Episcopal Ring with Amethyst setting used by Bishop O'Regan. Episcopal Ring with Sapphire setting used by Bishop Duggan. Mitre worn by Bishop Loras. Quaint Swiss Mitre used by Archbishop Henni. Curiously-embroidered bead-and-silver Mitre used by Bishop Cretin. Silver Crosier owned by Archbishop Henni. Jeweled Mitre used by the first Bishop of Green Bay. Episcopal Ring set with Emerald surrounded with Diamonds given by Archbishop Henni to Bishop Flasch. Wooden Crosier used by Bishop Loras. Lock of Bishop Smyth's Hair. Lock of Bishop Loras' Hair. Gold Episcopal Ring worn by Bishop Baltas Jeweled Mitre owned by Bishop Juncker. Lock of Bishop Cretin's Hair. Crosier given to Bishop McMullin by Archbishop Feehan. Copy used by Archbishop Ireland when he delivered his famous address on the occasion of the inauguration of the World's Congresses, Chicago.

Case 8.

Gold-Cloth Mitre, embroidered with Silver, used by Bishop England. Silver Ciborium used by Bishop England. Bishop Clancy's Coat of Arms. Lock of Bishop Reynold's Hair. Episcopal Ring worn by Bishop Chanche. Cross worn by Bishop Clancy. Jeweled Mitre worn by Archbishop Allemany. Curious old Crosier of Tortoise Shell and Silver used by Bishop Garcia-Moreno, First Bishop of California. Gold Cross and Chain, Episcopal Ring with Amethyst setting willed by Bishop O'Connell to the Bishops' Memorial Hall. Quaint old Mitre used by Archbishop Blanchet. Jeweled Mitre in which the Murdered Archbishop Seghers was consecrated, also used by Bishop Demers. Seal of Bishop Garcia-Moreno. Episcopal Ring worn by Bishop Gartland. Part of Bishop Gartland's Vestments, taken from his grave when his body was removed to the Cathedral, Mobile. Stole of painted velvet worn by Bishop Byrne. Pectoral Cross, Chain and Ring worn by Bishop O'Gorman. Bishop O'Gorman's Seal. Large Silver Crosier used by Bishop Portier. Bishop Portier's Mitre. Mitre worn by Bishop Pellicier. Gold-embroidered Mitre worn by Bishop Miege, S. J. Wood Carving from old Texas Mission.

Case 9.

Artistically embroidered Chasuble, Stole, Maniple, Chalice Veil and Burse, the handiwork of Miss Mary Gwendeline Caldwell. Bell made 1776, from the Mission Church, Cahokia, Illinois.

Cases 11, 12, 13, 14, 15.

Relics of Catholic Soldiers, Statesmen, Missionaries, Priests and Members of Religious Orders. Gold-embroidered Chasuble used by Father Marquette, gift of Bishop Borgess. Quaint old Chasuble used by Father Badin, first Priest ordained in the United States. Sword carried through the Mexican War and Late Civil War by General James Shields. Mitres worn by first Trappist Abbot and the first Benedictine Abbot of the United States. Medals, Coins, etc. Relics and Souvenirs of the Seton Family, gifts of Rt. Rev. Robert Seton, D. D. Relics of the Carroll Family, gifts of Mrs. Rebecca Carroll. Several Albums of Photographs of Catholic Priests, gift of Mr. Edwin Edgerly. Pictures illustrating American History. Photographs of many Catholic Editors. Life-sized Paintings of James A. McMaster, P. V. Hickey, John Boyle O'Reilly, William J. Onahan, Cardinals Newman and Manning, Shakespeare, Orestes A. Brownson, John Gilmary Shea, Miss Eliza Allen Starr, Richard H. Clark, LL.D., etc.

CATHOLIC HISTORICAL COLLECTIONS OF AMERICA.

Dept. B.

A small exhibit of Manuscripts from the Catholic Archives of America, established at Notre Dame, 1866. Autograph Letters of all the deceased Bishops of the United States. Specimens of Papal Bulls. Documents of historic interest. Maps illustrating work of early Missionaries. Handwriting of Catholic Priests and Laymen.

Dept. C.

The Catholic Reference Library of America. First Volume Bound of the Catholic Miscellany, 1822. The Jesuit, 1829. Literary and Catholic Sentinel, 1825. The Pilot, 1826. The Freeman's Journal, 1840. Catholic Diary, 1833. Catholic Telegraph, 1821. Le Propagateur Catalogue, 1843. The Catholic Mirror, 1849. The Catholic Herald, 1833, etc. Specimens of early Catholic Magazines, Pamphlets and rare Books.

FORT WAYNE, IND.

St. Augustine's Cathedral School.

MALE DEPT.—*Brothers of the Holy Cross.*
FEMALE DEPT.—*Sisters of Providence, Vigo County.*

2 Volumes: Reading, Physiology, Civil Government, Christian Doctrine, Orthography, Arithmetic, Grammar, United States History, Bible History, Geography, Drawing, Literature, Physics, Modern History, Astronomy, Algebra, Church History, Logic, Chemistry, Business Forms, Phonography and Typewriting. 2 Volumes: Standard Time, Rhetoric, Ancient History, Natural Philosophy, Astronomy, 3 Volumes Theory of Music.

St. Mary's School.—*Brothers of the Holy Cross.*

Christian Doctrine, United States History, Compositions, English and German Translations, Penmanship, Map Drawing, Geography, Grammar, Orthography, Freehand Drawing and Bible History.

St. Patrick's School.—*Sisters of Providence.*

Christian Doctrine, Penmanship, Compositions, Arithmetic, Geography, Music, Language Lessons, Grammar, Orthography, Bible History, United States History, Church History and General History.

St. Paul's School.—*Sisters of the Poor Handmaids of Christ.*

Christian Doctrine, Geography, Arithmetic, Orthography, Compositions, United States History and Grammar.

St. Peter's School.—*School Sisters of Notre Dame.*

Christian Doctrine, Letter Writing, Penmanship, Language Lessons, Orthography, Geography, United States History and Bible History.

ACADEMY, IND.

St. Vincent's School.—*Sisters of the Holy Cross.*

Christian Doctrine, Letter Writing, French Translations, Arithmetic, Orthography, United States History and Book-Keeping.

ANDERSON, IND.

St. Mary's School.—*Sisters of the Holy Cross.*

Arithmetic, Geography, Grammar, United States History, Algebra and Physiology.

AVILLA, IND.

St. Augustine's School.—*Secular Teachers.*
Christian Doctrine, Arithmetic, Compositions, Geography and Grammar.

COLUMBIA CITY, IND.

St. Joseph's School.—*Sisters of St. Agnes.*
Christian Doctrine, Grammar, United States History, Church History, Freehand Drawing, Arithmetic, Geography, Compositions.

CHESTERTON, IND.

St. Patrick's School.—*Secular Teachers.*
Bible History, United States History, Arithmetic, Grammar and Geography.

CRAWFORDSVILLE, IND.

St. Bernard's School.—*Sisters of the Holy Cross.*
History, Arithmetic, Chemistry, Botany, Rhetoric, Geometry, Literature, Algebra, Grammar and Geography.

CROWN POINT, IND.

St. Mary's School.—*Sisters of St. Agnes.*
Bible History, Arithmetic, Grammar, United States History and Geography.

St. Joseph's School.—*Sisters of St. Agnes.*
Christian Doctrine, Arithmetic, Geography, United States History, Grammar, Algebra and Physiology.

DELPHI, IND.

St. Joseph's School.—*Sisters of Providence.*
2 Volumes: Christian Doctrine, Penmanship, Language Lessons, Arithmetic, Orthography, Geography, Grammar, Bible History, Letters, Book-Keeping, Algebra, Rhetoric, Physical Geography, Literature and Physics.

EARL PARK, IND.

St. Anthony's School.—*Miss Maggie Higgins.*
Geography, History and Physiology.

ELWOOD, IND.

St. Joseph's School.—*Miss Margaret Murphy.*
United States History and Compositions.

EGE, IND.

St. Mary's School.—*Sisters of St. Francis.*
United States History, Geography, Grammar and Natural Philosophy.

ELKHART, IND.

St. Vincent's School.—*Sisters of the Holy Cross.*
Penmanship, Grammar, Orthography and Compositions.

FOWLER, IND.

School of St. John the Evangelist.—*Sisters of St. Francis.*
Christian Doctrine, Arithmetic, Penmanship, Grammar and Compositions.

FT. WAYNE, IND.

St. Patrick's School.—*Sisters of Providence.*
Examination Papers: Christian Doctrine, Arithmetic, Bible History, Geography, United States History, Grammar, Orthography, Penmanship and Music.

GARRETT, IND.

St. Joseph's School.—*Sisters of the Most Precious Blood.*
Christian Doctrine, Penmanship, Language Lessons, Compositions, Arithmetic, United States History, Grammar, Physiology.

GOSHEN, IND.

St. John's School.—*Sisters of the Holy Cross.*
Geography, Arithmetic, Grammar, Orthography, Algebra, Book-Keeping and Composition.

HAMMOND, IND.

St. Joseph's School.—*Sisters of Providence.*
1 Volume Examination Papers: Christian Doctrine, Grammar, Arithmetic, Orthography, Letters, History, Book-Keeping, Language, Bible History, Geography and Catechism.

HESSE CASSEL, IND.

St. John's School.—*Sisters of the Third Order of St. Francis.*
United States History, Geography and Lessons in Reading.

HUNTINGTON, IND.

Sts. Peter and Paul's School.—*School Sisters of Notre Dame.*
Christian Doctrine, History, Penmanship, Geography, Arithmetic, Language and Letter Writing.

KENTLAND, IND.

St. John's School.—*Sisters of St. Francis.*
Geography, Arithmetic and Christian Doctrine.

KLAASVILLE, IND.

St. Anthony's School.—*Sisters of St. Francis.*
Letter Writing, Spelling, Geography and Arithmetic.

KOKOMO, IND.

St. Patrick's School.—*Sisters of the Poor Handmaids of Christ.*
Specimens of Letter Writing.

LAFAYETTE, IND.

St. Ignatius' School.—*Sisters of Providence.*
Christian Doctrine, Orthography, Music, Penmanship, Geography, Arithmetic, Botany and Natural Philosophy.

St. Mary's School.—*Brothers of the Holy Cross.*
Arithmetic, Orthography and Geography.

LAFAYETTE, IND.—Continued.

St. Ann's School.—*Sisters of Providence.*

1 Volume Examination Papers: Christian Doctrine, Sacred History, Arithmetic, Grammar, Penmanship, Orthography, United States History, Physiology and Music.

LACRO, IND.

St. Patrick's School.—*Sisters of St. Francis.*

Grammar, United States History and Geography.

LAPORTE, IND.

St. Rose's School.—*Sisters of the Holy Cross.*

Christian Doctrine, Compositions, Algebra, Geography, History, Grammar and Arithmetic.

LOGANSPORT, IND.

St. Joseph's School.—*School Sisters of Notre Dame.*

Christian Doctrine, Orthography, Letters, Language Lessons, Arithmetic, German Translations, Geography, Penmanship and Freehand Drawing.

School of St. Vincent de Paul.—*Sisters of the Holy Cross.*

Christian Doctrine, Arithmetic, Geography, History, Grammar, Algebra and Rhetoric.

MICHIGAN CITY, IND.

St. Mary's School.—*Sisters of the Holy Cross.*

History, Geography, Language, Orthography, Christian Doctrine, Arithmetic, Grammar, German Translations, Bible History, Algebra, Physiology, Rhetoric and Literature.

St. Stanislaus' School.—*Sisters of the Holy Cross.*

Orthography, Letter Writing, Penmanship and Translations.

MISHAWAKA, IND.

St. Joseph's School.—*Sisters of the Holy Cross.*

Christian Doctrine, Grammar, Geography, Composition, Arithmetic, Bible History, United States History.

MONROEVILLE, IND.

School of St. Rose of Lima.—*Secular Teachers.*

Christian Doctrine, United States History and Bible History.

MUNCIE, IND.

St. Lawrence's School.—*Sisters of St. Agnes.*

Orthography, Arithmetic, Language Lessons, Geography and Algebra.

NEW CORYDON, IND.

Holy Trinity School.—*Sisters of Most Precious Blood.*

Penmanship, Arithmetic and United States History.

NEW HAVEN, IND.

St. John the Baptist School.—*Sisters of St. Agnes.*

Christian Doctrine, Grammar, Arithmetic, History, Letter Writing, Business Forms, Book-Keeping, Geography and Map Drawing.

OTIS, IND.

School of the Sacred Heart of Jesus.—*Sisters of St. Francis.*

Letter Writing, Bible History, Geography, Arithmetic, Christian Doctrine, Translations, Polish and United States History.

PERU, IND.

School of St. Charles Borromeo.—*Sisters of Providence.*

2 Volumes: Christian Doctrine, Arithmetic, Penmanship, Letter Writing, Geography, United States History, Grammar, Book-Keeping, Natural Philosophy, Phonography, Bible History, Church History, Algebra, Civil Government, Literature.

PLYMOUTH, IND.

St. Michael's School.—*Sisters of the Holy Cross.*

Christian Doctrine, United States History, Letter Writing, Arithmetic and Penmanship.

RENSSALAER, IND.

St. Joseph's Normal Indian School.—*Sisters of the Most Precious Blood.*

Orthography, Bible and United States History, Grammar, Geography and Church History.

SHELDON, IND.

St. Aloysius' School.—*Sisters of St. Francis.*

Letter Writing, Grammar, Geography, Church History and Arithmetic.

SOUTH BEND, IND.

St. Hedwige's School.—*Sisters of the Holy Cross.*

Geography, Bible History, Grammar, Arithmetic, Language, Polish Translations, Object Lessons, Orthography, United States and Polish History and Book-Keeping.

St. Joseph's School.—*Sisters of the Holy Cross.*

Christian Doctrine, Grammar, Letter Writing, Orthography, Geography and Arithmetic.

St. Mary's School.—*Sisters of the Holy Cross.*

Christian Doctrine, United States History, Geography, Orthography, Letter Writing, Arithmetic and Grammar.

ST. JOHN, IND.

St. John's School.—*Secular Teachers.*

Grammar, United States History, Arithmetic, Geography and Orthography.

TIPTON, IND.

St. John's School.—*Secular Teachers.*

Arithmetic, Physiology, Penmanship and Freehand Drawing.

UNION CITY, IND.

   St. Mary's School.—*Sisters of the Holy Cross.*

      Church History, Grammar, Penmanship, Orthography, Arithmetic, Geography, Compositions, Rhetoric, Book-Keeping and United States History.

VALPARAISO, IND.

   St. Paul's School.—*Sisters of Providence.*

      1 Volume Examination Papers: Christian Doctrine, Geography, Arithmetic, Language, Bible History, Grammar, Literature, Geometry, Physics and Church History. Penmanship, United States History, Rhetoric, Music and Algebra.

WINAMAC, IND.

   St. Peter's School.—*Sisters of the Precious Blood.*

      History, Grammar, Physiology, Penmanship, Arithmetic, United States History and Orthography.

ORPHANAGE.

FORT WAYNE, IND.

   St. Vincent's Orphanage.—*Sisters of the Poor Handmaids of Christ.*

      Compositions, Grammar, Arithmetic, United States History and Bible History.

DIOCESE OF GREEN BAY, WIS.

RT. REV. SEBASTIAN G. MESSMER, D.D.

Diocesan Committee.

Rev. J. J. Fox.   Rev. P. A. McDermott, C. S. Sp.   Rev. W. J. Fitzmaurice.

ALCOVES 24 AND 25.

Portrait of Rt. Rev. Bishop Messmer.

ACADEMY.

MARINETTE, WIS.

   Academy of Lourdes.—*School Sisters of Notre Dame.*

      Christian Doctrine, Penmanship, Geography, Arithmetic, Language, Letter Writing.

PARISH SCHOOLS.

GREEN BAY, WIS.

Cathedral School.—*School Sisters of Notre Dame.*

4 Volumes: Christian Doctrine, Orthography, Arithmetic, Object Lessons, Language, Grammar, Geography, Etymology, Physiology, Letter Writing, Book-Keeping, Vocal Music Teaching, Crochet Bed Spreads, Specimens of Needle-Work, Embroidery, Lace-Work, Embroidered Banners and Kindergarten Work.

St. John's School.—*School Sisters of Notre Dame.*

4 Volumes: Christian Doctrine, Orthography, United States History, Geography, Penmanship, Composition, Drawing, Church History, Civil Government, Physical Geography, Arithmetic, Grammar and Physiology.

St. Vincent's School.—*School Sisters of Notre Dame.*

2 Volumes: Christian Doctrine, Arithmetic, Grammar, United States History, Orthography, Language and Object Lessons.

AHNAPEE, WIS.

St. Mary's School.—*School Sisters of Notre Dame.*

1 Volume: School Regulations, Historical Account of the School, Christian Doctrine, Arithmetic, Grammar, Geography, English and German Penmanship, Drawing, United States History, Letter Writing and Orthography.

ANTIGO, WIS.

St. John's School.—*Sisters of St. Francis.*

1 Volume: Arithmetic, Christian Doctrine, History, Penmanship, Book-Keeping, Letter Writing and Music.

APPLETON, WIS.

St. Joseph's School.—*School Sisters of Notre Dame.*

3 Volumes: Christian Doctrine, Orthography, Arithmetic, Bible History, Language, Pastel and Crayon Pictures and Pen Drawings.

St. Mary's School.—*Dominican Sisters.*

3 Volumes: Christian Doctrine, Arithmetic, Geography, Orthography, Object Lessons, Science, Grammar, History, Compositions, Penmanship, Physical Geography and Algebra.

BAY SETTLEMENT, WIS.

Holy Cross School.—*Sisters of St. Francis.*

Christian Doctrine, Orthography, Arithmetic, Grammar, Geography, United States History, Letter Writing and Map Drawing.

St. Francis' Convent School.—*Sisters of St. Francis.*

1 Volume: Christian Doctrine, Orthography, Arithmetic, Language, Geography and Specimens of Kindergarten Work.

BUCHANAN, WIS.

Holy Angels' School.—*Sisters of St. Agnes.*

2 Volumes: Christian Doctrine, Spelling, Arithmetic, Grammar, Geography, History, Freehand Drawing and Orthography.

CASIMIR, WIS.

St. Casimir's School.—*Sisters of St. Francis.*

1 Volume: Christian Doctrine, Arithmetic, Grammar, Orthography, German and English Translations, United States History, Geography and Freehand Drawing.

CATO, WIS.

St. Michael's School.—*Sisters of St. Francis.*

Christian Doctrine, Arithmetic, Grammar, Geography and Language Lessons.

CHILTON, WIS.

St. Mary's School.—*School Sisters of Notre Dame.*

1 Volume: Christian Doctrine, Arithmetic, Orthography, Penmanship, Letter Writing, Language, Grammar, German and English.

CLARK'S MILLS, WIS.

Immaculate Conception School.—*Sisters of St. Francis.*

Christian Doctrine, Arithmetic, Geography, Language, Grammar, German and English Translations.

DE PERE, WIS.

St. Mary's School.—*School Sisters of Notre Dame.*

2 Volumes: Christian Doctrine, Orthography, Geography, Language, Arithmetic, Grammar, United States History, Civil Government and Compositions.

FREEDOM, WIS.

St. Nicholas' School.—*School Sisters of Notre Dame.*

1 Volume: Christian Doctrine, Arithmetic, Grammar, Language, Geography, Compositions, Letter Writing, Penmanship and Bible History.

GRAND RAPIDS, MICH.

Sts. Peter and Paul's School.—*School Sisters of Notre Dame.*

2 Volumes: Christian Doctrine, Arithmetic, Grammar, Orthography, Penmanship, Language, Object Lessons, Drawing, United States History, Compositions, Physiology, Book-Keeping, Specimens of Object Drawings, Maps of Wisconsin and City of Grand Rapids.

LITTLE CHUTE, WIS.

District School.—*Sisters of Notre Dame.*

2 Volumes: Christian Doctrine, Orthography, Geography, Arithmetic, Language, Drawing, Grammar, Composition, Letter Writing, United States History and 1 Volume of Kindergarten Work.

LUXEMBURG, WIS.

St. Mary's School.—*Sisters of St. Francis.*

Arithmetic, Geography, Grammar, Penmanship, Orthography and Christian Doctrine.

MAPLE GROVE (KEWAUNEE), WIS.

St. Patrick's School.—*Sisters of Notre Dame.*

2 Volumes: Christian Doctrine, Arithmetic, Orthography, Grammar, Penmanship, Physiology, German Translations and Letter Writing.

MARINETTE, WIS.

St. Mary's Institute.—*School Sisters of Notre Dame.*

3 Volumes: Christian Doctrine, Arithmetic, Geography, Penmanship, United States History, Algebra, Civil Government, Physiology, General History, Physical Geography, Book-Keeping, Rhetoric, Bible History, Natural Philosophy, Algebra, Geometry, 1 Volume Music, Oil and Pastel Paintings, Crayon Pictures, Photographs, Needle and Crochet Work and Freehand Drawing.

MENASHA, WIS.

St. Mary's School.—*School Sisters of Notre Dame.*

2 Volumes: Christian Doctrine, Orthography, Geography, Language, Compositions, Grammar, Book-Keeping and Letter Writing.

St. Patrick's School.—*School Sisters of Notre Dame.*

2 Volumes: Christian Doctrine, Orthography, Language, Arithmetic, Algebra, United States History, Grammar, Physiology, Letter Writing, 14 Copy Books of Examination Papers.

NEW FRANKEN, WIS.

St. Kilians' School.—*Sisters of St. Francis.*

Christian Doctrine, Arithmetic, Geography, Language, Orthography, Penmanship, Bible History and United States History.

NEW KAUKAUNA, WIS.

Holy Cross School.—*Dominican Sisters.*

2 Volumes: Arithmetic, Orthography, Christian Doctrine, Object Lessons, United States History, Letter Writing, Physiology, Geography, Penmanship and Civil Government.

OCONTO, WIS.

St. Peter's School.—*Sisters of St. Joseph.*

Christian Doctrine, Orthography, Arithmetic, Penmanship, Letter Writing, Grammar, United States History, German and English Translations, Albums of Freehand Drawing.

OSHKOSH, WIS.

St. Mary's School.—*Sisters of St. Dominic.*

3 Volumes: Christian Doctrine, Orthography, Arithmetic, Geography, Penmanship, Letter Writing, German and English Translations and Albums of Freehand Drawing.

St. Peter's School.—*Sisters of St. Dominic.*

2 Volumes: Spelling, Christian Doctrine, Orthography, Language, Object Lessons, Geography, Penmanship, Kindergarten Work, Arithmetic, Grammar, United States History, Bible History, Physiology, Natural Philosophy and Map Drawing.

PORTAGE, WIS.

St. Mary's School.—*School Sisters of Notre Dame.*

3 Volumes: Christian Doctrine, Orthography, Language, Arithmetic, Geography, Grammar, Composition, United States History, Physiology, Map Drawing, Rhetoric, Natural Philosophy and Literature.

SHAWANO, WIS.

Sacred Heart School.—*Sisters of St. Joseph.*

1 Volume: Christian Doctrine, Arithmetic, Grammar, Geography, Bible History, Algebra, Botany, United States History, Civics, Compositions, Rhetoric, Geometry, Natural Philosophy, Physiology, Freehand Drawing and Map Drawings.

SOUTH KAUKAUNA, WIS.

St. Mary's School.—*Sisters of St. Francis.*

2 Volumes: Christian Doctrine, Language, Arithmetic, Orthography, Geography, Penmanship, Grammar and Album of Kindergarten Work.

STEVENS' POINT, WIS.

St. Peter's School.—*Sisters of Notre Dame.*

Christian Doctrine, Orthography, Grammar, Bible History, Compositions, Letter Writing and Penmanship.

St. Stephen's School.—*Sisters of Notre Dame.*

2 Volumes: Christian Doctrine, Orthography, Language, Penmanship, Arithmetic, Geography, Grammar, United States History, Book-Keeping, Algebra and Physiology.

STURGEON BAY, WIS.

Holy Guardian Angels' School.—*Sisters of St. Dominic.*

1 Volume: Christian Doctrine, Grammar, Arithmetic, Geography, United States History, Questions on Physics, Freehand Drawing, Language Lessons, Map Drawing.

TWO RIVERS, WIS.

St. Luke's School.—*Sisters of St. Agnes.*

1 Volume: Orthography, Christian Doctrine, Language, Letter Writing, Grammar, Arithmetic, United States History, Penmanship and Book-Keeping.

WAUSAU, WIS.

St. Mary's School.—*School Sisters of Notre Dame.*

2 Volumes: Language, Orthography, History, Arithmetic, Penmanship, Grammar, Christian Doctrine and Composition.

WEST DE PERE, WIS.

St. Joseph's School.—*Sisters of the Incarnate Word.*

3 Volumes: Christian Doctrine, Orthography, Arithmetic, Penmanship, Map Drawing, Language Lessons, Geography, Bible History, Grammar, United States History, Physics, Etymology, General History, Letter Writing, Physical Geography, Literature, Album of Music and Freehand Drawing.

WOODVILLE, WIS.

St. John's School.—*Sisters of St. Agnes.*

1 Volume: Christian Doctrine, Orthography, United States History, Geography, Arithmetic, Drawing, Civics, Physiology, Penmanship and Letter Writing.

INDUSTRIAL SCHOOL AND ORPHANAGE.

GREEN BAY, WIS.

St. Joseph's Orphan Asylum.—*School Sisters of Notre Dame.*

2 Volumes: Christian Doctrine, Orthography, Arithmetic, Grammar, United States History, Penmanship and Drawing.

KESHENA RESERVATION (Menominee Tribe), WIS.

St. Joseph's Indian Industrial School.

MALE DEPT.—*Franciscan Brothers.*
FEMALE DEPT.—*Sisters of St. Joseph.*

2 Volumes: Christian Doctrine, Geography, Arithmetic, Grammar, Orthography, Language, Map Drawing, Specimens of Linear Drawing. Shoes made by Indian Boys. Needle-Work, Crocheting, Plain Sewing by Indian Girls. Photographs. Miniature Engine Boiler by Indian Boy, Gabriel Tucker. Crayons of Grover Cleveland and George Washington

DIOCESE OF LA CROSSE.

RT. REV. JAMES SCHWEBACH, D. D.

ALCOVE 43.

ACADEMY.

PRAIRIE DU CHIEN, WIS.

St. Mary's Institute.—*School Sisters of Notre Dame.*

1 Framed View of St. Mary's Institute and Environs. 6 Albums Examination Papers (Class '92), 3 Herbariums, 3 Albums Examination Papers (Class '94), 10 Albums (Intermediate A): Bible History, Grammar, Compositions, Rhetoric, Arithmetic, Algebra, Book-Keeping, Geography, United States History and Physiology. 1 Album (Intermediate B) Examination Papers, 2 Albums (Preparatory) Examination Papers, 1 Album (Primary) Examination Papers, 3 Albums Shorthand, 1 Book "On the Prairie," 10 Albums Music, 1 Album Biographical Sketches, 11 Albums Art Work, 90 Booklets: Essays, Studies and Poems, 1 Painted Motto and 30 Oil Paintings.

PARISH SCHOOLS.

LA CROSSE, WIS.

St. Joseph's Cathedral School.—*Franciscan Sisters of P. A.*

4 Volumes: Christian Doctrine, Language, Grammar, Compositions, Arithmetic, Writing, Geography and United States History.

Holy Cross School.—*Franciscan Sisters of P. A.*

1 Volume Drawing, 2 Volumes: Christian Doctrine, Bible History, Language, Grammar, Translations, Compositions, United States History, Geography, Physiology and Penmanship.

Holy Trinity School.—*Franciscan Sisters of P. A.*

1 Volume Drawing, 2 Volumes: Christian Doctrine, Bible History, Grammar, Language, Compositions, Translations, Arithmetic, Penmanship, Geography and United States History.

St. James' School.—*Franciscan Sisters of P. A.*

1 Volume: Christian Doctrine, Bible History, Grammar, Arithmetic, Language, Compositions, United States History, Physiology, Civil Government, Book-Keeping, Commercial Law and Algebra.

St. John's School.—*Franciscan Sisters of P. A.*

1 Volume Drawing, 2 Volumes: Arithmetic, Book-Keeping, Civil Government, Commercial Law, Geography, Penmanship, Physiology, United States History, Bible History, Compositions and Translations.

St. Mary's School.—*Franciscan Sisters of P. A.*

1 Volume Drawing, 2 Volumes: Christian Doctrine, Bible History, Spelling, Language, Grammar, Compositions, Arithmetic, Writing, Geography and United States History.

St. Wenceslaus' School.—*Franciscan Sisters of P. A.*

2 Volumes: Christian Doctrine, Bible History, Spelling, Language, Grammar, Translations, Arithmetic, Geography, United States History, Penmanship, Compositions, Grammar, German and 1 Volume Drawing.

ASHLAND, WIS.

St. Agnes' School.—*Franciscan Sisters of P. A.*

1 Volume Drawing, 3 Volumes: Christian Doctrine, Bible History, Spelling, Language, Grammar, Translations, Rhetoric, Literature, Compositions, Spelling, Penmanship, Arithmetic, Algebra, Geometry, United States History, Physiology, Botany, Zoology and General History.

BAYFIELD, WIS.

Christ's School.—*Franciscan Sisters of P. A.*

1 Volume Map Drawing, 2 Volumes: Penmanship, Compositions, Language, Arithmetic, Catechism, Grammar, Geography, Bible History and United States History.

CHIPPEWA FALLS, WIS.

Notre Dame School.—*School Sisters of Notre Dame.*

1 Historical Chart, 1 Geological Chart, 1 Mechanical Drawing and 1 Landscape.

FOUNTAIN CITY, WIS.

St. Mary's School.—*Franciscan Sisters of P. A.*
1 Volume Drawing, 2 Volumes: Arithmetic, Geography, Compositions, Grammar, Language, Christian Doctrine, United States History, Physiology, Civil Government, Book-Keeping, Bible History and Penmanship.

MARSHFIELD, WIS.

St. Mary's School.—*School Sisters of Notre Dame.*
1 Volume Freehand Drawing, 2 Volumes: Christian Doctrine, Penmanship, Language, Arithmetic, Geography, Grammar, Composition, Orthography, Translations and United States History.

NEILLSVILLE, WIS.

St. Mary's School.—*Franciscan Sisters of P. A.*
1 Volume Freehand Drawing, 2 Volumes: Catechism, Bible History, Language, Grammar, Compositions, Translations, Arithmetic, Penmanship, Geography and United States History.

NEW RICHMOND, WIS.

Seat of Wisdom School.—*Sisters of St. Joseph.*
2 Volumes: Christian Doctrine, Arithmetic, Geography, United States History, Bible History, Physiology, Spelling, Grammar, Compositions, Penmanship, Algebra and Rhetoric.

PRAIRIE DU CHIEN, WIS.

St. Gabriel's School.—*School Sisters of Notre Dame.*
3 Volumes: Christian Doctrine, Arithmetic, Language, Geography, Grammar, Compositions, Natural Science, United States History, Algebra, Physiology, Penmanship, 1 Volume Book-Keeping and 1 Volume Drawing.

ST. MARY'S RIDGE, WIS.

St. Mary's School.—*Franciscan Sisters of P. A.*
1 Volume Drawing, 2 Volumes: Christian Doctrine, Bible History, Compositions, Translations, Arithmetic, United States History, Language, Grammar, Geography, Physiology and Penmanship.

SAUK CITY, WIS.

St. Aloysius' School.—*Franciscan Sisters of P. A.*
1 Volume Drawing, 2 Volumes: Arithmetic, Compositions, Arithmetic, Drawing, Geography, Grammar, Spelling, United States History, Catechism, German and Bible History.

DIOCESE OF MANCHESTER.

RT. REV. D. M. BRADLEY, D.D.

ALCOVE 53.

ACADEMIES AND HIGH SCHOOLS.

MANCHESTER, N. H.

St. Augustine's Academy.—*Brothers of the Sacred Heart.*
2 Volumes: Composition, Penmanship, Letter Writing, Book-Keeping. 133 Copy Books: Christian Doctrine, Geography, Algebra, Arithmetic, Map Drawing, Freehand Drawing. 21 Albums Linear Drawing, 1 Map of City of Manchester.

MANCHESTER, N. H.—Continued.

St. Joseph's High School.—*Christian Brothers.*

83 Albums: Christian Doctrine, Arithmetic, Orthography, United States History, General History, Compositions, Literature, Algebra, Geometry, Penmanship, Rhetoric, Physics, Physiology, Philosophy, Latin and French Translations, Mensuration, Typewriting, Drawing, Book-Keeping, Business Correspondence, Debates and 1 Album Photographs of the School, of Students and Buildings.

Academy of Jesu Marie.—*Sisters of the Holy Cross.*

4 Volumes: Christian Doctrine, Orthography, Arithmetic, Book-Keeping, Business Forms, Grammar and Dictations (French), 2 Pieces Ornamental Pen-Work.

Mt. St. Mary's Academy.—*Gray Nuns.*

9 Volumes: Christian Doctrine, History, Literature, Grammar, Geography, Arithmetic, French and Latin Translations, Geometry, Algebra, Book-Keeping, Natural Science, Rhetoric, Compositions, School Journal, Church History, Geometry, Geology, Chemistry, Astronomy, Physics, Botany, Bible History and United States History. 1 Volume Mt. St. Mary's Record.

St. Mary's Day Academy.—*Sisters of Mercy.*

1 Volume Examination Papers, 1 Volume Written Exercises, 1 Volume Phonography and Typewriting, Book-Keeping and Business Forms, 1 Volume Ancient, Modern and United States History (Topical Recitations), 1 Volume Composition, 2 Volumes English Literature, 19 Specimens Phonography, Typewriting and Penmanship.

PARISH SCHOOLS.

MANCHESTER, N. H.

St. Joseph's Cathedral School.—Female Dept.—*Sisters of Mercy*

6 Volumes: Christian Doctrine, Arithmetic, Orthography, Geography, United States History, Church and Bible History, Letter Writing, Compositions and Penmanship.

St. Agnes' School.—*Sisters of Mercy.*

4 Volumes: Christian Doctrine, Church, Bible, and United States History, Arithmetic, Grammar, Letter Writing, Language and Geography.

St. Raphael's School.—*Sisters of St. Benedict.*

14 Albums: Christian Doctrine, Arithmetic, Bible History, Orthography, Sacred History, Language, Grammar and Geography.

KEENE, N. H.

St. Joseph's School.—*Sisters of Mercy.*

3 Volumes: Christian Doctrine, Arithmetic, Language, Orthography, Bible History, United States History, Geography, Grammar and Compositions.

NASHUA, N. H.

St. Aloysius' School.

Male Dept.—*Brothers of the Sacred Heart.*

2 Volumes: Grammar, Orthography, Arithmetic, Geography, Letter Writing, Penmanship and Miscellaneous Exercises.

NASHUA, N. H.—Continued.

St. Aloysius' School.

FEMALE DEPT.—*Sisters of the Holy Cross.*

32 Albums: Christian Doctrine, Arithmetic, Orthography, Geography, Grammar, United States History, Book-Keeping, Drawing, Penmanship, Compositions, Literature, Sacred History.

School of the Sacred Heart.—*Sisters of Mercy.*

5 Albums: Christian Doctrine, United States History, Bible History, Physiology, Physical Geography, Algebra, Phonography, Typewriting, Orthography, Arithmetic, Geography and Kindergarten Work.

ORPHANAGE.

MANCHESTER, N. H.

St. Patrick's Orphanage.—*Sisters of Mercy.*

1 Volume: Specimens of Penmanship, Map Drawing and Freehand Drawing.

DIOCESE OF NATCHEZ.

RT. REV. THOMAS HESLIN, D. D.

ALCOVE 45.

ACADEMIES AND SELECT SCHOOLS.

BAY ST. LOUIS, MISS.

St. Stanislaus' Commercial School.—*Brothers of the Sacred Heart.*

4 Volumes Examinations and Exercises, 2 Volumes Book-Keeping, 1 Volume Trigonometry and Surveying, 2 Volumes: Rhetoric, Physics and Mathematics, 4 Volumes Examination Papers, 2 Volumes Specimens of Penmanship, 3 Volumes Linear Drawing, 3 Albums Pen-Work, 1 Volume Architectural Drawing, Crayon and Pen Drawing and Ornamental Writing, 1 Chart of Diocese, 1 Chart of Bay St. Louis and Environs. Plan of College Property.

St. Joseph's Academy.—*Sisters of St. Joseph.*

1 Volume: Christian Doctrine, Essays, Composition, Botany, Biographical Sketches, History, Grammar, Arithmetic, Algebra, Natural History, Map Drawing, Physiology, Astronomy and Physics.

CHATAWA, MISS.

St. Mary's Institute.—*School Sisters of Notre Dame.*

2 Volumes: Christian Doctrine, Church History, Penmanship, Language, Arithmetic, Geography, United States History, Algebra, Compositions.

GREENVILLE, MISS.

St. Rose of Lima's Academy.—*Sisters of Mercy.*

3 Volumes: Catechism, United States History, Geography, Map Drawing, Arithmetic, Spelling, Philosophy, Grammar, Music, Compositions, Ancient History, Mythology, Botany, Astronomy, Algebra, Physics, Physiology, Physical Geography, Biographical Sketches.

MERIDIAN, MISS.

St. Aloysius' Academy.—*Sisters of Mercy.*

2 Volumes: Catechism, Ancient History, Grammar, Mental Philosophy, Geometry, Algebra, Natural Philosophy, Astronomy, Rhetoric, Book-Keeping. 1 Volume Original Essays (with Photographs).

VICKSBURG, MISS.

St. Francis Xavier's Academy.—*Sisters of Mercy.*

7 Volumes: Catechism, Book-Keeping, Grammar, Geography, Arithmetic, Ancient and Modern History, Familiar Science, Philosophy, Drawing, Original Poem (Illustrated), Music, Geology, Chemistry, Mythology, Literature, History of Academy (with Photographic Views).

St. Aloysius' Commercial College.—*Brothers of the Sacred Heart.*

11 Albums Algebra, 10 Albums: History, Physics and Geometry, 9 Albums Mathematics, 17 Albums Book-Keeping, 23 Albums: History, Geography and Grammar, 16 Albums Rhetoric and Civil Government, 16 Albums Examination Papers, 4 Albums Christian Doctrine, Bible History, 15 Albums Christian Doctrine, 1 Album Phonography, 1 Album Arithmetic and Grammar, 86 Miscellaneous Exercises on the Different Studies, Freehand, Map and Mechanical Drawing, Pen-Work, Ornamental Writing, Photographs, Catalogue of College in Frame.

PARISH SCHOOLS.

NATCHEZ, MISS.

Cathedral School.

MALE DEPT.—*Brothers of the Sacred Heart.*

39 Albums, Book-Keeping, 7 Albums Geometry, 1 Album Algebra, 5 Albums Arithmetic, 34 Albums Home Exercises, 23 Albums Compositions, 7 Albums Trigonometry, 20 Albums Examination Papers, 8 Albums History, 62 Albums Penmanship, Specimens of Freehand Drawing, 1 Pastel Drawing, Ornamental Writing, Photographs and Examination Catalogues.

FEMALE DEPT.—*Sisters of Charity.*

8 Volumes: Arithmetic, Grammar, Literature, Geometry and Algebra.

St. Francis' School (Colored).—*Sisters of St. Francis.*

3 Volumes: Arithmetic, Grammar and Map Drawing.

BAY ST. LOUIS, MISS.

St. Rose's School (Colored).—*Sisters of St. Joseph.*

1 Volume: Catechism, Penmanship, Geography, Grammar, Spelling, Arithmetic and Map Drawing.

BILOXI, MISS.

Maris Stella School.—*Sisters of Mercy.*

14 Volumes: Christian Doctrine, Grammar, Geography, Astronomy, Philosophy, History, Rhetoric, Arithmetic, 1 Crayon Drawing.

JACKSON, MISS.

St. Joseph's School.—*Sisters of Mercy.*

1 Volume: Catechism, Church History, Geometry, Rhetoric, Algebra, Physiology, Ancient History, Grammar, Biography, Mythology, Arithmetic, Philosophy, Botany, Geography and History.

PASS CHRISTIAN, MISS.

St. Joseph's School.—*Sisters of Mercy.*

1 Volume: Catechism, Grammar, Arithmetic, Geography, Philosophy, Spelling, Church History and United States History.

TUCKER, MISS.

Holy Rosary Indian School.—*Sisters of Mercy.*

1 Volume: Catechism, Spelling, Arithmetic and Geography.

DIOCESE OF PITTSBURGH.

RT. REV. RICHARD PHELAN, D. D.

Diocesan Committee.

Rev. A. A. LAMBING.
Rev. REGIS CANEVIN.

Rev. MARTIN SINGER, O. S. B.
J. B. SULLIVAN, *Secretary.*

ALCOVES 47, 49 AND 51.

Portrait of Rt. Rev. Bishop Phelan.

COLLEGES, ACADEMIES AND SELECT SCHOOLS.

PITTSBURGH, PA.

Holy Ghost College.—*Fathers of the Holy Ghost.*

7 Volumes: Christian Doctrine, Book-Keeping, Rhetoric, Literature, Geometry, Trigonometry, Physics, Ancient and Modern History, Latin, Greek and French Compositions, Business Forms. 2 Volumes Original Essays on Columbus and Other Subjects in Latin, Greek, French, German and Polish. 1 Volume Mechanical and Freehand Drawing, 3 Framed Anatomical Drawings and 12 Framed Photographs of College and Students.

St. Mary's Academy.—*Sisters of Mercy.*

7 Volumes: Christian Doctrine, Arithmetic, Algebra, Geometry, Chemistry, Physiology, Astronomy, Physical Geography, Book-Keeping, Stenography, Typewriting, Latin, Greek, Compositions, American and European History, Maps. 1 Case Hand-Painted China and 4 Pieces Sewing and Embroidery. 3 Framed Maps.

PITTSBURGH, PA.—Continued.

Ursuline Convent.—*Ursuline Sisters.*

6 Volumes: Book-Keeping, Arithmetic, Geography, Algebra, English, French and German Compositions, Universal History, 2 Charts Church History, Botany, Geometry, 25 Mechanical and Crayon Drawings, 9 Maps, 1 Water Color and 9 Pieces Embroidery. 5 Miscellaneous Charts and 2 Framed Pictures. 1 Oil Painting of Columbus' Death.

ALLEGHENY, PA.

St. Benedict's Academy.—*Benedictine Sisters.*

16 Volumes: Catechism, Arithmetic, Geography, History, Grammar, Spelling, Algebra, Drawings, Bible History, Historical Chart Work, Map and Freehand Drawing and 1 Card Fancy Penmanship.

St. Ann's Academy.

1 Volume Christian Doctrine.

BEATTY, PA.

St. Vincent's College.—*Benedictine Fathers.*

9 Volumes: Christian Doctrine, Geography, Grammar, Spelling, Book-Keeping, Arithmetic, Algebra, Geometry, Trigonometry, Latin, Greek and German Exercises, Dogmatic Theology, Moral Theology, Church History, Mental Philosophy, Holy Scripture. Original Essays in 16 Languages: Latin, Greek, Hebrew, English, Spanish, Italian, Irish, Lutheran, Polish, Russian, Hungarian, Slavonian, Low German and Bohemian. 2 Volumes Photographs of Professors and Students. 3 Volumes Catalogues and 19 Framed Photographs.

St. Xavier's Academy.—*Sisters of Mercy.*

17 Volumes: Church History, Music, Stenography, Geography, Grammar, Essays, Literature, Freehand Drawing, 6 Charts of Church History, 6 Folios Natural History with Illustrations, 1 Folio of Botany with Illustrations, 1 Genealogical Chart of English and French Rulers and 1 Black Satin Screen Embroidery, 1 Volume Compositions, Poems and Essays, 5 Art Studies.

EBENSBURG, PA.

Mt. Gallitzin Academy.—*Sisters of St. Joseph.*

2 Volumes: Christian Doctrine, Arithmetic, Geography, Maps, Civil Government, History, Grammar, Literature and Spelling.

GREENSBURG, PA.

St. Joseph's Academy.—*Sisters of Charity.*

1 Volume: Christian Doctrine, Church History, Grammar with Words and their Derivation, Catechism, Orthography, Geometry, Algebra, Arithmetic, Natural Philosophy, Astronomy, Physical Geography, Botany, Physiology, Literature and History. 1 Volume Music, 1 Volume Water Colors, 3 Oil Paintings, 7 Hand-Painted Pieces of China.

HERMAN, PA.

St. Fidelis' College.—*Brothers of Mary.*

6 Volumes: Christian Doctrine, Arithmetic, Geography, Algebra, Geometry, Chemistry, Geology, English, Latin, Greek, German and French Compositions.

LORETTO, PA.

St. Aloysius' Academy.—*Sisters of Mercy.*

17 Volumes: Algebra, Geometry, Physical Culture, Physiology, Botany, Grammar, Essays on the Sciences, Geography, Map Drawing, 1 Relief Map of South America, 1 Chart American History, Science, Literature and Art, 1 Carved Easel and 1 Chart Universal Biography. 2 Art Studies.

PARISH SCHOOLS.

PITTSBURGH, PA.

Holy Cross School.—*Sisters of Charity.*

1 Volume: Christian Doctrine, Arithmetic, Grammar, United States History, Geography, Map Drawing, Dictations, Spelling and Pencil Sketches.

Sacred Heart School.—*Sisters of Charity.*

1 Volume: Christian Doctrine, Grammar, History, Spelling, Catechism, Arithmetic, Book-Keeping, Pencil Drawing and Geography.

St. Agnes' School.—*Sisters of Mercy.*

1 Volume: Christian Doctrine, Arithmetic, Algebra, Grammar, Geography, Spelling, Map Drawing and United States History.

St. Augustine's School.—*Sisters of St. Francis.*

6 Volumes: Christian Doctrine, Arithmetic, Dictation, History, Geography and Penmanship.

St. Benedict's School (Colored).—*Sisters of Mercy.*

1 Volume: Christian Doctrine, Arithmetic, Spelling, Dictations and 4 Pieces of Plain Sewing.

St. Bridget's School.—*Sisters of Mercy.*

5 Volumes: Christian Doctrine, Arithmetic, Grammar, Church History, United States History, Geography and Map Drawing.

St. James' School.—*Sisters of Charity.*

1 Volume: Christian Doctrine, History, Grammar, Arithmetic and Spelling.

St. John the Baptist's School.—*Sisters of Charity.*

1 Volume: Christian Doctrine, United States History, Orthography, Geography and Grammar.

St. John's School.—*Sisters of Charity.*

1 Volume: Christian Doctrine, Language, Geography, Arithmetic, Grammar and Drawing.

St. Kieran's School.—*Sisters of Charity.*

1 Volume: Christian Doctrine, Grammar, Catechism, Geography, History.

St. Malachy's School.—*Sisters of Charity.*

1 Volume: Christian Doctrine, Grammar, Arithmetic, Algebra, Book-Keeping, History and Stenography.

St. Mary of Mercy School.—*Sisters of Mercy.*

1 Volume: Christian Doctrine, Arithmetic, Grammar, Drawing, History and Geography.

PITTSBURGH, PA.—Continued.

St. Mary's School.—*Sisters of Mercy.*
2 Volumes: Christian Doctrine, Book-Keeping, Literature, Grammar, Algebra, Arithmetic, Geometry and Stenography. 1 Toscanellis Chart.

St. Michael's School.
MALE DEPT.—*Brothers of Mary.*
FEMALE DEPT.—*Sisters of St. Francis.*
18 Volumes: Christian Doctrine, Arithmetic, Penmanship, Drawing, Orthography, History, English and German Compositions, 48 Crayon Drawings, 10 Maps, 21 Architectural and Mechanical Drawings, 5 Volumes Arithmetic, Geography, Compositions, 5 Charts Writing.

St. Paul's School.—*Sisters of Mercy.*
MALE DEPT
3 Volumes: Christian Doctrine, Geography, Maps, History, Grammar, Arithmetic, 1 Folio of Map and Freehand Drawing, 2 Framed Maps.

FEMALE DEPT.
5 Volumes: Christian Doctrine, Arithmetic, Geography, Maps, History, Grammar, Letter Writing, Dictation, Colored Maps, Composition and 3 Folios of Freehand and Map Drawing.

St. Patrick's School.—*Sisters of Mercy.*
2 Volumes: Christian Doctrine, United States History, Grammar, Arithmetic and Dictation.

St. Peter's School.—*Sisters of St. Francis.*
5 Volumes: Arithmetic, Compositions, Penmanship, History, Geography, Dictations and Christian Doctrine.

St. George's School.—*Sisters of St. Francis.*
3 Volumes: Arithmetic, English and German Composition.

St. Joseph's School.—*Sisters of St. Francis.*
4 Volumes: Arithmetic and English and German Composition.

Sts. Peter and Paul's School.—*Sisters of Divine Providence.*
1 Volume: Arithmetic, Dictations and English and German Compositions.

ALLEGHENY, PA.

St. Andrew's School.—*Sisters of Mercy.*
2 Volumes. Catechism, History, Arithmetic, Grammar, Spelling, Derivation of Words and 1 Folio of Maps.

St. Joseph's School.—*Benedictine Sisters.*
2 Volumes: Christian Doctrine, Arithmetic, Grammar, Spelling, Derivation of Words and 1 Folio of Maps.

St. Mary's School.—*Benedictine Sisters.*
3 Volumes: Catechism, Book-Keeping, Arithmetic, History, Grammar, Spelling, English and German Composition. 13 Charts Drawing.

St. Peter's School.—*Sisters of Mercy.*
2 Volumes: Christian Doctrine, Grammar, Penmanship and Book-Keeping.

ALTOONA, PA.

St. John's Convent School.—*Sisters of Charity.*

1 Volume: Church History, Arithmetic, Algebra, Geometry, Astronomy, Maps, Natural Philosophy, History, Geography, Philosophy and Literature.

BRADDOCK, PA.

St. Thomas' School.—*Sisters of Mercy.*

1 Volume: Grammar, Christian Doctrine, United States History, Geography and Physiology.

BUTLER, PA.

St. Paul's School.—*Sisters of Mercy of Loretto.*

3 Volumes: Maps, Book-Keeping, Arithmetic, Etymology and Natural History.

St. Peter's School.—*Sisters of Mercy of Loretto.*

1 Historical Geographical Chart.

CHARTIERS, PA.

St. Francis de Sales' School.—*Sisters of St. Joseph.*

1 Volume: Christian Doctrine, Arithmetic, Geography and Language.

CONNELLSVILLE, PA.

Immaculate Conception School.—*Sisters of Mercy.*

7 Volumes: Church History, Etymology, Grammar, Arithmetic, Physiology, Rhetoric, Chronology, 2 Historical Geographical Charts.

GALLITZIN, PA.

Borough School.—*Sisters of St. Joseph.*

5 Volumes: Book-Keeping, Literature, Spelling, Geography, History, Grammar, Biography, Civil Government, Arithmetic, Map Drawing.

JOHNSTOWN, PA.

St. Columba's School.—*Sisters of Charity.*

1 Volume: Christian Doctrine, Arithmetic, Stenography, Grammar, History and Algebra.

St. John's School.—*Sisters of St. Joseph.*

9 Volumes: Christian Doctrine, Arithmetic, Drawing, Geography, History, Spelling, Algebra and Book-Keeping.

St. Joseph's School.—*Sisters of St. Francis.*

4 Volumes: Christian Doctrine, German and English Compositions.

St. Mary's School.—*Sisters of St. Francis.*

3 Volumes: Christian Doctrine, Arithmetic, English and German Compositions.

LATROBE, PA.

Holy Family School.—*Sisters of Mercy.*

2 Volumes: Christian Doctrine, Grammar, Latin Roots and English Derivations, Algebra, Arithmetic, Geography, Compositions, Stenography and Typewriting.

MILLVALE, PA.
St. Anthony's School.—*Sisters of St. Francis.*
4 Volumes: Arithmetic and English and German Compositions.

MT. OLIVER, PA
St. Joseph's School.—*Sisters of St. Francis.*
4 Volumes: Arithmetic, and English and German Compositions.

SCOTTDALE, PA.
St. John's School.—*Sisters of Charity.*
1 Volume: Christian Doctrine, Arithmetic, Geography, Compositions, History and Catechism.

SHARPSBURG, PA.
St. Joseph's School.—*Sisters of Charity.*
1 Volume: Catechism, United States History, Geography and Arithmetic.

St. Mary's School.—*Sisters of St. Francis.*
4 Volumes: Arithmetic, English and German Composition, History and Dictation.

TUNNELL HILL, PA.
Tunnell Hill School.—*Sisters of St. Joseph.*
2 Volumes: Geography, Arithmetic, History, Civil Government, Spelling, German, Book-Keeping and Physiology.

TURTLE CREEK, PA.
St. Coleman's School.—*Sisters of Mercy.*
1 Volume: Christian Doctrine, Familiar Science, Arithmetic, History, Geography and Grammar.

TYRONE, PA.
St. Matthew's School.—*Sisters of Mercy.*
1 Volume: Arithmetic and Compositions.

WILKINSBURG, PA.
St. James' School.—*Sisters of Charity.*
1 Volume: Catechism, Christian Doctrine, Algebra, Arithmetic, Grammar, Geography, Composition and Book-Keeping.

DIOCESE OF SIOUX FALLS.
RT. REV. M. MARTY, O.S.B., D.D.

ALCOVE 63.

ACADEMY.

SIOUX FALLS, S. D.
St. Rose's Academy.—*Ursuline Nuns.*
5 Volumes: Bible History, Compositions, Geography, Grammar, Biographies, Music, Freehand Drawing, Arithmetic, Algebra, Geography, Physiology and Map Drawing.

PARISH SCHOOLS.

SIOUX FALLS, S. D.

St. Michael's School.—*Ursuline Sisters.*

3 Volumes: Christian Doctrine, Orthography, Penmanship, Arithmetic, Letter Writing, Grammar, Geography, History, Biography, Church History and Map Drawing.

MILLBANK, S. D.

St. Lawrence's School.—*Ursuline Sisters.*

1 Volume: Orthography, Arithmetic, Letter Writing, Geography, Christian Doctrine, Sacred History, United States History, Object Drawing, Needle-Work, Grammar and Crochet Specimens.

MITCHELL, S. D.

Holy Family School.—*Sisters of St. Agnes.*

2 Volumes: Freehand Drawing, Grammar, Arithmetic, Book-Keeping, Algebra, Church History and United States History.

STEPHAN, S. D.

Immaculate Conception Indian Mission.—*Benedictine Sisters.*

2 Albums: Spelling, Arithmetic, Letter Writing and Map Drawing. 1 Embroidered Cushion.

STURGIS, S. D.

St. Martin's School.—*Benedictine Sisters.*

1 Volume: Arithmetic, Letter Writing, Geography, Grammar, Penmanship and Needle-Work.

YANKTON, S. D.

Sacred Heart School.—*Benedictine Sisters.*

5 Books: Geography, United States History, Grammar, Christian Doctrine, Orthography, Arithmetic and Letter Writing.

PINE RIDGE, S. D.

Sacred Heart Indian School.—*Franciscan Sisters.*

1 Album Letter Writing, 1 Album Penmanship, Specimens of Plain Needle-Work, Knitting, Crochet-Work, Weaving, Bead-Work and Embroidery.

Collective Exhibits and Groups of Exhibits from Religious Teaching Orders.

Brothers of the Christian Schools

(Frères des Ecoles Chretiennes.)

(EUROPE.)

REVEREND BROTHER JOSEPH, SUPERIOR-GENERAL, PARIS, FRANCE.

ALCOVES 105, 106, 107, 108, 109, 110, 111, 112, 113, 114 AND 115.

PARIS.

St. Nicholas' Professional School.

BRASS WORKS—Reliquary, Candelabra, Candlesticks and Grate Fender, Chandelier and Sanctuary Lamp, Set with Gems.

WOOD CARVING—37 Specimens.

FURNITURE—4 Pieces, Elegantly Carved and Polished.

TRAVELING APPURTENANCES—5 Trunks and Valises.

IRON WORK—36 Pieces of Machinery (Steel and Brass).

OPTICAL INSTRUMENTS—40 Instruments Including Telescopes, Microscopes, Surveying Instruments with Vernier Attachments.

ENGRAVING ON WOOD—6 Specimens.

MANUFACTURE OF BAND INSTRUMENTS—17 German-Silver and Brass Instruments.

MAP ENGRAVING—14 Specimens.

PRINTING AND BOOK-BINDING—24 Specimens.

MODELING IN CLAY—7 Specimens.

CLASS-WORK—9 Albums of Drawing (Linear and Ornamental), 18 Copy Books Catechism, 117 Copies Dictation, 6 Copy Books Style, 98 Copy Books Mathematics, 66 Copy Books Arithmetic, 11 Copy Books Natural History, 11 Copy Books Chemistry, 8 Copy Books Physics, 24 Copy Books Map Drawing.

St. Clothilde.

1 Volume Catechism, 20 Copy Books Composition, 70 Copy Books Writing, 6 Copy Books Stenography, 16 Copy Books Map Drawing.

St. Ambroise.

24 Copy Books Catechism, 1 Copy Book Literature, 22 Copy Books Geography, 17 Copy Books Writing, 3 Copy Books Stenography, 14 Copy Books Book-Keeping, 7 Copy Books Natural History, 4 Copy Books Geology, 7 Copy Books Chemistry, 9 Copy Books Physics.

PARIS.—Continued.

   St. Denis.
      15 Copy Books Language Lessons, 1 Album Geography.

   St. Joseph.
      3 Copy Books Class-Work.

   St. Sulpice.
      1 Volume Catechism.

   St. Germain L'Auxerrois.
      10 Copy Books Freehand Drawing, 1 Volume Ornamental Drawing.

BEAUVAIS.
      14 Copy Books Elements of Style, 1 Volume Writing, 157 Copy Books Writing, 9 Sets Book-Keeping, 10 Copy Books Pedagogy, 41 Copy Books Map Drawing, 11 Copy Books Horticulture, 1 Volume Plans (Buildings and Agricultural Machines), 20 Annals Agronomical Station, 1 Volume Results of Agricultural Labor from 1855 till 1892, 21 Copy Books Catechism, 110 Copy Books Language Lessons, 1 Volume Composition, 38 Copy Books Composition, 11 Copy Books Geometry, 80 Copy Books Mathematics, 80 Copy Books Arithmetic, 24 Copy Books Notes on Lessons on Reading.

BERGUES.
      1 Volume: Perspective, Reliefs, Plans.

ISSY-SUR-SEINE.
   St. Nicholas.
      6 Volumes Ornamental Drawing, 3 Volumes Linear.

IGNY (SEINE-ET-OISE).
   St. Nicholas.
      2 Volumes Geometrical Drawing, 1 Volume Ornamental Drawing.

ALAIS.
      4 Volumes Geometrical Drawing, 1 Volume Ornamental Drawing.

LAURAC.
      4 Copy Books of Class-Work, 1 Volume Resumé of Lessons in Agriculture, Botanical Specimens.

PRIVAS (ARDECHE).
      1 Volume Writing, 1 Volume Notes of Lessons in Agriculture. 4 Copy Books Map Drawing.

ARBOIS (JURA).
      1 Volume Ornamental Drawing, 2 Volumes Mechanical Drawing, 2 Volumes Linear Drawing.

BEAUNE (COTE D'OR).
      5 Copy Books Class-Work, 16 Copy Books Arithmetic, 21 Copy Books Map-Drawing, 40 Copy Books Writing, 1 Chart on the Phylloxera.

DIJON.

12 Volumes Class-Work, 1 Album of Surveying, 1 Volume Wines of Burgundy, 1 Volume Photographs, 2 Volumes Maps, 3 Volumes Linear Drawing, 1 Volume Ornamental, 1 Volume Relief, 1 Volume Washings, 1 Volume Sketches, 1 Volume Miscellaneous, 67 Copy Books Freehand Sketches of Objects, 4 Historical Maps Campaigns of Napoleon.

GRAY (HAUTE SAONE).

1 Album Pen and Water-Color Sketches, 2 Volumes Geography and History, 1 Volume Enlarged Reproductions.

ORMANS (DOUBS).

1 Volume Maps.

NEUFCHATEL (SWITZERLAND).

2 Volumes Drawings.

BEDARIEUX.

4 Copy Books Freehand Sketches and Finished Drawings.

BEZIERS (HERAULT).

50 Copy Books Dictation (Elementary Course), 42 Copy Books Dictation (Superior Course), 249 Copy Books Arithmetic, 38 Copy Books Algebra, 39 Copy Books Geometry, 33 Copy Books Map Drawing, 143 Copy Books Language Lessons, 24 Copy Books Records of Daily Lessons, 51 Copy Books Style, 135 Copy Books Writing, 13 Volumes Herbarium collected and arranged by Students, 2 Volumes Surveying, 4 Collections of Minerals and Shells, 5 Volumes Geometrical Drawing, 4 Volumes Ornamental Drawing, 1 Volume Sketches and Finished Drawings, 10 Copy Books Linear Drawing and 5 Copy Books Surveying.

CETTE (HERAULT).

68 Copy Books Dictation, 81 Copy Books Language Lessons, 158 Copy Books Writing, 22 Copy Books Lettering, 1 Volume Ornamental Drawing.

PEZENAS (HERAULT).

28 Copy Books Dictation, 53 Copy Books Language Lessons, 19 Copy Books Lettering, 1 Volume Linear Drawing.

MONTPELLIER.

115 Copy Books Dictation, 46 Copy Books Language Lessons, 30 Copy Books Algebra, 42 Copy Books Arithmetic, 100 Copy Books Writing, 1 Volume Geometrical Drawing.

CARCASSONNE (AUDE).

58 Copy Books Dictation, 152 Copy Books Language Lessons, 105 Copy Books Mathematics, 11 Copy Books Style, 20 Copy Books Maps, 64 Copy Books Linear Drawing, 5 Volumes Linear and Ornamental Drawing.

PERPIGNAN (PYRENEES ORIENT).

74 Copy Books Dictation, 12 Copy Books Lexicology and Style, 18 Copy Books Style, 69 Copy Books Language Lessons, 15 Copy Books Algebra, 23 Copy Books Geometry, 19 Copy Books Arithmetic, 18 Copy Books Book-Keeping, 6 Copy Books Natural History, 52 Copy Books Writing, 17 Copy Books Geography, 12 Copy Books History, 6 Copy Books Physics, 6 Copy Books Chemistry, 1 Copy Book Surveying, 2 Volumes Linear Drawing.

ST. LAURENT (SALANQUE).

19 Copy Books Dictation, 25 Copy Books Language Lessons, 1 Volume Linear Drawing.

BORDEAUX.

Schools: St. Paul, St. Eulalia, Sacred Heart, St. Julian, John Baptist de La Salle, Central High School.

1 Volume History, 4 Volumes Agriculture, 1 Copy Book Stenography, 2 Copy Books Arithmetic, 1 Collection Showing Wines, Vines, Soil and Shells found along the Basin of Gironde, 1 Chart Showing Region of Wines, and Geological Formation of the Basin, 2 Collections of Woods, 1 Volume Applied Botany, 4 Volumes Agriculture and Botany, 2 Volumes Ornamental Drawing, 1 Volume Perspective Drawing, 1 Volume Relief Drawing, 1 Volume Relief and Landscape Drawing, 3 Volumes Machine Drawing, 1 Volume Projections and Industrial Drawing, 1 Volume Sketches of Archæological Ornaments, 1 Volume Wines and Vines of Gironde, 1 Volume Heads and Landscapes, 1 Volume Industrial Drawing, 1 Volume Portraits and Landscapes, 1 Volume Pen Drawings, 1 Volume Heads after the Antique, 1 Monograph of Royal Bed (Renaissance), 3 Volumes Freehand Drawings, 2 Volumes Linear Drawings and Washings, 7 Volumes Linear Drawings for Monthly Competition, 6 Volumes Ornamental Drawings for Monthly Competition, 1 Volume Linear Drawing (4 Years' Course), 8 Copy Books Freehand Sketches, 32 Copy Books Linear Drawing, 1 Album Calligraphy.

AGEN.

2 Volumes Ornamental Drawing.

MARMANDE.

1 Volume Ornamental Drawing, 1 Volume Architectural Drawing and Plans, 50 Copy Book Linear Drawing.

HAVRE.

Schools: St Michael, Notre Dame, St. Maria.

2 Volumes Ornamental Drawing, 4 Volumes Linear Drawing, 1 Volume Mechanical Drawing, 5 Copy Books Ornamental Drawing, 59 Copy Books Daily Exercises, 31 Specimens of Writing, 70 Copy Books Business Forms, 35 Copy Books Map Drawing, 1 Volume Maps, 10 Charts showing imports of the City of Havre.

ROUEN.

96 Copy Books Daily Exercises, 9 Copy Books Book Keeping, 74 Copy Books Writing, 19 Copy Books Arithmetic, 3 Volumes Examination Papers, 3 Volumes Geometrical Drawings, 8 Volumes Ornamental Drawings.

CHARTRES.

2 Volumes Geometrical Drawing, 2 Volumes Architectural Drawing, 1 Volume Ornamental Drawing.

CAMBRAI.

2 Volumes Maps, 4 Volumes Linear Drawing, 1 Volume Ornamental Drawing.

DOUAI.

Wood Work—Specimens of Mortising, Cabinets, Doors, Windows and Stair Building.

Iron Work—Rulers, Compasses, Calipers, Iron Turning, Pulleys, Vises, Wrenches.

LILLE.

St. Pierre.

1 Volume Catechism, 1 Volume Æsthetics, 1 Volume Photographs of Buildings and Classes, 2 Copy Books Notes of Lessons on Preparing Patterns for Silk Weaving, 1 Volume Outline Drawing, 2 Volumes Patterns for Silk Weaving, 1 Volume Tapestry and Weaving Patterns, 1 Volume Figure Study (Preparatory for Engraving), 1 Volume Study of Heads (for Expression), 1 Volume Decorative Painting, 1 Volume Studies in Shading, 1 Volume Studies in Ornamental Drawing, 1 Volume Studies of Extremities and Heads, 8 Volumes Linear Drawing.

St. Luke.

2 Volumes Preparatory Drawings, 1 Volume Illuminated Drawings, 5 Volumes Architectural Drawings, 1 Volume Patterns and Decorative Painting, 1 Volume Drawings for Sculpture and Iron Work.

Commercial School.

1 Volume Course of Linear Drawing.

ST. AMAND LES EAUX (NORD).

11 Copy Books Arithmetic, 1 Copy Book of Stenography (System of Duploye by Bro. Bajule), 6 Volumes Stenography Applied to Other Lessons, 8 Volumes Stenography, 1 Volume Maps, 3 Albums Drawings, 1 Album Drawings of Scroll Work cut out with Pen-Knife.

CHAMBERRY (SAVOY).

15 Copy Books Catechism, 96 Copy Books Daily Exercises, 67 Copy Books Writing, 12 Copy Books Map-Drawing, 2 Volumes Colored Drawings, 5 Volumes Linear Drawings.

LA MOTTE (SAVOY).

1 Volume Catechism, 23 Copy Books Sacred History, 61 Copy Books Language Lessons, 82 Copy Books Arithmetic, 2 Copy Books Geometry, 1 Copy Book Descriptive Geometry, 1 Volume Specimen Writing, 2 Volumes Ornamental Writing, 21 Copy Books Writing, 8 Copy Books German, 40 Copy Books Italian, 90 Copy Books Writing, 1 Copy Book Civics, 52 Copy Books Map Drawing, 1 Volume Miscellaneous, 1 Volume Linear Drawing, 1 Volume Linear and Washings, 1 Volume Ornamental.

ANNECY.

33 Copy Books Catechism, 23 Copy Books Sacred History.

ST. ROCHE (SAVOY).

Specimens of Grafting.

LYON.

Ecole de La Salle.

8 Copy Books Catechism, 12 Copy Books Sketches from Objects, 34 Cards of Iron Forging, 1 Machine for Piercing, 1 Small Cannon, 4 Volumes Drawings, 2 Copy Books Conference on Hygiene, 18 Copy Books Sketches of Machines, 6 Sheets of Machine Drawing "Timed," 1 Volume Architectural Drawing, 1 Volume Descriptive Geometry.

ST. MARTIN D'AINAY.

41 Copy Books Class-Work, 4 Volumes Map Drawing, 11 Copy Books Freehand Drawing, 13 Copy Books Linear Drawing.

ST. ETIENNE (LOIRE).

Professional School.

1 Album Composition, 1 Album Geometry, 1 Album Arithmetic, 1 Album Algebra, 1 Album Writing, 5 Copy Books Book-Keeping, 2 Copy Books Notes on Lessons on Silk Weaving, 4 Patterns for Silk Weaving, 4 Copy Books Metallurgy, 2 Volumes Linear Drawing, 1 Volume Descriptive Geometry.

Deaf Mutes.

Pictures of Establishments, 3 Volumes for Teaching, 4 Objects for Teaching, 5 Books for Teaching, Photographs of Diplomas and Class.

NANTEZ.

1 Volume Projections, 2 Volumes Linear Drawings, 1 Volume Washings.

ANGERS.

1 Volume Linear Drawings.

MOULINS.

4 Copy Books Dictation, 5 Copy Books Style, 14 Copy Books Mathematics, 1 Volume Artistic Penmanship, 36 Copy Books Map Drawing, 14 Copy Books Freehand Sketches, 1 Volume Ornamental Drawing, 1 Volume Linear Drawing.

COMMENTRY.

1 Volume Writing, 2 Volumes Maps, 4 Volumes Linear Drawing, 1 Volume Mechanical Drawing and Washing, 1 Volume Mechanical Drawing and Plans, 1 Volume Freehand Sketches from Objects.

FOURCHAMBAULT.

6 Volumes Sketches from Objects, 1 Volume Linear Drawing.

LANDIVISIAU.

16 Copy Books Celtic Language.

MEZIERES.

1 Volume Ornamental Drawing, 1 Volume Geometrical Drawing.

CHARLEVILLE.

1 Volume Ornamental Drawing, 1 Volume Linear Drawing.

NANCY.

1 Volume Ornamental Drawing, 2 Volumes Geometrical Drawing.

TROYES.

1 Volume Relief Drawings, 1 Volume Ornamental Drawings, 1 Volume Freehand Sketches, 129 Copy Books Sketches, 13 Copy Books Linear Drawing.

ST. OMER (PAS DE CALAIS).

12 Volumes Ornamental Drawing, 1 Volume Construction, 1 Volume Projections, Shades and Perspective, 1 Volume Architectural and Mechanical, 1 Volume Divers Subjects, 2 Volumes Geometrical Tracings and Applications, 1 Volume Projections, 1 Volume Bridges and Plans, 1 Volume Descriptive Geometry, 1 Volume Washings in Colors.

HAZEBROUCK.
 11 Volumes Ornamental Drawings, 1 Volume Linear Drawing.

ST. AUBANT (TOULOUSE).
 13 Volumes Linear and Ornamental Drawings.

SPAIN.

COBRECES (SANTANDER).
 27 Copy Books Book-Keeping, 3 Copy Books Commercial Calculations, 3 Copy Books Surveying, 2 Large Maps.

CASTRO, URDIALES.
 5 Copy Books Language Lessons, 8 Copy Books Book-Keeping, 1 Volume Miscellaneous Work.

DUESTO-BILBAO.
 122 Specimen Sheets of Writing, 52 Copy Books Book-Keeping, 1 Volume Ornamental Drawing, 1 Volume Linear Drawing.

YEREZ.
 5 Copy Books Dictation, 12 Copy Books Arithmetic.

VALLADOLID.
 10 Copy Books Class-Work, 1 Copy Book Commercial Operation, 1 Copy Book Freehand Drawing, 1 Copy Book Linear Drawing, 1 Volume Map Drawing, 5 Maps, 7 Mounted Drawings.

ISLE OF MAURITIUS.

CUREPIPE.
 4 Copy Books on Cyclones.

ENGLAND.

LONDON.

Tooting College.

1 Volume Differential and Integral Calculus, 1 Volume Problems in Conic Sections, 1 Volume Mechanics, Optics and Hydrostatics, 1 Volume Notes on Chemistry, 14 Copy Books Notes on 50 Lectures on Electricity, 3 Copy Books Optics (Illustrations), 4 Copy Books Hydrostatics, 4 Copy Books Heat, 7 Copies Notes on Chemistry (Printed), 6 Josephian, Annual of the Old Boys' Society (Printed), Matriculation Examination of the London University in Mechanics, Algebra and Arithmetic, Riders in Geometry, Intermediate B. A. Examination (London University) in Mathematics, 6 Photographs of Grounds, Buildings, etc.

MANCHESTER.

St. Joseph's Industrial School.

6 Specimens of Wood Carving with Original Sketches, 2 Specimens (small) Cabinet Making, 18 Photographs of Boys and Building.

Brothers of the Christian Schools
(UNITED STATES).
Provincials of Districts.

Brother JUSTIN, New York.   Brother PAULIAN, St. Louis.
Brother QUINTINIAN, New York.   Brother BETTELIN, San Francisco.
Brother ROMUALD, Baltimore.

ALCOVES 61, 75, 77, 78, 79, 96, 97, 98, 99, 100, 101, 102, 103.

COLLEGES, ACADEMIES AND SELECT SCHOOLS.

AMAWALK, N. Y., Archdiocese of New York.

St. Joseph's Normal College.

Collection of Drawings, Illustrating the Christian Brothers' System. 38 Volumes Drawing by the Students. Display of Text Books: Spelling (3), Grammar (2), Commercial Law and Book-Keeping (3), Reading (7), Arithmetic (5), Mensuration, Hints on Teaching, Notes on Teaching, Hymn Book, Roll Books, Monthly Examination Register and Many Volumes of Other Publications. A Series of Drawing Books (Linear and Freehand), 12 Books Including Two for the Teacher. 6 Boxes of Botanical Specimens. A Collection of Woods, A Chart on Grammar, A Chart on Geography, Testimonials for School Work, Phonographic Chart for Simultaneous Teaching, Relief Maps of New York, Philadelphia, Washington and Niagara Falls, 1 Volume for the Development of Solids.

AMMENDALE, MD., Archdiocese of Baltimore.

Ammendale Normal Institute.

PREPARATORY DEPT.

1 Relief Map of Baltimore, 2 Volumes of Artistic Writing and Lettering, 2 Volumes of Map-Drawing, 22 Volumes of Freehand Drawing, 17 Volumes of Linear Drawing, 20 Copy Books of Projections, 1 Volume Essays on Methods of Teaching.

GLENCOE, MO., Archdiocese of St. Louis.

Preparatory Normal School.

Detailed Plans of Normal-School Property; Plans of Building; 4 Specimens Framed; Photograph of Building (Framed); Album of Photographic Views of Building, Grounds and Students. Class-Work of Students as Follows: Life and Voyages of Columbus, Illustrated with Maps; Lecture Accompanying Stereopticon Illustrations of United States History; 1 Album French Exercises, Co-Ordination of Reading and Composition and Language Exercises, 1 Album Grammar, 1 Album Arithmetic, 1 Album Penmanship, 2 Albums (37 Copies) Map Drawing, 1 Album Algebra and Plane Geometry, 1 Album Solid and Spherical Geometry and Plane Trigonometry, 3 Albums Crayon and Freehand Drawing.

MARTINEZ, CAL., Archdiocese of San Francisco.

Normal Institute.

11 Volumes: Geography, Trigonometry, Mensuration, and Linear Drawing

ELLICOTT CITY, MD., Archdiocese of Baltimore.

Rock Hill College.

COLLEGIATE DEPT.

3 Volumes English Essays, 1 Volume Studies from Works of Cardinal Gibbons, 1 Volume Ancient History, 1 Volume Higher English Studies, 1 Volume Evidences of Religion, 1 Volume Mental and Moral Philosophy, 1 Volume Physics and Chemistry, 1 Volume Trigonometry, Surveying and Navigation, 1 Volume Geometry and Mensuration, 1 Volume Analytical Geometry, 1 Volume Calculus and Algebra, 1 Volume Greek Classics, 1 Volume Greek Exercises, 1 Volume Latin Classics, 1 Volume Perspective Drawing, 1 Volume Projections, 1 Volume Geometrical Drawing and Lettering, 1 Volume Exercises in English Rhetoric, 1 Volume Navigation Charts, 1 Volume Architectural Drawings (Advanced Course), 1 Volume Architectural Drawing (First Year), 1 Volume Machine Drawing, 1 Volume Engineering and Tinted Specimens, Botanical Specimens, Collected by J. R. Edgerton; Woods, from College Grounds, Collected by J. B. Edgerton; Geological Specimens from College Grounds, Collected by A. P. Meyer. Relief Map of Ellicott City, by A. P. Meyer. College Book Containing Prospectus, Diplomas, College Badges, Act of Incorporation, Examination Reports, Monthly Returns, Testimonials, Good Notes, Invitations and Programmes of College Entertainment, Photographs of Literary Societies, Reading Circles and Athletic Unions, Views of Scenery, etc., by the Class in Photography, and College Songs and Addresses.

PREPARATORY DEPT.

2 Volumes Christian Doctrine, 3 Volumes English Compositions, 1 Volume Sacred History, 2 Volumes English Grammar, 1 Volume Algebra and Arithmetic, 1 Volume Geometry and Mensuration, 1 Volume Geography, 3 Volumes Penmanship, 2 Volumes Practical Arithmetic, 3 Volumes Orthography and 1 Volume Object Drawing.

MEMPHIS, TENN., Diocese of Nashville.

Christian Brothers' College.

SENIOR CLASS.

12 Volumes: Latin, Greek, Chemistry, Astronomy, Logic, Algebra, Analytical Geometry, Calculus, English Literature, Examination Papers, Surveying and Navigation, Political Economy, Evidences of Religion, Church History, Compositions and Poems (from Memory), Readings, Papers on Macbeth, Questions on Reading, Illustrated Work on the Natural Sciences, and Book-Keeping.

JUNIOR CLASS.

12 Volumes Trigonometry, Surveying, Algebra, Compositions, Chemistry, Natural Philosophy, Rhetoric, Latin, Greek, Plane and Spherical Trigonometry, Algebra, English Literature, Examination Papers, Christian Doctrine, Rhetoric, Geometry, Trigonometry, Weekly Readings and Examinations and Answers to Questions in Literary Reading.

SOPHOMORE CLASS.

5 Volumes: Examinations in Christian Doctrine, Algebra, Geometry, Trigonometry, Natural Philosophy, Rhetoric, History, Book-Keeping and Modern History.

FRESHMAN CLASS.

4 Volumes: Arithmetic, Algebra, Geometry, Composition, Writing, Physical Geography, and Miscellaneous Class-Work.

MEMPHIS, TENN., Diocese of Nashville.—Continued.
Christian Brothers' College.

INTERMEDIATE CLASS.

3 Volumes: Examinations in Spelling, Catechism, History, Geography, Compositions and Map Drawing.

COMMERCIAL CLASS.

17 Volumes: Examination Papers in Christian Doctrine, Grammar, Civil Government, Book-Keeping, Rhetoric, Mensuration, Commercial Correspondence, Typewriting, Ornamental Penmanship, Orthography.

PRIMARY CLASS.

2 Volumes: Catechism, Geography and Arithmetic.

FIRST PREPARATORY CLASS.

1 Volume Examinations: Catechism, Geography, Grammar, Bible History, United States History and 1 Volume Class-Work.

SECOND PREPARATORY CLASS.

1 Volume Examination Papers.

MISCELLANEOUS.

2 Volumes of Photographic Views Showing Building, Classes and Pupils; 1 Photograph of Students, 1 Relief Map of Tennessee; 40 Crayon Drawings, 150 Mechanical and Architectural Drawings, 1 Show-Case Containing the Following Articles: 1 Volume Work of Rev. R. P. Petro Wantier, S. J. Printed in 1633; 1 Volume Bible for the Blind, 1 Volume Abridgment of the Christian Doctrine, in the Sioux (Dakota) Language, by Mgr. Ravoux, of St. Paul, Minn.; Typesetting and Printing was also done by the Author 1845. 1 Volume Syntagma Juris Universi, Printed in 1608. 1 Volume Imitation of Christ, Printed in 1699. 1 Volume Polyglot Edition Imitation of Christ, in Eight Languages. 1 Volume: Work on Climates of the United States and Canada, by C. E. Volney, 1803. I Volume: Paradisus Animæ Christianæ, Printed in 1675. 1 Volume Ammulus Memorialis, Printed in 1694. 1 Bible in Latin and German, with Annotations, in Latin, Hebrew and Greek, Printed in 1751. 1 Volume Trubner's Literature of Aboriginal American Languages. 1 Volume Containing Prayers of St. Nersetis, Printed in Thirty-Six Languages, from the Island of St. Laxanrus—Gift of George Arnold, Jr., to Brother Maurelian, President of the Christian Brothers' College, Memphis, Tenn. 1 Case Imitation of Precious Stones, Imported from Europe by the Christian Brothers' College, of Memphis, Tenn., and used for Class Instructions.

NEW YORK CITY, N. Y., Archdiocese of New York.
Manhattan College.

Natural Theology, Synoptic Analysis and Examination Papers; Evidences of Religion, Notes, Developments and Examination Papers; Apologetics, Notes, Doctrinal Notes on Sacraments, Decalogues, Hierarchy, etc., in Synoptic Form; Physiology, Synoptic Outline and Examination Papers; Logic, Summaries of Lessons, with Illustrations; Philosophy of Literature, Essays and Examination Papers; Political Economy and Government, Essays; Philosophy of History, Essays and Examination Papers; Literature (English and American), Notes and Biographical Sketches of Authors, with Extracts (Illustrated), Criticism; Essays on Subjects of the Hour; Topical Analysis of Ancient and Modern History; Examination Papers; Latin Translations, Grover Cleveland's Inaugural Address, 1893; History of England; Extracts from Lingard; Archbishop Corrigan's Pastoral Letter, 1889; Aristotle and the Christian Church (Azarias); Metres of Horace, Translation; Extracts from Quintilian and Horace; Mark Antony's Oration; De Bello Gallico;

NEW YORK CITY, N. Y., Archdiocese of New York.—CONTINUED.

Manhattan College.

Prose Composition, Exercises; Scansion, Virgil; Latin Syntax, Synopsis with Examples; Prize Examination Papers; Greek Translations, Extracts from Plato; Homer's Iliad, Lucian with Exercises in Syntax; Homer, Scanned and Translated with Notes, Extracts from Anabasis; Prose Composition Exercises; Examination Papers; French Translation: Grover Cleveland's Inaugural Address, 1893; Life of Firmin Suc; Extracts with Critical Notes; Sentences Illustrating Rules of Grammar; French-English and English French Exercises; Notes on Grammar with Exercises. Natural Science and Mathematics; Geology: Notes and Illustrations, Examination Papers; Astronomy: Notes and Illustrations, Examination Papers; Chemistry: Chart Containing Specimens Prepared by Students, Notes and Photographic Illustrations; Physics: Notes and Pen Illustrations; Physiology: Synopsis of Lectures, with Pen and Crayon Illustrations by the Students; Analytical Geometry: Examination Papers and Class-Work. Conic Sections: Examination Papers and Class-Work. Surveying and Navigation: Problems with Diagrams, Notes and Illustrations; Trigonometry: Class-Work, Problems with Diagrams; Geometry: Problems with Demonstrations; Algebra: Class-Work, Problems; Drawing: Application for Projection, Specimens of Work from Croton Aqueduct, Models and Plans of Cottages; Crayon-Work, Landscape and Figure Drawing.

BUSINESS DEPT.

Religion: Notes and Analysis of Lessons and Lectures. English: Essays on Business, Commerce, Historial Subjects, Letters. Penmanship: English, Plain and Round Hand. Business Calculations: Exercises in Counting-House Work, Class Exercises. Book-Keeping: Double-Entry Sets; Law (Commercial and Constitutional): Notes of Lectures Given by Professor. Phonography: Exercises in Elementary Study; Correspondence and Amanuensis Work. Typewriting: Elementary Exercises, Business Letters, Transcription of Phonographic Notes, Office-Work.

PREPARATORY DEPT.

Religion: Essays on Doctrinal Subjects; Penmanship, Class-Work, Business Letters Transcribed. English Grammar: Analysis and Parsing. Syntax, Common Errors Corrected, Extracts from Standard Authors and Examination Papers. History (Ancient and Modern): Synopsis of Lessons, Developments and Illustrations by Pupils. Geography (United States of America): Reproduction of Maps, Pen and Crayon Work, Notes. Geometry: Demonstrations of Theorems in Plane Geometry. Civil Government: Forms of Government, Rights of Citizens, Latin Elementary Studies: Translations from Cæsar and Ovid, Scansion and Examination Papers. Greek: Elementary Studies and Translations into English. Arithmetic: Solutions of Problems, Decimal System, Business Operations. Book-Keeping: Double-Entry, Algebra, Solution of Problems in Fractions.

De La Salle Institute.

14 Volumes Evidences of Religion; 11 Volumes Latin Translations; 1 Volume Latin Examination Papers; 6 Volumes English Grammar; 2 Volumes American Literature; 5 Volumes Greek; 1 Volume Compositions; 39 Volumes on Various Subjects; 4 Volumes Rhetoric; 1 Volume Rhetoric Examination Papers; 6 Volumes Arithmetic; 4 Volumes Algebra; 5 Volumes Geometry; 2 Volumes Geometry Examination Papers; 2 Volumes Mensuration; 3 Volumes Analytical Geometry; 5 Volumes Trigonometry; 2 Volumes Geography; 2 Volumes Surveying; 1 Volume Engineering; 1 Volume Engineering Examination Papers; 3 Volumes Chemistry; 2 Volumes Mechanics; 1 Volume Astronomy; 3 Volumes Natural Philosophy; 2 Volumes Physics. A Collection of Original Drawings of Surveying and Engineering; Development of Solids (by One of the Professors); 2 Volumes Business Forms and Book-Keeping; 2 Volumes Phonography; 15 Volumes Typewriting; 7 Volumes French; 3 Volumes German; 7 Volumes Penmanship; 7 Volumes Dictation; 3 Volumes Letters; 8 Volumes Linear Drawing and 1 Volume Freehand Drawing.

OAKLAND, CAL., Archdiocese of San Francisco.

St. Mary's College.

COLLEGE DEPT.

Model of College Building Accompanied by Architect's Plans and Photograph of College; 27 Mounted Charts, explaining principles of Phonography, by Brother Hyacinth; Photographs of Graduates.

COLLEGE DEPT.

413 Volumes: Essays in Greek and Latin, Examinations and Studies in Mental and Natural Philosophy, Religion, Mathematics, Hygiene; 7 Surveys of St. Mary's College.

BUSINESS DEPT.

53 Volumes: Book-Keeping, Mathematics, Essays, Religion; 186 Volumes of Phonographic Exercises and 23 Volumes Typewriting.

ART DEPT.

4 Volumes: Linear Drawing, Mechanical Drawing; 55 Studies in Crayon, Lead-Pencil and Water-Colors; 18 Pieces of Pen-Work.

PHILADELPHIA, PA., Archdiocese of Philadelphia.

La Salle College.

COLLEGE DEPT.—SENIOR CLASS.

1 Volume Quarterly Examination Papers: Evidences of Religion, Metaphysics, Mathematics, Philosophy of History, English Literature, Civics, Latin, Greek, French and German.

JUNIOR CLASS.

1 Volume Quarterly Examination Papers: Evidences of Religion, Logic, English Literature, History, Mathematics, Latin, Greek, French, German, Chemistry and Essay-Writing.

SOPHOMORE CLASS.

1 Volume Quarterly Examination Papers: Christian Doctrine, History, Rhetoric, English Literature, Mathematics, Physics, Latin, Greek, French and German.

FRESHMAN CLASS.

1 Volume Quarterly Examination Papers: Christian Doctrine, History, English Literature, Rhetoric, Mathematics, Physics, Book-Keeping, Latin, Greek, French, German and Essay-Writing.

PREPARATORY DEPT.—FIRST CLASS.

1 Volume Quarterly Examination Papers: Catechism, Spelling, Arithmetic, Algebra, Mensuration, Geometry, English Grammar, Compositions, Geography, History, Book-Keeping, Writing, Latin and German.

SECOND CLASS.

1 Volume Quarterly Examination Papers: Catechism, Spelling, Arithmetic, English Grammar, Compositions, Geography, History, Writing, Latin and German.

THIRD CLASS.

1 Volume Quarterly Examination Papers: Catechism, Spelling, Arithmetic, English Grammar, Compositions, Geography, United States History and Writing.

FOURTH CLASS.

1 Volume: Catechism, Spelling, Arithmetic, English Grammar, Geography, United States History, Compositions and Writing.

SAN FRANCISCO, CAL., Archdiocese of San Francisco.

Sacred Heart College.

Photographs, 10 Rolls of Honor, 15 Surveys, 9 Specimens of Ornamental Penmanship, 53 Albums Class-Work: Geometry, Trigonometry, Chemistry, Language, Religion; 26 Volumes Corrected and Uncorrected Essays, 304 Volumes of Examinations, Penmanship and Book-Keeping.

ST. LOUIS, MO., Archdiocese of St. Louis.

Christian Brothers' College.

UNDERGRADUATE DEPT.

1 Volume each: Integral Calculus, Astronomical Topics, Analytical Geometry, Differential Calculus, Topics, Essays and Criticisms, Philosophy of Literature and Rhetoric, Political Economy, 4 Volumes Classics and Philosophy.

SOPHOMORE CLASS.

2 Volumes: Classics and Mathematics.

FRESHMAN CLASS.

1 Volume each. Classics and Algebra, Trigonometry, History and Rhetoric, Algebra and Geometry, English Classics, Christian Doctrine, Compositions, Studies in English.

SUB-FRESHMAN CLASS.

1 Volume Classics.

FIRST ACADEMIC.

1 Volume each: Grammar, Arithmetic, Algebra, Natural Sciences and Christian Doctrine.

DRAWING CLASS.

44 Charcoal Studies of Head and Figure from Cast, 60 Charcoal Ornaments from Cast, 45 Charcoal Studies from Objects, 5 Crayon Drawings, 100 Architectural and Mechanical Drawings, 36 Sketches in Oil and Water Colors.

SUPERIOR COMMERCIAL CLASS.

9 Volumes Book-Keeping. 2 Volumes each: Correspondence, Arithmetic, Mensuration, Balance Sheets. 1 Volume each: Catechism, Commercial Law, Commercial Forms, Journalizing, 1 Album Penmanship, Programmes and Cards of Entertainments, etc., 1 Album Photographs of Classes and 1 Set of Interior Views of the College.

FIRST COMMERCIAL CLASS.

1 Volume Phonography.

ST. JOSEPH, MO., Diocese of St. Joseph.

St. Joseph's Commercial College.

11 Volumes: Christian Doctrine, Geometry, Penmanship, Algebra, Arithmetic, Typewriting, Mensuration, Geography, Grammar, Maps, Book-Keeping, Commercial Law, Composition "Our Class" and 1 Album Photographs of Building, Classes and Ground.

WASHINGTON, D. C., Diocese of Baltimore.

St. John's College.

ACADEMIC DEPT.

5 Albums Composition, 3 Albums Phonography, 1 Album Latin and Greek, 1 Album Ornamental Drawing, 1 Relief Map of the City of Washington and 8 Framed Crayon Drawings.

ALBANY, N. Y., Diocese of Albany.

Christian Brothers' Academy.

4 Volumes: Linear Drawing, 1 Volume Ornamental Drawing, 1 Photographic Album of Cadet Battalion, 2 Volumes Typewriting and Phonography, 1 Volume English Compositions, 1 Volume Latin and English, 1 Volume Mathematics, 1 Volume Trigonometry, 1 Volume Practical Exercise in Trigonometry, 7 Volumes Penmanship, 2 Volumes Language, 1 Volume German Penmanship, 3 Volumes Examination Papers, 5 Volumes Home Exercises, 4 Volumes Kindergarten Work, Specimens of Modeling in Clay (Kindergarten).

BALTIMORE, MD., Diocese of Baltimore.

Calvert Hall.

1 Album each: Water-Color Drawing, Water-Color Sketches, Marquetry, Greek, French, Analytical Geometry, Trigonometry, Chemistry, Physics, Geography, Mensuration, Rhetoric, Literature, Typewriting, Commercial Correspondence, History, Civics, Commercial Law, Map Drawing; 2 Albums each: Crayon Drawings, Pen-and-Ink Sketches, Leaves, Object and Ornamental Drawing, Algebra, Grammar, Compositions, Spelling; 3 Albums Latin and Catechism, 4 Volumes each: German, Surveying, 5 Albums each: Linear Drawing and Arithmetic; 6 Albums Phonography, 7 Relief Maps (Mashed Paper), 8 Albums Book-Keeping; 12 Volumes Collection for Object Lessons, 13 Framed Crayons, 21 Albums Perspective Drawings and 2 Framed Water Colors.

BURLINGTON, N. H., Diocese of Burlington.

St. Joseph's Academy.

11 Albums Examination Papers: Penmanship, Grammar, Arithmetic, Dictation, Letter Writing, Composition, Commercial Law, Christian Doctrine, 72 Copy Books Miscellaneous Subjects, 1 Album Monthly Bulletins, 1 Album Drawing and 23 Copy Books of Penmanship.

MANCHESTER, N. H., Diocese of Manchester.

St. Joseph's High School.

3 Albums Christian Doctrine, 3 Volumes Mensuration, 3 Volumes Algebra, 5 Volumes Composition, 3 Volumes Business Forms, 3 Volumes Arithmetic, 3 Volumes Latin Exercises, 3 Volumes Shorthand (Verbatim Reporting), 3 Volumes Geometry, 8 Volumes Book-Keeping, 10 Volumes Examination Papers, 2 Volumes Reports on Examination Papers, 15 Volumes Penmanship, Contrast Pages, 6 Volumes Drawing, 8 Volumes Class-Work, 2 Large Albums Drawing and 1 Album Photographs.

NEW ORLEANS, LA., Diocese of New Orleans.

St. Joseph's Commercial School.

21 Volumes: Mensuration, Compositions, Arithmetic, Book-Keeping, Catechism, Typewriting, Notes, Drawing, Penmanship and Monthly Examinations.

NEW YORK CITY, N. Y., Diocese of New York.

La Salle Academy.

3 Volumes Christian Doctrine, 11 Volumes Drawing, 13 Volumes Class-Work, 7 Volumes Book-Keeping, 3 Volumes Graded Stenography, 4 Volumes Graded Lessons in Typewriting, 4 Volumes Business Forms, Stenography and Typewriting, 4 Volumes Lessons in Letter Writing, 4 Volumes Civil Government, 4 Volumes Stenographic Notes and Transcripts of Addresses and Lectures, 2 Volumes Debates and 1 Volume Typewriting Recreations.

OAKLAND, CAL., Diocese of San Francisco.
St. Joseph's Academy.

5 Mechanical Drawings and Plans, 24 Volumes: Penmanship, Arithmetic, Religion, 19 Albums: Maps, Sketches, Mensuration, Geography, History, Orthography, Language, English, Mathematics, Book-Keeping and Christian Doctrine.

PROVIDENCE, R. I., Diocese of Providence.
La Salle Academy.

8 Copy Books Graded Exercises, 8 Copy Books each Latin and English Essays with Phonography, 1 Album each: Christian Doctrine, Photographs and Sketches, 12 Copy Books French (First Class), 7 Copy Books Greek, 14 Copy Books French (Second Class), 11 Copy Books English Essays, 17 Copy Books Christian Doctrine, 30 Copy Books Translations, Latin, French, 9 Copy Books Shorthand (Verbatim Reports), 10 Copy Books Reports of Cases (Supreme Court), Phonography and Typewriting, 32 Copy Books Phonography Applied to Algebra, Sacred History, Grammar and Geology. 4 Albums Class Debates, 3 Albums Specimens, Trigonometry and Surveying.

HALIFAX, N. S., Diocese of Halifax.
La Salle Academy.

1 Album Photographs, 3 Volumes Geometry, 3 Volumes Grammatical Analysis, 3 Volumes Phonography, 10 Volumes Letters, 6 Volumes Invoices and Letters, 4 Volumes Home Exercises, 8 Volumes Writing, 18 Volumes Arithmetic, 24 Volumes Drawing (Primary Grade), 11 Volumes Writing (Primary Grade), 33 Copy Books Book-Keeping, 8 Sheets of Drawing and 1 Map.

SACRAMENTO, CAL., Diocese of Sacramento.
Sacramento Institute.

14 Copy Books Arithmetic, 24 Copy Books Writing, 26 Copy Books Christian Doctrine, 38 Copy Books of Dictation, 3 Albums Essays, 2 Albums Arithmetic, 2 Albums Trigonometry, 2 Albums Surveying, 2 Albums Book-Keeping. 2 Albums Descriptive Geometry, 4 Albums Applied Geometry, 1 Journal, 1 Ledger, Specimens Business Department, Currency, Testimonials and Diplomas.

ST. PAUL, MINN., Diocese of St. Paul.
Cretin High School.

28 Volumes: Typewriting, Phonography, Penmanship, Geometry, Arithmetic, History, Mensuration, Miscellaneous Work, Language Lessons, Examination Papers, Book-Keeping, General History, Maps, Description of St. Paul, Christian Doctrine and Rules of Exchange.

TROY, N. Y., Diocese of Albany.
De La Salle Institute.

8 Volumes Book-Keeping, 3 Volumes and 13 Copy Books English Grammar, 4 Volumes and 104 Copy Books Phonography, 8 Volumes and 34 Copy Books Arithmetic, 2 Volumes Geography, 2 Volumes and 4 Copy Books Trigonometry and Surveying, 7 Volumes and 18 Copy Books Algebra, 2 Volumes Geometry and Mensuration, 2 Volumes Examination Papers, 8 Volumes Compositions, 1 Volume Physics and Chemistry, 1 Volume and 5 Copy Books Rhetoric, 14 Copy Books German, 1 Volume Physiology, 3 Volumes Essays, 2 Copy Books Mensuration, 5 Volumes Penmanship, 18 Copy Books Commercial Law, 2 Copy Books Macaulay's Essay on Dryden (Phonography), 12 Copy Books Notes on Balmes' Criterion, 5 Copy Books Notes on

TROY, N. Y., Diocese of Albany.—CONTINUED.

De La Salle Institute.

Hamlet, 1 Copy Book Civil Government (Phonography), 2 Albums Contrast Pages Writing, 16 Large Volumes Drawing (Linear and Freehand), 19 Drawings (Framed), 50 Large Drawings (Architectural, Mechanical, Ornamental and Figures), 1 Album Business Forms and Photographs.

N. B. This Institution has a display with the New York State Exhibit.

WESTCHESTER, N. Y., Diocese of New York.

Sacred Heart Academy.

48 Albums Linear Drawing, 3 Albums Freehand Drawing, 10 Volumes Map Drawing, 3 Small Volumes Freehand Drawing, 4 Volumes Plane Geometry, 8 Volumes Solid Geometry, 11 Volumes Physics, 8 Volumes Algebra, 11 Volumes Latin, 3 Volumes Book-Keeping, 2 Volumes Trigonometry, 5 Volumes: Christian Doctrine, English Grammar, French, Trigonometry, German, Arithmetic, Mensuration, Phonography, Natural Philosophy. 1 Volume Phonography, 1 Volume Typewriting, 1 Volume Arithmetic, 1 Volume Dictation, 1 Album Photographs, 44 Large Drawings (Geographical, Ornamental and Mechanical), 1 Scrap Book.

PARISH SCHOOLS.

ALBANY, N. Y., Diocese of Albany.

Cathedral School.

2 Volumes Book-Keeping, 4 Volumes Penmanship, 1 Volume Examination Papers, 4 Volumes Home Exercises, 1 Portfolio of Crayon, Linear and Water-Color Drawings, Portfolios Charts, Phonography Charts, and 1 Ecce Homo (Crayon).

St. John's School.

2 Volumes Class-Work.

BALTIMORE, Md., Archdiocese of Baltimore

St. Alphonsus' School.

1 Album each: Map Drawing, Mensuration, Composition, German Grammar, Business Forms, Pen-and-Ink Drawings and Ornamental Drawing. 3 Volumes each: German Translations, Catechism and Writing. 5 Volumes Crayon Drawings. 6 Volumes each: Arithmetic, English Grammar.

Immaculate Conception School.

1 Cartoon each: Figure Drawing, Freehand Drawing, Projections and Shadows, Penmanship, Class-Work, Pen-Work and Compositions, Typewriting and Class Reports. 2 Cartoons each: Linear Drawing, Geometrical Figures, Book-Keeping, and Headline Copies, 1 Cartoon Essays, Arithmetic, Mensuration, Phonography and Grammar, 1 Album Pictures of Classes.

St. John's School.

1 Folio each: Composition, Dictation, Punctuation, Arithmetic, Mensuration and Algebra, Catechism, Bible History, Politeness, Arithmetic and Spelling, Class-Work, Single and Double Entry Book-Keeping. 1 Complete Set Double-Entry Book-Keeping. 1 Volume each: Monthly and Quarterly Examinations, Weekly Reports, Specimens of Typewriting, Regulations and Means of Emulations, Roll-Book (Second Class), Photographs of Classes.

BALTIMORE, MD., Archdiocese of Baltimore.—Continued.

St. John's School.
1 Perspective Drawing of St. John's School, 1 Pen-and-Ink Sketch of a Bird, 2 Folios Grammar, Geography and History, 2 Volumes Home Exercises, 4 Volumes Linear Drawing, 14 Volumes Penmanship, Plans of New School.

St. Vincent's School.
11 Volumes: Ornamental, Linear and Map Drawing, Home Exercises, Book-Keeping, Catechism, Spelling, Arithmetic and Geography.

BROOKLYN, N. Y., Diocese of Brooklyn.

St. James' Commercial School.
28 Volumes Examination Papers, 19 Volumes Typewriting, 6 Volumes Shorthand (Transcribed), 3 Volumes Business Letter Writing, 4 Volumes Penmanship, 1 Volume Shorthand, Arithmetic and Literature, 11 Volumes Algebra, Arithmetic, Geometry, Shorthand, Typewriting. 3 Volumes Geometry. 3 Volumes: Algebra, Arithmetic, Geometry, Mensuration and Shorthand, 1 Volume Photographs.

BUFFALO, N. Y., Diocese of Buffalo.

St. Joseph's Cathedral School.
53 Volumes and 2 Albums: Map Drawing, Analysis, Drawing, Christian Doctrine, United States History, Geography, Mensuration, Book-Keeping and 4 Volumes Registers.

St. Bridget's School.
33 Albums: Book-Keeping, Arithmetic, Mensuration, Penmanship, Drawing, Business Forms, Typewriting, Letter Writing, History, Reports and Photographs.

St. Louis' School.
31 Volumes: Christian Doctrine, Bible History, English and German Grammar, Translations, Poetry, Arithmetic, Geography, United States History, Physiology and Penmanship.

CHICAGO, ILL., Diocese of Chicago.

St. Patrick's Commercial School.
5 Volumes Christian Doctrine, 4 Volumes Arithmetic, 12 Volumes Class-Work, 3 Volumes Grammar, 16 Volumes Book-Keeping (Actual Business Practice), 4 Volumes Book-Keeping (Theory), 3 Volumes Geography, Map Drawing, 6 Volumes Quarterly Examinations, 2 Volumes Business Correspondence in Shorthand and Typewriting, 2 Volumes Phonography, Business Forms and Correspondence; 3 Volumes Phonography (Three Years' Course), 3 Volumes Original Compositions, 3 Volumes History of the United States, 1 Volume Commercial Law, 1 Volume Natural Philosophy, 1 Volume Mensuration, 19 Volumes Penmanship, 1 Volume Photographs, Means of Education, Plan showing Method of teaching Book-Keeping, Photographs of School and Classes.

CHICOPEE, MASS., Diocese of Springfield.

St. Joseph's School.
21 Volumes Book-Keeping, 36 Volumes Specimen Sheets of Penmanship, 100 Penmanship Copy Books, 12 Volumes Class-Work Various Branches, 2 Volumes Specimens of Typewriting, 1 Volume Compositions, 8 Volumes Freehand and Linear Drawing, 4 Volumes Maps, Large Album Photographs of Schools, Church and Surroundings, Teachers, Graduates, Sodalities, Chancel Choir, Military Company, Classes, 2 Cabinets Silk Culture, Product of Silk-Worm from Egg of Moth to the Finished Articles; 2 Cabinets Cotton from Seed of Plant to the Finest Grade of Cloth; 1 Cabinet How Paper Is Made.

JERSEY CITY, N. J., Diocese of Newark.

Catholic Institute.

3 Architectural Designs (Framed), 1 Volume Linear Drawing, 1 Volume Map Drawing, 1 Volume Double-Entry Book-Keeping, 2 Volumes each: Grammar, Dictation, Arithmetic, History and Orthography. 1 Volume Homophonous Words, 1 Volume Phonographic Exercises, 1 Volume Business Correspondence and Mercantile Forms, 2 Volumes Specimen Sheets in Penmanship, 3 Volumes Freehand Drawing, 1 Volume Mensuration, 1 Volume Geographical Exercises and 1 Volume Grammatical Exercises.

KANSAS CITY, MO., Diocese of Kansas City.

St. Joseph's Cathedral.

2 Volumes Christian Doctrine and Bible History, 5 Volumes Book-Keeping, 4 Volumes Penmanship, 1 Volume Grammar, 1 Volume each: Commercial Law, Composition, Mensuration, Algebra, Map Drawing, United States History and Mathematics.

NEWARK, N. J., Diocese of Newark.

St. Patrick's Cathedral School.

1 Volume Stereography (By Brother Donatian, F. S. C.), 7 Volumes Linear and Mechanical Drawing, 4 Volumes Architectural and Mechanical Drawing, 1 Volume Colored Maps, 2 Volumes Penmanship, 1 Volume Mathematics, 5 Volumes Class-Work (First Class), 6 Volumes Freehand Drawing (First Class), 1 Volume Penmanship, 2 Volumes Class-Work (Second Class), 1 Volume Penmanship (Second Class), 4 Volumes Class-Work (Second Class), 1 Volume Class-Work (Third and Fourth Class), 1 Volume Monthly Examination Reports, Weekly Reports and Testimonials of Merit, 1 Volume School Register, 1 Album Varieties of Cloth, collected by Maurice J. Allen; 3 Charts Illustrating 21 Parts of an Incandescent Lamp, collected by George W. Delaney, Jr.; 2 Charts Illustrating the Process of Rubber Manufacture, collected by Matthew Walsh; 3 Charts Horology, collected by L. O. Shikluna, John Walsh and Matthew Sullivan; 1 Chart Illustrating the Manufacture of Buttons from Ivory Nut, collected by Gregory Morrissey; 1 Chart Illustrating Uses of Tool Steel, collected by Charles Norton; 4 Charts Food Products, collected by Manus T. O'Donnell and John V. Hanrahan; 2 Charts Illustrating Process of Tanning and the Finished Leather, collected by Francis N. Smith and Samuel J. Harrison; 1 Chart "Oil Paints," collected by Charles Shaffery; 1 Relief Map of the United States (Framed), 8 Relief Maps.

NEWBURGH, N. Y., Diocese of New York.

St. Patrick's School.

13 Cabinets for Object Lessons, 5 Books Linear Drawing, 19 Books Ornamental Drawing, 22 Compositions on Object-Lesson Cabinets, 14 Bound Copies Miscellaneous Work, 54 Sets Book-Keeping, Single and Double Entry, 213 Writing Copies, 5 Copy Books Mensuration, 7 Copy Books Grammar, 6 Copy Books Algebra, 20 Copy Books Arithmetic, 40 Copy Books "Home Exercises" and 17 Class Copy Books.

NEW YORK CITY, N. Y., Diocese of New York.

St. Alphonsus' School.

2 Volumes Book-Keeping, 1 Volume Mechanical Drawing, 1 Volume Christian Doctrine, 3 Volumes Penmanship, 1 Volume History, 1 Volume Spelling and 16 Volumes Exercise Work: Geography, Letter Writing, Grammar, Arithmetic.

NEW YORK CITY, N. Y., Diocese of New York.—Continued.

St. Brigid's School.

31 Volumes Book-Keeping, 52 Volumes "Home Exercise:" Grammar, Invention, Punctuation, Arithmetic, Algebra, Mensuration and Compositions, 47 Volumes Penmanship, 19 Volumes Penmanship and Business Forms, 32 Volumes Freehand Drawing, 8 Volumes Linear Drawing, 4 Volumes Map Drawing, 1 Volume Pen-Work, 27 Volumes Printing (Old English, Marking, French and Round Hand), 1 Album Photographs, 1 Album Showing Improvement in Writing.

Cathedral School.

6 Volumes Penmanship, 17 Volumes Book-Keeping, 4 Volumes "Home-Work" and "Class-Work," 4 Volumes Geometry, Algebra, History, Christian Doctrine, Geography, English Compositions and Bible History, 4 Volumes Monthly Examination Papers, 4 Volumes Contrast Pages Penmanship, 8 Relief Maps (Plaster), a Collection of Large Drawings, 7 Large Maps (Mounted), Crayon Portrait of Most Rev. Archbishop Corrigan, 26 Volumes Drawing, Map of New York and Vicinity (Papier Maché), 1 Volume Fancy Pen-Work, 1 Volume Gray's Elegy (Illustrated).

St. Gabriel's School.

17 Volumes Book-Keeping, 4 Volumes English Grammar, 10 Volumes "Home Work," 4 Volumes Geometry, 3 Volumes Mensuration, 2 Volumes Geography, 4 Volumes Arithmetic, 4 Volumes Compositions, 5 Volumes History, 4 Volumes Algebra, 2 Volumes Christian Doctrine, 8 Volumes Drawing, 9 Large Mounted Maps and Crayon Portrait of Mgr. Farley.

Holy Innocents' School.

12 Copy Books Geography, 13 Copy Books Arithmetic, 11 Copy Books Grammar, 8 Copy Books Catechism, 10 Copy Books History, 11 Copy Books Spelling and Dictation, 22 Copy Books Penmanship and 3 Copy Books Class-Work.

Immaculate Conception School (East 14th Street).

1 Volume each: Maps, Penmanship (Contrast Pages), Ornamental Drawing, Dictation Exercises, United States History, Practical Geometry, Orthography. 2 Volumes: Explanations of Christian Doctrine, Arithmetic, Grammar, Penmanship. 5 Volumes each: Business Letters and Wall Maps. 18 Volumes Exercises: Catechism, Arithmetic, Algebra and Mensuration. 33 Volumes Geography, 17 Volumes Book-Keeping, 2 Framed Pictures, 2 Charts Geometrical Figures and 2 Large Drawings of Ships.

Immaculate Conception School (East 151st Street).

1 Volume Graphic Scrap Book, 1 Volume Pictorial Scrap Book, 1 Volume Specimen Penmanship, 1 Set Relief Maps, 1 Chart of Monthly Lessons, 1 Volume Souvenir Album, 1 Volume "Deutsche Sprachlehre," 1 Volume Specimen Pages of Book-Keeping, 1 Copy of Business Forms, 2 Volumes Botanical Specimens, 5 Volumes Penmanship Copies, 5 Volumes Writing (Competitions), 44 Volumes Freehand Drawing, 100 Writing Copies and 5 Sets "Home Work."

St. James' School.

1 Volume each of Colored Maps, Linear Drawing, Geometrical Drawing, Plane and Spherical Geometry, Lessons in English, 2 Volumes each of Stone and Iron Work, Solid, Plane and Spherical Geometry, Literature and Composition, Business Forms, 4 Volumes each of Mensuration, Geometry, Commercial Correspondence, Analysis, Business Forms, Arithmetic and Algebra, 9 Volumes Penmanship.

NEW YORK CITY, N. Y., Diocese of New York.—Continued.

St. Joseph's School.
1 Volume each of Christian Doctrine, Geography, 2 Volumes each of Grammar, Map and Linear Drawing, 6 Volumes Mathematics and Book-Keeping, 14 Volumes Freehand Drawing, 16 Volumes Penmanship and 1 Album Photographs of Pupils.

St. Mary's School.
1 Volume each: Linear Drawing, Phonography, Geometry, Algebra. 2 Volumes of Christian Doctrine and History. 4 Volumes each: Class-Work and Geography. 9 Volumes each of Book-Keeping and Grammar. 18 Volumes each Freehand Drawing and Arithmetic.

St. Nicholas' School.
6 Volumes: Grammar, Religious Instructions, Bible History, Arithmetic, Algebra, Penmanship, Geography. 2 Volumes each Class-Work and Book-Keeping. 3 Volumes each Linear Drawing and Freehand Drawing. 4 Volumes Arithmetic. 8 Volumes each: German and English Penmanship and Freehand Drawing. 3 Large Framed Drawings.

St. Patrick's School.
1 Volume each: Book-Keeping, Grammar, Catechism and Mensuration. 2 Volumes each: Arithmetic, Linear and Ornamental Drawing. 4 Volumes Penmanship.

St. Peter's School.
10 Volumes Book-Keeping, 12 Volumes Penmanship, 17 Volumes Ornamental Drawing, 5 Volumes Geography, 2 Volumes Christian Doctrine, 12 Single Pieces Linear Drawing, 8 Pieces Ornamental Drawing, 7 Volumes Arithmetic, 21 Copy Books Grammar, 18 Volumes Compositions, 24 Volumes Mathematics, 4 Large Wall Maps, 1 Volume Linear Drawing (from Object).

St. Teresa's School.
23 Volumes Grammar, 27 Volumes Arithmetic, 17 Volumes Algebra, 16 Volumes Christian Doctrine, 10 Volumes Orthography, 17 Volumes Penmanship, 4 Volumes Geography, 5 Volumes Map Drawing, 3 Volumes Drawing and 1 Volume History.

NEW ORLEANS, LA.

St. Joseph's Commercial School.
21 Volumes: Mensuration, Compositions, Arithmetic, Book-Keeping, Catechism, Typewriting, Notes, Drawing, Penmanship and Monthly Examinations.

OAKLAND, CAL., Archdiocese of San Francisco.

St. Anthony's School.
14 Volumes Class-Work: Grammar, Spelling, Compositions, Language, History, Geography, Arithmetic, Book-Keeping, Mensuration, Dictation and Catechism.

St. Francis de Sales' School.
9 Volumes Penmanship, 2 Volumes Algebra, 3 Volumes Business Forms, 4 Volumes Spelling and Dictation, 7 Volumes Practical Arithmetic, 3 Volumes Christian Doctrine, 4 Volumes Geography, 3 Volumes Miscellaneous Work, 1 Volume Book-Keeping, 1 Volume Plane Trigonometry, 1 Volume Grammar and Parsing, 1 Volume Photographs, 1 Volume Spelling, Dictations and Letters, 2 Volumes Practical Arithmetic, Receipts, 1 Volume Spelling and Dictation, 1 Volume Mensuration of Solids and Algebra, 1 Volume Examinations in History and Biographies, 1 Volume Composition. Latin Exercises, Letters and Orders for Merchandise, 1 Volume Receipted Bills and Mensuration of Surfaces.

OAKLAND, CAL., Archdiocese of San Francisco.—CONTINUED.

St. Mary's School.

96 Booklets: Class-Work Arithmetic, Spelling, Language, Geography, History, Grammar, Drawing, Penmanship, Mensuration, Book-Keeping, Christian Doctrine and 1 Volume Photographs.

PATERSON, N. J., Diocese of Newark.

St. John's School.

1 Album each: Dictation, Arithmetic, Typewriting, Phonography, Language Exercises, Examination Papers, Compositions, Geography, Paraphrasing, Dictations, Development of History, Monthly Examination Reports, Large Maps, Linear Drawing, Business Forms, Mechanical Drawing. 2 Albums each: Ornamental Drawing, Specimen Copies, 3 Double Show-Cases Containing Object Lessons on Silk, Cloth, Cotton, Jute, Flax, Plush and Wood.

PHILADELPHIA, PA., Diocese of Philadelphia.

St. Agatha's School.

1 Album each: Algebra and Mensuration. 2 Albums each: Catechism, History, Arithmetic, Geography and Grammar.

St. Ann's School.

1 Album Architectural Drawing and Maps, 1 Volume Lettering and Elements of Drawing, 1 Volume Object and Ornamental Drawing, 6 Volumes Botanical Specimens, 2 Class Registers, Specimens of Monthly and Weekly Reports, 1 Photograph Album, 26 Albums Class-Work: Christian Doctrine, Church and Bible History, Orthography, Grammar, Profane History, Mathematical, Physical and Political Geography, Arithmetic, Algebra, Mensuration, Composition, Geometry, Phonography, Botany, Book-Keeping and 25 Copy Books of Penmanship.

Cathedral School.

19 Albums: Linear and Ornamental Drawing, Book-Keeping, Catechism, Penmanship, Grammar, Compositions, Mensuration, History, Arithmetic, Geography, Algebra, Dictations, Business Forms, Phonography, Typewriting, Spelling and Botany.

St. Charles' School.

1 Album each: Compositions, Penmanship, Dictation, Sacred History, Letter Writing, Spelling, Bills and Receipts and Book-Keeping, 2 Volumes United States History; 3 Albums each: Geography, Christian Doctrine, Mensuration and Arithmetic; 4 Volumes Grammar; 2 Volumes Penmanship and 60 Sheets Drawing.

St. Michael's School.

1 Album each: Catechism, United States History, Bible History, Algebra, Mensuration, Arithmetic, Geography, Spelling, Book-Keeping, Bills and Receipts, Phonography, Drawing, 50 Home Exercises, 50 Copy Books and 1 Pastel Painting.

Our Mother of Sorrows' School.

1 Album each: Writing, Dictation, Algebra, Church History and Geography; 2 Albums each: Catechism, History, Grammar and Arithmetic.

St. Patrick's School.

1 Album each: Mensuration, Algebra, Arithmetic, Book-Keeping, History, Grammar, Dictation and Catechism.

PHILADELPHIA, PA., Diocese of Philadelphia.—CONTINUED.

St. Paul's School.

1 Album each: Spelling, Geography and History. 2 Albums each: Grammar, Mensuration and Specimens of Penmanship. 3 Albums Arithmetic. 2 Bound Volumes Specimens of Penmanship, 20 Miscellaneous Exercise Copy Books and 38 Model Copies.

St. Peter's School.

1 Volume Mensuration, 2 Volumes Arithmetic and Book-Keeping, 1 Volume Grammar, 1 Volume Geography, 1 Volume Bills of Sale, 1 Volume Translations, 3 Volumes Linear Drawing, 1 Volume Mechanical Drawing, 3 Volumes Architectural Drawing, 3 Volumes Ornamental Drawing, 1 Volume Map Drawing, 33 Mounted Maps, 2 Albums Water-Colors and Pastel Painting, 1 Volume Pen-and-Ink Sketches, 1 Volume Specimens of Writing (English and German), 6 Class Registers, 1 Collection Minerals, 1 Collection of Woods, 1 Collection Leather, 1 Collection Grains, Seeds and Spices.

SAN FRANCISCO, CAL., Diocese of San Francisco.

St. Peter's School.

3 Volumes Algebra, 6 Volumes Arithmetic, 4 Volumes Bible History, 28 Volumes Book-Keeping, 3 Volumes Christian Doctrine, 6 Volumes Compositions, 4 Volumes Dictation, 4 Volumes Drawing, 1 Volume Examination Papers, 1 Volume Geography, 1 Volume Geometrical Drawing, 1 Volume Grammar, 3 Volumes Home-Work, 2 Volumes Language, 1 Volume Map Drawing, 3 Volumes Mensuration, 8 Volumes Penmanship, 2 Volumes Series Copy Books, 1 Volume United States History, 1 Photograph Album, Framed Pen-Work and Framed Drawings.

ST. JOSEPH, MO., Diocese of St. Joseph.

St. Patrick's School.

9 Volumes: Christian Doctrine, Sacred History, Geography, Arithmetic, Grammar, Commercial Correspondence, Penmanship, Class-Work, 2 Volumes Book-Keeping, and 1 Album Views of Building, Classes, Grounds and Church.

ST. LOUIS, MO., Diocese of St. Louis.

Annunciation School.

6 Volumes: Spelling, Penmanship, Catechism, History, Mensuration, Compositions and Christian Doctrine.

St. Bridget's School.

COMMERCIAL CLASS.

St. Bridget's Book of Records, 2 Volumes each: Practical Book-Keeping, Compositions, Catechism, Bible History, Mathematics, Language Lessons, Geography, History, Notes and Telegrams, Examination Papers, Typewriting and Shorthand, Penmanship and Letters. 1 Volume Maps and 5 Volumes Mensuration.

FIRST CLASS.

1 Volume Penmanship, 4 Volumes: Letters, Grammar, Catechism and Arithmetic.

SECOND CLASS.

2 Volumes each: Catechism, Grammar, Geography, Arithmetic and Penmanship.

THIRD CLASS.

3 Volumes Miscellaneous Exercises and 1 Volume Arithmetic.

ST. LOUIS, MO., Diocese of St. Louis.—Continued

St. Lawrence's School.

1 Volume each: Grammar, Christian Doctrine, Bible History, Book-Keeping, Algebra, Mensuration, Penmanship, History, Geography and Dictation. 4 Volumes Arithmetic.

St. Malachy's School.

9 Volumes: Book-Keeping, Penmanship, Catechism, Geography, Grammar, History, Arithmetic, Business Forms, Mensuration, Algebra, Shorthand, Typewriting, Orthography, Freehand and Map Drawing.

St. Vincent's School.

16 Volumes: Penmanship, Mensuration, Grammar, Catechism, Arithmetic, Typewriting, Phonography and Algebra.

TEMESCAL, CAL., Diocese of San Francisco.

Sacred Heart School.

79 Booklets: Arithmetic, Grammar, Language, Geography, History, Penmanship, Book-Keeping, Mensuration, Algebra and Catechism, 1 Volume Photographs.

TOLEDO, OHIO, Diocese of Cleveland.

St. Francis de Sales' School.

45 Albums History, 15 Albums Book-Keeping, 80 Albums Arithmetic, 102 Albums Penmanship, 27 Albums Compositions, 16 Albums Mensuration, 4 Volumes Penmanship (Contrast Pages), a Series of Large Maps, 156 Small Maps, 54 Albums Christian Doctrine, 40 Albums Spelling, 35 Albums Geography, 10 Albums Abbreviations.

WEST OAKLAND, CAL., Diocese of San Francisco.

St. Joseph's Institute.

50 Volumes: Arithmetic, Language, Penmanship, Geography, Mensuration, Christian Doctrine, Book-Keeping. 33 Albums: History, Geography, Christian Doctrine, Monthly Reports and Rolls of Honor.

YONKERS, N. Y., Diocese of New York.

St. Mary's School.

4 Volumes Drawing and 34 Copy Books, Specimens of Penmanship, Arithmetic, Christian Doctrine, Grammar and Geography.

INDUSTRIAL SCHOOLS.

EDDINGTON, PA., Diocese of Philadelphia.

St. Francis' Industrial School.

Specimens of Plumbing, Carpentry, Forging and Stone Cutting. 1 Album each: Compositions, Language Lessons, Algebra, Geography and History. 2 Albums each: Ornamental Drawing, Spelling, Grammar and Catechism. 3 Albums each: Penmanship and Arithmetic and 7 Albums Linear Drawing.

FEEHANVILLE, ILL., Diocese of Chicago.
St. Mary's Training School.
12 Pairs Shoes, 4 Pairs Slippers, 12 Suits Boys' Clothing, 2 Volumes Specimens Printing, 2 Volumes Annual Reports, 2 Volumes Photographs of Classes and Shops, 2 Volumes Catechism, 2 Volumes Book-Keeping, 1 Volume Biographies, 1 Volume Spelling, 1 Volume Class Exercises, Specimens of Work in Knitting and Sewing.

NEW YORK CATHOLIC PROTECTORY.

WESTCHESTER, N. Y., Archdiocese of New York.
499 Copy Books: Penmanship, Daily Exercises, Weekly and Monthly Composition, 29 Copy Books Christian Doctrine, 138 Copy Books Arithmetic, 28 Copy Books Composition, 148 Copy Books Exercises in English Grammar, 30 Copy Books Synopsis of History of State of New York, 20 Copy Books History of the United States, 129 Copy Books Composition, Dictation, Grammar, History, Civil Government and Examination Papers, 22 Exercise Copy Books of Phonography, 19 Copy Books Typewriting, 2d Large Volumes Freehand Drawing, 8 Exercise Copy Books "The Holy Land: The Israelites—Their History," 28 Medium Volumes Drawing, 2 Large Volumes Freehand Drawing, 3 Volumes Mechanical Drawing, 1 Large Volume Projections, 192 Large Drawings (Figure, Ornamental and Mechanical), 9 Geographical Plaster Casts, 4 Suits of Boys' Clothes, 1 Dozen Pairs Shoes, 1 Wax Figure, 1 Dozen Pairs Stockings, 4 Specimens Chair Caning, 6 Electrotype Plates. Books and Pamphlets from the Printing Office, 1 Picture of the Building, Grounds, etc., 50 Copies of "Sketch of the Protectory," 1863-1893.

TROY, N. Y., Diocese of Albany.
Male Orphan Asylum.
16 Volumes: Drawing, Arithmetic, Writing, Dictation, Map Modeling, Freehand Drawing, Catechism, Map Drawing and Photographs. 1 Volume Contrast Pages Writing.

UTICA, N. Y.
St. Vincent's Industrial School.
8 Volumes Class-Work: Christian Doctrine, Penmanship, Composition, History, Grammar, 1 Volume Letter Writing, 1 Crayon Portrait, 46 Crayon Drawings (Framed), 26 Plaster Casts, 2 Frames Photographs, 51 Pieces Wood Carving, 12 Panels Pyrography, 16 Drawings from Photo-Etchings, 1 Chart Illustrated Stocking Industry, Samples of Stockings Made by Pupils.

Brothers of Mary.

Mother House, Dayton, Ohio.
REV. L. BECK, PROVINCIAL.

ALCOVES 55, 89, 91, 93 AND 95.

COLLEGES AND ACADEMIES.

DAYTON, OHIO, Diocese of Cincinnati.
St. Mary's Institute.
STUDENTS' WORK.
19 Volumes: Grammar, Rhetoric, Composition, Literature, United States History, Map Drawing, Geography, Commercial Law, Business Forms,

DAYTON, OHIO, Diocese of Cincinnati.—Continued.

St. Mary's Institute.

STUDENTS' WORK.

Arithmetic, Algebra, Geometry, Trigonometry, Physics, Chemistry (Actual Laboratory Work), 3 Volumes Book-Keeping (Actual Business Practice), 1 Volume Typewriting, 2 Volumes Phonography, 3 Volumes Penmanship, 1 Volume Pen Drawing, 1 Volume Color Studies, 4 Volumes Freehand Drawing, 1 Volume Landscapes, 17 Large Architectural Drawings (Actual Measurement), 20 Large Crayon Drawings, 6 Water Colors from Still Life, 5 Crayon Drawings from Cast, 22 Water-Color Studies, 1 Large Linear Drawing (Lavis).

NORMAL WORK.

10 Pen Drawings; "Our Father" and "In Memoriam;" Pen Drawings by Members of the Faculty; Set of Catalogues; Set of Photographs: Buildings, Classes, Laboratories, Societies, Sodalities, etc., by Members of the Faculty; a Grand Course of Linear Drawing.

Preparatory Normal School.

NORMAL WORK.

62 Specimens of Floral Environs with Description, 70 Specimens of Penmanship, 30 Pen Drawings, 50 Crayon Outlines from the Cast, 32 Crayon Drawings from the Flat, 8 Crayon Drawings from the Object, 31 Crayon Drawings from the Cast, 6 Crayons from Relief, 3 Pastel Drawings, 5 Charcoal Drawings, 6 Water Colors from Still Life, 6 Water-Color Studies (Copied), 6 Etchings, 15 Specimens of Automatic Pen-Work, 3 Topographical Maps (Actual Surveys), 4 Architectural Drawings (Actual Measurement), 27 Mechanical Measurement, 4 Architectural Drawings (Actual Measurement), 3 Mechanical Drawings (Lavis), 2 Architectural Drawings Perspective (Actual Measurement), Orders of Architecture Constructed from Scale, 7 Gothic Constructions, 1 Relief Map of St. Mary's Institute Grounds (Actual Surveys).

STUDENTS' WORK.

3 Volumes Christian Doctrine, 3 Volumes Bible History and Church History, 6 Volumes English and German Compositions and Commercial Law, 6 Volumes English and German Dictations, Exercises and Grammar, 1 Volume Rhetoric and Literature, 1 Volume United States History, Ancient History and General Geography, 1 Volume Medieval History, 5 Volumes Book-Keeping (Actual Business Practice), 3 Volumes Physics, 1 Volume Chemistry, 9 Volumes Arithmetic, Geography and Geometry, 1 Volume Trigonometry, 1 Volume Surveying and Leveling (Comprising Actual Surveys made by the Pupils), 3 Volumes Linear Drawing (Actual Measurement), 5 Volumes Freehand Drawing, 6 Volumes Penmanship, Pen Drawing (Original and Copied), 1 Volume Conventional Drawings from Flower Forms (in Original Designs), 1 Volume Isometrical Drawings and Parallel Perspective, 1 Volume Angular Perspective, 1 Volume Repertory of Music Performed by the Faculty and Pupils of the Preparatory Normal School, Examination Papers of the Principles of Music, Original Compositions, Melodies Written from Memory, 1 Volume Sepia Paintings, 1 Ecclesiastical Map of the United States, Normal Work by Members of the Faculty, Specimens of Blue Printing.

HONOLULU, HAWAIIAN ISLANDS.

St. Louis' College.

5 Volumes: Compositions, Arithmetic, Algebra and Trignometry. 2 Volumes Freehand Drawing, 1 Volume Geography, 1 Volume Map Drawing, 1 Volume Penmanship, 20 Pen Drawings, 2 Large Water-Color Scenes.

NORMAL WORK.

1 Large Oil Painting (Burning of Lake of Kilauea).

STOCKTON, CAL., Diocese of San Francisco.

St. Mary's College.

1 Mechanical Drawing (by the Brothers), 8 Drawings by the Students, 23 Volumes of Class-Work, Arithmetic, Composition, Dictation, Sketches, Maps, Examinations, Penmanship.

SAN ANTONIO, TEXAS, Diocese of San Antonio.

St. Mary's College.

NORMAL WORK.

1 Set of Photographs of Buildings, Classes, Societies and Picnic Views, by a Member of the Faculty. 10 Volumes Language, Orthography, Composition, Letter Writing, Grammar, United States History, Geography, Arithmetic, Penmanship, Literature, Algebra, Geometry, Book-Keeping, Trigonometry, Chemistry, Physics, Physiology. 1 Volume Penmanship, 1 Volume Book-Keeping. 5 Volumes Object Drawing, Map Drawing, Physical Geography. 1 Volume Linear Drawing (Actual Measurement), 1 Volume Shorthand, 1 Volume Typewriting and 1 Set Photographs.

PARISH SCHOOLS.

ALLEGHENY, PA., Diocese of Pittsburgh.

St. Mary's School.

14 Volumes: English and German Dictations, Arithmetic, Compositions, English and German Letter Writing, United States History, Geography, German, Geography, Dictations, Christian Doctrine, Penmanship, Drawing and Arithmetic.

BALTIMORE, MD., Diocese of Baltimore.

St. Martin's Academy.

3 Volumes: Spelling, Penmanship, Dictations, Letters and Compositions; 1 Volume Map Drawing; 2 Volumes Typewriting; 18 Charts of Drawing, 57 Volumes Book-Keeping, 16 Volumes Compositions.

St. James' School.

12 Albums: English and German Grammar, Spelling, English and German Compositions, Translations, English and German Penmanship, Arithmetic, Business Forms, 5 Volumes Elementary Drawing and 83 Specimens Free-hand Drawing.

St. Michael's School.

12 Volumes: Arithmetic, Business Forms, English and German Composition, English and German Language Lessons, English and German Spelling, English and German Penmanship, English and German Dictations.

CHICAGO, ILL., Diocese of Chicago.

St. Francis' School.

1 Volume Christian Doctrine, 1 Volume Sacred History, 3 Volumes German Language, 1 Volume English and German Penmanship, 3 Volumes English Language, 1 Volume United States History, Geography, 1 Volume Arithmetic, Commercial Law, Book-Keeping, 3 Volumes Freehand Drawing, 1 Volume Linear Drawing, Map Drawing, 5 Large Crayons, 1 Drawing of St. Francis' School.

CHICAGO, ILL., Diocese of Chicago.—CONTINUED.

St. Michael's School.

4 Volumes: English Dictation, Grammar, Composition, 1 Volume United States History, 1 Volume Arithmetic, 3 Volumes German Language, 1 Volume Pen-Work, Civics and Music, 4 Volumes Freehand Drawing, 4 Volumes Specimens of Penmanship, Maps, Cards of Linear Drawing, Map Drawing.

CINCINNATI, OHIO., Diocese of Cincinnati.

St. Joseph's School.

1 Volume Christian Doctrine, 5 Volumes: English and German Compositions, Letters, 3 Volumes English and German Dictations, 1 Volume Business Letters, 2 Volumes General Class-Work, 1 Volume United States History, Geography, 4 Volumes Freehand Drawing, 1 Volume Linear Drawing, Map Drawing; 30 Specimens Large Crayon Drawings and 60 Specimens of English and German Penmanship.

St. Mary's School.

10 Volumes: English and German Grammar, Compositions, Letter Writing, Translations, Dictations, Practical Arithmetic, United States History, Mensuration, Intellectual Arithmetic, Geography, Algebra, Penmanship, 4 Volumes Freehand Drawing.

CLEVELAND, OHIO, Diocese of Cleveland.

St. John's Cathedral School.

13 Volumes: Christian Doctrine, Mechanical Drawing, Geography, Map Drawing, Orthography, Dictations, Letter Writing, Compositions.

St. Mary's Assumption School.

3 Volumes: Drawing, Arithmetic, Grammar, Geography, United States History and Letter Writing.

St. Mary's School.

4 Volumes: English and German Compositions, Grammar, Dictations, United States History, English and German Penmanship, Arithmetic, 1 Volume Freehand Drawing and 1 Volume Linear Drawing.

St. Patrick's School.

62 Volumes: Drawing, Dictations, Algebra, Book-Keeping, United States History, Grammar, Language, Business Forms, Christian Doctrine, Commercial Arithmetic, Mechanical Problems and Bible History.

COLUMBUS, OHIO, Diocese of Columbus.

Holy Cross School.

2 Volumes: Language, Grammar, 1 Volume Orthography, 1 Volume Geography, 2 Volumes United States History, 2 Volumes Maps, 5 Volumes Freehand Drawing, Christian Doctrine, 1 Volume Auto-Biographies of Pupils.

COVINGTON, KY., Diocese of Covington.

St. Joseph's School.

11 Volumes: Arithmetic, Grammar, Geography, Book-Keeping, Map Drawing, Analysis and Compositions.

DAYTON, OHIO, Diocese of Cincinnati.

Holy Trinity School.

1 Volume Grammar, 3 Volumes German and English Compositions, 1 Volume Penmanship, 1 Volume Maps, 5 Volumes Freehand Drawing, 1 Volume Linear Drawing.

Emmanuel's School.

1 Volume English and German Compositions, Letter Writing, 3 Volumes Arithmetic and Mensuration, 1 Volume Map Drawing, 2 Volumes Freehand Drawing, 100 Specimens Freehand Drawing, 1 Volume Language, 4 Copy Books Specimens of Class-Work, 6 Copy Books Specimens Penmanship.

HILO, HAWAIIAN ISLANDS.

St. Mary's School.

1 Volume Penmanship, Pen Drawing, 1 Volume General Class-Work, 12 Specimens Freehand Drawing, 10 Maps of the Hawaiian Islands.

NEW ORLEANS, LA., Diocese of New Orleans.

St. Alphonsus' School.

1 Volume Programmes of Studies and Time Tables, Photographic View of New Orleans, with Compositions by Pupils of High Class, Book-Keeping, Christian Doctrine, Literature, Universal History, Arithmetic, Algebra, Geometry, Phonography, Physics, Commercial Law, 5 Volumes Class-Work, 65 Copy Books, 50 Specimens Large Crayon Drawings, 6 Albums Drawing, 1 Volume Drawing (Specimen), 7 Specimens of Linear Drawing, 1 Set Photographs of School and Pupils.

NEW YORK CITY, N. Y., Diocese of New York.

St. John the Baptist's School.

4 Volumes: German and English Grammar and Translations, German and English Dictations and Compositions, German and English Penmanship.

Our Lady of Sorrows' School.

1 Volume Grammar and Compositions, 1 Volume German Dictations. 1 Volume Penmanship and Translation and 1 Volume Arithmetic.

PITTSBURGH, PA., Diocese of Pittsburgh.

St. Michael's School.

18 Volumes: Arithmetic, Christian Doctrine, Penmanship, Drawing, Orthography, History, English and German Compositions, 48 Crayon Drawings, 10 Maps, 21 Architectural and Mechanical Drawings, 5 Volumes: Arithmetic, Geography and Compositions.

SAN ANTONIO, TEXAS, Diocese of San Antonio.

San Fernando School.

1 Volume General Class-Work, English and Spanish Penmanship.

SAN FRANCISCO, CAL., Diocese of San Francisco.

St. Joseph's Grammar School.

NORMAL WORK.

Relief Maps of California, San Joaquin and of vicinity of San Francisco; 1 Catalogue.

SAN FRANCISCO, CAL., Diocese of San Francisco.—Cont'd.

St. Joseph's Grammar School.

STUDENTS' WORK.

13 Relief Maps, 9 Relief Figures, 1 Framed Course of Study; 73 Volumes: Christian Doctrine, Reading, Grammar, Ancient and Modern History, United States History, Geography, Penmanship, Composition, Rhetoric, Literature, Freehand Drawing, Linear Drawing, Elocution, Algebra, Geometry, Trigonometry, Natural Philosophy, Chemistry, Book-Keeping, Arithmetic, Commercial Calculations, Commercial Law, Shorthand, 1 Album Photographs (Classes), 21 Sets of Book-Keeping, 170 Large Drawings.

WAILUKU, HAWAIIAN ISLANDS.

Catholic Mission.

1 Volume: Class-Work and Elementary Drawing, 1 Volume Penmanship, 25 Specimens Freehand Drawing and 1 Photograph of Professors and Pupils.

WINNEPEG, MANITOBA, CANADA.

St. Mary's School.

1 Volume Grammar, 1 Volume Dictation, 1 Volume Compositions, 2 Volumes Arithmetic, 3 Volumes Penmanship, 35 Specimens of Linear Drawing and 1 Volume Freehand Drawing.

Brothers of the Sacred Heart.

REV. BROTHER ATHANASIUS, PROVINCIAL.

ALCOVES 61 AND 63.

COLLEGES, ACADEMIES AND SELECT SCHOOLS.

NATCHEZ, MISS., Diocese of Natchez.

Cathedral Commercial School.

39 Albums Book-Keeping, 7 Albums Geometry, 1 Album Algebra, 5 Albums Arithmetic, 34 Albums Home Exercises, 23 Albums Compositions, 7 Albums Trigonometry, 20 Albums Examination Papers, 8 Albums History, 62 Albums Penmanship, Specimens of Freehand Drawing, 1 Pastel Drawing, Ornamental Writing, Photographs and Examination Catalogues.

BAY ST. LOUIS, MISS., Diocese of Natchez.

St. Stanislaus' Commercial School.

2 Volumes Book-Keeping, 1 Volume Trigonometry and Surveying, 2 Volumes Rhetoric, Physics and Mathematics, 4 Volumes Examination Papers, 2 Volumes Specimens of Penmanship, 3 Volumes Linear Drawing, 3 Albums of Pen-Work, 1 Volume Architectural Drawing, Crayon and Pen Drawing, Ornamental Writing, 1 Diocesan Chart, 1 Chart of Bay St. Louis and Environs. Plan of College Property.

DONALDSONVILLE, LA., Archdiocese of New Orleans.
St. Joseph's Institute.
6 Volumes: Penmanship, Compositions, Algebra, Trigonometry, Arithmetic, Grammar and Photographs.

MANCHESTER, N. H., Diocese of Manchester.
St. Augustine's Academy.
2 Volumes: Compositions, Penmanship, Letter Writing, Book-Keeping, 133 Copy Books, Geography, Christian Doctrine, Algebra, Arithmetic. Map Drawing, Freehand Drawing, 21 Albums Linear Drawing and 1 Map of the City of Manchester.

MOBILE, ALA., Diocese of Mobile.
St. Vincent's Academy.
1 Framed Specimen of Writing, 1 Framed Photograph and Drawing.

NASHUA, N. H., Diocese of Manchester.
St. Aloysius' School.
2 Volumes: Grammar, Orthography, Letter Writing, Penmanship and Miscellaneous Exercises.

NEW ORLEANS, LA., Archdiocese of New Orleans.
St. Aloysius' Institute.
9 Volumes: Penmanship, Examination Papers, Letter Writing, Rhetoric, Algebra, Arithmetic, Grammar, Book-Keeping, History, Geometry, French, Spanish, Compositions, Geography, Map Drawing, Bible History and Essays.

THIBODEAUX, LA., Archdiocese of New Orleans.
Thibodeaux College.
5 Volumes: Compositions, Physics, Algebra, Phonography, Book-Keeping, Penmanship, French Exercises, Arithmetic, Orthography, Geography, Map Drawing, Trigonometry, Surveying, 1 Album Linear and Freehand Drawing and Photographs.

VICKSBURG, MISS., Diocese of Vicksburg.
St. Aloysius' Commercial College.
11 Albums Algebra, 10 Albums History, Physics and Geometry, 9 Albums Mathematics, 17 Albums Book-Keeping, 23 Albums History, Geography, Grammar, 16 Albums Rhetoric and Civil Government, 16 Albums Examination Papers, 4 Albums Christian Doctrine and Bible History, 15 Albums Christian Doctrine, 1 Album Phonography, 1 Album Arithmetic and Grammar, 86 Miscellaneous Exercises in the Different Studies, Freehand, Map and Mechanical Drawing, Pen-Work, Ornamental Writing, Photographs, Catalogue of College (Framed).

PARISH SCHOOLS.

AUGUSTA, GA., Diocese of Savannah.
St. Patrick's School.
3 Volumes: Penmanship, Business Forms, Book-Keeping, Grammar, Arithmetic. Examination Papers, Algebra, Geometry, United States History, Letter Writing, Pen-Work and Catalogue of School.

INDIANAPOLIS, IND., Diocese of Vincennes.

St. John's School.

1 Volume Book-Keeping and Business Forms and 1 Volume Graded Penmanship; Photographs.

St. Patrick's School.

5 Volumes: Business Forms, Letter Writing, Arithmetic, Geography, Algebra, Geometry, United States History, Pen-Work and Catalogue of the School.

MOBILE, ALA., Diocese of Mobile.

Cathedral School.

2 Volumes: Penmanship, Compositions, Arithmetic, Book-Keeping and Photographs.

St. Vincent's School.

5 Albums: Map Drawing, Book-Keeping, Literature, Penmanship, Arithmetic, Letter Writing and Exercises on Miscellaneous Studies.

Sisters of Charity (Emmittsburg, Md.).

ALCOVE 52.

ACADEMIES.

EMMITTSBURG, MD., Diocese of Baltimore.

St. Joseph's Academy.

3 Volumes: Christian Doctrine, Arithmetic, Geography, Grammar, General History, Rhetoric, Astronomy, Physics, Physical Geography, United States History, Geology, French Translations, Illustrated Geography, Bible History, Typewriting, Phonography, Physiology, Church History, Chemistry, Botany, Complete Set of Photographic Views of the Institution, Album of Crayon and Map Drawing, 1 Large Oil Painting of Cardinal Gibbons, Pastel Paintings, Subjects: "Sacred Heart," "St. Joseph," "Country Boy and Girl," "Sacred Heart on Silk," "Pope Pius IX;" Landscapes, 1 Case Fancy Lace and Painting on Celluloid, 1 Harp with Oil Painting, 3 Piano Scarfs, Songs Written on Parchment (Framed); 1 Oak Rocker (Embroidered).

RICHMOND, VA., Diocese of Richmond.

St. Joseph's Academy.

4 Volumes: Arithmetic, Geography, Grammar, Algebra, Literature, Language, Ancient and Modern History, Book-Keeping, Composition, Drawing, Geometry, Phonography, Rhetoric, Physiology and Typewriting.

PARISH SCHOOLS.

BALTIMORE, MD., Diocese of Baltimore.

Immaculate Conception School.

18 Volumes: Christian Doctrine, Arithmetic, Geography, Orthography, Grammar, Algebra, United States History, Bible History, Book-Keeping, Geometry, Physiology, Natural Philosophy and General History.

BALTIMORE, MD., Diocese of Baltimore.—CONTINUED.

St. John's School.

56 Albums: Christian Doctrine, History, Geography, Language, Algebra, Grammar, Arithmetic, Rhetoric, Physiology, Physics, General History, Drawing, Book-Keeping.

St. Vincent's School.

33 Volumes: Grammar, Christian Doctrine, Arithmetic, Geography, Algebra, Bible History, Rhetoric, Logic, Mental Philosophy, Compositions, Civics, Roman History, Map Drawing, Music.

CHICAGO, ILL., Diocese of Chicago.

St. Columba's School.

16 Volumes: Kindergarten, Class-Work, Mathematics, Language, Science, English and Church History, Map Drawing, Photographs, 4 Pastel Paintings, 4 Pen Sketches and 7 Paintings from Object.

St. Patrick's School (GIRLS).

7 Volumes Graded Class-Work, from 2d to 8th Grade, 1 Volume Work from 1st to 2d Academic, 1 Volume Leaves from Our Alma Mater, 1 Volume Freehand Drawing, 1 Album Photographs, 1 Volume Miscellaneous Items, 1 Volume Kindergarten, 5 Paintings, 2 Drawings, 7 Maps, Fancy Work and Plain Sewing.

DENVER, COL., Diocese of Denver.

Immaculate Conception School.

3 Volumes: Freehand Drawing, Grammar, United States History.

EMMITTSBURG, MD., Diocese of Baltimore.

St. Euphemia's School.

4 Volumes: Christian Doctrine, Orthography, Grammar, Geography, Spelling, Arithmetic, Bible History, Book-Keeping, Compositions, Algebra, Physics, Phonography, Literature, Biography, Pen-Work, Map Drawing, United States History, Penmanship.

LA SALLE, ILL., Diocese of Peoria.

St. Vincent's School.

5 Volumes: Christian Doctrine, Orthography, Grammar, History, Book-Keeping, Physical Geography, Phonography, Typewriting, Drawing and 13 Specimens of Pastel Painting.

MOBILE, ALA., Diocese of Mobile.

St. Vincent's School.

2 Volumes: Christian Doctrine, Orthography, Arithmetic, Literature, Compositions, Algebra, Map Drawing, Physical Geography, Drawing and Historical Sketch of the State of Alabama.

NATCHEZ, MISS., Diocese of Natchez.

St. Joseph's School.

11 Volumes: Arithmetic, Literature, Geometry and Algebra.

NORFOLK, VA., Diocese of Richmond.

St. Mary's School.

2 Volumes: Christian Doctrine, Orthography, Letter Writing, Arithmetic, Algebra, Book-Keeping, Geography, Natural Philosophy, Physiology and Drawing.

PORTSMOUTH, VA., Diocese of Richmond.

St. Joseph's School.

2 Volumes: Christian Doctrine, Arithmetic, Bible History, Geography, Language, Algebra, Geometry, Book-Keeping, Civil Government, Compositions.

RICHMOND, VA., Diocese of Richmond.

St. Patrick's School.

3 Volumes: Catechism, Arithmetic, Compositions, Geography, Dictations, Grammar, United States History, Language Lessons, Algebra, Geometry, Book-Keeping, Civil Government, Literature, Physiology, Rhetoric, Phonography and Typewriting.

SAN FRANCISCO, CAL., Diocese of San Francisco.

St. Patrick's School.

5 Volumes: Class-Work of 3d, 4th, 5th Grades including Spelling, Grammar, Language, Compositions, Word Analysis, Geography, United States History, Physiology, Catechism, 1 Album Specimen of Display Work.

St. Vincent's School.

1 Crayon Sacred Heart, 3 Crayon Studies from Models, 3 Oil Paintings, 21 Volumes Class-Work by Pupils of the Rhetoric Class, 1st, 2d, 3d, 4th, 5th and 6th Grades, including: Grammar, Spelling, Word Analysis, Compositions, Letter Writing, Literature, Geography, United States History, Bible History, Arithmetic, Algebra, Geometry, Astronomy, Physiology, Physics, Drawing, Catechism, 1 Volume Maps and 1 Volume Charts.

ORPHANAGES AND INDUSTRIAL SCHOOLS.

BALTIMORE, MD., Diocese of Baltimore.

St. Vincent's Infant Asylum.

1 Album Kindergarten Work.

BUFFALO, N. Y., Diocese of Buffalo.

St. Vincent's Orphanage and Industrial School.

1 Isabella Gown, 1 Empire Night Gown, 1 Linen Lawn Dress (Made by Hand), 1 Child's Embroidered Silk Dress, 2 Child's Aprons (Crochet Tops, Trimmed with Gold and Pink), 1 Velvet Embossed Card Case, 1 Velvet Embossed Broom Case, 1 Dining-Room Table Center-Piece (Embroidered in Silk Floss), 1 Center-Piece (Embossed Violets), 1 Set Doilies, Photographs of Buildings, School Room, Bake Room and Kitchen; 6 Volumes: Arithmetic, Geography, Grammar, Christian Doctrine, History and Physiology.

CHICAGO, ILL., Diocese of Chicago.

St. Vincent's Infant Asylum.

1 Volume Kindergarten Work.

RICHMOND, VA., Diocese of Richmond.
St. Joseph's Asylum.
5 Volumes: Christian Doctrine, Orthography, Arithmetic, Book-Keeping, Grammar, United States History, Language, Geography, Phonography, Typewriting and Letter Writing.

SAN FRANCISCO, CAL., Diocese of San Francisco.
St. Francis' Technical School.
DRESSMAKING DEPT.
No. 1—Fancy Waist of White Crepe; Yoke and Cuffs of Fine Tucks and Drawn-Work. No. 2—Child's Dress of White India Silk; Full Skirt, Shirred Yoke, Finished with Rosettes of Baby Ribbon. No. 3.—Gentleman's Dressing Gown of Garnet Cloth; Lined with Quilted Satin (Tan), Collar and Cuffs Embroidered in Forget-Me-Nots.

EMBROIDERY DEPT.
No. 7—Address of Institution, Specimens of Darning and Embroidery, Lizzie Dormberger. No. 8—Tea Cloth, Linen Damask Embroidered. No. 9—Banneret Embroidered.

EMBROIDERY.
"Flowers of the Pacific Coast," by Ella Spalding, Embroidered in 108 Shades of Twist, Representing a Basket of California's Choicest Blossoms, White Satin Slippers Embroidered in Gold Bullion, by Ella Spalding, Pair Suspenders Embroidered in Chenille and Mounted by Nellie Lillas, Specimens of Embroidery, 1 Volume and a Fancy Scarf, by Nellie Lillas and a Fancy Scarf (Orange) by Maggie Daly.

FINE SEWING DEPT.
Tea Cloth by Annie Brierton, Home Industry—Specimens of Letters in Drawn-Work by Mary Driscoll, Specimens of Needle-Work (2 Volumes) Infant's Cloak, India Silk by Inserting in Darning, Infant's Cloak, Bengaline Silk, French Pattern in Fancy Stitching; Child's Dress, Bengaline Silk, Fine Drawn-Work, Having One Thread of Material Between Pattern.

Mt. St. Joseph's Infant Asylum.
7 Volumes from 2d, 3d, 4th and 5th Grades: Arithmetic, Spelling, Grammar, Geography, United States History, 1 Volume Work by Children Seven and Eight Years Old, 1 Album Photographs.

Mt. St. Joseph's Kindergarten.
3 Albums.

Roman Catholic Orphan Asylum.
10 Volumes: Arithmetic, Grammar, Geography, United States History, Literature, Dictation, Letter Writing, Book-Keeping, Physiology, Astronomy, Physics, Christian Doctrine, 11 Volumes Penmanship, 4 Charts of Drawing and 2 Specimens of Embroidery.

Sisters of Divine Providence.
ALCOVE 66.

ACADEMIES.

CASTORVILLE, TEXAS, Diocese of San Antonio.
Academy of Sisters of Divine Providence.
3 Albums: Christian Doctrine, Orthography, Arithmetic, Grammar, Geography, United States History, Bible History, Letter Writing and Drawing. 1 Album of Academies and Parochial Schools Taught by the Sisters of Divine Providence in Texas and Louisiana. Collection of Needle-Work and Crochet.

CASTORVILLE, TEXAS, Diocese of San Antonio.—CONTINUED

Divine Providence Academy.

Painting of Mother House, Novitiate and Vicinity, 1 Banner Representing Sisters of Divine Providence, in the Old and the New World, by Sister M. Gonzaga. 1 Banner Raised Embroidery, 1 Crochet Baby Clothes, 1 Album of Academy and Parish School. 1 Volume: Essays, Diagrams, Mathematics, 10 Pages Fancy Work and 18 Drawing Books.

CLARKSVILLE, TEXAS, Diocese of Dallas.

St. Joseph's Convent.

1 Painted Scarf, Celluloid, 1 Painted Handkerchief Case, 1 Celluloid Banner "Hail Columbia" and 7 Books, Essays and Mathematics.

JEFFERSON, TEXAS, Diocese of Dallas.

St. Mary's Convent.

1 Key Holder, Embroidered Violin, 1 Knit Cape, 2 Pages Fancy Work, 2 Books of Essays and 6 Books of Drawing.

NATCHITOCHES, LA., Diocese of Natchitoches.

St. Mary's Academy.

13 Copy Books School-Work 1 Copy Book Linear Drawing. 4 Copy Books Map Drawing.

PALESTINE, TEXAS, Diocese of Galveston.

St. Mary's Convent.

1 Painted Plush Scarf, 1 Page Fancy Work in Album and 5 Volumes of Essays.

PITTSBURGH, PA., Diocese of Pittsburgh.

Sts. Peter and Paul's School.

1 Volume: Arithmetic, Dictations and English and German Compositions.

SAN ANTONIO, TEXAS, Diocese of San Antonio.

St. Joseph's Academy.

1 Banner of Gold Embroidery, 2 Pages Fancy Work, 3 Books of Essays and 3 Volumes of Drawing.

TEMPLE, TEXAS, Diocese of Galveston.

St. Mary's Institute.

1 Volume Essays and 1 Volume Map Drawing.

PARISH SCHOOLS.

ALEXANDRIA, LA., Diocese of Natchitoches.

St. Francis Xavier's School.

3 Volumes of Essays and 2 Volumes Drawing, 1 Page Fancy Work in Album.

BERNARDO PRAIRIE, TEXAS.

Parochial School.

1 Page of Fancy Work in Album.

CASTROVILLE, TEXAS, Diocese of San Antonio.
St. Louis' School.
3 Books Essays and Mathematics, 1 Volume Essays, Biographies, Mathematics and 3 Books Drawing.

COLUMBUS, TEXAS, Diocese of San Antonio.
St. Mary's School.
1 Page Fancy Work in Album and 1 Book Drawing.

DANVILLE, TEXAS, Diocese of Galveston.
1 Book Essays.

DUBINA, TEXAS, Diocese of Galveston.
St. Edward's School.
2 Pages Fancy Work in Album.

ELLINGER, TEXAS, Diocese of Galveston.
St. Mary's School.
1 Page Fancy Work in Album.

FREDERICKSBURG, TEXAS, Diocese of San Antonio.
Sts. Peter and Paul's School.
1 Page Fancy Work in Album.

FREIBURG, TEXAS, Diocese of Galveston.
St. John's School.
3 Books Essays and 2 Books Map Drawing.

GALVESTON, TEXAS, Diocese of Galveston.
St. Joseph's School.
1 Page Fancy Work, 4 Books Essays and 2 Books Map Drawing.

HIGH HILL, TEXAS, Diocese of San Antonio.
St. Mary's School.
3 Books Essays and Examinations and 4 Books Drawing.

MENTZ, TEXAS, Diocese of Galveston.
St. Roches' School.
Specimens of Fancy Work.

NATCHITOCHES, LA., Diocese of Natchitoches.
St. Mary's Academy.
13 Volumes School-Work, 1 Book Drawing and 4 Books Map Drawing.

NEW BRAUNFIELD, TEXAS, Diocese of San Antonio.
Sts. Peter and Paul's School.
1 Page Fancy Work in Album.

PINEVILLE, LA., Diocese of Natchitoches.

Sacred Heart School.
1 Book Essays.

SEDALIA, MO., Diocese of Kansas City.

St. Vincent's School.
2 Books Essays.

SEDAN, TEXAS, Diocese of San Antonio.

St. Paul's School.
1 Page Fancy Work.

SCHULENBURG, TEXAS, Diocese of San Antonio.

St. Rose's School.
1 Crochet Cape, 1 Page Fancy Work, 9 Books Essays, and 3 Books Drawing.

St. Joseph's School.
5 Books Essays and Exercises, 9 Books Drawing, 3 Albums Freehand Drawing, Laces and Embroidery from Different Schools of Sisters of Divine Providence, 1 Oil Painting of Convent School at Clarksville, Texas.

WEIMER, TEXAS, Diocese of San Antonio.

St. Michael's School.
3 Books Compositions, Letter Writing and 1 Page Fancy Work in Album.

Dominican Sisters.
See Part III. and Diocesan Exhibits.

Sisters of St. Francis of Oldenburg, Ind.

Mother House, Oldenburg, Ind.

ALCOVE 65.

ACADEMY.

OLDENBURG, IND., Diocese of Vincennes.

Academy of the Immaculate Conception.
16 Volumes: Christian Doctrine, Arithmetic, Orthography, Grammar, Geography, United States History, Composition, Physiology, Natural History, Rhetoric, School Journal, Penmanship, Literature, Botany, Biography, Algebra, Mythology, Chemistry, Civil Government, German Essays, Bible History, Business Forms, Typewriting, Music, Drawing, Oil Paintings, Portrait of Father J. Randolph, Landscapes, Church Vestments (in Gold Cloth), Embroidery, Pastel Painting, Freehand Drawing, Set of School Books, Book Specimens of Fancy Work, 2 Painted Panels, 1 Infant's Outfit, 1 Glove Box, 1 Case Fancy Work.

PARISH SCHOOLS.

OLDENBURG, IND., Diocese of Vincennes.
St. Mary's School.
1 Volume: Christian Doctrine, Arithmetic, Geography, United States History, Grammar, English and German Penmanship, Orthography, Book-Keeping and Freehand Drawing.

CINCINNATI, OHIO, Diocese of Cincinnati.
St. Bonaventura's School.
2 Volumes Class-Work.

St. Michael's School.
2 Volumes Class-Work and 1 Volume Drawing.

COVINGTON, KY., Diocese of Covington.
St. Aloysius' School.
5 Volumes: Arithmetic, Spelling, Geography, Bible History, Penmanship, Compositions, German, United States History and Christian Doctrine.

DOVER, IND., Diocese of Vincennes.
St. John's School.
1 Volume Class-Work.

EVANSVILLE, IND., Diocese of Vincennes.
St. Mary's School.
1 Volume Class-Work.

INDIANAPOLIS, IND., Diocese of Vincennes.
St. Bridget's School.
1 Volume Class-Work.

St. Mary's School.
1 Volume Class-Work.

LAWRENCEBURG, IND., Diocese of Vincennes.
St. Lawrence's School.
1 Volume Class-Work.

MORRIS, IND., Diocese of Vincennes.
St. Anthony's School.
1 Volume Class-Work and 1 Volume Drawing.

NEW ALBANY, IND., Diocese of Vincennes.
St. Mary's School.
1 Volume Bound Copy Books.

NEW ALSACE, IND., Diocese of Vincennes.
   St. Paul's School.
      1 Volume Class-Work and 1 Volume Drawing.

RUSHVILLE, IND., Diocese of Vincennes.
   St. Mary's School.
      1 Volume Class-Work and 1 Volume Drawing.

ST. LOUIS, MO., Diocese of St. Louis.
   Holy Trinity School.
      2 Volumes Drawing.

ST. PETER, IND., Diocese of Vincennes.
   St. Peter's School.
      1 Volume Class-Work and 1 Volume Drawing.

ST. WENDEL, IND., Diocese of Vincennes.
   St. Wendel's School.
      1 Volume Class-Work.

SEDANSVILLE, OHIO, Diocese of Cincinnati.
   Mary of Help School.
      1 Volume Class-Work and 1 Volume Drawing.

SHELBYVILLE, IND., Diocese of Vincennes.
   St. Joseph's School.
      1 Book of Crocheting.

YORKVILLE, IND., Diocese of Vincennes.
   St. Martin's School.
      1 Volume Class-Work and 1 Volume Drawing.
   Sisters of St. Joseph.
      See Part III. and Diocesan Exhibits.

Sisters of Loretto.

Mother House, Loretto, Ky.

ALCOVES 62 AND 64.

ACADEMIES.

LORETTO, KY., Diocese of Louisville.
   Loretto Academy.
      9 Volumes: Christian Doctrine, Geography, Logic, Astronomy, Botany (Illustrated), Arithmetic, Grammar, United States History, Physiology, Ancient History, Algebra, Book-Keeping, Literature. Rhetoric, Modern History, Natural History, Physical Geography, Typewriting, Map Drawing, Musical Arrangement, Key to Ray's Geometry.

LORETTO, KY., Diocese of Louisville.—CONTINUED.

Loretto Academy.

FANCY WORK.

1 Plush Fire Screen, Arrasene Embroidery, 1 Hand-Painted Celluloid Calendar, 1 Child's Dress of Fine Linen trimmed with Lace and Insertion, 1 Hand-Painted Glassine Jewel Case, 1 Crayon, 4 Pastels, a Collection of Historical Letters from Rev. Chas. Nerinckx's handwriting, covering events in Europe from 1802 to 1814.

NORMAL WORK.

1 Benediction Cope and Preaching Stole of White Watered Silk (Hand Made and Worked in Gold Bullion). 1 Gold Vestment (Original Designs Embroidered in Spangles and Chenille). 1 Hand-Made Point-Lace Surplice, 1 Table Cover of Linen Drawn-Work, 2 Point-Lace Handkerchiefs, 1 Water Pitcher and Tray Cloth of Hand-Painted China. 1 Life-sized Crayon of Rt. Rev. W. G. McCloskey, D. D., Bishop of Louisville; 1 Original Operetta (Music Composed by a Sister of Loretto); 1 Celluloid Photographic Album containing views about Loretto (Amateur Work); 1 Poem "A Legion of Antioch," by a Sister of Loretto; 1 Dialogue "Hannchen" (Translated from French into German by a Sister of Loretto); 1 Hymn "O Queen Immaculate!"

CAPE GIRARDEAU, MO., Diocese of St. Louis.

St. Vincent's Academy.

7 Volumes: Christian Doctrine, Book-Keeping, Geography, United States History, Grammar, Natural Philosophy, Astronomy, Chemistry, Botany, General History, Literature, Logic, Geology and Mental Philosophy.

COLORADO SPRINGS, COL., Diocese of Denver.

Loretto Academy.

2 Volumes: Christian Doctrine, Spelling, Reading, Grammar, Arithmetic, Algebra, Geography, Physiology, History, Ancient and Modern History, Rhetoric, Compositions and Physical Geography.

DENVER, COL., Diocese of Denver.

St. Mary's Academy.

1 Volume: Christian Doctrine, Orthography, History, Grammar, Arithmetic, Geography, Book-Keeping, Geology, Natural Philosophy, Rhetoric, Mythology, Botany. 1 Royal Folio of Crayons and Paintings, 7 Cards of Kindergarten, 2 Volumes of "Convent Echo," 1 Portfolio of Pen and Pencil Drawings, 3 Map Charts, 8 Cards illustrating position of hands on the Key Board, 4 Books of Pictorial Designs.

ELIZABETHTOWN, KY., Diocese of Louisville.

St. Mary's Academy.

1 Blue Silk Dress (Point-Lace Trimming), 1 Point-Lace Fichu.

FLORISSANT, MO., Diocese of St. Louis.

Loretto Academy.

10 Volumes: Christian Doctrine, Algebra, Mensuration, Astronomy, Botany, Chemistry, Geology and Rhetoric.

ST. JOHN'S (HARDIN CO.), KY., Diocese of Louisville.

Bethlehem Academy.

1 Volume: Composition, Arithmetic, Algebra, Grammar, Botany, Astronomy, Physiology and 1 Table Scarf.

LAS CRUCES, NEW MEX., Vicariate-Apostolic of Arizona.

Visitation Academy.

2 Volumes: Christian Doctrine, Arithmetic, Sacred History, Natural Philosophy, Physiology, English and Spanish Translations, United States History, Geography, Orthography, Grammar, Algebra, Book-Keeping, Compositions, Civil History, Geology and Physics.

LAS VEGAS, NEW MEX., Diocese of Santa Fe.

Immaculate Conception Academy.

2 Volumes: Christian Doctrine, Arithmetic, Algebra, Astronomy, Botany, Chemistry, Geology, Geometry, Grammar, Geography; Bible, Natural, United States and Ancient History; Mental, Moral and Natural Philosophy; Physiology, Phonography, Rhetoric, Orthography, Translations (Spanish and Latin).

LEBANON, KY., Diocese of Louisville.

St. Augustine's Academy.

1 Volume: Christian Doctrine, United States History, Ancient History, Arithmetic, Grammar and Geography.

LOUISVILLE, KY., Diocese of Louisville.

St. Benedict's Academy.

4 Volumes: Arithmetic, Catechism, Grammar, Geography, United States History, Map Drawing, Physiology, Natural History, Compositions, General History, Phonography, Zoology, Rhetoric, Book-Keeping, Bible History, Algebra and Botany.

MONTGOMERY, ALA., Diocese of Mobile.

Academy of St. Mary.

6 Volumes: Christian Doctrine, Spelling, Arithmetic, Algebra, Book-Keeping, Rhetoric, Grammar, Science, Compositions, Astronomy, Literature, Music, Drawing, Geography, United States History, Physiology, Botany and Sketches.

FANCY WORK.

1 Landscape in Oil, 2 Sets of Scarfs Etched in Silk, 1 Pair Pillow Shams of Net-Work done on Linen, 2 Crochet Dresses (Silk Trimmings), 1 Shawl Crochet in Ice Wool, 1 White Zephyr Crochet Fascinator (Edged with Silk Floss), 1 Pink Head Dress (Zephyr and Silk Trimming), 1 Tapestried Sampler, 1 Head-Rest of Plush (Silk Embroidery), 1 Cape Crochet (Zephyr with Silk Trimmings), 2 Plain Baby Socks of Crochet-Work, 1 Pair Crochet Mittens, 1 Plush Piano Cover, 1 Dress Shirt, 1 Dresser Scarf, 1 Oil Painting, life size, of Rev. B. J. Flaget, First Bishop of Kentucky; 1 Chocolate Set of Hand-Painted China.

MORA, NEW MEX., Diocese of Santa Fe.

Academy of the Annunciation.

2 Volumes: Christian Doctrine, Arithmetic, Geography, United States History, Orthography, Translations (English and Spanish).

ST. LOUIS, MO., Diocese of St. Louis.

Loretto Academy.

1 Mater Dolorosa (Pen-Work, by a Sister of Loretto).

SANTA FE, NEW MEX., Diocese of Santa Fe.

Academy of Our Lady of Light.

>5 Volumes: Christian Doctrine, Book-Keeping, Arithmetic, Geography, Grammar, United States History, Orthography, Botany, Physical Culture, Algebra, Chemistry, Compositions, General History, Literature, Penmanship, Natural Philosophy, Physiology, Phonography, English and Spanish Translations.

SOCORRO, NEW MEX., Diocese of Santa Fe.

Academy of Our Lady of Mt. Carmel.

>6 Volumes: Christian Doctrine, Spelling, Geography, Arithmetic, History, Compositions, Essays, Penmanship, Physiology and Music.

TAOS, NEW MEX., Diocese of Santa Fe.

>1 Crochet Shawl, 1 Knitted Banner, 1 Crochet Thread Tidy, 1 Card Crochet, Specimens of Silk Lace, 1 Crochet Neck-Tie, 1 Pair Fancy Knitted Silk Mittens, 1 Piano Solo, "I Stand On Memory's Golden Shore."

PARISH SCHOOLS.

BERNALILLO, NEW MEX., Diocese of Santa Fe.

Sacred Heart School.

>1 Volume: Photographs, Spelling, Arithmetic, Grammar, History and Translations.

Sacred Heart Industrial Indian School.

>1 Volume: Photographs, Christian Doctrine, Grammar, Geography, United States History and Hygiene.

EL PASO DEL NORTE, TEXAS, Vicariate-Apostolic of Arizona.

Sacred Heart School.

>2 Volumes: Christian Doctrine, Arithmetic, Algebra, Grammar, United States History, Typewriting, Music, Book-Keeping and Physiology.

KANSAS CITY, MO., Diocese of Kansas City.

St. Patrick's School.

>4 Volumes: Christian Doctrine, Arithmetic, Grammar, United States History, Geography, Letter Writing, Compositions, General History, Physics, Geology, Physiology, Astronomy, Specimens of Penmanship and Business Forms.

ST. LOUIS, MO., Diocese of St. Louis.

St. Kevin's School.

>3 Volumes: Christian Doctrine, Bible History, Grammar, Arithmetic, Algebra, Geography, Physical Geography, United States History and General History.

St. Michael's School.

>3 Volumes: Christian Doctrine, Bible History, Grammar, United States History, Geography, Philosophy, Book-Keeping, Arithmetic, Orthography and Drawing.

ST. LOUIS, MO., Diocese of St. Louis.—Continued.

Sisters of Mercy.

See Part III. and Diocesan Exhibits.

Sisters of Notre Dame.

Various Branches. See Part III. and Diocesan Exhibits.

School Sisters of Notre Dame.

Mother House, Western Province, Milwaukee, Wis.
Mother House, Eastern Province, Baltimore, Md.

ALCOVES 1, 2, 3, 4, 59, 60.

BALTIMORE, MD., Diocese of Baltimore.

Institute of Notre Dame.

1 Volume Music, 2 Volumes Mechanical Drawing, 1 Silk Map of Maryland, 12 Oil Paintings, 1 Pen Picture, 1 Picture Tapestry Painting, 1 Original Painting, 1 Lace Embroidered Handkerchief, 1 Embroidered Center-Piece, 2 Volumes Specimens of Needle-Work, 7 Hand-Painted China Pieces, 1 Herbarium, 2 Framed Drawings of the Institute, 1 Volume German Essays, 27 Volumes: Language, Essays, Geography, Penmanship, Grammar Arithmetic, Catechism, Bible History, United States History, Geometry, Trigonometry, Geology, Physiology, Compositions, Algebra, Spelling, Map Drawing, Elementary Science, General History, Literature, Book-Keeping and 2 Volumes Object and Cast Drawings.

CHATAWA, MISS., Diocese of Natchez.

St. Mary's Institute.

1 Volume: Christian Doctrine, Church History, Penmanship, Language, Arithmetic, Geography, Algebra, United States History, Compositions and 1 Herbarium.

EMBLA, MD., Diocese of Baltimore.

Notre Dame of Maryland.

1 Volume Latin, 6 Volumes French, 1 Volume German, 1 Volume Art, 2 Herbariums, 5 Volumes Drawing, 45 Volumes: Christian Doctrine, Geography, Grammar, Arithmetic, Trigonometry, Geometry, Algebra, Geology, Physiology, Mental Philosophy, United States History, Bible History, Botany, Church History, Astronomy, Literature, 4 Oil Paintings, Chemistry and Book-Keeping.

FT. LEE, N. J., Diocese of Newark.

Institute of Holy Angels.

15 Volumes: Christian Doctrine, Grammar, Composition, Reading, Arithmetic, Geography, French, German, Spelling, Physics, Book-Keeping, Algebra, 1 Volume Class Drawing and 1 Oil Painting.

MARINETTE, WIS., Diocese of Green Bay.

Academy of Lourdes.
4 Volumes: Christian Doctrine, Algebra, Arithmetic, General History, Physics, Geography, Civil Government, Book-Keeping, Church History, Bible History, United States History, Compositions, Commercial Geography, Astronomy, Language, Penmanship, Spelling, Science and Botany.

St. Mary's Institute.
3 Volumes. Christian Doctrine, Arithmetic, Geography, Penmanship, United States History, Algebra, Civil Government, Physiology, General History, Book-Keeping, Rhetoric, Bible History, Natural Philosophy, Geometry, 1 Volume Music, Pictures, Oil and Pastel Paintings, Crayon Pictures, Photographs, Needle-Work, Crocheting and Freehand Drawing.

MILWAUKEE, WIS., Diocese of Milwaukee.

Notre Dame Convent.
21 Large Oil Paintings, 1 Volume Music, 1 Volume "Responses" Compiled and Arranged by the School Sisters of Notre Dame, 1 Globe Wax Flowers, 1 Globe Wax Vegetables, 1 Globe Wax Fruit, 1 Globe Wax Confectionery, 1 Painted and Embroidered Souvenir Album, 2½ Yards Knitted Lace, 14 Medium-sized Oil Paintings.

St. Mary's Day and Select School.
8 Volumes: Natural Science, Language, History, Bible History, Mensuration, Mathematics, Civil Government, Christian Doctrine, Grammar, Geography, Spelling, 2 Volumes Freehand Drawing, 1 Volume Kindergarten, 2 Volumes Music, 1 Volume Book-Keeping, 20 Card-Board Prisms and 2 Volumes Mechanical Drawing.

PRAIRIE DU CHIEN, WIS., Diocese of La Crosse.

St. Mary's Institute.
1 Framed View of St. Mary's Institute and Environs, 6 Volumes Examination Papers, Class '92. Intermediate A: 10 Albums, Bible History, Grammar, Composition, Rhetoric, Algebra, Arithmetic, Book-Keeping, Geography, United States History. Intermediate B: 1 Album Examination Papers. Preparatory: 1 Volume Examination Papers. Primary: 1 Volume Examination Papers. 3 Albums Shorthand, 1 Book "On the Prairie," 10 Albums Music, 1 Album Biographical Sketches, 11 Albums Art Work, 1 Painted Motto and 30 Oil Paintings.

QUINCY, ILL., Diocese of Alton.

St. Mary's Institute.
11 Volumes: Mathematics, Chemistry, Literature, Mythology, Civil Government, Physics, Geometry, Algebra, Physiology, United States History, Bible and Ancient History, Catechism, 1 Volume German, 2 Volumes Arithmetic, 2 Volumes Music, 1 Herbarium, 4 Scrap Books, 18 Photographic Views, 4 Cases of Natural History, 1 Embroidered Altar Cloth, 1 Embroidered Center-Piece, 1 Embroidered Tray Cloth, ½ Dozen Doilies, 6 Pictures in Oil, Pastel and Crayon, 1 Handkerchief—Roman Embroidery, 4 Essays from Graduating Class of '93, Photographs of Class of '93 and 1 Embroidered Letter Case.

PARISH SCHOOLS.

AHNAPEE, WIS., Diocese of Green Bay.

St. Mary's School.
1 Volume: School Regulations, Historical Account of the Schools, Christian Doctrine, Arithmetic, Grammar, Geography, English and German Penmanship, Drawing, United States History, Letter Writing and Orthography.

APPLETON, WIS., Diocese of Green Bay.

St. Joseph's School.

3 Volumes: Christian Doctrine, Orthography, Bible History, Arithmetic, Language, Pastel, Crayon and Pen Drawing.

BALTIMORE, MD., Diocese of Baltimore.

St. Alphonsus' School.

3 Volumes: Language, Arithmetic, Spelling, Geography, Grammar, United States History, Bible History, German, Penmanship and Compositions.

St. Ann's School.

5 Volumes: Christian Doctrine, Arithmetic, Geography, Grammar, Language, United States History, Bible History, Spelling, Language, Penmanship, Algebra, Physiology and Book-Keeping.

St. James' School.

4 Volumes: Christian Doctrine, Language, Penmanship, Spelling, Catechism, Compositions, United States History, German and Bible History.

St. Leo's School.

2 Volumes: Language, Arithmetic, Geography, Spelling, Penmanship, Catechism, Bible History and Grammar, United States History.

St. Wenceslaus' School.

1 Volume: Writing, Language, Arithmetic, Geography, Compositions, Catechism, Spelling and Bohemian.

BARTON, WIS., Diocese of Milwaukee.

St. Mary's School.

1 Volume: Language, Penmanship, Geography, Arithmetic, Christian Doctrine, Geography, Grammar, German, United States History and Compositions.

BELLEVILLE, ILL., Diocese of Belleville.

St. Luke's School.

1 Volume: Christian Doctrine, Penmanship, Language, Arithmetic, Geography, United States History, Physiology, Book-Keeping and 2 Volumes Drawing.

St. Peter's School.

1 Volume Drawing, 1 Volume: Penmanship, Arithmetic, Language, Spelling, Grammar, Catechism, German, United States History. 1 Volume Needle-Work.

BUFFALO, N. Y., Diocese of Buffalo.

St. Mary's School.

7 Volumes: Kindergarten Occupation, Grammar, Penmanship, United States History, Mechanical Drawing, Arithmetic, Compositions, Dictations, Geography, Spelling, Book-Keeping, 4 Pictures in Needle-Work, 1 Bracket of Leather Flowers and 1 Wax Cross and Roses.

CANTON, MASS., Diocese of Boston.

St. John's School.

4 Volumes: Language, Arithmetic, Geography, Spelling, Grammar, United States History, Physiology, Christian Doctrine, Kindergarten, Bible History and Algebra.

CANTONVILLE, MD. Diocese of Baltimore.

St. Mark's School.

1 Volume: Geography, Arithmetic, Algebra, Composition, Grammar, Sacred History and Catechism.

CHICAGO, ILL., Diocese of Chicago.

St. Mary's School.

7 Volumes: Penmanship, Geography, Grammar, Rhetoric, Christian Doctrine, Arithmetic, Chemistry, Drawing, United States History, Spelling, Book-Keeping, German and Physiology, Algebra, Compositions and 2 Volumes Drawing.

St. George's School.

2 Volumes: Penmanship, Grammar, Compositions, Arithmetic, United States History, Spelling, Christian Doctrine, Bible History, German and Geography.

St. Michael's School.

11 Volumes English Work, 7 Volumes German Work, 1 Volume English and German Work, 1 Volume Ornamental Pen-Work, 14 Volumes Drawing, Freehand and from Model, Map Drawing, Crayon and Pastel Drawing, 1 Oil Painting, Celluloid, Knitting, Crocheting, Plain Sewing, Embroidery and Fancy Work.

St. Paul's School.

17 Volumes: English and German Class-Work, Physiology, Hygiene, Arithmetic, Language, Grammar, Penmanship, Spelling, Compositions, Letter Writing, Translations. 9 Volumes Drawing: Map, Linear and Freehand Drawing. Specimens of Needle-Work and Kindergarten.

CHIPPEWA FALLS, WIS., Diocese of La Crosse.

Notre Dame School.

2 Volumes: Christian Doctrine, Orthography, History, Geography, Language, Grammar, Arithmetic, Civil Government and Compositions.

DE PERE, WIS., Diocese of Green Bay.

St. Mary's School.

2 Volumes: Christian Doctrine, Orthography, History, Geography, Language, Grammar, Arithmetic, Civil Government and Compositions.

ESCANABA, MICH., Diocese of Marquette.

St. Joseph's School.

2 Volumes: Arithmetic, Penmanship, Catechism, Language, Spelling, United States History, Grammar, Bible History, Compositions, Physiology, Church History, Algebra, Rhetoric, American Literature, General History and Civil Government.

FT. MADISON, IOWA, Diocese of Davenport.

St. Mary's School.

1 Volume: Bible History, Penmanship, Language, Arithmetic, Geography, United States History, Catechism, German, 1 Embroidered Center-Piece.

FT. WAYNE, IND., Diocese of Ft. Wayne.

St. Mary's School.

2 Volumes: Penmanship, Language, Arithmetic, German, Christian Doctrine, United States History, Language Lessons, Grammar, Geography and 1 Volume Drawing.

St. Peter's School.

1 Volume: Christian Doctrine, Language, Arithmetic, Geography, Grammar, German, Penmanship and 2 Volumes Freehand Drawing.

FREEDOM, WIS., Diocese of Green Bay.

St. Nicholas' School.

1 Volume: Christian Doctrine, Arithmetic, Grammar, Language, Geography, Compositions, Letter Writing, Penmanship and Bible History.

GRAND RAPIDS, MICH., Diocese of Grand Rapids.

St. James' School.

3 Volumes: Christian Doctrine, Arithmetic, Penmanship, Drawing, Geography, Language and Compositions.

St. Mary's School.

1 Volume: Penmanship, Language, Arithmetic, Geography, United States History, Compositions, German Translations and Drawing.

GRAND RAPIDS, WIS., Diocese of Green Bay.

Sts. Peter and Paul's School.

2 Volumes: Christian Doctrine, Arithmetic, Grammar, Orthography, Penmanship, Language, Object Lessons, Drawing, United States History, Compositions, Physiology, Book-Keeping, Specimens of Object Drawing, Map of Wisconsin and City of Grand Rapids.

GREEN BAY, WIS., Diocese of Green Bay.

Cathedral School.

4 Volumes: Christian Doctrine, Orthography, Arithmetic, United States History, Penmanship, Geography, Grammar, Etymology, Physiology, Letter Writing, Book-Keeping, Vocal Music Teaching, Crochet Bead-Work, Crochet Bed-Spreads, Specimens of Needle-Work, Embroidery and Lace-Work, Embroidered Banners and Kindergarten.

St. John's School.

4 Volumes: Christian Doctrine, Orthography, United States History, Compositions, Geography and Penmanship, Drawing, Civil Government, Arithmetic, Grammar and Physiology.

St. Vincent's School.

2 Volumes: Christian Doctrine, Arithmetic, Grammar, United States History, Orthography, Language and Object Lessons.

HIGHLAND, ILL., Diocese of Alton.

St. Paul's School.

1 Volume: Penmanship, Language, Arithmetic, Geography, United States History, Spelling, Catechism, Bible History and German.

HUNTINGTON, IND., Diocese of Ft. Wayne.
Sts. Peter and Paul's School.
1 Volume: Christian Doctrine, Penmanship, Book-Keeping, United States History, Arithmetic, Geography, Bible History, Spelling, Catechism and 1 Volume Drawing.

KENOSHA, WIS., Diocese of Milwaukee.
St. George's School.
1 Volume: Language, Spelling, Arithmetic, Christian Doctrine, Geography, United States History, Penmanship and German.

LITTLE CHUTE, WIS., Diocese of Green Bay.
District School.
2 Volumes: Christian Doctrine, Orthography, Geography, Arithmetic, Language, Drawing, Grammar, Compositions, Letter Writing, United States History and 1 Volume Kindergarten.

LOGANSPORT, IND., Diocese of Ft. Wayne.
St. Joseph's School.
1 Volume: Penmanship, Christian Doctrine, Language, Compositions, Letter Writing, Arithmetic, United States History, Spelling, Grammar, German and 1 Volume Freehand Drawing.

LOUISVILLE, KY., Diocese of Louisville.
St. Boniface's School.
1 Volume: Penmanship, Language, Arithmetic, Geography, United States History, Christian Doctrine, Spelling, Compositions, Grammar and German.

MAPLE GROVE (KEWAUNEE), WIS., Diocese of Green Bay.
St. Patrick's School.
2 Volumes: Christian Doctrine, Arithmetic, Orthography, Grammar, Penmanship, Physiology, German Translations and Letter Writing.

MALDEN, MASS., Diocese of Boston.
Immaculate Conception School.
3 Volumes: Christian Doctrine, Spelling and Grammar; 1 Volume each: Grammar, Compositions, Elementary Science, United States History; 2 Volumes Arithmetic and Algebra, 3 Volumes Geography and Map Drawing, 3 Volumes Drawing and 2 Booklets of Kindergarten.

MARSHFIELD, WIS., Diocese of La Crosse.
St. Mary's School.
1 Volume: Freehand Drawing; 2 Volumes: Christian Doctrine, Penmanship, Language, Arithmetic, Geography, Grammar, Compositions, Orthography, Translations and United States History.

MENASHA, WIS., Diocese of Green Bay.
St. Patrick's School.
2 Volumes: Christian Doctrine, Arithmetic, Language, Orthography, Algebra, United States History, Grammar, Physiology, Letter Writing and 14 Copy Books of Examination Papers.

St. Mary's School.
2 Volumes: Christian Doctrine, Orthography, Geography, Language, Compositions, Book-Keeping and Letter Writing.

MILWAUKEE, WIS., Diocese of Milwaukee.

St. Anthony's School.
1 Volume: Penmanship, Arithmetic, Language, Geography, United States History, Bible History, German, Reading, Grammar and Compositions.

St. Francis' School.
1 Volume: Penmanship, Geography, Language, Arithmetic, History, Reading, Grammar, Compositions, German, Bible History, Catechism, United States History, 1 Volume Drawing.

Holy Trinity School.
2 Volumes Drawing, 1 Volume Christian Doctrine, Penmanship, Arithmetic, Geography, Natural Science, German, United States History, Grammar, Book-Keeping and Compositions.

St. Joseph's School.
2 Volumes: Penmanship, Language, Arithmetic, Geography, United States History, Natural Science, Grammar, German and 1 Volume Drawing.

St. Josaphat's School.
1 Volume: Christian Doctrine, Arithmetic, Language, Geography, Grammar, Penmanship, Polish History, Compositions, Catechism and 1 Volume Freehand Drawing.

St. Michael's School.
1 Volume Drawing, 1 Volume: Penmanship, Language, Spelling, German, Language, Arithmetic, History and Compositions.

MT. CALVARY, WIS., Diocese of Milwaukee.

Our Lady of Mt. Carmel School.
1 Volume Needle-Work.

NEW YORK, N. Y., Diocese of New York.

Assumption School.
5 Volumes: Compositions, History, Geography, Arithmetic, German, Orthography, Grammar and Christian Doctrine.

St. Joseph's School (East 87th Street).
8 Volumes: Grammar, Compositions, Geography, United States History, Spelling, Christian Doctrine, Arithmetic, Book-Keeping and Bible History.

NEW ORLEANS, LA., Diocese of New Orleans.

St. Mary's Assumption School.
2 Volumes: Penmanship, Arithmetic, Language, Geography, Bible History, German, 1 Plush Drapery and 1 Book of Needle-Work.

PEORIA, ILL., Diocese of Peoria.

St. Joseph's School.
2 Volumes Drawing, 1 Volume: Language, Arithmetic, Geography, Grammar, Compositions, United States History, Spelling, German, Catechism, Bible History and 1 Volume Specimens of Sewing.

St. Patrick's School.
1 Volume: Christian Doctrine, Arithmetic, Geography, Penmanship, Language, United States History, Spelling and 1 Volume Book-Keeping.

PHILADELPHIA, PA., Diocese of Philadelphia.

St. Bonifacius' School.
1 Volume Class Drawings.

St. Peter's School.
1 Volume Map Drawings.

PORTAGE, WIS., Diocese of Green Bay.

St. Mary's School.
3 Volumes: Christian Doctrine, Orthography, Language, Arithmetic, Geography, Grammar, Compositions, United States History, Physiology, Map Drawing, Rhetoric, Natural Philosophy and Literature.

PRAIRIE DU CHIEN, WIS., Diocese of La Crosse.

St. Gabriel's School.
3 Volumes: Christian Doctrine, Arithmetic, Language, Geography, Grammar, Compositions, Natural Science, United States History, Algebra, Physiology, Penmanship, 1 Volume Book-Keeping and 1 Volume Drawing.

QUINCY, ILL., Diocese of Alton.

St. Boniface's School.
2 Volumes: Penmanship, Language, Catechism, Compositions, Geography, Arithmetic, Christian Doctrine, United States History, Spelling, Translations.

St. Francis' School.
1 Volume: Christian Doctrine, Penmanship, Geography, Language, Arithmetic, United States History, Grammar and German.

ROXBURY, MASS., Diocese of Boston.

School of Our Lady of Perpetual Help.
1 Volume Specimens of Sewing, 6 Volumes: Penmanship, Language, Geography, Spelling, Grammar, Catechism, Algebra, United States History, Physiology, Civil Government, Astronomy and Book-Keeping.

ST. CHARLES, MO., Diocese of St. Louis.

St. Peter's School.
1 Volume: Arithmetic, Penmanship, Language, German, Geography, Dictation and History.

ST. DONATUS, IOWA, Diocese of Dubuque.

St. Donatus' School.
6 Volumes: Christian Doctrine, Arithmetic, Geography, Compositions, Physiology, Map Drawing, Language.

ST. LOUIS, MO., Diocese of St. Louis.

St. Alphonsus' School.
12 Volumes: Christian Doctrine, Language, Drawing, Penmanship, Arithmetic, United States History, Spelling, Grammar, Book-Keeping, Physiology, Hygiene, Natural Science, Compositions, Civil Government, Bible History, Algebra and Rules of Etiquette.

ST. PAUL, MINN., Diocese of St. Paul.

Assumption of the B. V. M.

2 Volumes Freehand Drawing.

STEVEN'S POINT, WIS., Diocese of Green Bay.

St. Peter's School.

Christian Doctrine, Orthography, Grammar, Bible History, Compositions, Letter Writing and Penmanship.

St. Stephen's School.

2 Volumes: Christian Doctrine, Orthography, Language, Penmanship, Arithmetic, Geography, Grammar, United States History, Book-Keeping, Algebra and Physiology.

WABASHA, MINN., Diocese of Winona.

St. Felix School.

1 Volume Specimen Sewing.

WASHINGTON, D. C., Diocese of Baltimore.

St. Mary's School.

4 Volumes: Freehand Drawing, Writing, Spelling, Language, Arithmetic, Geography, Grammar, Composition, German and Christian Doctrine.

WAUSAU, WIS., Diocese of Green Bay.

St. Mary's School.

4 Volumes: Freehand Drawing, Writing, Spelling, Language, Arithmetic, Geography, Grammar, Compositions, German and Christian Doctrine.

WASHINGTON, MO., Diocese of St. Louis.

St. Francis Borgia's School.

1 Volume: Christian Doctrine, Arithmetic, Penmanship, Language, Geography, United States History, Drawing, Translations, 5 Photographs of School and Churches.

INDUSTRIAL SCHOOLS AND ORPHANAGES.

GREEN BAY, WIS., Diocese of Green Bay.

St. Joseph's Orphanage.

2 Volumes: Christian Doctrine, Orthography, Arithmetic, Grammar, United States History, Penmanship and Drawing.

HARBOR SPRINGS, MICH., Diocese of Grand Rapids.

Indian Industrial School.

1 Volume: Penmanship, Geography, Language, Arithmetic, Compositions, Bible History, Christian Doctrine, 1 Volume Specimens of Needle-Work, 1 Volume Freehand Drawing.

NEW ORLEANS, LA., Diocese of New Orleans.

St. Joseph's Orphanage.

1 Volume: Language, Penmanship, Arithmetic, Catechism and German.

Sisters of the Precious Blood.

Mother House, O'Fallon, Mo.

ALCOVE 57.

O'FALLON, MO., Diocese of St. Louis.

St. Mary's Institute.

1 Volume Sketch of General Method of Teaching and Course of Study; Antipendium—Art Embroidery; Photograph St. Mary's Institute.

ST. LOUIS, MO., Diocese of St. Louis.

St. Elizabeth's Institute.

2 Volumes: Etiquette, Geography, United States History, Sacred History, English and German Translations, Method in Music Domestic Economy, Culinary Department, Calligraphy, German Exercises, Arithmetic, Compositions, Epistolary Correspondence (German and English), Book-Keeping and 1 Album Drawing. Antipendium, Art Embroidery, Peacock-Blue Plush Piano Cover, Set for Dresser (Scarf and 5 Small Pieces), Piano Cover, Pillow Shams, Table Scarf, Chair Scarf, Dresser Scarf, Infant's Shirt, Piano-Stool Cover, Linen Apron, Modern Lace, Ladies' Black Mittens (Silk), Infant's Jacket, Hood, Socks, Handkerchief Case containing 6 Hemstitched Handkerchiefs, 5 Pencil Drawings, Specimens of Pastel, Oil Painting.

St. Agatha's School.

Christian Doctrine (German), Church History (German), Grammar, Exercises in German, German Composition, Orthography, Arithmetic, Penmanship, Kindergarten Work: Folding, Intertwining, Embroidery, Drawing, Perforating and Cutting.

St. Augustine's School.

Arithmetic, German and English Penmanship, Grammar, Orthography.

OLD MONROE, MO., Diocese of St. Louis.

Immaculate Conception School.

Christian Doctrine, Penmanship.

OMAHA, NEB., Diocese of Omaha.

St. Joseph's School.

English and German Penmanship, Arithmetic and Geography.

St. Mary Magdalene's School.

English and German Penmanship and Grammar.

OTTAWA, OHIO, Diocese of Cleveland.

Sts. Peter and Paul's School.

1 Volume: Orthography, Bible History, Compositions, Arithmetic, Church History, Christian Doctrine.

RENSSAELER, IND., Diocese of Ft. Wayne.

St. Joseph's Normal Indian School.

Orthography, United States History, Bible History, Grammar, Geography and Church History.

RIVIER AUX VASES, MO., Diocese of St. Louis.
Sts. Philip and James' School.
Grammar, Arithmetic, German and English Penmanship.

FALLS CITY, NEB., Diocese of Lincoln.
St. Francis' School.
Arithmetic, Algebra, Grammar, Geography, History and Physiology.

FLORISSANT, MO., Diocese of St. Louis.
Sacred Heart School.
Christian Doctrine, Grammar, Geography, German Compositions, Orthography, Arithmetic, History, German and English Penmanship.

GARRETT, IND., Diocese of Ft. Wayne.
St. Joseph's School.
Christian Doctrine, Penmanship, Language, Compositions, Arithmetic, United States History, Grammar and Physiology.

GLANDORF, OHIO, Diocese of Cleveland.
Catholic District School.
1 Volume: Christian Doctrine, German, Arithmetic, Spelling, Definitions.

NEW CORYDON, IND., Diocese of Ft. Wayne.
Holy Trinity School.
Penmanship, Arithmetic and United States History.

JOSEPHVILLE, MO., Diocese of St. Louis.
St. Joseph's School.
Grammar, English and German Penmanship

ST. PETER'S, MO., Diocese of St. Louis.
All Saints' School:
Christian Doctrine, Grammar, Arithmetic, German, Letter Writing, History, Physiology, German and English Penmanship.

TIPTON, MO., Diocese of St. Louis.
St. Andrew's School.
English and German Penmanship, English and German Translations, Arithmetic.

WINAMAC, IND., Diocese of Ft. Wayne.
St. Peter's School.
History, Grammar, Physiology, Penmanship, Arithmetic, United States History, Orthography.

ZELL, MO., Diocese of St. Louis.
St. Joseph's School.
English and German Grammar, English and German Penmanship and Orthography.

Sisters of Providence.

Mother House, St. Mary's, Vigo Co., Ind.

ALCOVE 65.

ACADEMIES.

FT. WAYNE, IND., Diocese of Ft. Wayne.
St. Augustine's Academy.
2 Volumes Examination Papers: Christian Doctrine, Church History, Standard Time, Algebra, Rhetoric, Ancient and Modern History, Natural Philosophy, Astronomy, Literature, Penmanship, Arithmetic, Orthography, Geography, 3 Volumes Theory of Music and Literature.

GALESBURG, ILL., Diocese of Peoria.
St. Joseph's Academy.
4 Volumes: Christian Doctrine, Arithmetic, Geography, Algebra, Natural Philosophy, Physical Geography, History, Literature, Rhetoric, Chemistry, Bible History, Orthography, Grammar, Penmanship and Drawing.

KANSAS CITY, MO., Diocese of Kansas City.
Sacred Heart Academy.
2 Volumes Examination Papers: Christian Doctrine, Music, Arithmetic, Geography, History, Orthography and Grammar.

PORT HURON, MICH., Diocese of Detroit.
Sacred Heart Academy.
1 Volume Examination Papers: Christian Doctrine, Bible History, Arithmetic, Geography, Algebra, Ancient and Modern History, United States History, Literature, Rhetoric, Astronomy, Physics, Geology, Logic and Table Etiquette.

ST. MARY'S OF THE WOODS, IND., Diocese of Vincennes.
St. Rose's Academy.
Map of Battlefield of Gettysburg, 3 Volumes: Christian Doctrine, Arithmetic, Geography, Church History, Algebra, United States History, Geology, Grammar, Civil Government, Literature, Physics, Music, Penmanship, Map Drawing and Music Literature.

NEWPORT, KY., Diocese of Covington.
St. Martin's Academy.
1 Volume Grammar, Compositions, History, Arithmetic and Specimens of Fancy Needle-Work.

PARISH SCHOOLS.

CHICAGO, ILL., Diocese of Chicago.
St. Philip's School.
1 Volume: Christian Doctrine, Bible History, Church History, Orthography, Physiology, Arithmetic, Grammar, Geography, United States History and Map Drawing.

CHICAGO, ILL., Diocese of Chicago.—Continued.

School of Our Lady of Sorrows.

1 Volume: Christian Doctrine, Orthography, Arithmetic, Grammar, Geography and Drawing.

School of the Seven Dolors.

3 Volumes: Christian Doctrine, Arithmetic, Geography, Physical Geography, Grammar, United States History, Orthography and Literature.

CHELSEA, MASS., Diocese of Boston.

St. Rose's School.

3 Volumes: Christian Doctrine, Arithmetic, Geography, Grammar, Rhetoric, Literature, Algebra, History, Phonography and Drawing.

CONNERSVILLE, IND., Diocese of Vincennes.

St. Gabriel's School.

1 Volume: Christian Doctrine, Arithmetic, Geography, Orthography, Physical Geography, Grammar, Compositions, United States History and Music.

DELPHI, IND., Diocese of Ft. Wayne.

St. Joseph's School.

2 Volumes: Christian Doctrine, Arithmetic, Orthography, Bible History, Book-Keeping, Grammar, Geography, Physics, Literature, Rhetoric and Penmanship.

EAST SAGINAW, MICH., Diocese of Grand Rapids.

St. Mary's School.

4 Volumes: Christian Doctrine, Arithmetic, Geography, United States History, Penmanship, Algebra, Geometry, Physics, Botany, Compositions and Music.

FT. WAYNE, IND., Diocese of Ft. Wayne.

St. Augustine's Cathedral School.

Reading, Physiology, Civil Government, Christian Doctrine, Orthography, Arithmetic, United States History, Bible History, Grammar, Geography, Drawing, Literature, Physics, Modern History, Astronomy, Algebra, Church History, Logic, Chemistry, Business Forms, Phonography and Typewriting.

St. Patrick's School.

Examination Papers: Christian Doctrine, Arithmetic, Bible History, Geography, United States History, Grammar, Orthography, Penmanship and Music.

FRENCHTOWN, IND., Diocese of Vincennes.

Sacred Heart School.

1 Volume Examination Papers: Language, Arithmetic, United States History, Book-Keeping, Grammar, Christian Doctrine and Spelling.

GREENCASTLE, IND., Diocese of Vincennes.

St. Paul's School.

2 Volumes: Arithmetic, Grammar, Spelling, Penmanship, Catechism and History.

EVANSVILLE, IND., Diocese of Vincennes.

Holy Trinity School.

> 1 Volume Examination Papers: Spelling, Language, Catechism, History, Geography, Bible History, Book-Keeping, Grammar, Music, German Translations and Phonography.

HAMMOND, IND., Diocese of Ft. Wayne.

St. Joseph's School.

> 1 Volume Examination Papers: Language, Bible History, Arithmetic, Geography and Catechism.

INDIANAPOLIS, IND., Diocese of Vincennes.

St. Patrick's School.

> Christian Doctrine, History, Geography, Grammar, Phonography, Bible History, Spelling, Penmanship and Drawing.

St. James' School.

> 2 Volumes Examination Papers: Literature, History, Christian Doctrine, Geography, Algebra, Arithmetic, Grammar, Bible History, Spelling, Physiology, Sacred History, Business Letters, Compositions. Map Drawing and Physical Geography.

JEFFERSONVILLE, IND., Diocese of Vincennes.

St. Augustine's School.

> 2 Volumes Examination Papers: Music, Christian Doctrine, Algebra, History, Bible History, Language, Geography, Spelling and Drawing.

LAFAYETTE, IND., Diocese of Ft. Wayne.

St. Ann's School.

> 1 Volume Examination Papers: Christian Doctrine, Sacred History, Arithmetic, Grammar, Penmanship, Orthography, United States History, Physiology and Music.

St. Ignatius' School.—*Sisters of Providence.*

> Christian Doctrine, Orthography, Music, Penmanship, Geography, Arithmetic, Botany, Natural Philosophy.

LOCKPORT, ILL., Diocese of Peoria.

Sacred Heart School.

> 2 Volumes Examination Papers: Christian Doctrine, Arithmetic, Spelling, Geography, United States History, Rhetoric, Modern History and Book-Keeping.

LOOGOOTEE, IND., Diocese of Vincennes.

St. John's School.

> 1 Volume Examination Papers: Christian Doctrine, Arithmetic, Spelling, Language, United States History, Algebra, Literature and Rhetoric.

MADISON, IND., Diocese of Vincennes.

St. Michael's School.

> 1 Album of Elementary Drawing.

NEW ALBANY, IND., Diocese of Vincennes.

Holy Trinity School.

1 Volume: Christian Doctrine, Arithmetic, History, Music, Rhetoric, Literature, United States History, Composition, Physics, Civil Government and Algebra.

PERU, IND., Diocese of Ft. Wayne.

St. Charles' School.

2 Volumes: Bible History, Christian Doctrine, Grammar, Arithmetic, Penmanship, Church History, Algebra, Book-Keeping, Phonography, Civil Government, Literature and Natural Philosophy.

RICHMOND, IND., Diocese of Vincennes.

St. Mary's School.

2 Volumes Examination Papers: Christian Doctrine, History, Orthography, Arithmetic, Grammar, Geography, United States History, Algebra and Compositions.

ST. MARY'S OF THE WOODS, IND., Diocese of Vincennes.

St. John's School.

4 Volumes: Grammar, Geography, Christian Doctrine, United States History, Drawing and Physiology.

SAGINAW, MICH., Diocese of Grand Rapids.

St. Andrew's School.

4 Volumes: Christian Doctrine, Geography, Bible History, Penmanchip, Orthography, United States History, Church History, Algebra, Logic, General History, Questions on Natural Science and Compositions.

SEYMOUR, IND., Diocese of Vincennes.

St. Ambrose's School.

1 Volume Examination Papers: Christian Doctrine, Bible History, Arithmetic, Grammar, Orthography, Geography, United States History, Compositions.

TERRE HAUTE, IND., Diocese of Vincennes.

St. Benedict's School.

1 Volume Examination Papers: Arithmetic, German, Spelling, Letter Writing, Drawing, United States History, Map Drawing and Specimens of Embroidery.

St. Joseph's School.

2 Volumes: Spelling, Arithmetic, Geography, Christian Doctrine, Grammar, Language, Letter Writing, Vocal Music, Drawing and Geography.

VINCENNES, IND., Diocese of Vincennes.

St. John's School.

1 Volume Examination Papers: Christian Doctrine, Bible History, Spelling, Grammar, Arithmetic, United States History and Penmanship.

VALPARAISO, IND., Diocese of Ft. Wayne.

St. Paul's School.

1 Volume Examination Papers: Christian Doctrine, Bible History, Arithmetic, Penmanship, United States History, Grammar, Rhetoric, Physics, Music and Algebra.

WASHINGTON, IND., Diocese of Vincennes.
St. Mary's School.
1 Volume Examination Papers: Arithmetic, Spelling, Language, German Language, Freehand, Drawing, Grammar, Letter Writing and Geography.

YPSILANTI, MICH., Diocese of Detroit.
St. John's School.
2 Volumes Examination Papers: Catechism, Arithmetic, Penmanship, Music, Bible History, United States History, Rhetoric, Phonography, Typewriting, Church History and Algebra.

Ursuline Sisters.
See Part III. and Diocesan Exhibits.

Visitation Nuns.
See Part III. and Diocesan Exhibits.

Individual or Special Exhibits.

WASHINGTON, D. C., Archdiocese of Baltimore.
Catholic University of America.
Its establishment decreed by the Third Plenary Council of Baltimore in 1884.

THE CHANCELLOR OF THE UNIVERSITY, THE ARCHBISHOP OF BALTIMORE, HIS EMINENCE, JAMES CARDINAL GIBBONS, D.D.

THE RECTOR OF THE UNIVERSITY, THE RT. REV. JOHN J. KEANE, D.D., BISHOP OF AJASSO.

Photographic Group of Prelates of Third Plenary Council of Baltimore, Water-Color Pictures of Divinity Hall and McMahon Hall of Philosophy; India-Ink Sketch of Dwelling Halls for Lay Students, Topographic Map Showing Present and Proposed Buildings, Printed Prospectus and Year Book.

AMAWALK, N. Y., Archdiocese of New York.
St. Joseph's Normal College.—*Christian Brothers.*
1 Set of Books for Simultaneous Teaching of Freehand and Crayon Drawing, 1 Set for Simultaneous Teaching of Linear Drawing—including Projections, Shades and Shadows, also Teacher's Hand-Book; 1 Set for teaching: Reading, Spelling, Grammar, Book-Keeping, Commercial Law, Mensuration, Philosophy of Literature, Christian Philosophy, etc.; 1 Set of Books for teaching Penmanship; the De La Salle Normal Manual or Management of the Christian Schools, the Blessed De La Salle and His Educational Methods.

BALTIMORE, MD.
Star of the Sea School.
See Diocese of Baltimore, Part II., and Sisters of Charity, B. V. M., Part III.

BORDEAUX, FRANCE.
Brother Leobert.
Album of Calligraphy, Complete System of Methods Used by the Brothers of the Christian Schools in Teaching Writing.

CAHOKIA, ILL., Diocese of Belleville.
Holy Family Church.
Old Church Bell, cast in 1776, 14 inches high and 44 inches in circumference, gift of the King of France and first bell used west of the Alleghany Mountains.

CARLSBOURG, BELGIUM.
Brother Alexis.
1 Set of School Maps, 1 Set of Copy Books for Teaching Map Drawing, 1 Relief Map of the Province of Belgium, 1 Relief Map for Instructing Children in Elements of Geography, Submersible Relief Map, Set of Wall Maps, Atlases, Text Books, Globes, Hypsometrical Casts and Relief Maps for Teaching Geography.

Columbian Library of Catholic Authors for the United States of America.

Catholic Educational Exhibit.—Rt. Rev. J. L. SPALDING, *President.*

Several Thousand Volumes by Catholic Authors, Contributed by Authors and Publishers in the United States, England, Canada, Ireland. (Catalogue to be published at a future day.)

CHICAGO, ILL., Archdiocese of Chicago.

Rev. J. J. Carroll.—*Pastor St. Thomas' Church, Hyde Park.*

Manuscript Translation of Letter from Our Holy Father, Pope Leo XIII., Dated July 20, 1892, into the Irish Language.

COAL CITY, ILL., Archdiocese of Chicago.

Rev. A. De Paradis.

Illuminated and Illustrated Volume of the Magnificat in 150 Languages.

COLUMBUS, OHIO, Diocese of Columbus.

Papal Josephinum College.—Rev. JOSEPH JESSING, *President.*

ALCOVES 80, 82 AND 84.

This college is the property of the Propaganda at Rome, and includes an Ecclesiastical Seminary, a Classical and Scientific School, preparatory for the Seminary, and a School for Orphans, with an Industrial Department for Wood-Carving, Statuary, etc.

Bound Volumes of the "Ohio Waisenfreund," edited and printed at the College.

Map of the World from the first half of the 16th Century, by Sebastian Munster, Born 1489.

Map of North and South America, from the middle of the 17th Century, by the Dutch writer, O. Dapper.

Map of North America, from the 17th Century, with the following titles: "Amerique Septentrionalis. Carte d' un tres grand Pays entre le Noveau Mexique at la Mer Glaciale dedi*e & Guillaume, III^s Roy de la Grande Bretagne Par le R. P. Louis de Hennepin, Mission: Recol: et Not: Apost: Chez A. V. Someren a Amsterdam, 1698." This is the first Map on which the Mississippi River and the Great Lakes are represented.

Map of the territory lying between the Atlantic and the Mississippi, from the 17th Century, sketched by Father Hennepin and engraved by A. V. Someren.

Map of the Hemispheres, from the middle of the 18th Century, Drawn in 1744, by Joseph Antone Ferrari, of Milan, in the City of Venice.

Framed photographs and other pictures.

Noteworthy old books. "St. Antoninus, Summa Theologica," printed by Nicholaus Jensen in 1479. St. Anthony, the author, born in the year 1389, Archbishop of Florence from 1446 to 1459, in which year he died. "Platina, De Vitis Pontificum Romanorum," Latin History of the Pontiffs, from St Peter to Paul II. The Author, Bartholomew Platina, was born in 1421 and died in 1481, as librarian of the Vatican in Rome. Printed by Anthony Koburger, Nurenberg, 1481. "Quadragesimale Discipuli," a book of Latin Lenten Sermons, printed by John Otman in Reutligen, in 1489. "Exercitium

COLUMBUS, OHIO, Diocese of Columbus.—Continued.

Papal Josephinum College.—Rev. Joseph Jessing, President.

Grammaticale Puerorum," printed in Germany in 1504. The book is printed in Gothic Characters, the explanatory text being mostly in Latin throughout the book.

"Cursus Librorum Philosophiæ Naturalis." This book was written by the Franciscan Monk, Nicolaus de Orbelli, who lived in the 15th Century. Latin and printed in Gothic characters at Basil in 1503. "Disputatio Excellentium Doctrum Johannis Eccii et Andreæ Carolostadii et Dr. Johannis Eccii et D. Martini Lutheri, Augustiani, quæ cepit IIII. Julii 1519—— In 1519 several debates were held at Leipsig, Dr. Eck being on one side and Dr. Carlstadt and Dr. Martin Luther on the other. The principal disputation was on the Primacy of the Roman Pontiff. The debate begun on June 27, 1519, between Eck and Carlstadt, and was continued from July 4th to July 14th, between Eck and Luther. The book on exhibition is the original record of this discussion, and was taken down in shorthand during the course of the dispute, and immediately afterward printed at Leipsig.

"Canones Apostolorum," Veterum Conciliorum Constitutiones, Decreta Pontoficum Antiquiora, De Primatu Romanæ Ecclesiæ—Apostolic canons, Constitutions of the old councils, Decrees of the earlier Popes, about the Primacy of the Roman Church. This book was printed at Munich in 1525.

"Chronicle of the Old Christian Churches," from Eusebius, Ruffinus, etc. This book was printed at Strasburg by George Ulrich of Andla in 1530. It is a church history of the first centuries, and probably the first and oldest church history printed in the German language.

"Altercatio Synagogæ et Ecclesiæ" in Latin and was printed at Cologne by Melchor Novesianus, 1537.

Photographs of the Rector, Rev. Jos. Jessing, professors, students, choir, drum corps, orphans and shops in the industrial printing and household departments of Josephinum College.

Books printed at Josephinum College.

Illustrated catalogue of ecclesiastical works of art, such as statues, altars, etc., made in art department of Josephinum College.

4 catalogues of Josephinum College, for years 1889, 1890, 1891, 1892.

Group—"Thou Art Peter." True imitation on a reduced scale of a life size group, carved at Josephinum College.

"The High Altar," built in strictly Gothic style, of the best American oak wood, with red and white mahogany. Height of altar, 28 feet, length of altar table, 9 feet. Carved and built at the Industrial School of Josephinum College.

56 examination copies containing exercises in Latin, Greek, German and English, Universal History, United States History, Geography, Arithmetic and Natural Science.

41 Albums containing written exercises from pupils of the Sexta: Catechism in English, Latin and German and translations; German composition, Universal History, United States History, Geography, and Gabelsberger's Stenography in English and German.

Albums containing exercises of the pupils of the Quinta: Doctrina Christiana in English, Latin and German languages and translations, Universal History, United States History, Geography, Arithmetic, Zoology and Gabelsberger's Stenography.

Exercises from the pupils of the Quarta: Doctrina Christiana, the Latin, English and German languages. Latin, English and German ti nslations; general composition, German Literature, Universal History, Unit 1 States History, Geometry, Physics, and Gabelsberger's Stenography in th Latin and German Languages, and business and reporter's style in the English language.

COLUMBUS, OHIO, Diocese of Columbus.—Continued.

Papal Josephinum College.—Rev. Joseph Jessing, *President.*

Exercises from the students of the Secunda: Doctrina Christiana in the English and German languages; Logica Scholastica: The figures of the Syllogism; Translations in Latin, Greek, German and English languages. German Literature, Algebra, Physics and Stenography.

Photograph of the Columbus statue erected October 12th, 1892, on the 400th Anniversary of the Discovery of America. Statue stands in the yard of Josephinum College. Designed by Alphons Pelzer, and executed in sheet copper by W. H. Mullins, of Salem, Ohio. The statue stands 9 feet high.

COUNCIL BLUFFS, IOWA.

St. Francis' Academy.

See Diocese Davenport, Part II. and Sisters of Charity B. V. M., Part III.

DETROIT, MICH., Diocese of Detroit.

Pernin's Shorthand Institute.

Diploma, Prospectus, Manual of Phonography, Practical Reporter and Monthly Stenographer.

EMMITTSBURG, MD., Diocese of Baltimore.

Mt. St. Mary's College.—*Secular Clergy.*

Photographic Views of Buildings, Chapel Grounds, Classes, Brass Band and Athletic Club.

HOLYOKE, MASS., Diocese of Springfield.

St. Jerome's Catholic Total Abstinence, Benevolent and Literary Society.

Photographs of Buildings, Meeting Hall, Reading Rooms, Library Billiard Rooms, Gymnasium, Bath Rooms, Armory, Parlor, Spiritual Director, Officers, Guards, Drum Corps and Base-Ball Team.

JASPER, IND.

Jasper College.

See Diocese Vincennes, Part II. and Benedictine Fathers, Part III.

KANSAS CITY, MO.

Annunciation School.

See Diocese Kansas City, Part II. and Sisters of Charity B. V. M., Part III.

LEWISTON, IDAHO.

See Vicariate Apostolic, Part II. and Sisters of St. Francis, Part III.

LOUISVILLE, KY., Diocese of Louisville.

Mrs. M. W. T. Ward.

Oil Painting "St. Augustine in Ecstasy."

MEMPHIS, TENN., Diocese of Nashville.

St. Patrick's School.

See Diocese of Nashville, Part II. and Sisters of Charity of Nazareth, Part III.

MEMPHIS, TENN., Diocese of Nashville.—CONTINUED.

Ashe Art School.—*Miss M. L. Ashe, Principal.*

Cotton Panel, Blooms, Balls and matured Cotton, Miss Annie Rhea; Cotton Panel with Matured Cotton, Mrs. E. M. Brown; Cotton Panel with Matured Cotton, Miss Leingfield; Corn Panel, Miss M. L. Ashe; Corn Panel, Mrs. E. M. Brown; "Good Luck" (Old Negro Woman in Rags), Miss Madge Rogers; "Contentment" (Negro Boy Eating Apples), Miss Annie Rhea; Portrait of Col. J. B. Ashe (in Continental Uniform), Miss Ashe; Vase of Chrysanthemums, Miss M. L. Ashe; Vase of Magnolias, Miss Annie Rhea; Wine and Grapes, Miss Minnie Brown; Panel Cotton Growing, Miss M. L. Ashe; Panel "A Yard of Tennessee Cloth," Mrs. M. Chandler. (All the above in pastel.) "Head of a Young Girl," Etching on Silk, Miss A. A. Ashe; 1 Landscape, Miss A. A. Ashe; "Head of an Old Woman," from life, Miss M. L. Ashe; "Basket of Grapes," Mrs. Hunt; "Flowers," Miss Hunt; "Watermelon" (Oil), Mrs. N. Chandler; "A Study in Pink" (Oil), M. L. Ashe; "Aunt Rachel," M. L. Ashe.

NEW LEXINGTON, OHIO.

St. Aloysius' Academy.

See Diocese Columbus, Part II. and Sisters St. Francis, Part III.

NEW YORK CITY, N. Y., Diocese of New York.

Brother Innocentinian.—*De La Salle Institute, Christian Brothers.*

1 Album Development of Solids.

Miss M. G. Caldwell.—*First Foundress Catholic University.*

Embroidered Vestment.

NOTRE DAME, IND., Diocese of Ft. Wayne.

Notre Dame University.

See Congregation of the Holy Cross and Ft. Wayne Diocese.

OGDENSBURG, N. Y.

St. Mary's Academy.

See Diocese Ogdensburg, Part II. and Gray Nuns, Part III.

OTTAWA, OHIO, Diocese of Cleveland.

Rev. N. H. Nosbisch.

2 Volumes, the Works of St. John Chrysostom, Printed 1633.

OTTAWA, ONT., CANADA, Diocese of Ottawa.

Rev. Æneas MacDonald Dawson.—*F. R. S. of the Senate.*

Ossian's Epic Poems translated into Latin by Rev. Alexander MacDonald.

PINE BLUFF, ARK.

Annunciation Academy and Colored Industrial Institute.

See Diocese Little Rock, Part II. and Sisters of Charity of Nazareth, Part III.

PARIS, FRANCE.

Freres des Ecoles Chretiennes.—*Brothers of the Christian Schools.*

Sets of Plaster Casts, Models in Wood and Zinc to aid in Teaching Drawing, Set of Charts for Illustrating Descriptive Geometry, Set of Wall Charts for Teaching Crayon, Linear Drawing; Set of Text Books.

PHILADELPHIA, PA., Diocese of Philadelphia.
American Catholic Historical Society.

Autograph Letter of Thomas Burke of North Carolina.
Autograph Letter of Ædanus Burke of South Carolina.
Manuscript Document of Chas. Carroll, 1st and 2d.
Bishop Carroll's Funeral Oration on Washington with Autograph Letters of both.
Autograph Letter of Charles Carroll. Autograph Letter of Bishop F. P. Kenrick. American Museum, Volume 1, 1787. De La Porteric's Boston Pastoral, 1799. M. Carey's History of Yellow Fever, 1793. Carroll's Address to Catholics, 1784. United States Catholic Miscellany, Volume 2, 1824.
Pious Guide, Georgetown, 1792. Huby's Spiritual Retreat, Philadelphia, 1792. Houdet's Morality, Philadelphia, 1796. Unerring Authority, Lloyd, Philadelphia, 1789. England's Conversion and Reformation, Antwerp, 1725. England's Conversion and Reformation, Lancaster, Pa., 1813. Lingard's England, 1st American Edition, Volume 1, 1827. Butler's Lives, first American Edition, Volume 1, 1822. Lloyd's System of Shorthand, 1819. Silhouette and Home of Thomas Lloyd. Original Seal of Maryland. Prayer-Book owned by Captain Maguire, 1790.
Cross made from First Altar erected in Pennsylvania.
Medals on Board. Pectoral Cross of Abp. Hughes. Pectoral Cross of Bishop Chanche. Pectoral Cross of Bishop Gartland. Pectoral Cross of Bishop Van de Velde. Seal and Chain of Bishop M. O'Connor. Thomas á Kempis (in German), Germantown, 1795. Pise's History of Church, Volume 1, Baltimore, 1827. Alexandria Controversy, Georgetown, 1817. O'Gallagher on Penance, New York, 1815.
Blosius' Answer (German), Lancaster, 1796. Bishop Fenwick's Webbe's Masses. Sacred Concert at St. Augustine's, 1810. Devotions for Catholic Blind, Philadelphia. Pastorine's History of Church, First American Edition, 1807. Laity's Directory, New York. 1822. United States Catholic Directory for 1833. Two Church Music Books, 1787 and 1791. The Metropolitan, Baltimore, 1830. Catholic Christian Instructed, Philadelphia, 1786. Carey's Douay Bible, 1790. Prospectus announcing same. Carey's New Testament, 1805. The Jesuit, Volume 1, Boston, 1829. Catholic Herald, Volume 1, Philadelphia, 1833. Ring of Bishop M. O'Connor. Book Plate of Chas. Carroll, Sr. Signature of Lionel Brittin. Father Farmer's Reliquary. Miniature of Rev. S. S. Cooper.
Father Mathew's Autograph. Archbishop Wood's Catechism and Ordination. Autograph of Judge Gaston of North Carolina. Catalogue of Bishop Conwell's Library (Mss.), Goshenhoppen Register. Bishop McGill's Faith the Victory, Richmond, 1865.
Bishops Egan and Conwell's Mitre. Bishop Neuman's Mitre. Gallitzin Letter (Frame 1). Loretto Mission, Kentucky. Picture of Archbishop Carroll, 1812. Old Panel from St. Inigoe's, Md.

Catholic Total Abstinence Union.

Chart giving history of the Union, pamphlets, Portrait in oil of Father Mathew.

League of the Sacred Heart.

65 Volumes of Publications, Diplomas in Latin and English, Charts, Statistics and Almanacs, Devotional Pictures, Circulars for the promotion of Religion, Morality and Education.

REIMS, FRANCE.
Brother Arille.

3 Volumes: Original Methods for Teaching Drawing and Design, Perspective, Decorative, etc.

SHAMOKIN, PA.
St. Stanislaus' School.
See Diocese of Harrisburg, Part II., and Felician Sisters, Part III.

ST. AUGUSTINE'S, FLA.
St. Joseph's Academy.
See Diocese of St. Augustine, Part II., and Sisters of St. Joseph, Part III.

ST. MEINRAD, IND.
St. Meinrad's College.
See Diocese of Vincennes, Part II., and Benedictine Fathers, Part III.

GEORGETOWN, D. C.
Visitation Convent.
See Diocese of Baltimore, Part II., and Visitation Nuns, Part III.

PART II.

CLASSIFICATION OF EXHIBITS BY DIOCESES.

ARCHDIOCESE OF BALTIMORE.

His Eminence, James Cardinal Gibbons, D.D.

Portrait in Oil of His Eminence, The Cardinal.

UNIVERSITY.

WASHINGTON, D. C.

Catholic University of America.—Rt. Rev. John J. Keane, D. D., *Rector.*

Photographic Group of Prelates, Third Plenary Council of Baltimore, which created the University; Water-Color Picture of Divinity Hall and McMahon Hall of Philosophy; India-Ink Sketch of Dwelling Halls for lay Students, Topographical Map showing present and proposed Buildings; Prospectus and Year Book.

COLLEGES.

EMMITTSBURG, MD.

Mt. St. Mary's College.—*Secular Clergy.*

Photographic Views of Buildings, Chapel Grounds, Classes, Brass Bands and Athletic Club.

ELLICOTT CITY, MD.

Rock Hill College.—*Christian Brothers.*

3 Volumes English Essays, 1 Volume Studies from Works of Cardinal Gibbons, 1 Volume Ancient and Modern History, 1 Volume Higher English Studies, 1 Volume Evidences of Religion, 1 Volume Mental and Moral Philosophy, 1 Volume Physics and Chemistry, 1 Volume Trigonometry, Surveying and Navigation, 1 Volume Geometry and Mensuration, 1 Volume Analytical Geometry, 1 Volume Calculus and Algebra, 1 Volume Greek Classics, 1 Volume Greek Exercises, 1 Volume Latin Classics, 1 Volume Perspective Drawing, 1 Volume Projections, 1 Volume Geometrical Drawing and Lettering, 1 Volume Exercises in English Rhetoric, 1 Volume Navigation Charts, 1 Volume Architectural Drawings (Advanced Course), 1 Volume Architectural Drawings (First Year), 1 Volume Machine Drawing, 1 Volume Isometrical Drawing, 1 Volume Engineering and tinted specimens, botanical specimens by J. R. Edgerton, Woods from College Grounds by J. B. Edgerton, Geological Specimens from College Grounds by A. P. Meyer, Relief Map of Ellicott City by A. P. Meyer, College Book Containing Prospectus, Diplomas, College Badge, Act of Incorporation, Examination Reports, Monthly Returns, Testimonials, Good Notes, Invitations and Programmes of College Entertainments, Photographs of Literary Societies, Reading Circles and Athletic Unions; Views of Scenery, etc., by the Class in Photography, College Songs and Addresses.

PREPARATORY DEPT.

2 Volumes Christian Doctrine; 3 Volumes English Compositions; 1 Volume Sacred History; 2 Volumes English Grammar; 1 Volume Algebra and Arithmetic; 1 Volume Geometry and Mensuration; 1 Volume Geography; 3 Volumes Penmanship; 2 Volumes Practical Arithmetic; 2 Volumes Orthography; 1 Volume Object Drawing.

WASHINGTON, D. C.

St. John's College.—*Christian Brothers.*

ACADEMIC DEPT.

5 Albums of Composition; 3 Albums of Phonography; 1 Album of Latin and Greek; 1 Album Ornamental Drawing; 1 Relief Map of the City of Washington; 8 Framed Crayon Drawings.

AMMENDALE, MD.

Ammendale Normal Institute.—*Christian Brothers.*

PREPARATORY DEPT.

1 Relief Map of Baltimore; 2 Volumes Artistic Writing and Lettering; 2 Volumes Map Drawing; 22 Volumes Freehand Drawing; 17 Volumes of Linear Drawing; 20 Copies of Projections.

ACADEMIES.

BALTIMORE, MD.

Calvert Hall Institute.—*Christian Brothers.*

84 Albums: Water-Color Drawings and Sketches, Crayon Drawings, Pen-and-Ink Sketches, Collection of Leaves, Marquetry, Object, Ornamental and Linear Drawing, Catechism, Greek, Latin, French, German, Algebra, Analytical Geometry, Trigonometry, Surveying, Physics, Chemistry, Mensuration, Arithmetic, Geography, Grammar, Rhetoric, Literature, Typewriting, Composition, Phonography, Commercial Correspondence, History, Civics, Commercial Law, Spelling, Book-Keeping, Map Drawing, 12 Collections for Object Teaching, 7 Relief Maps, 13 Framed Crayons, 2 Framed Water Colors.

BALTIMORE, MD.—Continued.

Institute of Notre Dame.—*School Sisters of Notre Dame.*

1 Volume Music, 2 Volumes Kindergarten, 3 Volumes Freehand Drawing, 2 Volumes Mechanical Drawing, 1 Volume Botanical Souvenirs, 1 Silk Map of Maryland, 1 Motto on Silk, 18 Oil Paintings, 1 Lace Handkerchief, 1 Embroidered Handkerchief, 1 Embroidered Center-Piece, 2 Volumes Specimens of Needle-Work, 7 Hand-Painted Pieces (China), 1 Herbarium, 2 Framed Drawings of Institute, 1 Volume German Essays, 41 Volumes: Language, Numbers, Geography, Grammar, Writing, Arithmetic, Catechism, United States History, Bible History, Composition, Algebra, Spelling, Elementary Science, Map Drawing, General History, Literature and Book-Keeping.

St. Martin's Academy.—*Brothers of Mary.*

3 Volumes: Spelling, Penmanship, Dictations, Letters and Compositions; 1 Volume Map Drawing, 2 Volumes Typewriting, 18 Charts of Drawing, 57 Volumes Book-Keeping, 16 Volumes Compositions.

EMMITTSBURG, MD.

St. Joseph's Academy.—*Sisters of Charity.*

3 Volumes: Christian Doctrine, Arithmetic, Geography, Grammar, General History, Rhetoric, Astronomy, Physics, Physical Geography, United States History, French Translations, Illustrated Geography Bible History, Typewriting, Phonography, Arithmetic, Physiology, Geology, Church History, Chemistry, Arithmetic, Botany, Complete set of Photographic views of the Institution, Album of Crayon and Map Drawing, one Large Oil Painting of Cardinal Gibbons, Pastel Paintings—Subjects: "Sacred Heart," "St. Joseph," "Country Boy and Girl," Sacred Heart on Silk .'ope Pius IX., Landscapes, 1 Case Fancy Lace and Painting on Celluloid, 1 Harp with Oil Painting, 3 Piano Scarfs, Songs Written on Parchment (Framed) and 1 Oak Rocker (embroidered).

GEORGETOWN, D. C.

Visitation Academy.—*Visitation Sisters.*

5 Historical Charts, 2 Genealogical Charts, 1 Chart Crown Heads of Europe in family groups, 4 Paintings, 1 small Photo of Cotton Plant.

GOVANSTOWN, MD.

Notre Dame of Maryland.—*School Sisters of Notre Dame.*

1 Volume Latin, 1 Volume French, 1 Volume German, 1 Volume Music, 1 Volume Art, 2 Volumes Herbarium, 3 Volumes Drawings. 45 Volumes: Science, Object Lessons, Language, Spelling, Geography, Grammar, Arithmetic, Algebra, Natural History, United States History, Bible History, Physics, Geometry, Trigonometry, Geology, Physiology, Natural History, Natural Philosophy, Mental Philosophy, Botany, Rhetoric, Church History, Book-Keeping, Astronomy, Literature, Christian Doctrine.

PARISH SCHOOLS.

BALTIMORE, MD.

Immaculate Conception School.

Male Dept.—*Christian Brothers.*

19 Albums: Linear and Ornamental Drawing, Projections, Writing, Book-Keeping, Compositions, Arithmetic, Mensuration, Phonography, Typewriting, Pen-Work and Photographs.

BALTIMORE, MD.—Continued.

Immaculate Conception School.

FEMALE DEPT.—*Sisters of Charity.*

18 Volumes: Christian Doctrine, Arithmetic, Geography, Orthography, Grammar, Algebra, United States History, Bible History, Book-Keeping, Geometry, Physiology, Natural Philosophy and General History

St. Alphonsus' School.

MALE DEPT.—*Christian Brothers.*

28 Albums: Map and Crayon Drawing, Mensuration, Arithmetic, Composition, German Grammar and Translation, Catechism, Business Forms, Writing, Ornamental Lettering and Pen-and-Ink Drawing.

FEMALE DEPT.—*School Sisters of Notre Dame.*

3 Volumes: Language Lessons, Arithmetic, Spelling, Geography, Grammar, United States History, Composition, Catechism, Bible History, German and Writing.

St. Ann's School.—*School Sisters of Notre Dame.*

5 Volumes: Catechism, Arithmetic, Geography, Grammar, Language, United States History, Bible History, Spelling, Writing, Algebra, Physiology, Book-Keeping.

St. James' School.

MALE DEPT.—*Brothers of Mary.*

12 Albums: English and German Grammar and Spelling, English and German Translations, English and German Writing, Arithmetic and Business Forms; 5 Volumes Elementary Drawing.

FEMALE DEPT.—*School Sisters of Notre Dame.*

4 Volumes: Language, Writing, Spelling, Arithmetic, Geography, Grammar, Catechism, Composition, United States History, Bible History, German.

St. John's School.

MALE DEPT.—*Christian Brothers.*

52 Volumes: Catechism, Composition, Dictation, Punctuation, Geography, Grammar, History, Arithmetic, Mensuration, Algebra, Bible History, Writing, Home Exercises, Linear and Ornamental Drawing, Typewriting, Monthly and Quarterly Examination Reports, Weekly Reports, Regulations and Means of Emulation, 1 Perspective Drawing of School and 1 Pen Drawing of Bird, Plan of New School, Photographs.

FEMALE DEPT.—*Sisters of Charity.*

56 Albums: Christian Doctrine, Arithmetic, Geography, Language, History, Algebra, Grammar, Rhetoric, Physiology, Physics, General History, Drawing and Book-Keeping.

St. Leo's School.—*School Sisters of Notre Dame.*

2 Volumes: Language, Grammar, Arithmetic, Geography, Spelling, Writing, Catechism, Bible History.

St. Martin's School.

MALE DEPT.—*Brothers of Mary.*

15 Copy Books Composition, 57 Copy Books Book-Keeping, 2 Volumes Typewriting, 3 Volumes Crayon Drawings. 3 Volumes: Composition, Letter Writing, Dictation and Writing.

BALTIMORE, MD.—Continued.

St. Michael's School.

MALE DEPT.—*Brothers of Mary.*
12 Volumes: Arithmetic, Business Forms, English and German Grammar, English and German Language Exercises, Spelling, English and German Dictation and Composition, Writing, Translation.

FEMALE DEPT.—*School Sisters of Notre Dame.*
1 Volume: Language, Writing, Grammar, Arithmetic, Geography, Catechism, Composition, Spelling, German.

Star of the Sea School.—*Sisters of St. Joseph.*

Examination Papers: Catechism, Literature, Civil Government, United States History, Book-Keeping, Arithmetic, Compositions, Ornamental Writing, Map Drawing and Drawing.

St. Vincent's School.

MALE DEPT.—*Christian Brothers.*
11 Volumes: Ornamental, Linear and Map Drawing; Home Exercises, Book-Keeping, Catechism, Spelling, Arithmetic, Geography.

FEMALE DEPT.—*Sisters of Charity.*
33 Volumes: Christian Doctrine, Arithmetic, Geography, Grammar, Algebra, Bible History, Rhetoric, Logic, Mental Philosophy, Composition, Civics, Roman History, Map Drawing and Music.

St. Wenceslaus' School.—*School Sisters of Notre Dame.*

1 Volume: Writing, Language, Arithmetic, Geography, Composition.

CATONSVILLE, MD.

St. Mark's School.—*School Sisters of Notre Dame.*

1 Volume: Geography, Arithmetic, Algebra, Grammar, Composition, Sacred History, Catechism.

EMMITTSBURG, MD.

St. Euphemia's School.—*Sisters of Charity.*

3 Volumes: Christian Doctrine, Orthography, Grammar, Geography, Arithmetic, Bible History, Book-Keeping, Compositions, Algebra, Physics, Phonography, Literature, Biography, Pen-Work, Map Drawing. 1 Volume: Christian Doctrine, Orthography, Grammar, Arithmetic, Geography, United States History and Penmanship.

LONACONING, MD.

St. Mary's School.—*Sisters of St. Joseph.*

Examination Papers: Catechism, Bible History, Church History, Literature, Science, Rhetoric, Civil Government, United States History, Geography, Book-Keeping, Geometry, Algebra, Arithmetic and Compositions.

WASHINGTON, D. C.

St. Mary's School.—*School Sisters of Notre Dame.*

4 Volumes: Drawing, Writing, Spelling, Language Lessons, Arithmetic, Geography, Grammar, Composition, Catechism, German.

WESTERNPORT, MD.

St. Peter's School.—*Sisters of St. Joseph.*

Examination Papers: Catechism, Bible History, Science, Geography, Algebra, Arithmetic, Compositions, United States History and Drawing.

ORPHANAGE.

BALTIMORE, MD.

St. Vincent's Infant Asylum.—*Sisters of Charity.*

1 Album Kindergarten Work.

ARCHDIOCESE OF BOSTON.

MOST REV. JOHN J. WILLIAMS, D. D.

ACADEMIES.

BOSTON, MASS.

Academy of Notre Dame.—*Sisters of Notre Dame.*

5 Volumes: Drawing, Botany, Literature, Christian Doctrine and specimens of Needle-Work.

CHELSEA, MASS.

St. Rose's Academy.—*Sisters of Providence.*

1 Volume: Arithmetic, Orthography, Physical Geography, Physiology, Grammar, Christian Doctrine, Rhetoric, Literature, Algebra, History, Phonography and Letters.

LOWELL, MASS.

St. Patrick's Academy.—*Sisters of Notre Dame.*

2 Volumes Needle-Work, 1 Volume: Christian Doctrine, English Compositions, Spanish Translations, French Translations, German Poems, Latin Translations, 1 Volume: Geology, Botany, Chemistry, Mathematics, Geometry and Commercial Forms.

ROXBURY, MASS.

Notre Dame Academy.—*Sisters of Notre Dame.*

1 Volume English and American Literature. 1 Volume: Zoology, Astronomy, Chemistry and Compositions.

PAROCHIAL SCHOOLS.

BOSTON, MASS.

St. Joseph's School.—*Sisters of Notre Dame.*

1 Volume specimens Sewing, 1 Volume Drawing, 1 Volume: Grammar, United States History, Sacred History, Geography, Arithmetic, Compositions, Christian Doctrine, Literature and Penmanship.

BOSTON, MASS.—Continued.

St. Mary's School.

2 Volumes: Christian Doctrine, History, Business Letters, Grammar, Compositions, Geography, Penmanship, Literature, Arithmetic, Algebra, Botany and Sacred History.

CANTON, MASS.

St. John's School.—*Sisters of Notre Dame.*

1 Volume Kindergarten Work, 3 Volumes: Language, Geography, Spelling, Arithmetic, Grammar, United States History, Christian Doctrine, Physiology, Bible History and Algebra.

CHELSEA, MASS.

St. Rose's School.—*Sisters of Providence.*

MALE DEPT.

1 Volume Class-Work: Drawing, Spelling, Christian Doctrine, Abbreviations, Writing, Arithmetic, Geography, Grammar, Sacred History, Map Drawing, United States History and Miscellaneous.

FEMALE DEPT.

1 Volume Class-Work, Christian Doctrine, Bible History, Reading, Spelling, Grammar, Arithmetic, Drawing, Geography and Map Drawing.

EAST BOSTON, MASS.

Our Holy Redeemer High School.—*Sisters of Notre Dame.*

1 Volume: Literature, Astronomy, Philosophy, Book-Keeping, Music, History, Algebra, Civil Government, Mineralogy and Botany.

Holy Redeemer School.
Assumption School.
Sacred Heart School.
—*United Work, Sisters of Notre Dame.*

2 Volumes: Christian Doctrine, Geography, Grammar, United States History, Compositions, Bible History, Language, Zoology, Book-Keeping, Botany, 1 Volume specimens of Sewing.

LAWRENCE, MASS.

St. Mary's School.—*Sisters of Notre Dame.*

1 Volume Examination Papers: Literature, United States History, Book-Keeping, Astronomy, Mathematics, Algebra, Philosophy, Penmanship, Poetry, Compositions, Literature, Geography, Grammar, Language, Catechism and Music.

LOWELL, MASS.

St. Patrick's School.—*Sisters of Notre Dame.*

4 Volumes Needle-Work, 1 Volume: Compositions, Literature, Astronomy, History, Algebra, Geography, Arithmetic, Language and Grammar.

LYNN, MASS.

St. Mary's School.—*Sisters of Notre Dame.*

2 Volumes: Literature, Book-Keeping, Botany, Music, Algebra, Physiology, Conchology, Geology, Arithmetic, Compositions, United States History, Geography, Essays, Sacred History, Grammar, English History and Zoology, 1 Volume Drawing.

SALEM, MASS.

St. James' School.—*Sisters of Notre Dame.*

1 Volume Methods in Teaching Geography, 1 Volume Topical Synopsis of Geography and 1 Volume Outline of Geography.

SOMMERVILLE, MASS.

St. Joseph's School.—*Sisters of Notre Dame.*

1 Volume Drawing, 2 Volumes: Christian Doctrine, Language, Grammar, Geography, English Literature, Algebra, Architecture, Natural Science, Arithmetic, Book-Keeping, Music and 1 Volume Science (Work of small children).

WALTHAM, MASS.

St. Joseph's School.—*Sisters of Notre Dame.*

1 Volume (High-School Grade): Essays, Grammar, United States History, English Literature, American Literature, Church History, Algebra, Book-Keeping, Astronomy, Natural Philosophy, Botany, 1 Volume (Grammar Grades).

Archdiocese of Chicago.

See Diocesan Exhibit, Part I.

ARCHDIOCESE OF CINCINNATI.

MOST REV. WM. H. ELDER, D. D.

ACADEMIES.

DAYTON, OHIO.

St. Mary's Institute.—*Brothers of Mary.*

STUDENTS' WORK.

19 Volumes: Grammar, Rhetoric, Composition, Literature, Map Drawing, Geography, Commercial Law, Business Forms, Arithmetic, Algebra, Geography, Trigonometry, Physics, Chemistry (Actual Laboratory Work), 3 Volumes Book-Keeping (Actual Business Practice), 1 Volume Phonography, 1 Volume Typewriting, 3 Volumes Penmanship, 1 Volume Pen Drawing, 1 Volume Color Studies, 4 Volumes Freehand Drawing, 1 Volume Landscapes, 17 Large Architectural Drawings (Actual Measurement), 20 Large Crayon Drawings, 6 Water-Colors from Still Life, 5 Crayon Drawings from Cast, 22 Water-Color Studies and 1 Large Drawing (Lavis).

NORMAL WORK.

10 Pen Drawings; "Our Father" and "In Memoriam," Pen Drawings by Members of the Faculty, Photographs of Buildings, Classes, Laboratories, Societies, Sodalities, etc., by Members of the Faculty, a Grand Course of Linear Drawing.

DAYTON, OHIO.—Continued.

Preparatory Normal School.

NORMAL WORK.

62 Specimens of Floral Environs with Description, 70 Specimens of Penmanship, 30 Pen Drawings, 50 Crayon Outlines from Cast, 32 Crayon Drawings from the Flat, 8 Crayon Drawings from the Object, 31 Crayon Drawings from the Cast, 6 Crayons from Relief, 3 Pastel Drawings, 5 Charcoal Drawings, 6 Water Colors from Still Life, 6 Water-Color Studies (Copied), 6 Etchings, 15 Specimens of Automatic Pen-Work, 3 Topographical Maps (Actual Measurement), 27 Mechanical Measurements 4 Architectural Drawings (Actual Measurement), 3 Mechanical Drawings (Lavis), 2 Architectural Drawings Perspective (Actual Measurement), Orders of Architecture Constructed from Scale, 7 Gothic Constructions, 1 Relief Map of St. Mary's Institute Grounds (Actual Surveys).

STUDENTS' WORK.

3 Volumes: Christian Doctrine, 3 Volumes Bible History and Church History, 6 Volumes English and German Compositions, and Commercial Law, 6 Volumes: English and German Dictations, Exercises and Grammar, 1 Volume Rhetoric and Literature, 1 Volume United States, Ancient and Bible History, Medieval History, General Geography, 5 Volumes Book Keeping (Actual Business Practice), 3 Volumes Physics, 1 Volume Chemistry, 9 Volumes Arithmetic, Geography and Geometry, 1 Volume Trigonometry, 1 Volume Surveying and Leveling (Actual Surveys and Measurements), 5 Volumes Freehand Drawing, 6 Volumes Penmanship, 3 Volumes Linear Drawing, Pen Drawing (Original and Copied), 1 Volume Conventional Drawing from Flower Forms in Original Designs, 1 Volume Repertory of Music performed by the Faculty and the Students of the Preparatory Normal School, 1 Volume of Isometrical Drawings and Parallel Perspective, 1 Volume of Angular Perspective, Original Compositions and Melodies written from memory, 1 Volume Sepia Painting, 1 Ecclesiastical Map of the United States, Normal Work by Members of the Faculty, Specimens of Blue Printing.

PARISH SCHOOLS.

CINCINNATI, OHIO.

St. Bonaventura's School.—*Sisters of St. Francis.*

2 Volumes Class-Work.

St. Joseph's School.—*Brothers of Mary.*

1 Volume Christian Doctrine, 5 Volumes: English and German Compositions, Letters, 3 Volumes English and German Dictations, 1 Volume Business Letters, 2 Volumes Class-Work, 1 Volume United States History, Geography, 4 Volumes Freehand Drawing, 1 Volume Linear Drawing, Map Drawing, 30 Specimens of Large Crayon Drawings, 60 Specimens of English and German Penmanship.

St. Mary's School.

10 Volumes: English and German Grammar, Compositions, Letter Writing, Translations, Dictations, Practical Science, Practical Arithmetic, United States History, Mensuration, Intellectual Arithmetic, Geography, Algebra, Penmanship, 4 Volumes Freehand Drawing and 1 Volume Linear Drawing.

DAYTON, OHIO.

St. Francis' School.—*Ursuline Sisters.*

1 Volume: Christian Doctrine, German Exercises, Compositions and Arithmetic.

DAYTON, OHIO.—Continued.

Holy Trinity School.

> 12 Volumes: Grammar, German and English Compositions, Penmanship, Maps, Drawing.

Emmanuel School.—*Brothers of Mary.*

> 1 Volume English and German Compositions and Letter Writing, 3 Volumes Arithmetic and Mensuration, 1 Volume Map Drawing, 2 Volumes Freehand Drawing, 100 specimens of Freehand Drawing, 1 Volume Language, 4 Copy Books specimens of Class-Work, 6 Volumes specimens of Penmanship.

Archdiocese of Dubuque.
See Diocesan Exhibit, Part I.

Archdiocese of Milwaukee.
See Diocesan Exhibit, Part I.

Archdiocese of New Orleans.
See Diocesan Exhibit, Part I.

Archdiocese of New York.
See Diocesan Exhibit, Part I.

Archdiocese of Philadelphia.
See Diocesan Exhibit, Part I.

Archdiocese of San Francisco.
See Diocesan Exhibit, Part I.

ARCHDIOCESE OF ST. LOUIS.
Most Rev. Peter R. Kenrick, D. D.

COLLEGES AND ACADEMIES.

ST. LOUIS, MO.

Christian Brothers' College.—*Christian Brothers.*

Under-Graduate Dept.

> 1 Volume each: Entegral Calculus, Astronomical Geometry, Differential Calculus, Topics, Essays, Criticism, Philosophy of Literature, Political Economy, Rhetoric and 4 Volumes Classics and Philosophy.

ST. LOUIS, MO.—CONTINUED.

Christian Brothers' College.—*Christian Brothers.*

SOPHOMORE CLASS.
2 Volumes: Classics and Mathematics.

SUB-FRESHMAN CLASS.
1 Volume Classics.

FRESHMAN CLASS.
1 Volume each: Classics, Trigonometry, Algebra, Geometry, English Classics, Rhetoric, Christian Doctrine, Compositions and Studies in English.

FIRST ACADEMIC.
1 Volume each: Grammar, Arithmetic, Algebra, Natural Science and Christian Doctrine.

DRAWING CLASS.
44 Charcoal Studies of Head and Figure from cast, 60 Charcoal Ornaments from Cast, 45 Charcoal Studies from Objects, 5 Crayon Drawings, 100 Architectural and Mechanical Drawings, 36 Sketches in Oil and Water Color.

FIRST COMMERCIAL CLASS.
1 Volume Phonography.

SUPERIOR COMMERCIAL CLASS.
9 Volumes Book-Keeping, 2 Volumes each: Correspondence, Arithmetic, Mensuration, Balance Sheets, 1 Album Penmanship, Programmes, Photographs and 1 Set Interior Views of College.

Loretto Academy.—*Sisters of Loretto.*
1 Mater Dolorosa, Executed in Pen-Work by a Sister of Loretto.

St. Elizabeth's Institute.—*Sisters of the Precious Blood.*
3 Volumes: Etiquette, Geography, United States History, Sacred History, English and German Translations, Method of Music, Domestic Economy, Culinary Department, Caligraphy, German Exercises, Arithmetic, Compositions, Epistolary Correspondence (German and English), Book-Keeping, 1 Album Drawing, 1 Antipendium, Art Embroidery, Peacock-Blue Piano Cover, Set for Dresser (5 Small Pieces and Scarf), Piano Cover, Pillow Shams, Table Cover, Table Scarf, Dresser Scarf, Infant's Shirt, Piano-Stool Cover, Linen Apron, Modern Lace, Ladies' Black Silk Mittens, Infant's Jacket, Hood and Socks, Hemstitched Handkerchiefs in Case, 5 Pencil Drawings, Specimens of Pastel and Oil Paintings.

St. Joseph's Academy.—*Sisters of St. Joseph.*
13 Volumes: Church History, Rhetoric, Stenography, Algebra, Latin, Geometry, Geology, Physiology, Geography, Fine Arts, Arithmetic, Christian Doctrine, Grammar, Zoology, Book-Keeping, Mythology, History, Language, Map Drawing, Astronomy, Moral Philosophy, 1 Volume Literature, 4 Mounted Maps, 1 India-Ink Picture, 6 Pieces Illuminated Work, 1 Lace Rochet Alb, Drawn-Thread Table Cloth, 5 Wash-Silk Embroidered Table Scarfs, 12 Doilies, 2 Lace Doilies, 1 Silk Embroidered Handkerchief, 3 Tray Covers, in Wash Silk, 3 Silk Picture Scarfs, 2 Photograph Holders, Embroidered Cushions, 3 Plaques, 1 Tambourine Bolten Cloth, 1 Table Mat, 1 Ciborium Cover, 1 Watch Pocket, 1 Lace Needle Book, 3 Panels in Embroidery, 9 Oil Paintings, Sketch Book, Botanical Book, Album of Flowers from Nature.

Ursuline Academy.—*Ursuline Sisters.*
6 Volumes: Language, Compositions, Grammar, Arithmetic, Orthography, Definitions, History, Familiar Science, Chemistry, Physiology, Natural Philosophy, Ethics, Civil Government, Astronomy, Literature, Mythology, Classical Mythology, Biography and Algebra.

ARCADIA, MO.

Arcadia College.—*Ursuline Sisters.*

4 Volumes: Christian Doctrine, Grammar, Spelling, Geography, United States History, Etiquette, Civil Government, Physical Geography, Arithmetic, Algebra, Literature, Physiology, Rhetoric, Biography, Stenography, Astronomy, Chemistry, Botany, Mythology, Ancient and Modern History, Trigonometry, Logic, Compositions, Music, Essays, Map Drawing, Pen-Work and Colored Drawing.

CAPE GIRARDEAU, MO.

St. Vincent's Academy.—*Sisters of Loretto.*

7 Volumes: Christian Doctrine, Book-Keeping, Geography, Bible History, United States History, Grammar, Philosophy, Astronomy, Chemistry, Botany, Logic, Geology, Literature.

FLORISSANT, MO.

Loretto Academy.—*Sisters of Loretto.*

10 Volumes: Christian Doctrine, Exercises in Teaching, Algebra, Mensuration, Astronomy, Botany, Chemistry, Geology and Rhetoric.

GLENCOE, MO.

Preparatory Normal School.—*Christian Brothers.*

Detailed Plans of the Normal-School Property and Buildings, 4 Specimens Framed Photographs of Building, 1 Album Photographic Views of Grounds, Building, Students; Class-Work of Students as follows: "Life and Voyage of Columbus," Illustrated with Maps, Lecture accompanying Stereopticon Illustrations of United States History and French Exercise Album, Co-Ordination of Reading and Compositions, Language Exercises, 1 Album Grammar, 1 Album Photographs, 1 Album Arithmetic and 1 Album Penmanship.

Preparatory Normal Institute.—*Christian Brothers.*

37 Copy Books Map Drawing, 1 Album Algebra and Plane Geometry, 1 Album Spherical and Solid Geometry, 1 Album Plane Trigonometry, 3 Albums Crayon and Freehand Drawing.

O'FALLON, MO.

St. Mary's Institute.—*Sisters of the Precious Blood.*

1 Volume Sketch of General Method of Teaching and Course of Study; Antipendium—Art Embroidery, Photographs of St. Mary's Institute.

PARISH SCHOOLS.

ST. LOUIS, MO.

Annunciation School.—*Christian Brothers.*

6 Volumes: Spelling, Penmanship, History, Mensuration, Compositions and Christian Doctrine.

Holy Trinity School.—*Sisters of St. Francis.*

2 Volumes Drawing.

ST. LOUIS, MO.—Continued.

Holy Name School.—*Sisters of St. Joseph.*
 3 Volumes: Christian Doctrine, Arithmetic, Language, Geography, Mental Arithmetic, United States History, Practical Arithmetic, Orthography, Essays and Letter Writing.

St. Agatha's School.—*Sisters of the Precious Blood.*
 Christian Doctrine (German), Church History (German), Grammar, Exercises in German, German Compositions, Orthography, Arithmetic, Penmanship; 4 Volumes Kindergarten Work: Intertwining, Embroidery, Drawing, Perforating and Cutting; Photographs of School and Pupils.

St. Aloysius' School.—*Secular Teachers.*
 10 Volumes: Language, Arithmetic, Christian Doctrine, Geography, United States History, Bible History, Spelling, Physiology, Drawing and Writing.

St. Alphonsus' School.—*School Sisters of Notre Dame.*
 12 Volumes: Christian Doctrine, Drawing, Penmanship, Arithmetic, United States History, Spelling, Grammar, Book-Keeping, Physiology, Hygiene, Science, Civil Government, Algebra, Rules of Etiquette and Physiology.

St. Anthony's School.—*Secular Teachers.*
 1 Volume: Penmanship, Geography, Language, Arithmetic, United States History, Bible History, Spelling, Physiology, Drawing.

St. Augustine's School.—*Sisters of the Precious Blood.*
 Arithmetic, Grammar, English and German Penmanship, Orthography.

St. Bridget's School.
 COMMERCIAL CLASS:
 St. Bridget's Book of Records, 2 Volumes each: Practical Book-Keeping, Compositions, Catechism, Bible History, Mathematics, Language Lessons, Geography, History, Notes and Telegrams, Examination Papers, Typewriting and Shorthand, Penmanship and Letters. 1 Volume Maps and 5 Volumes Mensuration.
 FIRST CLASS.
 1 Volume Penmanship, 4 Volumes: Letters, Grammar, Catechism and Arithmetic.
 SECOND CLASS.
 2 Volumes each: Catechism, Grammar, Geography, Arithmetic and Penmanship.
 THIRD CLASS.
 3 Volumes Miscellaneous Exercises and 1 Volume Arithmetic.

St. John's School.—*Sisters of St. Joseph.*
 1 Volume: Catechism, Notes, Algebra, Dictation, History, Letter Writing, Grammar, Essays, Spelling, Literature, Philosophy, Physiology, Geography, Arithmetic and Civil Government; Vestments used at Mass.

St. Kevin's School.—*Sisters of Loretto.*
 3 Volumes: Christian Doctrine, Bible History, Grammar, Arithmetic, Algebra, Geography, Physical Geography, United States History and General History.

St. Lawrence O'Tool School.—*Sisters of St. Joseph.*
 3 Volumes: Christian Doctrine, Bible History, Drawing, Spelling, Grammar, Essays, Arithmetic and United States History.

St. Lawrence's School.—*Christian Brothers.*
 1 Volume each: Grammar, Christian Doctrine, Bible History, Algebra, Book-Keeping, Mensuration, Penmanship, History, Geography, Dictations; 2 Volumes each: Arithmetic (First Class) and Arithmetic (Second Class).

ST. LOUIS, MO.—Continued.

St. Michael's School.—*Sisters of Loretto.*
3 Volumes: Christian Doctrine, Bible History, United States History, Grammar, Geography, Philosophy, Book-Keeping, Arithmetic, Orthography and Drawing.

St. Malachy's School.—*Christian Brothers.*
9 Volumes: Book-Keeping, Penmanship, Catechism, Geography, Grammar, History, Arithmetic, Business Forms, Mensuration, Algebra, Stenography, Typewriting, Orthography, Freehand and Map Drawing.

St. Patrick's School.—*Sisters of St. Joseph.*
3 Volumes: Geography, Grammar, Book-Keeping, Christian Doctrine, Spelling, Definitions, United States History, Physical Geography, Physiology and German Exercises.

St. Vincent's School.—*Christian Brothers.*
16 Volumes: Christian Doctrine, Penmanship, Mensuration, Grammar, Arithmetic, Typewriting, Phonography and Algebra.

Ursuline Day School.—*Ursuline Sisters.*
4 Volumes: Compositions, Grammar, Christian Doctrine, Arithmetic, Rhetoric, Etymology, United States History, Civil Government, Logic, Ancient and Modern History, Mythology, Physiology, Chemistry, Literature, Botany, Physics, Astronomy, Mathematics; 4 Paintings, 1 Ciborium Cover, 1 Missal Cover, 1 Stand Cover, 2 Embroidered Handkerchiefs and 1 Cravat Case.

FLORISSANT, MO.

Sacred Heart School.—*Sisters of the Precious Blood.*
Christian Doctrine, Grammar, Geography, Orthography, German Compositions, History, Arithmetic, German and English Penmanship.

JOSEPHVILLE, MO.

St. Joseph's School.—*Sisters of Precious Blood.*
Grammar, English and German Penmanship.

OLD MONROE, MO.

Immaculate Conception School.—*Sisters of the Precious Blood.*
Christian Doctrine, Penmanship (German and English).

RIVIERE AUX VASES, MO.

Sts. Philip and James' School.—*Sisters of Precious Blood.*
Grammar, Arithmetic, German and English Penmanship.

ST. CHARLES, MO.

St. Peter's School.—*School Sisters of Notre Dame.*
1 Volume: Arithmetic, Penmanship, Language, German, Geography, Dictation and History.

ST. PETER, MO.

All Saints' School.—*Sisters of the Precious Blood.*
Christian Doctrine, Grammar, Arithmetic, German, Letter Writing, History, Physiology and German and English Penmanship.

TIPTON, MO.

St. Andrew's School.—*Sisters of the Precious Blood.*
English and German Penmanship, English and German Translations and Arithmetic.

ZELL, MO.

St. Joseph's School.—*Sisters of the Precious Blood.*

English and German Grammar, English and German Penmanship and Orthography.

SPECIAL SCHOOL.

ST. LOUIS, MO.

Mariæ Consilia Deaf-Mute School.—*Sisters of St. Joseph.*

1 Volume: Language, Catechism. History, Arithmetic and Geography.

ARCHDIOCESE OF SANTA FE.

MOST. REV. JOHN B. SALTPOINTE, D.D.

ACADEMIES.

SANTA FE, NEW MEX.

Academy of Our Lady of Light.—*Sisters of Loretto.*

5 Volumes: Christian Doctrine, Book-Keeping, Arithmetic, Geography, Grammar, United States History, Orthography, Botany, Physical Geography, Physical Culture, Algebra, Chemistry, Compositions, General History, Literature, Penmanship, Natural Philosophy, Physiology, Phonography, English and Spanish Translations.

LAS VEGAS, NEW MEX.

Immaculate Conception Academy.—*Sisters of Loretto.*

2 Volumes: Christian Doctrine, Arithmetic, Algebra, Astronomy, Botany, Chemistry, Geology, Geometry, Grammar, Geography, Bible, Natural, United States and Ancient History; Mental, Moral and Natural Philosophy; Physiology, Phonography, Rhetoric, Orthography, Translations (Spanish and Latin), Arithmetic.

MORA, NEW MEX.

Academy of the Annunciation.—*Sisters of Loretto.*

2 Volumes: Christian Doctrine, Arithmetic, Geography, United States History, Orthography, Translations of English and Spanish.

SOCORRO, NEW MEX.

Academy of Our Lady of Mt. Carmel.—*Sisters of Loretto.*

6 Volumes: Christian Doctrine, Spelling, Geography, Arithmetic, History, Compositions, Essays, Penmanship, Physiology and Music.

TAOS, NEW MEX.

Public School.—*Sisters of Loretto.*

1 Crochet Shawl; 1 Knitted Banner; 1 Crochet Thread Tidy; 1 Card Crochet Specimens of Silk Lace; 1 Crochet Necktie; 1 Pair Fancy Knitted Silk Mittens; 1 Piano Solo, "I Stand On Memory's Golden Shore."

PARISH SCHOOLS.

BERNALILLO, NEW MEX.

Sacred Heart School.—*Sisters of Loretto.*

1 Volume: Photographs, Spelling, Arithmetic, Grammar, History and Translations.

INDUSTRIAL SCHOOL,

BERNALILLO, NEW MEX.

Sacred Heart Industrial Indian School.—*Sisters of Loretto.*

1 Volume: Photographs, Christian Doctrine, Grammar, Geography, United States History, Hygiene.

ARCHDIOCESE OF ST. PAUL.

MOST REV. JOHN IRELAND, D. D.

ACADEMIES.

ST. PAUL, MINN.

Cretin High School.—*Christian Brothers.*

28 Volumes: Phonography, Typewriting, Penmanship, Geography, Arithmetic, History, Mensuration, Miscellaneous Work, Language, Examination Papers, Book-Keeping, General History, Maps, Description of St. Paul, Christian Doctrine and Rules of Exchange.

FARIBAULT, MINN.

Bethlehem Academy.—*Dominican Sisters.*

1 Volume: Catechism, United States History, Algebra, Compositions, Book Keeping, Irish History, Literature and English History.

FRONTENAC, MINN.

Villa Maria Academy.—*Ursuline Sisters.*

1 Volume Printed Periodical; Photographs and Botanical Specimens.

PARISH SCHOOLS.

MINNEAPOLIS, MINN.

Holy Rosary School.—*Dominican Sisters.*

4 Volumes Examination Papers: Arithmetic, Christian Doctrine, Language, Geography, Reading, Grammar, Maps, United States History, Physiology, Algebra, Literature, Book-Keeping, Latin, Orthography, Modern History, Rhetoric and Geometry.

ST. PAUL, MINN.

Assumption School.—*School Sisters of Notre Dame.*
2 Volumes Freehand Drawing.

DIOCESE OF ALBANY.

RT. REV. FRANCIS McNEIRNY, D. D.

ACADEMIES.

ALBANY, N. Y.

Christian Brothers' Academy.—*Christian Brothers.*

4 Volumes Linear Drawing, 1 Volume Ornamental Drawing, 1 Volume Photographs of Cadet Battalion, 2 Volumes Typewriting and Phonography, 4 Volumes Phonography, 1 Volume English Compositions, 1 Volume Latin and English, 1 Volume Mathematics, 1 Volume Trigonometry, 1 Volume Practical Exercises, 1 Volume German Penmanship, 7 Volumes Penmanship, 2 Volumes Language Exercises, 3 Volumes Examination Papers, 5 Volumes Home Exercises, 4 Volumes Kindergarten Work and Specimen of Modeling in Clay (Kindergarten).

TROY, N. Y.

De La Salle Institute.—*Christian Brothers.*

8 Volumes Book-Keeping, 3 Volumes and 13 Copy Books English Grammar, 4 Volumes and 104 Copy Books Phonography, 8 Volumes and 34 Copy Books Arithmetic, 2 Volumes Geography, 2 Volumes and 4 Copy Books Trigonometry and Surveying, 7 Volumes and 18 Copy Books Algebra, 2 Volumes Geometry and Mensuration, 2 Volumes Mensuration, 2 Volumes Examination Papers, 8 Volumes Compositions, 1 Volume Physics and Chemistry, 1 Volume and 5 Copy Books Rhetoric, 14 Copy Books German, 1 Volume Physiology, 3 Volumes Essays, 5 Volumes Penmanship, 18 Copy Books Commercial Law, 2 Copy Books Macaulay's Essays on Dryden (Phonography), 12 Copy Books Notes on Balmes' Criterion, 5 Copy Books Notes on Hamlet, 1 Copy Book Civil Government (Phonography), 2 Albums Contrast Pages Writing, 16 Volumes Linear and Freehand Drawing, 19 Framed Drawings, 50 Large Drawings (Mechanical, Freehand, Architectural, Ornamental and Figures), 1 Album Business Forms and Photographs.

N. B. This institution has a display with the New York State Exhibit.

PARISH SCHOOLS.

ALBANY, N. Y.

Cathedral School.—*Christian Brothers.*

2 Volumes Book-Keeping, 4 Volumes Penmanship, 1 Volume Examination Papers, 4 Volumes Home Exercises, Portfolio of Crayon, Linear and Water-Color Drawings, Portfolio of Charts, Phonography and Ecce Homo (Crayon).

St. John's School.—*Christian Brothers.*

2 Volumes Class Work.

ORPHANAGE.

TROY, N. Y.

Catholic Male Orphan Asylum.—*Christian Brothers.*

16 Volumes: Drawing, Contrast Writing, Dictation, Map Modeling, Freehand Drawing, Catechism, Map Drawing and 1 Volume of Photographs.

DIOCESE OF ALTON.

RT. REV. JAMES RYAN, D.D.

PARISH SCHOOLS.

ALTON, ILL.

St. Patrick's School.—*Ursuline Sisters.*

1 Volume: Catechism, Arithmetic, Compositions, Map Drawing, Geography, United States History, Grammar, Language, Spelling and Penmanship.

QUINCY, ILL.

St. Mary's Institute.—*School Sisters of Notre Dame.*

11 Volumes: Mathematics, Astronomy, Chemistry, Literature, Mythology, Civil Government, Physics, Geometry, Algebra, Physiology, Geology, Rhetoric, Compositions, Geography, Language, Orthography, Phonography; United States, Bible and Ancient History; Catechism, 1 Volume Herbarium, 2 Volumes Arithmetic, 2 Volumes Music, 1 Volume German, 4 Scrap Books, 18 Photographs, 4 Specimens Natural History, 1 Embroidered Altar-Piece, 1 Embroidered Center-Piece, 1 Embroidered Tray Cloth, ½ Dozen Embroidered Doilies.

HIGHLAND, ILL.

St. Paul's School.—*School Sisters of Notre Dame.*

1 Volume: Penmanship, Language, Arithmetic, Geography, Compositions, United States History, Spelling, Catechism and Bible History.

QUINCY, ILL.

St. Boniface's School.—*School Sisters of Notre Dame.*

2 Volumes: Penmanship, Language, Compositions, Arithmetic, Geography, Christian Doctrine, United States History, Spelling, Translations and Catechism.

St. Francis' School.—*School Sisters of Notre Dame.*

1 Volume: Penmanship, Arithmetic, United States History, Geography, Translations and Catechism.

DIOCESE OF BELLEVILLE.
RT. REV. JOHN JANSSEN, D.D.

BELLEVILLE, ILL.

St. Luke's School.—*School Sisters of Notre Dame.*

1 Volume: Christian Doctrine, Penmanship, Language, Arithmetic, Geography, United States History, Physiology, Book-Keeping, 2 Volumes Drawing.

St. Peter's School.—*School Sisters of Notre Dame.*

1 Volume Drawing. 1 Volume: Penmanship, Arithmetic, Language, Geography, United States History, Spelling, Grammar, Compositions, Christian Doctrine, German, Drawing.

CAHOKIA, ILL.

Old Church Bell, cast in 1776, 14 inches high and 44 inches in circumference; gift of the King of France, and first bell used West of the Alleghany Mountains.

Diocese of Brooklyn.
See Diocesan Exhibit, Part I.

Diocese of Buffalo.
See Diocesan Exhibit, Part I.

DIOCESE OF BURLINGTON.
RT. REV. LOUIS DE GOESBRIAND, D.D.

BURLINGTON, VT.

St. Joseph's Academy.—*Christian Brothers.*

11 Albums Examination Papers: Penmanship, Arithmetic, Dictation, Spelling, Grammar, Letter Writing, Composition, Christian Doctrine, Commercial Law, 72 Copy Books Miscellaneous Subjects, 1 Album Monthly Bulletins, 1 Album Drawing and 23 Copy Books of Penmanship.

Diocese of Cleveland.
See Diocesan Exhibit, Part I.

DIOCESE OF COLUMBUS.

RT. REV. JOHN AMBROSE WATTERSON, D. D.

COLLEGE AND ACADEMY.

COLUMBUS, OHIO.

Papal Josephinum College.—Rev. JOSEPH JESSING, *President.*

This college is the property of the Propaganda at Rome, and includes an Ecclesiastical Seminary, a Classical and Scientific School, preparatory for the Seminary, and a School for Orphans, with an Industrial Department for Wood-Carving, Statuary, etc.

ALCOVES 60, 62 AND 64.

Bound Volumes of the "Ohio Waisenfreund," edited and printed at the College.

Map of the World from the first half of the 16th Century, by Sebastian Munster, Born 1489. Map of North and South America, from the middle of the 17th Century, by the Dutch writer, O. Dapper. Map of North America, from the 17th Century, with the following titles: "Amerique Septentrionalis. Carte d' un tres grand pays entre le noveau Mexique at la Mer Glaciale dediće à Guillaume, III. Roy de la Grande Bretagne, Par le R. P. Louis de Hennepin, Mission Recol. et Not. Apost. Chez. A. V. Someren à Amsterdam, 1698." This is the first Map on which the Mississippi River and the Great Lakes are represented. Map of the territory lying between the Atlantic and the Mississippi, from the 17th Century, sketched by Father Hennepin and engraved by A. V. Someren. Map of the Hemispheres, from the middle of the 18th Century, drawn in 1744, by Joseph Antone Ferrari, of Milan, in the City of Venice. Framed photographs and pictures. Noteworthy old books: "St. Antoninus, Summa Theologica," printed by Nicholaus Jensen in 1479. St. Anthony, the author, born in the year 1389, Archbishop of Florence from 1446 to 1459, in which year he died. "Platina, De Vitis Pontificum Romanorum," Latin History of the Pontiffs, from St. Peter to Paul II., 1464 to 1474; the author, Bartholomew Platina, was born in 1421 and died in 1481, as librarian of the Vatican in Rome—by Anthony Koburger, Nurenberg, 1431. "Quadragesimale Discipuli," a book of Latin Lenten Sermons, printed by John Otman in Reutligen, in 1489.

"Exercitum Grammaticale Puerorum," printed in Germany in 1504. The book is printed in Gothic Characters, the explanatory text being mostly in Latin throughout the book.

"Cursus Librorum Philosophiæ Naturalis." This book was written by the Franciscan Monk, Nicolaus de Orbelli, who lived in the 15th Century. Latin and printed in Gothic characters at Basil in 1503. "Disputatio Excellentium Doctrum Johannis Eccii et Andreæ Carolastadii et Dr. Johannis Eccii et D. Martini Lutheri, Augustiani, quæ cepit IIII. Julii 1519.— In 1519 several debates were held at Leipsig, Dr. Eck being on one side and Dr. Carlstadt and Dr. Martin Luther on the other. The principal disputation was on the Primacy of the Roman Pontiff. The debate began on June 27, 1519, between Eck and Carlstadt, and was continued from July 4th to July 14th, between Eck and Luther. The book on exhibition is the original record of this discussion, which was taken down in shorthand during the course of the dispute, and printed immediately afterward at Leipsig.

COLUMBUS, OHIO.—Continued.

Papal Josephinum College.—Rev. Joseph Jessing, *President.*

"Canones Apostolorum," Veterum Conciliorum Constitutiones, Decreta Pontificum Antquiora, De Primatu Romane Ecclesiæ-Apostolic Canons, Constitutions of the old councils, Decrees of the earlier Popes, about the Primacy of the Roman Church. This book was printed at Munich in 1525.

"Chronicle of the Old Christian Churches," from Eusebius, Ruffinus, etc. This book was printed at Strasburg by George Ulrich of Andla in 1530. It is a church history of the first centuries, and probably the first and oldest church history printed in the German language.

"Altercatio Synagogue et Ecclesiæ" in Latin and was printed at Cologne by Melchor Novesianus, 1537.

Photographs of the Rector, Rev. Jos. Jessing, professors, students, choir, drum corps, orphans and shops in the industrial printing and household departments of Josephinum College.

Books printed at Josephinum College.

Illustrated catalogue of ecclesiastical works of art, such as statues, altars, etc., made in art department of Josephinum College.

4 catalogues of Josephinum College, for years 1889, 1890, 1891, 1892.

Group—"Thou Art Peter." True imitation on a reduced scale of a life-size group, carved at Josephinum College.

"The High Altar," built in strictly Gothic style, of the best American oak, with red and white mahogany. Height of altar, 28 feet, length of altar table, 9 feet. Carved and built at the Industrial School of Josephinum College.

56 examination copies containing exercises in Latin, Greek, German and English, Universal History, United States History, Geography, Arithmetic and Natural Science.

41 Albums containing written exercises from pupils of the Sexta: Catechism in English, Latin and German and translations; German composition, Universal History, United States History, Geography, and Gabelsberger's Stenography in English and German.

Albums containing exercises of the pupils of the Quinta: Doctrina Christiana in English, Latin and German languages and translations, Universal History, United States History, Geography, Arithmetic, Zoology and Gabelsberger's Stenography.

Exercises from the pupils of the Quarta: Doctrina Christiana in the Latin, English and German languages. Latin, English and German translations; general Composition, German Literature, Universal History, United States History, Geometry, Physics, and Gabelsberger's Stenography in the Latin and German Languages, and business and reporter's style in the English language.

Exercises from the students of the Secunda: Doctrina Christiana in the English and German languages; Logica Scholastica: The figures of the Syllogism; Translations in Latin, Greek, German and English languages. German Literature, Algebra, Physics and Stenography.

Photograph of the Columbus statue erected October 12th, 1892, on the 400th Anniversary of the Discovery of America. Statue stands in the yard of Josephinum College. Designed by Alphons Pelzer, and executed in sheet copper by W. H. Mullins, of Salem, Ohio. The statue stands 9 feet high.

NEW LEXINGTON, OHIO.

St. Aloysius' Academy.—*Sisters of St. Francis.*

3 Volumes Examination Papers: Grammar, Compositions, Algebra, Astronomy, Book-Keeping, Arithmetic, History, Physical Geography, Drawing, 1 Landscape (water color), 1 Cross painted and embroidered on cloth, 1 Picture Flowers on Silk, Sewing.

PARISH SCHOOL.

COLUMBUS, OHIO.

Holy Cross School.—*Brothers of Mary.*

2 Volumes Language Exercises and Grammar, 1 Volume Orthography, 1 Volume Geography, 2 Volumes United States History, 2 Volumes Maps, 5 Volumes Freehand Drawing and Christian Doctrine, 1 Volume Autobiographies of Pupils.

Diocese of Covington.

See Diocesan Exhibit, Part I.

DIOCESE OF DALLAS.

RT. REV. EDWARD FITZGERALD D. D., ADMINISTRATOR.

CLARKSVILLE, TEXAS.

St. Joseph's Convent.—*Sisters of Divine Providence.*

1 Painted Scarf, 1 Celluloid painted handkerchief Case, 1 Celluloid Banner, "Hail Columbia," and 7 Books of Essays and Mathematics.

JEFFERSON, TEXAS.

St. Mary's Convent.—*Sisters of Divine Providence.*

1 Key Holder, Embroidered Violin, 1 Knit Cape, 2 Books of Essays and 6 Books of Drawing.

DIOCESE OF DAVENPORT.

RT. REV. HENRY COSGROVE, D.D.

ACADEMY.

COUNCIL BLUFFS, IOWA.

St. Francis' Academy.—*Sisters of Charity, B. V. M.*

1 Pastel Crayon: Angelic Tribute to St. Cecelia, 1 Original crayon portrait of Young Girl and 1 Landscape in water colors.

PARISH SCHOOLS.

FT. MADISON, IOWA.

St. Mary's School.—*Sisters of St. Francis of P. A.*

1 Volume: Bible History, Penmanship, Language, Arithmetic, Geography, United States History, Catechism, German and 1 Center-Piece.

WEST POINT, IOWA.

St. Mary's School.—*Sisters of St. Francis of P. A.*
2 Volumes: Christian Doctrine, Bible History, Orthography, Arithmetic, Language Lessons, Grammar, Geography, United States History, Letter Writing, Penmanship and English and German Translations.

Diocese of Denver.
See Diocesan Exhibit, Part I.

Diocese of Detroit.
See Diocesan Exhibit, Part I.

Diocese of Fort Wayne.
See Diocesan Exhibit, Part I.

DIOCESE OF GALVESTON.
RT. REV. N. A. GALLAGHER, D. D.

ACADEMIES.

PALESTINE, TEXAS.
St. Mary's Convent.—*Sisters of Divine Providence.*
1 Painted Plush Scarf, 1 Page Fancy Work in Album and 5 Books of Essays.

TEMPLE, TEXAS.
St. Mary's Institute.—*Sisters of Divine Providence.*
1 Book of Essays and 1 Book Map Drawing.

PARISH SCHOOLS.

BERWARDO PRAIRIE, TEXAS.
Parochial School.—*Sisters of Divine Providence.*
1 Page Fancy Work in Album.

ELLINGER, TEXAS.
St. Mary's School.—*Sisters of Divine Providence.*
1 Page Fancy Work in Album.

FREIBURG, TEXAS.

St. John's School.—*Sisters of Divine Providence.*
3 Books of Essays and 2 Books Map Drawing.

GALVESTON, TEXAS.

St. Joseph's School.—*Sisters of Divine Providence.*
1 Page Fancy Work in Album, 4 Books of Essays and 2 Books of Map Drawing.

MENTZ, TEXAS.

St. Roches' School.—*Sisters of Divine Providence.*
Specimens of Fancy Work.

DIOCESE OF GRAND RAPIDS.
RT. REV. HENRY JOSEPH RICHTER, D. D.

PARISH SCHOOLS.

GRAND RAPIDS, MICH.

St. Alphonsus' School.

2 Volumes: Penmanship, Catechism, Literature, Geometry, Physics, Geology, Commercial Law, Music, Essays, Book-Keeping.

St. James' School.—*School Sisters of Notre Dame.*

2 Volumes: Christian Doctrine, Penmanship, Arithmetic, Drawing, Language, Geography, Compositions, Dictations, Bible History, Grammar, Physiology, United States History, Algebra, Book-Keeping, Civil Government, Rhetoric and 1 Volume Drawing.

St. Mary's School.

1 Volume: Penmanship, Language Arithmetic, Geography, United States History, Compositions, German Translations and Drawing.

MT. PLEASANT, MICH.

Sacred Heart School.

1 Volume: Geometry, Geology, Literature, Physiology, Arithmetic, Geography, United States History, Grammar, Compositions, Catechism, Spelling, Language and Numbers.

SAGINAW, MICH.

St. Andrew's School.—*Sisters of Providence.*

4 Volumes: Christian Doctrine, Geography, Bible History, Penmanship, Orthography, United States History, Church History, Algebra, Logic, General History, Questions on Natural Science and Compositions.

EAST SAGINAW, MICH.

St. Mary's School.—*Sisters of Providence.*

4 Volumes: Christian Doctrine, Arithmetic, Geography, United States History, Penmanship, Algebra, Geometry, Physics, Botany, Compositions and Music.

TRAVERSE CITY, MICH.

St. Francis' School.

1 Volume School-Work, Grades 2 to 10 with Photographs and Illustrations.

INDUSTRIAL SCHOOL.

HARBOR SPRINGS, MICH.

Indian Industrial School.

1 Volume: Penmanship, Arithmetic Language, Compositions, Bible History, Christian Doctrine, 1 Volume specimens of Needle-Work, 1 Volume Freehand Drawing, 1 Suit Boy's Clothes, 1 Child's Flannel Skirt, 3 Muslin Undergarments, 1 Woolen Comforter, 1 Cassimere Dress, 3 Pairs Knitted Hose, 1 Challis Dress, 1 Crochet Hand-Bag, 2 Embroidered Panels and 1 Knitted Bed-Spread.

Diocese of Green Bay.

See Diocesan Exhibit, Part I.

DIOCESE OF HARRISBURG.

RT. REV. THOMAS MCGOVERN, D.D.

SHAMOKIN, PA.

St. Stanislaus' School.—*Felician Sisters.*

1 Framed Picture, 1 Framed Motto, 1 Crochet Curtain, 1 Embroidered Scarf and 1 Silk Spider-Web.

DIOCESE OF HELENA.

RT. REV. JOHN B. BRONDAL, D.D.

HELENA, MONT.

St. Peter's School.—*Ursuline Sisters.*

3 Carved Cases, 8 Framed Crayon Pictures, 4 Oil Paintings, 1 Blanket and 1 Case Needle-Work.

DIOCESE OF JAMESTOWN.

RT. REV. JOHN SHANLEY, D.D.

GRAND FORKS, S. D.

St. Bernard's Ursuline Convent.—*Ursuline Sisters.*

4 Volumes: Diacritical Marking, Grammar, Rhetoric, Latin, German and French Exercises, Ancient and Modern History, Christian Doctrine, Algebra, Chemistry, Astronomy, Geology, Book-Keeping, Stenography, Typewriting, 2 Albums Photographs and Music.

DIOCESE OF KANSAS CITY.

Rt. Rev. John Joseph Hogan, D.D.

ACADEMIES.

KANSAS CITY, MO.

Sacred Heart Academy.—*Sisters of Providence.*

2 Volumes: Christian Doctrine, Music, Arithmetic, Geograpny, History, Orthography and Grammar.

St. Teresa's Academy.—*Sisters of St. Joseph.*

3 Volumes: Christian Doctrine, Geometry, Logic, Botany, Book-Keeping, Chemistry, Geology, Physiology, Original Drafts of Quarterly Examinations.

PARISH SCHOOLS.

KANSAS CITY, MO.

Annunciation School.—*Sisters of Charity, B. V. M.*

1 Volume: Maps, Sketches, Mensuration, Arithmetic and Diagraming Sentences.

St. Joseph's Cathedral.—*Christian Brothers.*

2 Volumes: Christian Doctrine, Bible History, 5 Volumes Book-Keeping, 4 Volumes Penmanship, 1 Volume Grammar, 1 Volume each: Commercial Law, Compositions, Mensuration, Algebra, Map Drawing, United States History and Mathematics.

St. Patrick's School.—*Sisters of Loretto.*

4 Volumes: Christian Doctrine, Arithmetic, Grammar, United States History, Geography, Letter Writing, Compositions, General History, Physics, Geology, Physiology, Astronomy, Specimens of Penmanship and Business Forms.

SEDALIA, MO.

St. Vincent's School.—*Sisters of Divine Providence.*

2 Books Essays.

Diocese of La Crosse.

See Diocesan Exhibit, Part I.

DIOCESE OF LINCOLN.

Rt. Rev. Thomas Bonacum, D.D.

FALLS CITY, NEB.

St. Francis' School.—*Sisters of Providence.*

Specimens Arithmetic, Algebra, Grammar, History and Physiology.

DIOCESE OF LITTLE ROCK.
RT. REV. EDWARD FITZGERALD, D. D.

ACADEMIES.

PINE BLUFF, ARK.

Annunciation Academy.—*Sisters of Charity of Nazareth.*

1 Volume Freehand and Map Drawing, 5 Albums Specimens of Botany, 1 Volume Book-Keeping, 8 Volumes Christian Doctrine, 1 Volume: Essays, Orthography, Grammar, United States History, Geography, Modern and Ancient History, Arithmetic, Algebra, Book-Keeping, Typewriting, Stenography, Natural Philosophy, Geology, Chemistry, Mythology, Botany, Rhetoric, Logic, Astronomy; 22 Plain Drawings, 3 Crayons, 17 Oil Paintings, 1 Polish Painting, 3 Crystal Pearl Paintings, 1 Pastel, 39 Specimens of Embroidery, 1 Chart of Pine Bluff and Environs and 1 Catalogue of Academy.

INDUSTRIAL SCHOOL.

PINE BLUFF, ARK.

Colored Industrial School.—*Sisters of Charity of Nazareth.*

2 Volumes Arithmetic, 2 Volumes Geography, 2 Volumes Orthography, 1 Volume Map Drawing. 2 Volumes United States History, Grammar; Plain Sewing, Popular Science, Dressmaking, Specimens of Cotton and Cotton Bales.

DIOCESE OF LOUISVILLE.
RT. REV. WILLIAM GEORGE MCCLOSKEY, D. D.

ACADEMIES.

LOUISVILLE, KY.

St. Benedict's Academy.—*Sisters of Loretto.*

4 Volumes: Arithmetic, Catechism, Grammar, Geography, United States History, Map Drawing, Physiology, Natural History, Compositions, General History, Phonography, Zoology, Rhetoric, Book-Keeping, Bible History, Algebra and Botany.

ELIZABETHTOWN, KY.

St. Mary's Academy.

1 Blue Silk Dress, Point-Lace Trimming, 1 Point-Lace Fichu.

ST. JOHN'S, KY.

Bethlehem Academy.—*Sisters of Loretto.*

1 Volume: Compositions, Arithmetic, Algebra, Grammar, Botany, Astronomy, Physiology and 1 Table Scarf.

LEBANON, KY.

St. Augustine's Academy.—*Sisters of Loretto.*

1 Volume: Christian Doctrine, United States History, Ancient History, Arithmetic, Grammar and Geography.

PARISH SCHOOL.

LOUISVILLE, KY.

St. Boniface's School.—*School Sisters of Notre Dame.*

1 Volume: Penmanship, Language, Arithmetic, Geography, United States History, Catechism, Spelling, Compositions, Grammar and German.

Diocese of Manchester.

See Diocesan Exhibit, Part I.

DIOCESE OF MARQUETTE.

RT. REV. JOHN VERTIN, D.D.

PARISH SCHOOL.

ESCANABA, MICH.

St. Joseph's School.—*School Sisters of Notre Dame.*

2 Volumes: Arithmetic, Penmanship, Catechism, Language, Spelling, United States History, Grammar, Bible History, Compositions, Physiology, Church History, Algebra, Rhetoric, American Literature, General History and Civil Government.

DIOCESE OF MOBILE.

RT. REV. JEREMIAH O'SULLIVAN, D.D.

ACADEMIES.

MOBILE, ALA.

Academy of the Visitation.—*Sisters of the Visitation.*

2 Volumes: Christian Doctrine, Sacred History, Arithmetic, Algebra, Geometry; 1 Volume United States History, Freehand Drawing, 1 Album Theory of Music, Water-Color Crayon, Pastel Paintings, Photographs and Penmanship.

St. Vincent's Academy.—*Brothers of the Sacred Heart.*

1 Framed specimen of Writing, 1 Framed Photograph and Drawing.

BIRMINGHAM, ALA.

Holy Angels' Academy.—*Benedictine Sisters.*

3 Volumes: Christian Doctrine, Church History, Penmanship, Compositions, History, Arithmetic, Grammar, Business Forms, Chemistry, Astronomy, Dictation, Music, Language, United States History, Geography and Map Drawing.

St. Paul's School.—*Benedictine Sisters.*

1 Volume: Sacred History, Compositions, Astronomy, Dictations, Letters, Geography, Arithmetic, Language and Spelling.

MONTGOMERY, ALA.

Academy of St. Mary.—*Sisters of Loretto.*

6 Volumes: Christian Doctrine, Spelling, Arithmetic, Algebra, Book-Keeping, Rhetoric, Grammar, Science, Compositions, Astronomy, Literature, Music, Drawing, Geography, United States History, Physiology, Botany and Sketches.

FANCY WORK.

1 Landscape in Oil; 2 Sets of Scarfs stitched in Silk; 1 Pair Pillow Shams of net-work done on linen; 2 Crochet Dresses, silk trimmings; 1 Shawl Crochet in ice wool; 1 White Zephyr Crochet Fascinator, edged with silk Floss; 1 Pink Head-Dress worked in Zephyr, silk trimmings; 1 Tapestried Sampler; 1 Head-Rest of Plush, silk embroidery; 1 Cape Crochet in Zephyr, silk trimmings; 2 Plain Baby Socks of Crochet Work; 1 Pair Crochet Mittens; 1 Plush Piano Cover; 1 Dress Shirt; 1 Dresser Scarf; 1 Oil Painting, life size, of Rt. Rev. B. J. Flaget, First Bishop of Kentucky; 1 Chocolate Set of hand-painted China.

PARISH SCHOOLS.

MOBILE, ALA.

Cathedral School.—*Brothers of the Sacred Heart.*

2 Volumes: Penmanship, Compositions, Arithmetic, Book-Keeping and Photographs.

St. Vincent's School.

5 Albums: Map Drawing, Book-Keeping, Literature, Penmanship, Arithmetic, Letter Writing, Grammar and Miscellaneous Studies.

DIOCESE OF MONTEREY AND LOS ANGELES.

RT. REV. FRANCIS MORA, D. D.

ACADEMY.

LOS ANGELES, CAL.

St. Mary's Academy.—*Sisters of St. Joseph.*

5 Mounted Maps.

DIOCESE OF NASHVILLE.

VERY REV. P. J. GLEESON, V. G.

COLLEGE AND ACADEMY.

MEMPHIS, TENN.

Christian Brothers' College.—*Christian Brothers.*

SENIOR CLASS.

12 Volumes: Latin, Greek, Chemistry, Astronomy, Logic, Algebra, Analytical Geometry, Calculus, English Literature, Examination Papers (in Surveying and Navigation), Political Economy, Evidences of Religion, Church History, Compositions and Poems (from Memory), Readings, Papers on Macbeth, Questions on Reading, Illustrated Work on the Natural Sciences and Book-Keeping.

JUNIOR CLASS.

12 Volumes: Trigonometry Surveying, Algebra, Compositions, Chemistry, Natural Philosophy, Rhetoric, Latin, Greek, Plane and Spherical Trigonometry, English Literature, Examination Papers on Christian Doctrine, Rhetoric, Geometry, Trigonometry, Weekly Readings and Examinations and Answers to Questions in Literary Reading.

SOPHOMORE CLASS.

5 Volumes: Examinations in Christian Doctrine, Algebra, Geometry, Trigonometry, Natural Philosophy, Rhetoric, History, Book-Keeping and Modern History.

FRESHMAN CLASS.

4 Volumes: Arithmetic, Algebra, Geometry, Composition, Writing, Physical Geography and Miscellaneous Class-Work.

INTERMEDIATE CLASS.

3 Volumes: Examinations in Spelling, Catechism, History, Geography, Compositions and Map Drawing.

COMMERCIAL CLASS.

17 Volumes: Examination Papers in Christian Doctrine, Grammar, Civil Government, Book-Keeping, Rhetoric, Mensuration, Commercial Correspondence, and Typewriting; Ornamental Penmanship, Examination in Orthography.

PRIMARY CLASS.

2 Volumes: Catechism, Geography and Arithmetic.

FIRST PREPARATORY CLASS.

1 Volume Examinations: Catechism, Geography, Grammar, Bible History, United States History and 1 Volume Class-Work.

SECOND PREPARATORY CLASS.

1 Volume Examination Papers.

MISCELLANEOUS.

2 Volumes of Photographic Views, showing Building, Classes and Pupils; 1 Photograph of Students, 1 Relief Map of Tennessee, 40 Crayon Drawings, 150 Mechanical and Architectural Drawings, 1 Show-Case containing the following articles: 1 Volume, Work of Rev. R. P. Petro Wantier, S. J., Printed in 1633. 1 Volume Bible for the Blind, 1 Volume Abridgment of the Christian Doctrine, in the Sioux (Dakota) Language, by Mgr. Ravoux,

MEMPHIS, TENN.—CONTINUED.

Christian Brothers' College.—*Christian Brothers.*

MISCELLANEOUS.

of St. Paul, Minn.; type-setting and printing was also done by the Author. 1846. 1 Volume Syntagma Juris Universi, printed in 1609. 1 Volume Imitation of Christ, Printed in 1699. 1 Volume, Polyglot Edition, Imitation of Christ in Eight Languages. 1 Volume: Work on Climates of the United States and Canada, by C. F. Volney, 1803. 1 Volume: Paradisus Animæ Christianæ, Printed in 1675. 1 Volume Ammulus Memorialis, Printed in 1694. 1 Bible in Latin and German, with annotations, in Latin, Hebrew and Greek, Printed in 1751. 1 Volume Trubner's Literature of aboriginal American languages. 1 Volume containing Prayers of St. Nersetis, printed in thirty-six Languages from the Island of St. Lazanrus; gift of George Arnold, Jr., to Brother Maurelian, President of the Christian Brothers' College, Memphis, Tenn. 1 Case imitation of Precious Stones, imported from Europe and used for class instructions.

NASHVILLE, TENN.

St. Bernard's Academy.—*Sisters of Mercy.*

2 Volumes: Christian Doctrine, Orthography, United States History, Mensuration, Grammar, Natural Philosophy, Biography, Book-Keeping and Rhetoric.

PARISH SCHOOLS.

NASHVILLE, TENN.

St. Joseph's School.—*Sisters of Mercy.*

7 Volumes: Christian Doctrine, Orthography, Grammar, Arithmetic, Geography, Algebra, Modern History, Bible History and Penmanship.

St. Patrick's School.—*Sisters of Mercy.*

49 Albums: Spelling, Grammar, Geography, Catechism, Arithmetic, History, Letter Writing, Map Drawing and Algebra.

CLARKSVILLE, TENN.

St. Mary's School.—*Dominican Sisters.*

6 Volumes: Numbers, Penmanship, Spelling, Drawing, Language, Reading, Christian Doctrine, Arithmetic, Compositions.

MEMPHIS, TENN.

St. Patrick's School.—*Sisters of Charity (Nazareth, Ky.).*

10 Volumes: Christian Doctrine, Orthography, Arithmetic, Geography, Bible History, Grammar, United States History, Algebra, Ancient History, Rhetoric, Literature, Civil Government, Geometry, Mythology, Map Drawing, 3 Oil Paintings, Crayon Drawings (Figures and Ornaments).

Ashe Art School.

Cotton Panel, Blooms, Balls and Matured Cotton, Miss Annie Rhea; Cotton Panel with Matured Cotton, Mrs. E. M. Brown; Cotton Panel with Matured Cotton, Miss Leingfield; Corn Panel, Miss M. L. Ashe; Corn Panel, Mrs. E. M. Brown; "Good Luck" (Old Negro Woman in rags), Miss Madge Rogers; "Contentment" (Negro Boy eating apples), Miss Annie Rhea;

MEMPHIS, TENN.—Continued.

Ashe Art School.

Portrait of Col. J. B. Ashe (in Continental Uniform), Miss Ashe; Vase of Chrysanthemums, Miss M. L. Ashe; Vase of Magnolias, Miss Annie Rhea; Wine and Grapes, Miss Minnie Brown; Panel Cotton Growing, Miss M. L Ashe; Panel "A Yard of Tennessee Cotton," Mrs. M. Chandler. (All the above Pastel.) "Head of a Young Girl," Etching on Silk, Miss A. A. Ashe; 1 Landscape, Miss A. A. Ashe; "Head of an Old Woman," from life, Miss M. L. Ashe; "Basket of Grapes," Mrs. Hunt; "Flowers," Miss Hunt; "Watermelon" (Oil), Mrs. N. Chandler.

Diocese of Natchez.

See Diocesan Exhibit, Part I.

DIOCESE OF NATCHITOCHES.

RT. REV. ANTHONY DURIER, D. D.

ACADEMY.

NATCHITOCHES, LA.

St. Mary's Academy.—*Sisters of Divine Providence.*
13 Volumes Class-Work, 1 Book Drawing and 4 Books of Map Drawing.

PARISH SCHOOLS.

ALEXANDRIA, LA.

St. Francis Xavier's School.—*Sisters of Divine Providence.*
3 Volumes of Essays, 2 Books Drawing, 1 Page of Fancy Work in Album.

PINEVILLE, LA.

Sacred Heart School.—*Sisters of Divine Providence.*
1 Volume of Essays.

DIOCESE OF NESQUALLY.

RT. REV. ÆGIDIUS JUNGER, D. D.

PARISH SCHOOL.

SEATTLE, WASH.

Sacred Heart School.—*Sisters of St. Dominic.*
8 Volumes: Christian Doctrine, Numbers, Spelling, Language, Geography, Object Lessons, Drawing, Writing, Reading, United States History, Compositions, Grammar, Physics, Arithmetic, Zoology, Botany, Map Drawing, Physiology, Painting (water colors) and Photographs of each grade.

DIOCESE OF NEWARK.

RT. REV. WINARD MICHAEL WIGGER, D.D.

ACADEMIES.

FORT LEE, N. J.

Institute of the Holy Angels.—*School Sisters of Notre Dame.*

15 Volumes: Christian Doctrine, Grammar, Compositions, Reading, Arithmetic, Geography, French, German, Spelling, Physics, Algebra, Geometry, Book-Keeping, 1 Volume Class-Drawing and 1 Large Oil Painting.

JERSEY CITY, N. J.

Catholic Institute.—*Christian Brothers.*

3 Architectural Designs (Framed), 1 Volume Linear Drawing, 1 Volume Double-Entry Book-Keeping, 2 Volumes each: Dictation, Grammar, Arithmetic, History and Orthography, 1 Volume Homophonous Words, 1 Volume Phonographic Exercises, 1 Volume Business Correspondence and Mercantile Forms, 2 Volumes specimen sheets of Penmanship, 3 Volumes Freehand Drawing, 1 Volume Mensuration, 1 Volume Geographical Exercises, 1 Volume Grammatical Exercises.

PARISH SCHOOLS.

NEWARK, N. J.

St. Patrick's Cathedral.—*Christian Brothers.*

1 Volume Stereography, by Brother Donatian, F.S.C., 74 Volumes Linear Drawing, 1 Volume Architectural and Mechanical Drawing, 1 Volume Colored Maps, 2 Volumes Penmanship, 1 Volume Mathematics, 5 Volumes Class-Work (First Class), 6 Volumes Freehand Drawing (First Class), 1 Volume Penmanship (Second Class), 4 Volumes Class-Work (Third Class), 1 Volume Class-Work (Third and Fourth Classes), 1 Volume Monthly Examination Reports, Weekly Reports and Testimonials of Merit; 1 Volume School Register, 1 Album Varieties of Cloth, collected by Maurice I. Allan, 3 Charts illustrating 21 Parts of an Incandescent Lamp, collected by Geo. W. Delaney, Jr., 2 Charts illustrating the manufacture of Rubber from the raw material, collected by Matthew Walsh; 3 Charts of Horology, collected by L. O. Shikluna, John Walsh and Matthew Walsh; 1 Chart illustrating the manufacture of buttons from the Ivory Nut, collected by Gregory Morrissey; 1 Chart illustrating the use of tool steel, collected by Charles Norton; 4 Charts of Food Product, collected by Manus T. O'Donnell and John V. Hanrahan; 2 Charts illustrating process of tanning and finishing forms of Leather, collected by Francis N. Smith and Samuel J. Harrison; 1 Chart Oil-Paints, Chas. Shaffery; 1 Framed Relief Map of United States and 8 Relief Maps.

ORANGE VALLEY, N. J.

Our Lady of the Valley School.—*Sisters of St. Joseph.*

3 Albums Drawing and 1 Album Maps.

PATERSON, N. J.

St. John's School.—*Christian Brothers.*
1 Album each: Dictation, Arithmetic, Typewriting, Phonography, Language Exercises, Examination Papers, Geography, Compositions, Paraphrasing, Development of History, Monthly Examination Papers, Reports, Large Maps, Linear Drawing, Business Forms, Mechanical Drawing. 2 Albums each: Ornamental Drawing, Specimen Copies; 3 Double Show-Cases containing Object Lessons on Silk, Silk Cloth, Cotton, Jute, Flax, Plush and Wood.

DIOCESE OF OMAHA.

RT. REV. R. SCANNELL, D. D.

PARISH SCHOOLS.

OMAHA, NEB.

St. Joseph's School.—*Sisters of the Precious Blood.*
English and German Penmanship, Arithmetic, Geography.

St. Mary Magdalene's School.—*Sisters of the Precious Blood.*
English and German Penmanship, Grammar.

DIOCESE OF OGDENSBURG.

RT. REV. HENRY GABRIELS, D. D.

ACADEMY.

OGDENSBURG, N. Y.

St. Mary's Academy.—*Gray Nuns.*
11 Volumes Class-Work: History, Catechism, Orthography, Algebra, Geometry, Drawing, Geography, Map Drawing, Physical Geography, Grammar, Physics, Astronomy, Language, Arithmetic, French, Compositions, Economics, Book-Keeping, Typewriting, Latin, Botany, Zoology, Chemistry, 16 Photographs and 1 Volume History of St. Mary's Academy.

DIOCESE OF PEORIA.

RT. REV. J. L. SPALDING, D. D.

Portrait in Oil of Bishop Spalding.

ACADEMIES.

PEORIA, ILL.

Academy of Our Lady of the Sacred Heart.—*Sisters of St. Joseph.*
3 Volumes: Grammar, Arithmetic, Geography, History, Literature, Philosophy, Language, Rhetoric, Algebra, Geology, Zoology, Mythology, Astronomy, Modern History, Stenography, Christian Doctrine, Memoirs and Book-Keeping.

GALESBURG, ILL.

St. Joseph's Academy.—*Sisters of Providence.*

4 Volumes: Christian Doctrine, Arithmetic, Geography, Algebra, Natural Philosophy, Physical Geography, History, Literature, Rhetoric, Geometry, Chemistry, Bible History, Orthography, Grammar and Drawing.

NAUVOO, ILL.

St. Mary's Benedictine Academy.—*Benedictine Sisters.*

4 Volumes: Christian Doctrine, Arithmetic, Algebra, German Translations, Orthography, French Translations, Latin, Botany, Descriptive Astronomy, Phonography, Grammar, Photographs, Specimens of Freehand and Map Drawing.

OTTAWA, ILL.

St. Francis Xavier's Academy.

4 Volumes: Christian Doctrine, Spelling, Arithmetic, Grammar, Geography, Object Lessons (Drawing), Physical Geography and Music.

PARISH SCHOOLS.

PEORIA, ILL.

St. Patrick's School.—*Sisters of Notre Dame.*

1 Volume: Christian Doctrine, Arithmetic, Geography, Penmanship, Spelling and 1 Volume Book-Keeping.

St. Joseph's School.—*Sisters of Notre Dame.*

2 Volumes Drawing. 1 Volume: Language, Arithmetic, Geography, Grammar, Compositions, United States History, Spelling, German, Catechism, Bible History and 1 Volume specimens of Sewing.

St. Mary's School.—*Sisters of St. Joseph.*

7 Volumes: Penmanship, Geography, Grammar, Christian Doctrine, Rhetoric, Algebra, Geometry, Drawing, United States History, Arithmetic, Spelling, Book-Keeping and German.

CHAMPAIGN, ILL.

St. Mary's School.—*School Sisters of Notre Dame.*

2 Volumes Drawing. 7 Volumes: Christian Doctrine, Language, Penmanship, Spelling, Grammar, Geography, Compositions, Rhetoric, Arithmetic, Algebra, Geometry, United States History, Ancient History, Physiology, Physics and Map Drawing.

DANVILLE, ILL.

St. Patrick's School.—*Sisters of the Holy Cross.*

1 Volume Specimen Writing.

LOCKPORT, ILL.

Sacred Heart School.—*Sisters of Providence.*

2 Volumes: Christian Doctrine, Arithmetic, Spelling, Geography, United States History, Rhetoric, Modern History and Book-Keeping.

LA SALLE, ILL.

St. Vincent's School.—*Sisters of Charity.*

5 Volumes: Christian Doctrine, Orthography, Grammar, History, Book-Keeping, Physical Geography, Phonography, Typewriting, Drawing and 13 Specimens of Pastel Painting.

Diocese of Pittsburgh.

See Diocesan Exhibit, Part I.

DIOCESE OF PROVIDENCE.

RT. REV. MATTHEW HARKINS, D. D.

PROVIDENCE, R. I.

La Salle Academy.—*Christian Brothers.*

8 Copy Books Graded Exercises. 8 Copy Books each: Latin, English Essays and Phonography; 1 Album each: Christian Doctrine, Photographs and Sketches; 12 Copy Books French (First Class), 7 Copy Books French (Second Class), 11 Copy Books English Essays, 17 Copy Books Religion; 30 Copy Books: Translations, Latin, French, etc.; 9 Copy Books Shorthand (Verbatim Reporting); 10 Copy Books Reports on Cases in Supreme Court; Phonography applied to Algebra, Sacred History, Grammar, Geology; 4 Albums Class Debates, 3 Albums Specimens Trigonometry and Surveying

DIOCESE OF RICHMOND.

RT. REV. A. VAN DE VYVER, D. D.

ACADEMY.

RICHMOND, VA.

St. Joseph's Academy.—*Sisters of Charity.*

4 Volumes: Arithmetic, Geography, Grammar, Algebra, Literature, Language, Ancient and Modern History, Book-Keeping, Composition, Drawing, Geometry, Phonography, Rhetoric, Physiology and Typewriting.

PARISH SCHOOLS.

RICHMOND, VA.

St. Patrick's School.—*Sisters of Charity.*

3 Volumes: Catechism, Arithmetic, Compositions, Geography, Dictations, Grammar, United States History, Language Lessons, Algebra, Geometry, Book-Keeping, Civil Government, Literature, Physiology, Rhetoric, Phonography and Typewriting.

NORFOLK, VA.

St. Mary's School.—*Sisters of Charity.*

2 Volumes: Christian Doctrine, Orthography, Letter Writing, Arithmetic, Algebra, Book-Keeping, Geography, Natural Philosophy, Physiology and Drawing.

PORTSMOUTH, VA.

St. Joseph's School.—*Sisters of Charity.*

2 Volumes: Christian Doctrine, Arithmetic, Bible History, Geography, Language, Algebra, Geometry, Book-Keeping, Civil Government, Compositions.

ORPHANAGE.

RICHMOND, VA.

St. Joseph's Asylum.—*Sisters of Charity.*

5 Volumes: Christian Doctrine, Orthography, Arithmetic, Book-Keeping, Grammar, United States History, Language, Geography, Phonography, Typewriting and Letter Writing.

DIOCESE OF SACRAMENTO.

RT. REV. PATRICK MONOGUE, D. D.

COLLEGE AND ACADEMIES.

SACRAMENTO, CAL.

Sacramento Institute.—*Christian Brothers.*

14 Copy Books Arithmetic, 24 Copy Books Writing, 25 Copy Books Christian Doctrine, 38 Copy Books Dictation, 3 Albums Essays, 2 Albums Arithmetic, 2 Albums Book-Keeping, 2 Albums Descriptive Geometry, 1 Ledger, 1 Journal, Specimens of Business-Department Currency, Testimonials, Diplomas, etc.

MARYSVILLE, CAL.

College of Notre Dame.—*Sisters of Notre Dame.*

Christian Doctrine, Bible History, Language, Orthography, Arithmetic, United States History, Grammar, Geography, Letter Writing, Literature, Rhetoric, Church History, Algebra, Geometry, Book-Keeping, Chemistry, Needle-Work, Map Drawing, Tapestry, Photographs.

EUREKA, CAL.

St. Joseph's Convent—*Sisters of Mercy.*

Specimens of Map Drawing, Freehand Drawing, Chronological Map and Specimens of Illuminated Writing.

GRASS VALLEY, CAL.

Mt. St. Mary's Academy.—*Sisters of Mercy.*

38 Albums: Christian Doctrine, Grammar, United States History, Orthography, Geography, Spelling, Book-Keeping, Compositions, Algebra, General History, Vocal Music, Freehand Drawing, Map Drawing, Oil Painting, Photographs, Pastels, Fancy Hair-Work, Embroidered Scarfs and specimens of Botany.

ORPHANAGE.

GRASS VALLEY, CAL.

St. Patrick's Orphan Asylum.—*Sisters of Mercy.*

Spelling, Arithmetic, Letter Writing, Object Drawing, Photographs.

DIOCESE OF SAN ANTONIO.

RT. REV. JOHN C. NERAZ, D. D.

COLLEGE AND ACADEMIES.

SAN ANTONIO, TEXAS.

St. Joseph's Academy.—*Sisters of Divine Providence.*

1 Gold-embroidered Banner, 2 Pages Fancy Work, 3 Books of Essays and 3 Books of Drawing.

St. Mary's College.—*Brothers of Mary.*

10 Volumes Exercises: Orthography, Compositions, Letter Writing, Grammar, United States History, Geography, Arithmetic, Penmanship, Literature, Algebra, Geometry, Book-Keeping, Trigonometry, Chemistry, Physics and Physiology; 1 Volume Penmanship, 1 Volume Book-Keeping, 5 Volumes Object Drawing, Map Drawing and Physical Geography; 1 Volume Linear Drawing, from Actual Measurement, 1 Volume Shorthand, 1 Volume Typewriting and 1 Set of Photographs of Buildings, Classes, Societies and Picnic Views, by a Member of the Faculty.

CASTROVILLE, TEXAS.

Divine Providence Academy.—*Sisters of Divine Providence.*

Painting of Mother House, Novitiate and Vicinity, 1 Banner Representing Sisters of Divine Providence, in the Old and the New Worlds, by Sister M. Gonzaga, 1 Banner Raised Embroidery, 1 Crochet Baby Clothes, 1 Album of Academy and Parish School, 1 Volume Essays, Diagrams, Mathematics, 10 Pages Fancy Work and 18 Drawing Books, 3 Albums: Christian Doctrine, Orthography, Arithmetic, Grammar, Geography, Bible History, Letter Writing and Drawing; 1 Album of Academies and Parish Schools taught by the Sisters of Divine Providence in Texas and Louisiana, Collection of Needle-Work and Crochet.

PARISH SCHOOLS.

SAN ANTONIO, TEXAS.
San Fernando School.—*Brothers of Mary.*
1 Volume each: General Class-Work, English and Spanish Translations and Penmanship.

CASTROVILLE, TEXAS.
St. Louis' School.—*Sisters of Divine Providence.*
3 Books Essays and Mathematics, 1 Volume Essays, Biographies, Mathematics and 3 Books Drawing.

COLUMBUS, TEXAS.
St. Mary's School.—*Sisters of Divine Providence.*
1 Page Fancy Work in Album and 1 Book Drawing.

DANVILLE, TEXAS.
Sisters of Divine Providence.
1 Book Essays.

DUBINA, TEXAS.
St. Edward's School.
2 Pages Fancy Work in Album.

FREDERICKSBURG, TEXAS.
Sts. Peter and Paul's School.—*Sisters of Divine Providence.*
1 Page Fancy Work in Album.

HIGH HILL, TEXAS.
Sisters of Divine Providence.
3 Books Essays and Examination Papers and 4 Books Drawing.

NEW BRAUNFELS, TEXAS.
Sts. Peter and Paul's School.—*Sisters of Divine Providence.*
1 Page of Fancy Work in Album.

SCHULEMBURG, TEXAS.
St. Joseph's School.—*Sisters of Divine Providence.*
2 Albums: Freehand Drawing, Laces, Embroidery, from different schools, taught by the Sisters of Divine Providence, 1 Oil Painting from Convent School, Clarksville, 5 Books Essays and Exercises and 9 Books Drawing.

St. Rose's School.
1 Crochet Cape, 1 Page Fancy Work, 9 Books of Essays and 3 Drawing Books.

SEDAN, TEXAS.
St. Paul's School.—*Sisters of Divine Providence.*
1 Page Fancy Work.

WEIMER, TEXAS.

St. Michael's School.—*Sisters of Divine Providence.*

3 Books: Compositions, Letter Writing and 1 Page Fancy Work.

DIOCESE OF ST. AUGUSTINE.
RT. REV. JOHN MOORE, D. D.

ACADEMY.

ST. AUGUSTINE, FLA.

St. Joseph's Academy.—*Sisters of St. Joseph.*

10 Albums Grammar, 10 Albums Arithmetic, 4 Albums Algebra, 8 Albums Book-Keeping, 13 Albums Music, 6 Volumes Biographies, 1 Volume Poems, 1 Volume Compositions, 10 Junior Examination Papers, 10 Examination Papers by Colored Pupils, 36 Senior Examination Papers, 2 Pen-Drawing Books, 3 Copy-Books, 43 Kindergarten Books, 54 Primary Books, Needle-Work, 2 Yards Black Lace, 7½ Yards Insertion, 2¾ Yards Alencon, 4¾ Yards Guipure, 3 Yards Duchesse, 3 Yards Torchon, 1 Yard White Guipure, 3 Small Crayons, 1 Lace Cushion, 2 Herbariums—Pascue Florida. A Monthly edited by the Pupils, "The Glorification of Columbus."

DIOCESE OF SAVANNAH.
RT. REV. T. A. BECKER, D. D.

PARISH SCHOOL.

AUGUSTA, GA.

St. Patrick's School.—*Brothers of the Sacred Heart.*

3 Volumes: Penmanship, Business Forms, Book-Keeping, Grammar, Arithmetic, Examination Papers, Algebra, Geometry, United States History, Letter Writing, Pen-Work and Catalogue of the School.

Diocese of Sioux Falls.
See Diocesan Exhibit, Part I.

DIOCESE OF SPRINGFIELD.
RT. REV. THOMAS D. BEAVEN, D. D.

PARISH SCHOOLS.

SPRINGFIELD, MASS.

Sacred Heart School.—*Sisters of Notre Dame.*

1 Volume: Church History, English History, Geography, Grammar, Zoology, Astronomy, Botany, Arithmetic, Algebra, United States History, Book-Keeping, Literature, Spelling. 1 Volume Specimens of Needle-Work.

CHICOPEE, MASS.

St. Joseph's School.—*Christian Brothers.*

21 Volumes: Book-Keeping, 36 Volumes Specimen Sheets of Penmanship, 100 Copy Books, 12 Volumes Class-Work various branches, 2 Volumes Specimens of Typewriting, 1 Volume Compositions, 8 Volumes Freehand and Linear Drawing, 4 Volumes Maps, Large Album Photographs of Schools, Church, Surroundings, Teachers, Graduates, Sodalities, Chancel Choir, Military Company, Classes, etc., Cabinets, Silk Culture—Product of Silk-Worm from Egg of Moth to the finished Articles, 2 Cabinets Cotton—from Seed to the finest grade of cloth. 1 Cabinet—How Paper Is Made.

HOLYOKE, MASS.

St. Jerome's Catholic Total Abstinence, Benevolent and Literary Society.

Photographs of Buildings, Meeting Hall, Reading Rooms, Library, Billiard Rooms, Gymnasium, Bath Rooms, Armory, Parlor, Spiritual Director, Officers, Guards, Drum Corps and Base-Ball Team.

WORCESTER, MASS.

St. John's School.—*Sisters of Notre Dame.*

1 Volume Drawing. 1 Volume: United States History, Geography, Grammar, Arithmetic, Language, Christian Doctrine and Compositions.

St. John's High School.—*Sisters of Notre Dame.*

1 Volume: Church History, Sacred History, Physical Geography, Astronomy, Algebra, Book-Keeping. United States History, Arithmetic, Map Drawing and Architectural Drawing.

DIOCESE OF ST. JOSEPH.

RT. REV. MAURICE F. BURKE, D. D.

ST. JOSEPH, MO.

St. Joseph's Commercial College.—*Christian Brothers.*

11 Volumes: Christian Doctrine, Geometry, Penmanship, Geography, Grammar, Maps, Book-Keeping, Commercial Law, Composition "Our Class" and 1 Album Photographs of Building, Classes and Ground.

St. Francis de Sales' School.—*Sisters of St. Joseph.*

1 Volume: Drawing, Physiology, Philosophy, Rhetoric, Algebra, Grammar, Geography, Map Drawing, Book-Keeping.

St. Patrick's School.—*Christian Brothers.*

9 Volumes: Christian Doctrine, Sacred History, Geography, Arithmetic, Grammar, Commercial Correspondence, Penmanship, Class-Work, 2 Volumes Book-Keeping and 1 Album Views of Building, Classes, Grounds and Church.

DIOCESE OF SYRACUSE.

RT. REV. P. A. LUDDEN, D. D.

UTICA, N. Y.

St. Vincent's Industrial School.

8 Volumes Class Work: Christian Doctrine, Penmanship, Arithmetic, Compositions, History, Grammar, 1 Volume Letter Writing, 1 Crayon Portrait of Rt. Rev. Bishop Ludden, 46 Crayon Drawings (Framed), 26 Plaster Casts, 2 Framed Photographs, 51 Wood Carvings, 13 Panels of Pyrography, 16 Drawings for Photo-Etching, 1 Chart illustrating Stocking Industry, Samples of Stockings made by Pupils.

DIOCESE OF VINCENNES.

RT. REV. FRANCIS SILAS CHARTARD, D. D.

COLLEGES AND ACADEMIES.

JASPER, IND.

Jasper College.—*Benedictine Fathers.*

1 Volume: Christian Doctrine, Arithmetic, Geography, Algebra, Ancient and Modern History, Geometry, Trigonometry, Natural Philosophy, Physiology, German Translations, Compositions, Penmanship, Latin Class-Work, Phonography, Commercial Law and Book-Keeping.

ST. MEINRAD, IND.

St. Meinrad's College.—*Benedictine Fathers.*

1 Volume: Christian Doctrine, Bible History, Latin, English Compositions and Essays, German Exercises, Ancient History, Algebra, Arithmetic, Geometry, Logic, English, German and Latin Translations, Moral Theology, Papers on the Decalogue and Holy Scripture (English and Latin).

FERDINAND, IND.

Academy of the Immaculate Conception.—*Benedictine Sisters.*

1 Embroidered Vestment.

OLDENBURG, IND.

Academy of the Immaculate Conception.—*Sisters of St. Francis.*

16 Volumes: Christian Doctrine, Arithmetic, Orthography, Grammar, Geography, United States History, Composition, Physiology, Natural History, Penmanship, Literature, Botany, Rhetoric, School Journal, Biography, Algebra, Mythology, Chemistry, Civil Government, German Essays, Bible History, Business Forms, Typewriting, Music, Drawing, Oil Paintings, Portrait of Father J. Randolph, Landscapes, Church Vestments (in gold cloth), Embroidery, Pastel Painting, Freehand Drawing, Set of Text-Books, Book specimens of Fancy Work, 2 Painted Panels, 1 Infant's Outfit, 1 Glove Box and 1 Case of Fancy Work.

ST. MARY'S OF THE WOODS, IND.

St. Mary's Institute.—*Sisters of Providence.*

Map of the Battlefield of Gettysburg. 3 Volumes: Christian Doctrine, Arithmetic, Geography, Church History, Algebra, United States History, Geology, Grammar, Civil Government, Literature, Physics, Music, Penmanship, Map Drawing and Music Literature.

PARISH SCHOOLS.

VINCENNES, IND.

St. John's School.—*Sisters of Providence.*

1 Volume: Christian Doctrine, Bible History, Spelling, Grammar, Arithmetic, United States History, Penmanship.

DOVER, IND.

St. John's School.—*Sisters of St. Francis.*

1 Volume Class-Work.

EVANSVILLE, IND.

Holy Trinity School.—*Sisters of Providence.*

1 Volume Examination Papers: Spelling, Language, Catechism, United States History, Geography, Bible History, Book-Keeping, Grammar, Music, German Translations and Phonography.

St. Mary's School.—*Sisters of St. Francis.*

1 Volume Class-Work.

FRENCHTOWN, IND.

Sacred Heart School.—*Sisters of Providence.*

1 Volume: Language, Arithmetic, United States History, Book-Keeping, Grammar, Christian Doctrine and Spelling.

GREENCASTLE, IND.

St. Paul's School.—*Sisters of Providence.*

2 Volumes: Arithmetic, Grammar, Spelling, Penmanship, Catechism and History.

INDIANAPOLIS, IND.

Sacred Heart School.—*Sisters of St. Joseph.*

3 Volumes: Grammar, Arithmetic, German, Botany and Geography.

St. Bridget's School.—*Sisters of St. Francis.*

1 Volume Class-Work.

St. James' School.—*Sisters of Providence.*

2 Volumes: Literature, History, Christian Doctrine, Geography, Algebra, Arithmetic, Grammar, Bible History, Spelling, Physiology, Sacred History, Business Letters, Compositions, Maps and Physical Geography.

St. John's School.—*Brothers of the Sacred Heart.*

1 Volume: Book-Keeping and Business Forms, 1 Volume Graded Penmanship and Photographs.

INDIANAPOLIS, IND.—Continued.

St. Mary's School.—*Sisters of St. Francis.*
1 Volume Class-Work.

St. Patrick's School.—*Brothers of Sacred Heart.*
5 Volumes: Business Forms, Letter Writing, Arithmetic, Geography, Algebra, Geometry, United States History, Penmanship, Catalogue of School.

St. Patrick's School.—*Sisters of Providence.*
Christian Doctrine, United States History, Geography, Grammar, Phonography, Bible History, Spelling, Penmanship and Drawing.

JEFFERSONVILLE, IND.

St. Augustine's School.—*Sisters of Providence*
2 Volumes: Christian Doctrine, Music, Algebra, Geography, Bible History, Language, Spelling and Drawing.

LAWRENCEBURG, IND.

St. Lawrence's School.—*Sisters of St. Francis.*
1 Volume Class-Work.

LOOGOOTEE, IND.

St. John's School.—*Sisters of Providence*
1 Volume: Christian Doctrine, Arithmetic, Language, Spelling, United States History, Algebra, Literature and Rhetoric.

MADISON, IND.

St. Michael's School.—*Sisters of Providence.*
1 Album Elementary Drawing.

MORRIS, IND.

St. Anthony's School.—*Sisters of St. Francis.*
1 Volume Class-Work and 1 Volume Drawing.

NEW ALBANY, IND.

Holy Trinity School.—*Sisters of Providence.*
1 Volume: Christian Doctrine, Arithmetic, History, Music, Rhetoric, Literature, United States History, Composition, Physics, Civil Government and Algebra.

NEW ALSACE, IND.

St. Paul's School.—*Sisters of St. Francis.*
1 Volume Class-Work and 1 Volume Drawing.

OLDENBURG, IND.

St. Mary's School.—*Sisters of St. Francis.*
1 Volume: Christian Doctrine, Arithmetic, Geography, United States History, Book-Keeping, Grammar, English and German Penmanship, Orthography, Freehand Drawing.

RICHMOND, IND.

St. Mary's School.—*Sisters of Providence.*

2 Volumes: Christian Doctrine, History, Orthography, Arithmetic, Grammar, Geography, United States History, Algebra and Compositions.

RUSHVILLE, IND.

St. Mary's School.—*Sisters of St. Francis.*

1 Volume Class-Work and 1 Volume Drawing.

SEYMOUR, IND.

St. Ambrose's School.—*Sisters of Providence.*

1 Volume: Christian Doctrine, Bible History, Arithmetic, Grammar, Orthography, Geography, United States History, Compositions.

SHELBYVILLE, IND.

St. Joseph's School.—*Sisters of St. Francis.*

1 Book Crocheting.

ST. MARY'S OF THE WOODS, IND.

St. John's School.—*Sisters of Providence.*

4 Volumes: Grammar, Geography, Christian Doctrine, United States History, Drawing and Physiology.

ST. PETER, IND.

St. Peter's School.—*Sisters of St. Francis.*

1 Volume Class-Work, 1 Volume Drawing.

ST. WENDEL, IND.

St. Wendel's School.—*Sisters of St. Francis.*

1 Volume Class-Work.

TERRE HAUTE, IND.

St. Benedict's School.—*Sisters of Providence.*

1 Volume: Arithmetic, German, Spelling, Letter Writing, United States History, Map Drawing and Specimens of Embroidery.

St. Joseph's School.—*Sisters of Providence.*

2 Volumes: Spelling, Grammar, Arithmetic, Geography, Christian Doctrine, Language, Letter Writing, Vocal Music, Drawing.

WASHINGTON, IND.

St. Mary's School.—*Sisters of Providence.*

1 Volume: Arithmetic, Spelling, Language, German, Drawing, Grammar, Letters, Geography.

YORKVILLE, IND.

St. Martin's School.—*Sisters of St. Francis.*

1 Volume Class-Work and 1 Volume Drawing.

INDUSTRIAL SCHOOL.

CONNERSVILLE, IND.

St. Gabriel's Industrial School.—*Sisters of Providence.*

1 Volume: Christian Doctrine, Arithmetic, Geography, Orthography, Physical Geography, Grammar, Compositions. United States History and Music.

DIOCESE OF WHEELING.

RT. REV. JOHN J. KAIN, D. D.

WHEELING, W. VA.

Cathedral School.—*Sisters of Charity.*

1 Volume Maps.

DIOCESE OF WINONA.

RT. REV. JOSEPH B. COTTER, D. D.

WABASHA, MINN.

St. Felix's School.—*School Sisters of Notre Dame.*
1 Volume Specimens of Sewing.

Wabasha Convent.—*Sisters of Notre Dame.*
1 Volume Specimens of Sewing.

VICARIATE-APOSTOLIC OF ARIZONA.

RT. REV. P. BOURGADE, D. D.

ACADEMY.

LAS CRUCES, NEW MEX.

Visitation Academy.—*Sisters of Loretto.*

2 Volumes: Christian Doctrine, Arithmetic, Sacred History, Natural Philosophy, Physiology, English and Spanish Translations, United States History, Geography, Orthography, Grammar, Algebra, Book-Keeping, Compositions, Civil History, Geology and Physics.

VICARIATE-APOSTOLIC OF IDAHO.

RT. REV. A. J. GLORIEUX, D.D.

LEWISTON, IDAHO.

    St. Aloysius' Academy.—*Sisters of St. Francis.*

        Maps of the United States in Clay and Specimens of Clay Objects, Typewriting, Phonography, Photograph of Bishop Glorieux, Freehand Drawing and Embroidery.

VICARIATE-APOSTOLIC OF NORTH CAROLINA.

RT. REV. LEO HAID, D.D., O.S.B.

COLLEGES AND ACADEMIES.

BELMONT, N. C.

    St. Mary's College.—*Benedictine Fathers.*
        1 Photograph of Building.

    Sacred Heart Academy.—*Sisters of Mercy.*
        1 Photograph of Building.

WILMINGTON, N. C.

    St. Mary's College.—*Benedictine Fathers.*
        6 Photographs: Parlor, Refectory, Recitation Room, Dramatic Hall, Science Room and Play Grounds.

    St. Mary's Seminary.—*Sisters of Mercy.*
        1 Photograph of Building.

    Academy of Incarnation.—*Sisters of Mercy.*
        1 Photograph of Building.

PARISH SCHOOLS.

WILMINGTON, N. C.

    St. Thomas' School.—*Sisters of Mercy.*
        1 Photograph of Building.

    Parish School (Colored).—*Sisters of Mercy.*
        1 Photograph of Building.

PART III.

CLASSIFICATION OF EXHIBITS BY RELIGIOUS TEACHING ORDERS.

Benedictine Fathers.

COLLEGES AND ACADEMIES.

BEATTY, PA., Diocese of Pittsburgh.

St. Vincent's Seminary and College.

9 Volumes: Christian Doctrine, Arithmetic, Geography, Grammar, Spelling, Book-Keeping, Algebra, Geometry, Trigonometry, Latin, Greek and German Exercises, Dogmatic Theology, Moral Theology, Church History, Mental Philosophy, Holy Scripture, Original Essays in Sixteen Languages: Latin, Greek, Hebrew, English, Spanish, Italian, Irish, Lithuanian, Polish, Russian, Hungarian, Slavonian, Low German and Bohemian. 3 Photographs of Professors and Students and 3 Catalogues.

BELMONT, N. C., Vicariate-Apostolic of North Carolina.

St. Mary's College.

1 Photograph of Building.

JASPER, IND., Diocese of Vincennes.

Jasper College.

Specimens of Class-Work in Christian Doctrine, Grammar, Composition, Arithmetic, Algebra, Geometry and Trigonometry, Geography, History, Natural Philosophy, Physiology, Exercises in German and Latin, Stenography, Book-Keeping, etc., with Outline of Methods of Teaching.

ST. MEINRAD, IND., Diocese of Vincennes.

St. Meinrad's College.

1 Volume: Christian Doctrine, Bible History, Latin and English Compositions, Essays, German Exercises, Ancient History, Algebra, Arithmetic, Geometry, Logic, English, German and Latin Translations, Moral Theology, Papers on the Decalogue and Holy Scripture (English and Latin).

WILMINGTON, N.C., Vicariate-Apostolic of North Carolina.

St. Mary's College.

6 Photographs: Parlor, Refectory, Recitation Room, Science Room, Dramatic Hall and Play Grounds.

Congregation of the Holy Cross.

NOTRE DAME, IND.

University of Notre Dame du Lac.

Full-length life-size Portrait in oil of Very Rev. E. Sorin, C. S. C., Founder of the University. Ten Portraits in oil-work by Professor Gregori and his Pupils of the Art School, Notre Dame. Topographical Survey of the University Precincts, Scale 1:792, drawn by class of 1893. Samples of work done in iron by students first year's course Practical Mechanics. Samples of work done in wood by students of the Institute of Technology, Notre Dame. Crayons from life and casts by students of Professor Ackerman's Class. Blue prints and examples of linear drawing from Institute of Technology. Photographs made by class of Photo-Micrography. Twenty-six bound Volumes of the Notre Dame Scholastic, illustrating work of the students in classes of English Composition, Rhetoric, English Literature and Belle Letters. Specimens of books printed and published at Notre Dame. Bound volumes of the Ave Maria, printed and published at Notre Dame. Paintings and Lithographs illustrating the growth of Notre Dame. A few Photographs and Souvenirs of persons connected with the University of Notre Dame du Lac. One hundred and twenty Photographs of the Department of Experimental Bacteriology; Photo-Micrography; Electrical Engineering; Art Schools; Libraries; Physical Cabinets; Lecture Rooms and Laboratory; Department of Natural History; Law School; College of Music; Gymnasium; Institute of Technology; School of Manual Labor; Normal School; Theological Seminary of the Holy Cross; Literary, Athletic and Aquatic Associations; Chemical Department; Observatory and the various Colleges, Halls and Dormitories of the University made by the members of Father Alexander Keroch's Photograph Class. Twelve Photographs of Gregori's famous Mural frescoes in the Columbian Gallery, Notre Dame.

CATHOLIC HISTORICAL COLLECTIONS OF AMERICA.

Dept. A.

THE BISHOP'S MEMORIAL HALL.

Life-sized portraits in oil of Bishop Carroll, Bishop Egan, Bishop Connanner, Bishop Flaget, Archbishop Hughes and Bishop Luers by Gregori; Bishop Persico; Cardinal Manning by Carnivale; Bishop England by Irish Arbit; Abbot Smith by Healy; Bishop Fenwick by P. Wood; Bishop Chabrat by Du Bois; Cardinal Franchi by Carnivale; Cardinal McCloskey, Archbishop Kenrick and Archbishop Spalding by Gregori; Archbishop Conwell by Nagle; Archbishop Purcell by Wood; Bishop Kelly by Wood; Cardinal Ledochowski by Carnivale; Cardinal Simeoni by Carnivale; Father Badin by

CATHOLIC HISTORICAL COLLECTIONS OF AMERICA.
Dept. A.

THE BISHOPS' MEMORIAL HALL.—CONTINUED.

Clement; Father Junipero Serra by Wood; John Gilmary Shea and Orestes A. Brownson by Gregori; Bishop Rosati by Gregori; life-size portrait in crayon of Bishop Cretin by Gregori; Photographs and Engravings of deceased Bishops; Original Manuscripts of sermons preached by various American Bishops.

CASE 1.

Gold-embroidered and jeweled Mitres used by the First Bishops of Baltimore. Precious Mitre worn by Most Rev. Archbishop Spalding. Gothic Mitre designed by Pugin, used by Archbishop Bayley when he imposed the Biretta Rosa on Cardinal McCloskey. Gold-embroidered red velvet Mitre used by Archbishop Kenrick of Baltimore. Gold-plated Crosier used by the early Archbishops of Baltimore. Mitten of white wool worn by Pope Pius IX. when he gave his last blessing to the attendants surrounding his deathbed. Red silk Zuchetto worn by Pius IX. when elected Pope. Lock of the Hair of Pius IX. and pieces of his Cassock, Mantle and Surplice enshrined in a gold Casket. Gold Chalice used by several Popes and Cardinals. White silk Zuchetto worn by Pope Leo XIII. Gold Chalice made 1524, owned and used by Archbishop Carroll, gift of Bishop Borgess. Crosier of Olive Wood from Garden of Gethsemene, inlaid with silver, mother-of-pearl, ebony and ivory, supposed to have been given to the first American Bishop by the Bishop who consecrated him, Rt. Rev. Dr. Wormesley of England. Pen and Holder used to sign the decrees of the Third Plenary Council of Baltimore. Original Miniature of Pope Leo XIII. Gold Pen and Holder used by Bishop Keane when writing the statutes of the Catholic University of America. Several miniatures and photographs of Baltimore dignitaries. Gold Cross and Chain worn by Archbishop Eccleston when consecrated, also worn by Archbishop Elder when consecrated Bishop of Natchez. German Bible in 2 Volumes printed in German at Nuremberg, 1470. Catholic Bible printed 1473, five months before birth of Martin Luther.

CASE 2.

Gold-embroidered Mitre used by Bishop Penalvery Cardenas, First Bishop of Louisiana and the Floridas, gift of Archbishop Janssens. Gold-embroidered Mitre worn by Rt. Rev. Bishop Dubourg and successor in Diocese of New Orleans. Gold Mitre worn by Archbishop Odin when first Bishop of Galveston. Pectoral Cross and Chain worn by Bishop Dubourg. Gold Episcopal Ring worn by Archbishop Blanc. Episcopal Ring worn by Archbishop Odin. Silver Mission Chalice used by Archbishop Odin and Archbishop Perche. Pallium with jeweled Clasps, worn by Archbishop Leray. White linen Mitre used by Archbishop Perche. Mozetta of purple moire antique worn by Archbishop Leray. Gold Mitre worn by Bishop Verot, First Bishop of St. Augustine. Decoration and Cross of the Holy Sepulchre, presented to Archbishop Perche. Holy Bible, first Catholic Bible published in the United States, 1790. Bible printed in 1805, owned and used by Mother Seton, first Sister of Charity in the United States. Catholic New Testament published in English in 1682. Silver Cruets and Salver used in the Cathedral of New Orleans. Rare Engravings and Photographs of Personages connected with Archdiocese of New Orleans.

CASE 3.

Curious old Mitre used by First Bishop of Louisville. Wooden Crosier used by Bishop Flaget. Gold pectoral Cross used by Bishop Flaget. Gold-embroidered Sandals used by Bishop Flaget. Silver and Gold Mission Chalice used by Bishop Bruté. Gold-embroidered Red Mitre used by Bishop Bruté. Jeweled Mitre worn by Bishops De la Hailandiere and Bazin. Richly embroidered Mitre used by Bishop de St. Palais. Silver Crosier given to Bishop Bruté by the Archbishop of Vienna. Gold-plated Crosier used by the Second Bishop of Vincennes and his Successors. Lock of

CATHOLIC HISTORICAL COLLECTIONS OF AMERICA.

Dept. A.

CASE 3.—CONTINUED.

Bishop Bazin's Hair. Pocket Missal, 1647, used by Bishop Bruté. Gold-lined Silver Ciborium used by the early Missionaries of Southern Indiana. Gold-lined Pyx used on early Missions of Vincennes. Gold-embroidered Mitre used by Bishop Luers. Gold Episcopal Ring used by Bishop Luers. Gold-embroidered Mitre used by Bishop Miles and his Successors. Silver and Gold Chalice used by early Missionaries of Northern Indiana. Mitre worn by Bishop Rappe. Gold Episcopal Cross and Chain used by Bishops Rappe and de Goesbriand. Seal of Bishop Gilmour. Daguerreotypes and Photographs of Dignitaries of Indiana and Kentucky.

CASE 4.

Beautiful English Mitre of exquisite Needle-Work used by the Bishop Fenwick of Cincinnati. Embroidered Mitre used by Bishop Rosecrans. Precious Mitre used by Archbishop Purcell. Flemish Mitre used by Bishop Lefevere. Jeweled Mitre used by Bishop Baraga and Successors. Gold-embroidered Silver Cloth Mitre used by Bishop Borgess. Pewter Chalice used by early Jesuit Missionaries of Michigan, also by Father Richard. Silver and Gold Crosier given to Archbishop Purcell by the Germans of Cincinnati. Cane containing relic of a Saint, used by Bishop Baraga. Curious semi-circular Mitre used by Bishop Young. Exquisitely Chiseled Crosier of Silver and Ebony given to Bishop Lefevere of Detroit by Bishop Mallou of Bruges. Quaint old Pyx in the form of a Silver Cross used by the early Missionaries of Ohio. Silver Pax used by Deacons at Solemn High Mass. Sub-Deacons' Pax. Lock of Archbishop McHale's Hair. Bishop Reze's Seal. Gold-embroidered Gauntlets used by Bishop Lefevere.

CASE 5.

Jeweled Mitre used by Bishop Conwell gift of Archbishop Ryan. Precious Mitre used by Bishop Neumann. Gold-plated Silver Cross worn by Bishop Egan. Gold-embroidered White Gauntlets used by Bishop Egan. Silver Chalice used by Rev. Prince Gallitzin. Episcopal Ring worn by Bishop Conwell. Gold-embroidered and Jeweled Mitre worn by Bishop Hendricken. Jeweled Mitre used by Bishop Shannahan. Cane used by Rev. Prince Gallitzin. Silver and Bronze Medals of Cathedral, Philadelphia. Writing of St. Liguori, attested by Bishop Neumann. Bronze Medals of Archbishop Wood and St. Charles Seminary. Photographs of Philadelphia Dignitaries.

CASE 6.

Gold-embroidered Roman Mitre used by the First Bishops of New York. Precious Mitre used by Archbishop Hughes. Gold Pectoral Cross used by Archbishop Hughes and Bishop de Goesbriand. Cardinal's Biretta, Zuchetto and Mozetta worn by Cardinal McCloskey. Lock of Cardinal McCloskey's Hair in a Jeweled Locket. Jeweled Mitre worn by Bishop Bacon. Lock of Cardinal de Cheverus' Hair. Cross blessed by Bishop de Cheverus, First Bishop of Boston. Precious Mitre worn by Bishop Fitzpatrick. Lock of Bishop Tyler's Hair. Embroidered Mitre used by Bishop Galberry. Mitre worn by Bishop O'Reilly who was drowned at sea. Mitre used by Bishop McFarland. Jeweled Crosier used by Bishop Timon of Buffalo. Cardinal's Hat used by Cardinal Jocobini. Several rare old Daguerreotypes and Books owned by Eastern Bishops. Pen and Holder used by John Gilmary Shea LL. D. when writing the last pages of his History. Pencil used by Father Lambert LL. D. when writing his famous book "Notes on Ingersoll."

CASE 7.

Gold-embroidered Silk Mitre used by Bishop Quarter. Pectoral Cross and Chain worn by Bishop Vandevelde. Pectoral Cross worn by Bishop O'Regan. Gold Cross and Chain used by the Fourth Bishop of Chicago. Gold-embroidered Mitre used by Bishop Foley. Episcopal Ring with Amethyst Setting used by Bishop O'Regan. Episcopal Ring with Sapphire

CATHOLIC HISTORICAL COLLECTIONS OF AMERICA.

Dept. A.

CASE 7.—CONTINUED.

Setting used by Bishop Duggan. Mitre worn by Bishop Loras. Quaint Swiss Mitre used by Archbishop Henni. Curiously embroidered Bead-and-Silver Mitre used by Bishop Cretin. Silver Crosier owned by Archbishop Henni. Jeweled Mitre used by the First Bishop of Green Bay. Episcopal Ring set with Emerald surrounded with Diamonds given by Archbishop Henni to Bishop Flasch. Wooden Crosier used by Bishop Loras. Lock of Bishop Smyth's Hair. Lock of Bishop Loras' Hair. Gold Episcopal Ring worn by Bishop Baltus. Jeweled Mitre owned by Bishop Juncker. Lock of Bishop Cretin's Hair. Crosier given to Bishop McMullin by Archbishop Feehan. Copy used by Archbishop Ireland when he delivered his famous address on the occasion of the Inauguration of the World's Congresses, Chicago.

CASE 8.

Gold Cloth Mitre embroidered with Silver used by Bishop England. Silver Ciborium used by Bishop England. Bishop Clancy's Coat of Arms. Lock of Bishop Reynold's Hair. Episcopal Ring worn by Bishop Chanche. Cross worn by Bishop Clancy. Jeweled Mitre worn by Archbishop Alemany. Curious old Crosier of Tortoise Shell and Silver used by Bishop Francis Garcia Moreno, First Bishop of California. Gold Cross and Chain, Episcopal Ring with Amethyst Setting, willed by Bishop O'Connell to the Bishops' Memorial Hall. Quaint old Mitre used by Archbishop Blanchet. Jeweled Mitre in which the murdered Archbishop Seghers was consecrated, also used by Bishop Demers. Seal of Bishop Francis Garcia Moreno. Episcopal Ring worn by Bishop Gartland. Part of Bishop Gartland's vestments taken from his grave when his body was removed to the Cathedral, Mobile. Stole of painted velvet worn by Bishop Byrne. Pectoral Cross, Chain and Ring worn by Bishop O'Gorman. Bishop O'Gorman's Seal. Large Silver Crosier used by Bishop Portier. Bishop Portier's Mitre. Mitre worn by Bishop Pelliser. Gold-embroidered Mitre worn by Bishop Miege, S. J. Wood-Carving from Old Texas Mission.

CASE 9.

Artistically embroidered Chasuble, Stole, Maniple, Chalice Veil and Burse (Handiwork of Miss Mary Guendaline Caldwell). Old Bell made 1776 from the Mission Church, Cahokia, Illinois.

CASES 11, 12, 13, 14, 15.

Relics of Catholic Soldiers, Statesmen, Missionaries, Priests and Members of Religious Orders. Gold-embroidered Chasuble used by Father Marquette, gift of Bishop Borgess. Quaint old Chasuble used by Father Badin, First Priest ordained in the United States. Sword carried through the Mexican and the Civil Wars by General James Shields. Mitres worn by First Trappist Abbot and the First Benedictine Abbot of the United States. Medals, Coins, etc. Relics and Souvenirs of the Seton Family, gifts of Rt. Rev. Robert Seton, D. D. Relics of the Carroll Family, gifts of Mrs. Rebecca Carroll. Several Albums of Photographs of Catholic Priests, gift of Mr. Edwin Edgerly. Pictures illustrating American History. Photographs of many Catholic Editors. Life-sized Paintings of James A. McMaster; P. V. Hickey; John Boyle O'Reilly; William J. Onahan; Cardinals Newman and Manning; Shakespeare; Orestes A. Brownson; John Gilmary Shea; Miss Eliza Allen Starr; Richard H. Clark, LL. D.

Dept. B.

A small exhibit of Manuscripts from the Catholic Archives of America, established at Notre Dame, 1866. Autograph Letters of all the deceased Bishops of the United States. Specimens of Papal Bulls. Documents of Historic Interest. Maps illustrating work of early Missionaries. Handwriting of Catholic Priest and Layman.

CATHOLIC HISTORICAL COLLECTIONS OF AMERICA.

Dept. C.

The Catholic Reference Library of America. First Volume bound of the Catholic Miscellany, 1822. The Jesuit, 1829. Literary and Catholic Sentinel, 1825. The Pilot, 1826. The Freeman's Journal, 1840. Catholic Diary, 1833. Catholic Telegraph, 1821. Le Propagateur Catalogue, 1843. The Catholic Mirror, 1849. The Catholic Herald, 1833, etc.,
Specimens of early Catholic Magazines, Pamphlets and rare books.

CHICAGO, ILL.

St. Columbkille's School.

1 Volume each: Language, Arithmetic, Catechism, Geography, History, Orthography and Book-Keeping.

FT. WAYNE, IND., Diocese of Ft. Wayne.

St. Mary's School.

Christian Doctrine, United States History, Compositions, English and German Translations, Penmanship, Map Drawing, Geography, Grammar, Orthography, Freehand Drawing and Bible History.

Cathedral School.

Grammar, Arithmetic, Christian Doctrine, Orthography, United States History, Bible History, Business Forms, Drawing, Algebra, Physiology, General History, Natural Philosophy, Phonography, Typewriting.

SPECIAL EXHIBIT.

Specimens Linear Drawing, 1 Volume Specimens of Map Drawing, 3 Volumes: Christian Doctrine, Grammar, Orthography, Geography, Penmanship, Arithmetic, United States History, Algebra, Book-Keeping, Commercial Law, Phonography, Ancient and Modern History, Natural Philosophy and Photographs.

LA FAYETTE, IND., Diocese of Ft. Wayne.

St. Mary's School.

Arithmetic, Orthography and Geography.

WEST SENECA, N. Y., Diocese of Buffalo.

St. John's Protectory and Orphanage.

Specimens of Printing and Electrotyping.

Fathers of the Holy Ghost.

PITTSBURGH, PA., Diocese of Pittsburgh.

Holy Ghost College.

6 Volumes: Christian Doctrine, Rhetoric, Literature, Geometry, Trigonometry, Physics, Ancient and Modern History, Latin, Greek and French Compositions; 2 Volumes Original Essays on Columbus and other subjects, in Latin, Greek, French, German and Polish, Mechanical and Freehand Drawing, 3 Framed Anatomical Drawings and 12 Framed Photographs of College and Students.

Franciscan Brothers.

COLLEGE AND ACADEMIES.

BROOKLYN, N. Y., Diocese of Brooklyn.

St. Francis' College.

8 Volumes: Geography, Christian Doctrine, Grammar, Arithmetic, Physiology, Rhetoric, Algebra, Greek, Geometry, Latin, History, Philosophy and Astronomy.

St. Leonard's Academy.

3 Volumes: Christian Doctrine, Arithmetic, Geography, Grammar, German, Mensuration, Algebra, Orthography, Composition, Stenography, Penmanship, Book-Keeping and Typewriting.

St. Patrick's Academy.

11 Volumes: Grammar, Mechanical Drawing, Algebra, United States History, Church History, Spelling, Arithmetic, Compositions, Geography, Penmanship, Geometry, Typewriting, Dictation and Shorthand.

Sacred Heart Institute.

7 Volumes: Catechism, Geography, Writing, Spelling, Arithmetic, United States History, Typewriting, Phonography, Grammar, Physiology, Mensuration, Compositions, Civics, Algebra, History, Book-Keeping and English Literature.

St. Vincent de Paul's Academy.

2 Volumes: Language, Grammar, Spelling, Christian Doctrine, Mechanical Drawing, Typewriting, Penmanship, Phonography, Book-Keeping, Letter Writing, Map Drawing, Arithmetic and Geography.

PARISH SCHOOLS.

BROOKLYN, N. Y., Diocese of Brooklyn.

Assumption School.

1 Volume: Christian Doctrine, United States History, Spelling, Grammar, Typewriting, Arithmetic, Book-Keeping, Compositions and Geography.

St. Anthony's School.

2 Volumes: Geography, Grammar, Civics, Catechism, Spelling, Compositions, Language, Arithmetic, Phonography, Typewriting, History, Physiology, Algebra, Physical Geography.

St. Ann's School.

4 Volumes: Catechism, Arithmetic, Geography, Grammar, Orthography, Business Forms, History, Civil Government, Algebra and Compositions.

St. Charles' School.

3 Volumes: Spelling, Writing, Arithmetic, Catechism, Geography, Dictations, Grammar, Maps, Geometry, Mensuration, Typewriting, English Literature, Algebra, Book-Keeping and Civil Government.

BROOKLYN, N. Y., Diocese of Brooklyn.—Continued.

St. Francis' School.

8 Volumes: Christian Doctrine, Arithmetic, Geography, Grammar, Physiology, Greek, Rhetoric, Algebra, Geometry, Latin, History, Philosophy and Astronomy.

St. Francis de Sales' School.

1 Volume: Spelling, Arithmetic, Grammar, Geography, Catechism and History.

St. John's School.

2 Volumes: Christian Doctrine, Arithmetic, Grammar, Geography and History.

St. John the Evangelist's School.

1 Volume: Grammar, Geography, United States History, Catechism, Book-Keeping, Composition, Mensuration, Civil Government, Phonography and Typewriting.

St. Mary Star of the Sea.

2 Volumes: Business Forms, Spelling, Arithmetic, History, Geography, Grammar, Composition, Dictation and Catechism.

St. Paul's School.

2 Volumes: Geography, Grammar, Spelling, Catechism and History.

St. Vincent de Paul's School.

2 Volumes: Christian Doctrine, Spelling, Language, Mechanical Drawing, Typewriting, Penmanship.

PHILADELPHIA, PA., Diocese of Philadelphia.

St. Vincent de Paul's School.

See Diocesan Exhibit.

KESHENA (Menominee Reservation), Diocese of Green Bay.

St. Joseph's Industrial School.

1 Volume: Bible History, Geography, United States History, Arithmetic, Spelling and Grammar.

Jesuit Fathers.

BUFFALO, N. Y., Diocese of Buffalo.

Canisius College.

7 Albums: Christian Doctrine, Geography, Bible History, Letter Writing, Analysis, Essays, Latin, German, Mathematics, History, Compositions, Greek, Algebra, Greek Translations, Philosophy, 1 Drama—"Columbus"; 1 Album of Photographs and 10 Drawings.

CLEVELAND, OHIO, Diocese of Cleveland.

St. Ignatius' College.
12 Volumes: Drawing, French, Phonography, Geography, Penmanship, English Compositions, Sacred History, German, Spelling, Map Drawing, Christian Doctrine, Algebra, Book-Keeping, Polyglot, Mathematics, History, Physics and Greek.

DENVER, COL., Diocese of Denver.

College of the Sacred Heart.
1 Volume: Mental Philosophy, Mathematics, United States History, Chemistry, Physics, Ancient History, Composition, Christian Doctrine, Arithmetic, Language, Latin, Grammatical Analysis, Book-Keeping, Orthography, Geography, Penmanship and 1 Volume of "The Highlander" (published monthly)

NEW ORLEANS, LA., Diocese of New Orleans.

College of the Immaculate Conception.
1 Volume: Electricity, Greek, Letters, Latin, Geometry and Algebra.

SANTA CLARA, CAL., Diocese of San Francisco.

Santa Clara College.
NORMAL DEPT.
5 Text Books in Mathematics by Rev. Jos. Bayma, S. J., Pen-Work by Professor of Penmanship, Descriptive Catalogues. Photographs of Students and Graduates. Apparatus used in Commercial Department.

STUDENTS' WORK.
14 Studies in Crayon, India Ink and Water Color; 21 Albums: Essays, Prose, Poetry and Latin; Moral and Natural Philosophy; Mathematics and Book-Keeping.

SAN FRANCISCO, CAL., Diocese of San Francisco.

St. Ignatius' College.
NORMAL DEPT.
Photographs of Students, Church, College, Museum, Library, Chemical and Physical Laboratories. 14 Albums: Essays, Translations, Examinations in Greek, Latin and English. Moral and Natural Philosophy, Mathematics, Book-Keeping. 1 Lecture—"The Atmosphere."

SAN JOSE, CAL., Diocese of San Francisco.

St. Joseph's College.
Photographs of Students, Church and College, 4 Volumes: Latin, Greek and English Exercises, Mathematics and Book-Keeping.

Lazarist Fathers.

SUSPENSION BRIDGE (Niagara University P. O.), N. Y., Diocese of Buffalo.

Niagara University.
Oil-Paintings of College and Seminary, Most Rev. Archbishop Lynch and Rt. Rev. Bishop Timon; Crayon Portraits of Rt. Rev. Bishop Ryan, D.D., Very Rev. R. E. V. Rice, Very Rev. P. V. Kavanaugh, C. M.; 4 Seminary O L. A. and C. Literary Scrolls, 4 B. L. A. Banners, 2 R. E. V. R. Banners, 1 N. U. G. C. Banners, 4 Basilian L. A. Scrolls, 3 R. E. V. L. R. L. A. Scrolls, 2 Souvenir Volumes, 10 Volumes Niagara Index, 3 Volumes "Index Niagarenses," a number of Copies of the "Index," 11 Small Pictures of Different Societies, 19 Mounted Photographs.

BROOKLYN, N. Y., Diocese of Brooklyn.

St. John's College.

1 Volume: Christian Doctrine, French Translations, Latin, Greek, Astronomy, Composition, Rhetoric and Geometry.

Congregation of St. Viateur.

KANKAKEE, ILL.

St. Viateur's College.—*Priests and Brothers of the Community of St. Viateur.*

1 Volume Class-Work (Preparatory Department), 2 Volumes Penmanship, 1 Volume Book-Keeping, 1 Volume Arithmetic, 1 Volume Spelling and Compositions, 1 Volume English Grammar, 1 Volume Rhetoric and Composition, 1 Volume History, Composition and Geography, 1 Volume Literary and Military Societies, 2 Volumes Latin and Greek, 1 Volume French and German, 1 Volume Mathematics and Science, 1 Volume Evidences of Religion, 1 Volume Intellectual Philosophy, 1 Volume Philosophy of History, 1 Volume: Ode—"The Cross and Columbus," 1 Volume "Epines et Fleurs," 1 Volume "Liola-Legende Indienne," 6 Volumes St. Viateur's College Journal, Photographs of Faculty, Students, Associations, College Buildings, Mineralogical, Entomological, Botanical and Conchological Specimens from College Museum.

PARISH SCHOOL.

CHICAGO, ILL.

Holy Name School.

3 Volumes Class-Work: Primary and Grammar Departments.

Benedictine Sisters.

ALCOVE 63.

ACADEMIES.

ALLEGHANY, PA., Diocese of Pittsburgh.

St. Benedict's Academy.

16 Volumes: Catechism, Arithmetic, Geography, History, Grammar, Spelling, Algebra, Drawing, Bible History, Historical Chart-Work, Map and Freehand Drawing, 1 Card Fancy Penmanship.

BIRMINGHAM, ALA., Diocese of Mobile.

Holy Angels' Academy.

1 Volume: Compositions, Language, Arithmetic, Christian Doctrine, Letters.

CHICAGO, ILL., Diocese of Chicago.
Sts. Benedict and Scholastica's Academy.
6 Volumes Class-Work, 12 Oil Paintings, 4 Water Colors, 5 Drawings from the Antique, Bullion and Silk Embroidery.

COVINGTON, KY., Diocese of Covington.
Academy of St. Walburg.
3 Volumes: Spelling, Grammar, Literature, Geography, Map Drawing, History and Music.

CANON CITY, COL., Diocese of Denver.
Mt. St. Scholastica's Academy.
2 Volumes: Christian Doctrine, Arithmetic, Geography, Grammar, Algebra, Geometry, Compositions, Physiology, Orthography, Literature, Phonography, Book-Keeping, Freehand Drawing and Physics.

FERDINAND, IND., Diocese of Vincennes.
Academy of the Immaculate Conception.
1 Embroidered Vestment.

NAUVOO, ILL., Diocese of Peoria.
St. Mary's Benedictine Academy.
4 Volumes: Christian Doctrine, Arithmetic, Algebra, German Translations, Orthography, French Translation, Latin, Botany, Descriptive Astronomy, Grammar, Photographs, Specimens of Freehand and Map Drawing.

PARISH SCHOOLS.

ALLEGHANY, PA., Diocese of Pittsburgh.
St. Joseph's School.
2 Volumes: Christian Doctrine, Arithmetic, Geography, Spelling, Derivation of Words and 1 Volume Maps.

St. Mary's School.
3 Volumes: Catechism, Book-Keeping, Arithmetic, History, Grammar, Spelling, English and German Composition.

BIRMINGHAM, ALA., Diocese of Mobile.
St. Paul's School.
1 Volume: Sacred History, Composition, Astronomy, Dictations, Letters, Geography, Arithmetic, Language and Spelling.

CHICAGO, ILL., Diocese of Chicago.
St. John Nepomucene's School.
3 Volumes English Studies, 2 Volumes Bohemian Studies.

St. Joseph's School.
12 Volumes Class-Work; 2 Volumes Drawing, Specimens of Crocheting, Plain Sewing and Drawn-Work, 5 Crayon Drawings and 2 Pastel Drawings.

MANCHESTER, N. H., Diocese of Manchester.
St. Raphael's School.
14 Albums: Christian Doctrine, Arithmetic, Bible History, Orthography, Sacred History, Language, Grammar and Geography.

STURGIS, S. D., Diocese of Sioux Falls.
St. Martin's School.
Geography, United States History, Grammar, Christian Doctrine, Bible History, Drawing, Composition, Book-Keeping and Orthography.

YANKTON, S. D., Diocese of Sioux Falls.
Sacred Heart School.
Arithmetic, Letter Writing, Geography, Grammar, United States History, Christian Doctrine, Book-Keeping, Orthography, Bible History.

STEPHAN, S. D., Diocese of Sioux Falls.
Immaculate Conception School (Indian Mission).
1 Volume: Freehand Drawing, Grammar, Arithmetic, Industrial Needle-Work, Letter Writing, Kindergarten Work, Weaving, Matting, Knitting and Photographs.

Dominican Sisters.

ALCOVE 4.

COLLEGE, ACADEMIES AND SELECT SCHOOLS.

SAN RAFAEL, CAL., Diocese of San Francisco.
College San Rafael.

NORMAL WORK.
5 Studies in life of St. Agnes, Water Color of College and 1 Album of Photographs.

STUDENTS' WORK.
14 Volumes: Grammar, Literature, Letter Writing, Rhetoric, Historical Essays, Physical Geography, United States and French History, Astronomy, Physiology, Natural Philosophy, Algebra, Geometry, Christian Doctrine, Historical Charts, English and Ancient History, Arithmetic, French, Civil Government, Trigonometry, Chemistry, Geology, Mythology, Class-Notes, Penmanship, Stenography. 1 Volume Water Colors and Sketches of California Missions.

NEW ORLEANS, LA., Diocese of New Orleans.
Dominican Academy (Dryades St.).
7 Volumes Book-Keeping, 1 Volume each of Arithmetic, Book-Keeping, Geometry, Trigonometry, Compositions, Letter Writing.

Dominican Academy (St. Charles Ave.).
13 Volumes Book-Keeping, 3 Volumes Arithmetic, 1 Volume each of Trigonometry, Algebra, French Translations, Questions and Annotations, 2 Volumes Essays, 5 Volumes Drawing, 15 Crayons, 7 Paintings, 4 Framed Photographs and 1 Volume Magazine Published by the Pupils.

NEW YORK CITY, N. Y., Diocese of New York.

Convent of the Holy Rosary.

18 Volumes: Christian Doctrine, History, Arithmetic, Reading, Compositions, Book-Keeping, Grammar, Geography, Spelling, Language, Kindergarten Work, 16 Photographs of Grades, 2 Felt Table-Scarfs, 9 Undergarments, 9 Gingham Dresses, 1 Child's Dress (Drawn-Work), 6 Throws, 3 Worked Splashers, 35 Needle Books, Cushions and Toys, 1 Pair Crochet Slippers and 4 Hemstitched Handkerchiefs.

Academy of the Holy Rosary.

37 Volumes: Arithmetic, Algebra, Book-Keeping, Geometry, Diagrams, Catechism, Dictation, Grammar, English Compositions, Map Drawing, German Compositions, Geography, German Penmanship, Music; 5 Framed Photographs, 2 Paintings on Glass, 2 Pictures, 1 Volume Book-Keeping, Kindergarten Work, Stenography and Typewriting, 3 Knitted Capes, 1 Knitted Sacque, 2 Pairs Slippers, 1 Velvet Photograph Case, 1 Silk-and-Wool Hood, 1 Silk Necktie, 1 Crochet Tie, 1 Crochet Cap, 1 Pair Crochet Leggins, 2 Lace Tidies, 1 Linen Handkerchief, 2 Calendars and 2 Cases (Celluloid).

SAN FRANCISCO, CAL., Diocese of San Francisco.

St. Agnes' Academy.

8 Volumes: Literature, Geography, Geometry, Geology, Astronomy, Algebra and Christian Doctrine.

St. Rose's Academy.

NORMAL DEPT.

1 Album California Wild Flowers and 1 Album Photographs of Students.

STUDENTS' WORK.

14 Volumes: Grammar, Literature, Rhetoric, Letter Writing, Historical Essays, Logic, Physical Geography, United States and French History, Astronomy, Physiology, Natural Philosophy, Etymology, Algebra, Geometry, Book-Keeping, Music, Christian Doctrine; 12 Volumes of Sketches of Old California Missions, 1 Volume "Columbus."

Academy of Immaculate Conception.

14 Volumes: Grammar, Language, Composition, Arithmetic, Algebra, Geometry, United States History, Physics, Chemistry, Stories of California Missions, Christian Doctrine; 1 Album Photographs and Maps.

STOCKTON, CAL., Diocese of San Francisco.

St. Agnes' Academy.

8 Volumes: Literature, Geometry, Geography, Geology, Astronomy, Algebra and Christian Doctrine.

PARISH SCHOOLS.

APPLETON, WIS., Diocese of Green Bay.

St. Mary's School.

3 Volumes: Christian Doctrine, Arithmetic, Geography, Orthography, Object Lessons, Science, Grammar, History, Compositions, Penmanship, Physical Geography and Algebra.

BELGIUM, WIS., Diocese of Milwaukee.

St. Mary's School.

1 Volume: History, Geography, Arithmetic, Spelling, Language, Catechism, Reading and Physiology.

BROOKLYN, N. Y., Diocese of Brooklyn.

All Saints' School.

2 Volumes: United States History, Grammar, Geography, Arithmetic, Compositions, German and Christian Doctrine.

St. Bernard's School.

1 Volume: Arithmetic, Geography, Painting, Spelling, United States History, Christian Doctrine.

St. Fidelis' School.

Christian Doctrine, Language, Arithmetic, Geography and Compositions.

Holy Family.

1 Volume: Penmanship, Bible History, United States History, Arithmetic, Composition, Geography, Translations, Letter Writing, Book-Keeping, Grammar and Drawing.

Holy Trinity School.

6 Volumes: Arithmetic, Geography, Composition, Grammar, History, Map Drawing, Christian Doctrine, Natural Philosophy, Natural History, Penmanship; 1 Volume Kindergarten Work.

St. Leonard of Port Maurice's School.

4 Volumes: Grammar, Spelling, Arithmetic, Geography, Philosophy, United States History and Kindergarten Work.

Sorrowful Mother's School.

1 Volume: Christian Doctrine, Arithmetic, Geography, Grammar Kindergarten Work, Compositions, United States and German History.

CALEDONIA, WIS., Diocese of Milwaukee.

St. Louis' School.

1 Volume: German and English Reading, Penmanship, Arithmetic, Spelling, Grammar, United States History, Geography and Christian Doctrine.

CHICAGO, ILL., Diocese of Chicago.

Immaculate Conception School.

5 Volumes Class-Work, 13 Framed Maps, 20 Specimens various kinds of Sewing, 2 Portfolios of Music, 1 Ship (Boys' Handiwork) and Photographs of School (Framed).

St. Jarlath's School.

8 Volumes: Catechism, Orthography, Language, Arithmetic, Letters, Penmanship, Geography, Map and Freehand Drawing, Bible History, Grammar, Compositions, Physiology, American Literature; Framed Drawings.

St. Thomas' School.

6 Volumes Class-Work, 1 Volume Drawing, 1 Volume Map Drawing, 1 Volume Paper Work, Framed Maps and Drawing.

CLARKSVILLE, TENN., Diocese of Nashville.
St. Mary's School.
6 Volumes: Numbers, Penmanship, Spelling, Drawing, Language, Reading, Christian Doctrine, Arithmetic, Compositions.

COVINGTON, KY., Diocese of Covington.
St. Joseph's School.
2 Volumes: Arithmetic, Map Drawing, Letters, Geography, Compositions, Christian Doctrine, Spelling and History.

DEFIANCE, OHIO, Diocese of Cleveland.
Our Lady of Perpetual Help.
6 Volumes: Dictations, Spelling, Language, Arithmetic, Christian Doctrine, Compositions, Letter-Writing, Geography, Drawing, Physics, Physiology.

ESCANABA, WIS., Diocese of Marquette.
St. Joseph's School.
2 Volumes: Penmanship, Spelling, Catechism, Geography, Composition, Grammar, Language, Arithmetic, Algebra, Physiology, Geometry, Rhetoric, General History, United States History, Bible History and Map Drawing.

FARIBAULT, MINN., Diocese of St. Paul.
Dominican School (Bethlehem Academy).
1 Volume: Catechism, United States History, Algebra, Composition, Book-Keeping, Irish History, Literature and English History.

GRAND RAPIDS, MICH., Diocese of Grand Rapids.
St. Alphonsus' School.
2 Volumes: Penmanship, Catechism, Literature, Geometry, Physics, Geology, Commercial Law, Music, Essays and Book-Keeping.

HIGHLANDS, COL., Diocese of Denver.
St. Dominic's School.
1 Volume: Christian Doctrine, Grammar, Orthography, Geography, Object Lessons, Map Drawing, Language, Vocal Music and Bible History.

KENOSHA, WIS., Diocese of Milwaukee.
St. George's School.
1 Volume: Penmanship, Language, Arithmetic, Geography, Grammar, Christian Doctrine, German and United States History.

MINERAL POINT, WIS., Diocese of Milwaukee.
St. Mary's School.
1 Volume: Compositions, German and English, 1 Crochet Cape, 1 Pair Knitted Hose, 2 Knitted Sacques, 1 Drawn Tidy, 1 Crochet Tidy, 3 Pairs Knitted Boots, 2 Satin Cushions, 1 Crochet Cushion, 1 Linen Apron, 3 Linen Handkerchiefs, 2 Samples Bead-Work and 2 Samples Lace-Work.

MINNEAPOLIS, MINN., Diocese of St. Paul.
Holy Rosary School.
4 Volumes Examination Papers: Arithmetic, Christian Doctrine, Language, Geography, Reading, Grammar, Maps, United States History, Physiology, Algebra, Literature, Book-Keeping, Latin, Orthography, Modern History, Rhetoric and Geometry.

MT. PLEASANT, MICH., Diocese of Grand Rapids.
Sacred Heart School.
1 Volume: Geometry, Geology, Literature, Physiology, Arithmetic, Geography, United States History, Grammar, Compositions, Catechism, Spelling and Language.

MAZOMANIE, WIS., Diocese of Milwaukee.
St. Barnabas' School.
1 Volume: Drawing, Catechism, Arithmetic, Geography, Language, Reading, Penmanship and Spelling.

NEWBURGH, N. Y., Diocese of New York.
St. Mary's School.
1 Volume: Compositions, Grammar, Arithmetic, Christian Doctrine, Geography, Spelling and Penmanship.

NEW KAUKAUNA, WIS., Diocese of Green Bay.
Holy Cross School.
2 Volumes: Arithmetic, Orthography, Christian Doctrine, Object Lessons, United States History, Letter Writing, Physiology, Geography, Penmanship and Civil Government.

NEW YORK CITY, N. Y., Diocese of New York.
St. John Baptist's School.
4 Volumes: Arithmetic, Geography, Catechism, Language Lessons, United States History, Bible History, German and Compositions.

St. Nicholas' School.
12 Volumes: German and English Grammar, Composition, United States History, Geography, Arithmetic, German and English Penmanship, German Dictation, Map and Mechanical Drawing; Book of Kindergarten Work, 2 Framed Photographs, 1 Apron, Knitted Cape, Lace Throw, 1 Satin Cushion, Satin Hand-Bag, Lace Tidy, Pair Shoes, 1 Pair Boots, 1 Pair Satin Slippers, 1 Drawn Throw and 1 Gingham Apron.

St. Vincent Ferrer's School.
18 Volumes: Christian Doctrine, Arithmetic, Geography, Grammar, United States History, Mechanical Drawing, Freehand Drawing, Language, Composition and Dictation.

OSHKOSH, WIS., Diocese of Green Bay.
St. Mary's School.
3 Volumes: Christian Doctrine, Orthography, Arithmetic, Geography, Penmanship, Letter Writing, German and English Translation, Album of Freehand Drawing.

St. Peter's School.
2 Volumes: Spelling, Christian Doctrine, Orthography, Language, Geography, Grammar, Compositions, United States History, Map Drawing, Physiology, Rhetoric, Natural Philosophy and Literature.

PORTAGE, WIS., Diocese of Green Bay.
St. Mary's School.
3 Volumes: Christian Doctrine, Orthography, Language, Arithmetic, Geography, Grammar, Compositions, United States History, Physiology, Map Drawing, Rhetoric, Natural Philosophy and Literature.

RACINE, WIS., Archdiocese of Milwaukee.

Holy Name School.
1 Volume: English Grammar, Catechism, Language, Reading, Spelling, Arithmetic, Geography and Mensuration.

St. Catherine's School.
4 Volumes: English and German Reading, Arithmetic, Geography, Spelling, Grammar, History, Algebra, Botany, Physiology, Composition, Language, Book-Keeping, Christian Doctrine; 1 Volume Essays from Sisters, 2 Lace Curtains, 1 Crayon (Infant Redeemer), 1 Painting, 1 Crayon.

St. Mary's School.
1 Volume: Catechism, Spelling, Arithmetic, Writing and Geography.

St. Joseph's School.
2 Volumes: Reading, Geography, Grammar, Catechism, Arithmetic, Language, Numbers.

St. Patrick's School.
1 Volume: Reading, Writing, Language, Spelling, Arithmetic, Grammar, Geography, United States History, Composition, Christian Doctrine and 1 Volume Drawing.

ROCKFORD, ILL., Diocese of Chicago.

St. James' School.
6 Volumes Class-Work, 2 Volumes Map Drawing, 2 Volumes Object Drawing and 1 Volume Penmanship.

SAGINAW, MICH., Diocese of Grand Rapids.

St. Joseph's School.
3 Volumes: Book-Keeping, Physics, Literature, Rhetoric, History, Reading, Bible History, Science, Spelling, Grammar, Arithmetic and Physiology.

SAN FRANCISCO, CAL., Diocese of San Francisco.

St. Boniface's School.
2 Volumes Catechism and Bible History, 2 Volumes Language and Compositions, 2 Volumes Geography and United States History, 3 Volumes Arithmetic, 1 Volume Products of California, 2 Volumes Penmanship, 2 Volumes English Compositions, 3 Volumes German Compositions and 1 Album Photographs.

SAN LEANDRO, CAL., Diocese of San Francisco.

Parish School.
1 Volume Photographs.

SAN RAFAEL, CAL., Diocese of San Francisco.

San Rafael's School.
3 Volumes: Arithmetic, Grammar, History, Penmanship, Rhetoric, Composition, French, German, Italian, History and Catechism. 1 Volume Photographs.

SEATTLE, WASH., Diocese of Nesqually.

Sacred Heart School.

4 Volumes: Mat Weaving, Sewing, Folding and Cutting. 8 Volumes: Christian Doctrine, Numbers, Spelling, Language, Drawing, Writing, Reading, United States History, Compositions, Grammar, Physics, Arithmetic, Zoology, Botany, Map Drawing and Photographs.

SPARTA, WIS., Diocese of La Crosse.

St. Patrick's School.

2 Volumes: Compositions, Geography, Grammar, Arithmetic, Language, Bible History, United States History, Algebra, Civil Government, Physiology, Book-Keeping, Commercial Law and Christian Doctrine.

STOCKTON, CAL., Diocese of San Francisco.

St. Joseph's Primary School.

2 Volumes: Arithmetic, Spelling, Language, Geography and Christian Doctrine.

STURGEON BAY, WIS., Diocese of Green Bay.

Holy Guardian School.

1 Volume: Christian Doctrine, Arithmetic, Grammar, Geography, United States History, Questions on Physics, Freehand Drawing, Language Lessons, Map and Linear Drawing.

TRAVERSE CITY, MICH., Diocese of Grand Rapids.

St. Francis' School.

1 Volume Class Work with Photographs and Illustrations.

VALLEJO, CAL., Diocese of San Francisco.

St. Vincent's School.

17 Sets Written Examinations, 7 Charts Grammar, Pen-Work, Colors, Tints and 1 Album Photographs.

ORPHANAGES.

BROOKLYN, N. Y., Diocese of Brooklyn.

Holy Trinity Orphan Asylum.

1 Volume: Christian Doctrine, Arithmetic, Penmanship, Grammar, Geography and United States History.

SAN FRANCISCO, CAL., Diocese of San Francisco.

St. Rose's Kindergarten.

Gifts and Occupations Illustrated.

SAN RAFAEL, CAL., Diocese of San Francisco.

San Rafael Kindergarten.

1 Album Kindergarten Work.

St. Joseph's Kindergarten.

1 Album Kindergarten Work.

VALLEJO, CAL., Diocese of San Francisco.
  St. Vincent's Kindergarten.
    Charts of Kindergarten Work.

Felician Sisters.

DETROIT, MICH., Diocese of Detroit.
  St. Mary's Institute.
    6 Volumes: Penmanship, Drawing, Book-Keeping, Grammar, Geography, Christian Doctrine, Compositions, Science, United States History, Polish History, Bible History, Polish Language; 20 Pieces Fancy Work, 1 Large Gold-embroidered Picture (Madonna, with Seals of Detroit and Poland).

SHAMOKIN, PA., Diocese of Harrisburg.
  St. Stanislaus' School.
    1 Picture Seeds Framed, 1 Motto Framed, 1 Crochet Curtain, 1 Embroidered Scarf and 1 Silk Spider-Web.

Sisters of the Holy Cross.

PARISH SCHOOLS.

ACADEMY, IND., Diocese of Ft. Wayne.
  St. Vincent's School.
    Christian Doctrine, Letter Writing, French Translations, Arithmetic, Orthography, United States History and Book-Keeping.

ANDERSON, IND., Diocese of Ft. Wayne.
  St. Mary's School.
    Arithmetic, Geography, Grammar, Botany, Rhetoric, United States History, Algebra and Physiology.

CRAWFORDSVILLE, IND., Diocese of Ft. Wayne.
  St. Bernard's School.
    History, Arithmetic, Chemistry, Botany, Rhetoric, Geometry, Literature, Algebra, Grammar and Geography.

DANVILLE, ILL., Diocese of Peoria.
  St. Patrick's School.
    1 Volume Specimen Writing.

ELKHART, IND., Diocese of Ft. Wayne.
  St. Vincent's School.
    Penmanship, Grammar, Orthography and Composition.

GOSHEN, IND., Diocese of Ft. Wayne.

St. John's School.

Geography, Grammar, Orthography, Algebra, Book-Keeping and Compositions.

LA PORTE, IND., Diocese of Ft. Wayne.

St. Rose's School.

Christian Doctrine, Geography, History, Grammar and Arithmetic.

LOGANSPORT, IND., Diocese of Ft. Wayne.

School of St. Vincent de Paul.

Christian Doctrine, Arithmetic, Geography, History, Grammar, Algebra and Rhetoric.

MICHIGAN CITY, IND., Diocese of Ft. Wayne.

St. Mary's School.

History, Geography, Grammar, Language, Orthography, Christian Doctrine, Arithmetic, German Translations, Bible History, Algebra, Physiology, Rhetoric and Literature.

St. Stanislaus' School.

Orthography, Penmanship, Letter Writing and Translations.

MISHAWAKA, IND., Diocese of Ft. Wayne.

St. Joseph's School.

Christian Doctrine, Grammar, Geography, Compositions, Arithmetic, Bible History and United States History.

MORRIS, ILL., Diocese of Chicago.

Immaculate Conception School.

1 Volume Maps and Examination Papers.

NASHUA, N. H., Diocese of Manchester.

St. Aloysius' School.

32 Albums: Christian Doctrine, Orthography, Arithmetic, Geography, United States History, Grammar, Book-Keeping, Drawing, Penmanship, Literature, Composition, Sacred History.

NEW ORLEANS, LA., Diocese of New Orleans.

St. Mary's Assumption School.

2 Volumes: Penmanship, Arithmetic, Language, Geography, United States History, Catechism, Grammar, Spelling, Bible History, German; 1 Plush Drapery and 1 Box Needle-Work.

PLYMOUTH, IND., Diocese of Ft. Wayne.

St. Michael's School.

Geography, Bible History, Grammar, Arithmetic and Language.

SOUTH BEND, IND., Diocese of Ft. Wayne.

St. Hedwige's School.

Geography, History, Catechism, Arithmetic, Language, Polish Translations, Object Lessons, Orthography, United States and Polish History and Book-Keeping.

St. Joseph's School.

Christian Doctrine, Bible History, Grammar, Letter Writing, Orthography, Geography and Arithmetic.

St. Mary's School.

Christian Doctrine, United States History, Geography, Orthography, Letter Writing and Arithmetic.

UNION CITY, IND., Diocese of Ft. Wayne.

St. Mary's School.

Church History, Grammar, Penmanship, Orthography, Arithmetic, Compositions, Rhetoric, Book-Keeping and United States History.

Gray Nuns.

ACADEMIES.

BUFFALO, N. Y., Diocese of Buffalo.

Holy Angels' Academy.

18 Volumes: Typewriting, Stenography, Catechism, Physical Geography, Analysis, Ancient History, Lessons in English, Arithmetic, Book-Keeping, Physics, Astronomy; 150 Specimens Botany, 33 Pieces Embroidery, 1 Eagle embroidered in Gold and 1 Volume Photographs.

Mt. St. Mary's Academy.

9 Volumes: Christian Doctrine, History, Arithmetic, Literature, Grammar, Geography, French and Latin Translations, Geometry, Algebra, Book-Keeping, Natural Philosophy, Rhetoric, Compositions and School Journals.

OGDENSBURG, N. Y., Diocese of Ogdensburg.

St. Mary's Academy.

11 Volumes: Christian Doctrine, United States History, Orthography, Geography, Civics, Arithmetic, Physiology (with Illustrations), Rhetoric, Grecian History, Astronomy, Physics, Book-Keeping, Algebra, Geometry, Language, Grammar, Freehand Drawing and Collection of Photographs.

PARISH SCHOOL.

BUFFALO, N. Y., Diocese of Buffalo.

Holy Angels' School.

11 Volumes: Penmanship, Grammar, United States History, Map Drawing and Compositions.

Ladies of the Sacred Heart of Mary.

ACADEMY.

BUFFALO, N. Y., Diocese of Buffalo.

St. Mary's Academy.

10 Oil Paintings. 77 Volumes and 5 Albums: Grammar, Book-Keeping, Geography, Physiology, Essays, Maps and Illustrated Stories.

PARISH SCHOOLS.

BUFFALO, N. Y., Diocese of Buffalo.

St. Joseph's Cathedral School.

12 Volumes: Spelling, Map Drawing, Arithmetic, History, Grammar, Geography and Catechism.

St. Nicholas' School.

2 Volumes: Analysis, Map Drawing, Grammar, Geography and United States History.

School of Our Lady of Mercy.

10 Volumes: Christian Doctrine, History, Arithmetic and Analysis.

CLEVELAND, OHIO, Diocese of Cleveland.

Holy Name School.

4 Volumes: Book-Keeping, Sacred History, United States History, Language, Grammar, Geography, Christian Doctrine, Drawing, Spelling, Music and Penmanship.

LANCASTER, N. Y., Diocese of Buffalo.

St. Mary's School.

9 Volumes: Arithmetic, Geography, Map Drawing, United States History and Christian Doctrine.

SANDUSKY, OHIO, Diocese of Cleveland.

Holy Angels' School.

1 Volume: Grammar, Christian Doctrine, Arithmetic, Orthography, Geography and United States History.

Sts. Peter and Paul's School.

1 Volume: Compositions, Catechism, Algebra, Book-Keeping, Arithmetic, Grammar, History and Map Drawing.

Ladies of the Sacred Heart.

SAN FRANCISCO, CAL., Diocese of San Francisco.

Academy of the Sacred Heart.

NORMAL DEPT.

12 Original Designs in Illumination of Magnificat, 1 Altar Card, 1 Illuminated Card, Signed M. Henggler, Photographs.

STUDENTS' WORK.

145 Volumes: Religion, Mental and Physical Science, Architecture, French, German and English Literature, Language, Mathematics, History; 14 Historical and Geographical Charts, 16 Volumes Herbaria, 18 Portfolios: Bands and Specimens of Needle-Work, Embroidery, Crochet, Lace, etc., 1 Volume Pen-and-Ink Drawing, Arithmetic, Etymology, United States History, French History and Sacred History.

Presentation Sisters.

ACADEMIES.

BERKELEY, CAL., Diocese of San Francisco.

Presentation Normal School.

Display Work, Drawing and Penmanship. 2 Volumes: Grammar, Compositions; English, Ancient, Bible and United States History; Arithmetic, Geography, Music and Christian Doctrine.

DUBUQUE, IOWA, Diocese of Dubuque.

Presentation Convent.

3 Volumes: Christian Doctrine, Grammar, Map Drawing, Letter Writing, Spelling, Arithmetic, Kindergarten Work, Natural Science, Book-Keeping, Stenography and Typewriting.

WAUKON, IOWA, Diocese of Dubuque.

Sacred Heart Convent.

2 Volumes: Arithmetic, Geometry, Algebra, Book-Keeping, Grammar, Geography, Literature, History and Drawing.

PARISH SCHOOLS.

BERKELEY, CAL., Diocese of San Francisco.

St. Joseph's School.

4 Volumes: Penmanship, Grammar, Spelling, Arithmetic, Compositions, Geography, Bible History, Catechism, Book-Keeping, Drawing, Physics and Astronomy.

DUBUQUE, IOWA, Diocese of Dubuque.

Sacred Heart School.

2 Volumes: Drawing, History, Book-Keeping, Christian Doctrine, Map Drawing and Grammar.

FARLEY, IOWA, Diocese of Dubuque.

St. Joseph's School.

Algebra, Arithmetic, Book-Keeping, History, Geography, Civil Government, United States History, Physiology and Spelling.

SAN FRANCISCO, CAL., Diocese of San Francisco.

Cathedral School.

2 Albums Writing, 1 Album Crochet Work, 1 Crayon Drawing of Most Rev. Archbishop Riordan, 1 Pastel Drawing, 1 Framed Piece of Needle-Work, 1 Map of California and 1 Fire Screen.

Sacred Heart Presentation Convent.

7 Volumes Copy Books, 3 Volumes Drawing, 7 Volumes Exercises, 5 Volumes Compositions, 5 Volumes Examination Lessons, 2 Volumes Algebra, 1 Painted Banner, 1 Set of Object Charts, 1 Photograph Album, 1 Album Paintings and 1 Album Needle-Work. 10 Volumes Class-Work: Grammar, Geography, United States History, Arithmetic, Astronomy, Christian Doctrine, 1 Album of Drawings, 1 Album of Penmanship, Display Work of Drawing and Designs.

Sacred Heart Kindergarten.

Specimens of Sewing, Drawing and Weaving.

St. Francis' Kindergarten.

1 Album Kindergarten Work.

Sisters of Charity (B. V. M.).

ACADEMIES.

ACKLEY, IOWA, Diocese of Dubuque.

Sacred Heart Academy.

7 Volumes: Map and Mechanical Drawing, Christian Doctrine, Arithmetic, Spelling, Recitation, Modern History, Physiology, Geometry, United States History and Kindergarten Work.

CEDAR RAPIDS, IOWA, Diocese of Dubuque.

St. Joseph's Academy.

7 Volumes: Christian Doctrine, United States History, Geography, Catechism, Language, Arithmetic.

CHICAGO, ILL.

St. Vincent's Academy.

15 Volumes Class-Work, 1 Volume Map Drawing, 2 Volumes Drawing, 2 Volumes Music and Framed Maps.

COUNCIL BLUFFS, IOWA, Diocese of Davenport.

St. Francis' Academy.

1 Landscape (Water Color), 1 Original Crayon and 1 Angelic Tribute to St. Cecelia.

DUBUQUE, IOWA, Diocese of Dubuque.

St. Joseph's Academy.

4 Volumes: Christian Doctrine, Astronomy, Geometry, Chemistry, Geology, Algebra, Physiology, Botany, Music, Philosophy, 1 Peacock worked on Silk, 1 Celluloid Painting.

PARISH SCHOOLS.

CHICAGO, ILL., Diocese of Chicago.

Annunciation School.

16 Volumes Class-Work; Framed Maps and Samples of Needle-Work, 7 Volumes Examination Papers.

Guardian Angel School.

2 Volumes Class-Work and 1 Volume Drawing.

Sacred Heart School.

19 Volumes Class-Work, 2 Volumes Music, 3 Volumes Map Drawing, 9 Pieces Framed Work, 1 Piece Modeling.

St. Agnes' School.

5 Volumes Class-Work and 1 Volume Drawing.

St. Aloysius' School.

11 Volumes Class-Work; 3 Volumes Music, Map Drawing and Needle-Work.

St. Bridget's School.

15 Volumes Class-Work, Framed Maps and Samples of Needle-Work.

St. Charles' School.

7 Volumes Class-Work and 4 Volumes Map Drawing.

St. Joseph's School.

6 Volumes Class-Work and 1 Volume Drawing.

St. Pius' School.

50 Volumes Graded School-Work and 29 Specimens of Map Drawings.

CLINTON, IOWA, Diocese of Dubuque.

St. Mary's School.

1 Album Map Drawing, 3 Albums Paper Folding and 1 Volume Book-Keeping. 6 Volumes: Geometry, Ancient History, Chemistry, Arithmetic, Map Drawing, Christian Doctrine, Composition, Mechanical Drawings and Kindergarten Work.

St. Martin's School.

2 Volumes: Christian Doctrine, Arithmetic, Geography, Epistolary Correspondence, Physiology, United States History, Language and Penmanship.

DUBUQUE, IOWA, Diocese of Dubuque.

St. Mary's School.

3 Volumes: Arithmetic, Spelling, Geography, Letter Writing, Map Drawing and Language.

St. Mary's German School.

12 Volumes: Christian Doctrine, Geography, Grammar, Orthography, Compositions, Drawing, Letter Writing, Kindergarten Work and Translations.

KANSAS CITY, MO., Diocese of Kansas City.

Annunciation School.

1 Volume: Maps, Sketches, Mensuration, Arithmetic and Diagraming Sentences.

St. Raphael's School.

4 Volumes: Compositions, Geography, Christian Doctrine, Music, Drawing, Catechism.

LE MARS, IOWA, Diocese of Dubuque.

St. James' School.

1 Volume: Christian Doctrine, Arithmetic, Geography, Grammar, Spelling, Reading and Map Drawing.

McGREGOR, IOWA, Diocese of Dubuque.

St. Mary's School.

2 Mounted Charts. Grammar, Geography, Map Drawing, Physiology, History and Drawing.

SAN FRANCISCO, CAL., Diocese of San Francisco.

St. Bridget's School.

STUDENTS' WORK.

10 Volumes Class-Work and 2 Volumes Drawing.

ACADEMIC DEPT.

1 Volume: Astronomy, Literature, Philosophy and Chemistry. 1 Volume: Christian Doctrine, Rhetoric, Composition and Modern History. 1 Volume: Botany, Zoology, Algebra and Geometry.

NORMAL WORK.

1 Herbarium of Flowers from the Pacific Coast, 1 Album containing Photographs of Church, School and Pupils.

Sisters of Charity (Greensburg).

ACADEMIES.

ALTOONA, PA., Diocese of Pittsburgh.

St. John's Convent School.

1 Volume: Church History, Arithmetic, Algebra, Geometry, Astronomy, Maps, Natural Philosophy, History and Literature.

GREENSBURG, PA., Diocese of Pittsburgh.

St. Joseph's Academy.

1 Volume: Christian Doctrine, Church History, Grammar with Words and their Derivations, Orthography, Algebra, Arithmetic, Natural Philosophy, Astronomy, Botany, Physical Geography, Physiology, Literature, History; 1 Volume Music, 1 Volume Water Colors, 3 Oil Paintings, 7 Hand-Painted Pieces of China.

PARISH SCHOOLS.

JOHNSTOWN, PA., Diocese of Pittsburgh.

St. Columba's School.

1 Volume: Christian Doctrine, Arithmetic, Stenography, Grammar, History and Algebra.

PITTSBURGH, PA., Diocese of Pittsburgh.

Holy Cross School.

1 Volume: Christian Doctrine, Arithmetic, Grammar, United States History, Geography, Map Drawing, Dictations, Book-Keeping, Pencil Drawing and Pencil Sketches.

Sacred Heart School.

1 Volume: Christian Doctrine, Book-Keeping, Grammar, History, Spelling, Pencil Drawings, Geography.

St. James' School.

1 Volume: Christian Doctrine, History, Grammar, Geography and Spelling.

St. Kieran's School.

1 Volume: Christian Doctrine, Arithmetic, Grammar, Algebra, Book-Keeping, Geography and History.

St. Malachy's School.

1 Volume: Christian Doctrine, Arithmetic, Geography, Algebra, Book-Keeping, History and Stenography.

SCOTTDALE, PA., Diocese of Pittsburgh.

St. John's School.

1 Volume: Christian Doctrine, Arithmetic, Geography, Compositions and History.

SHARPSBURG, PA., Diocese of Pittsburgh.

St. Joseph's School.

1 Volume: Christian Doctrine, United States History, Geography and Arithmetic.

WILKINSBURG, PA., Diocese of Pittsburgh.

St. James' School.

1 Volume: Christian Doctrine, Algebra, Arithmetic, Grammar, Geography, Compositions, Book-Keeping.

Sisters of Charity (Mt. St. Vincent).

NEW YORK CITY, N. Y., Diocese of New York.

Mt. St. Vincent on the Hudson.

82 Volumes: Bible History, Algebra, History, Geography, Astronomy, Greek, Latin, German, Logic, Essays, Physics, Rhetoric, Domestic Economy; 27 Copies Music, Christian Doctrine, 28 Copy Books Book-Keeping, 40 Illustrated Charts Natural Science, 12 Articles Honiton and Point-Lace, 10 Oil Paintings, 5 Crayon Pictures, 2 Paintings in Moist Colors, 9 Panel Photographic Views (Mt. St. Vincent), 4 Crayons, 1 Case: 12 Pieces Handmade Undergarments.

St. Gabriel's Academy.

24 Volumes: Grammar, Geography, Orthography, United States History, Natural Philosophy, Geometry, Algebra, Physiology, Catechism, Astronomy, French and English History, Penmanship, Rhetoric, Drawing and Book-Keeping.

St. Mary's Academy.

SENIOR DIVISION.

5 Volumes: Essays, Mathematics, Church History, Literature, Rhetoric, United States History, Geography, Astronomy, Physics and Physiology.

MIDDLE AND JUNIOR DIVISIONS.

5 Volumes: Christian Doctrine, Bible History, Arithmetic, Geography, Grammar and Drawing.

St. Paul's Academy (117th St.).

3 Volumes: Christian Doctrine, Arithmetic, Geography, Civil Government, English History, Astronomy, Philosophy, Grammar, Orthography, Composition, Literature and Drawing.

PARISH SCHOOLS.

BROOKLYN, N. Y., Diocese of Brooklyn.

St. Charles' School.

1 Volume: Grammar, Algebra, History, Geography, Arithmetic, Christian Doctrine, Civil Government, Business Forms, Dictation.

BROOKLYN, N. Y., Diocese of Brooklyn.—Continued.

St. Mary Star of the Sea.
4 Volumes: Arithmetic, History, Grammar, Geography, Spelling, Maps, Civil Government, Algebra, Rhetoric, Book-Keeping, Astronomy, Physiology and Composition.

St. Paul's School.
1 Volume: Geography, Maps, United States History, Catechism, Bible History, Arithmetic, Algebra, Rhetoric, Physiology, Civil Government and Drawing.

St. Stephen's School.
1 Volume: Geography, Maps, United States History, Catechism, Bible History, Arithmetic, Algebra, Rhetoric, Physiology, Civil Government and Drawing.

NEW ORLEANS, LA., Diocese of New Orleans.

St. Simeon's School.
13 Volumes: Penmanship, Arithmetic, Geography, Literature, Botany, Rhetoric, Physiology, Historical Anecdotes, Compositions, Music; 1 Volume Drawing and Photographs.

NEW YORK CITY, N. Y., Diocese of New York.

St. Augustine's School.
2 Volumes: Arithmetic, Spelling, Grammar, Composition, Geography, Penmanship, Language, Drawing and Reading.

St. Brigid's School.
10 Volumes: Arithmetic, Christian Doctrine, Grammar, Reading, United States History, Writing, Language, Physiology, Physics, Astronomy; 2 Framed Maps, 1 Large Volume Drawings, 5 Crayon Pictures, 3 Painted Pictures and 1 Painted Velvet Banner.

St. Gabriel's School.
11 Volumes: Grammar, Geography, United States History, Penmanship, Spelling, Drawing and Book-Keeping.

Holy Cross School.
3 Volumes: Reading, Language, Penmanship, Composition and Music.

Immaculate Conception School (East 14th St.).
24 Volumes: Christian Doctrine, Algebra, Grammar, Geography, Arithmetic, Geology, United States History, English History, Compositions, Penmanship.

St James' School.
4 Volumes: Penmanship, Arithmetic, Geography, Sewing, Drawing, Christian Doctrine, Grammar, Algebra, Music, Composition and Book-Keeping.

St. Joseph's School (87th St.).
4 Volumes: Arithmetic, Book-Keeping, Geography, History, Christian Doctrine and Bible History.

St. Lawrence's School.
6 Volumes: Reading, Writing, Spelling, Grammar, Geography, United States History, Composition and Christian Doctrine.

NEW YORK CITY, N. Y., Diocese of New York.—Continued.

St. Mary's School.
11 Volumes: Weaving, Catechism, Grammar, Arithmetic, Spelling, Dictations and Compositions.

St. Monica's School.
15 Volumes: Map Drawing, Christian Doctrine, History, Grammar, Geography, Civil Government, Penmanship, Geometry and Book-Keeping.

St. Peter's School.
6 Volumes: Christian Doctrine, Music, Algebra, Geometry, Arithmetic, Dictation and United States History.

St. Stephen's School.
8 Volumes: Book-Keeping, Algebra, Arithmetic, Dictation, United States History, Geometry, Grammar, Composition and Christian Doctrine.

HAVERSTRAW, N. Y., Diocese of New York.

St. Peter's School.
1 Volume: Arithmetic, Geography, Spelling, Grammar, United States History and Sewing.

KINGSTON, N. Y., Diocese of New York.

St. Joseph's School.
1 Volume: Geography, Grammar, Arithmetic, Physiology, Spelling, United States History and Catechism.

NEW BRIGHTON, N. Y., Diocese of New York.

St. Peter's School.
1 Volume: Christian Doctrine, Arithmetic, Spelling, Geography and Grammar.

NEWBURGH, N. Y., Diocese of New York.

St. Patrick's School.
24 Copy Books: Book-Keeping, Penmanship, Geography, Christian Doctrine, Geometry, Civil Government, History, Grammar, Literature and Specimens of Sewing.

NYACK, N. Y., Diocese of New York.

St. Ann's School.
7 Copy Books: Arithmetic, Grammar, Geography, Catechism, Dictations, History, Spelling, Numbers, Writing, Compositions and Drawing.

POUGHKEEPSIE, N. Y., Diocese of New York.

St. Mary's School.
1 Volume Arithmetic, Geography, Grammar, 17 Maps, 4 Cards Drawing, 2 Cards of Pasting.

RONDOUT, N. Y., Diocese of New York.

St. Mary's School.
3 Volumes: Catechism, Language, Arithmetic, Geography, Spelling, Grammar, United States History and Compositions.

ROSENDALE, N. Y., Diocese of New York.
  St. Peter's School.
    2 Volumes: Christian Doctrine, Church History, Geography, Spelling, Grammar, Arithmetic, Penmanship and Map Drawing.

SAUGERTIES, N. Y., Diocese of New York.
  St. Mary's School.
    2 Volumes: Christian Doctrine, Arithmetic, Spelling, Grammar, History, Language, Drawing and Numbers.

SING SING, N. Y., Diocese of New York.
  St. Augustine's School.
    5 Volumes: Christian Doctrine, Church History, Dictation, Arithmetic, Grammar, United States History, Penmanship, Reading, Composition, Map Drawing.

INDUSTRIAL SCHOOLS.

BROOKLYN, N. Y., Diocese of Brooklyn.
  St. Paul's Industrial School.
    5 Volumes: Christian Doctrine, Arithmetic, Geography, Grammar, United States Government, Maps, Photographs and Needle-Work.

  St. John's Home.
    2 Volumes: Christian Doctrine, Arithmetic, Spelling, Language, Geography, Drawing; 2 Volumes Kindergarten Work.

NEW YORK CITY, N. Y., Diocese of New York.
  Roman Catholic Male Orphan Asylum.
    Collection of Photographs.

WESTCHESTER, N. Y., Diocese of New York.
  New York Catholic Protectory.
    3 Embroidered Glove Cushions, 11 Pairs Kid Gloves, 3 Boards of Sample Lace, 5 Linen Embroidered Tray Covers, 4 Children's Bonnets, 3 Silk Neckties, 5 Ladies' Waists, 1 Lady's Morning Gown, 8 Gentlemen's Shirts, 1 Book of Stenography, 1 Embroidered Coverlet Patch-Work, 1 Wax Figure Dressed, 1 Night Dress, 3 Children's White Aprons, 4 Bonnet Stands, 1 Kid (Mounted), 7 Muslin Covers, 3 Sets of Underclothes, 19 Pictures, 1 Basket of Flowers, 6 Kindergarten Mats and 4 Glass Cases.

Sisters of Charity (Mt. St. Joseph, Ohio).

PARISH SCHOOLS.

CLEVELAND, OHIO.
  St. Wenceslaus' School.
    1 Volume: Arithmetic, Algebra, Christian Doctrine, United States History, Bible History, Geography, Book-Keeping, Compositions, Letter Writing, Grammar, Music, Drawing.

DENVER, COL., Diocese of Denver.

Sacred Heart School.

3 Volumes: Grammar, Letter Writing, Business Forms, Freehand Drawing, Penmanship, Algebra, United States History, Geography, Physiology, General History, Bible History, Geometry.

Immaculate Conception School.

3 Volumes: Christian Doctrine, Arithmetic, Geography, History, Orthography, Grammar, Physiology, Book-Keeping, Letter Writing, Penmanship, Freehand Drawing, Map Drawing and Music.

LIMA, OHIO, Diocese of Cleveland.

St. Rose of Lima's School.

1 Volume: Christian Doctrine, Philosophy, History, Arithmetic, Geography, Penmanship, United States History and Drawing.

PUEBLO, COL., Diocese of Denver.

St. Patrick's School.

1 Volume: Christian Doctrine, Arithmetic, Penmanship, United States History, Orthography, Pen and Freehand Drawing, Vocal Music, Object and Map Drawing.

WELLSVILLE, OHIO.

Immaculate Conception School.

1 Volume: Drawing, Catechism, United States History, Mental Arithmetic, Practical Arithmetic, Music and Grammar.

Sisters of Charity (Leavenworth).

DENVER, COL., Diocese of Denver.

Annunciation School.

1 Volume: Arithmetic, Geography, Christian Doctrine, Orthography, Bible History, Penmanship, Photographs.

LEADVILLE, COL., Diocese of Denver.

St. Mary's School.

1 Volume: Christian Doctrine, History, Arithmetic, Geography, Grammar, Algebra, Book-Keeping, Church History, Literature and Physics.

ORPHANAGE.

DENVER, COL., Diocese of Denver.

Mt. St. Vincent's Orphan Asylum.

1 Volume: Christian Doctrine, Geography, Arithmetic, Orthography, United States History, Object Lessons, Map Drawing and Freehand Drawing.

Sisters of Charity (Nazareth).

ALCOVES 54 AND 56.

ACADEMIES.

COVINGTON, KY., Diocese of Covington.

La Salette Academy.

6 Volumes: Christian Doctrine, Map Drawing, Spelling, Latin, Geometry, Algebra, Physiology, Practical Science, Arithmetic, Letter Writing, Bible History, Music and Book-Keeping.

LEXINGTON, KY., Diocese of Covington.

St. Catharine's Academy.

5 Volumes: Map Drawing, Arithmetic, Compositions, Christian Doctrine and Spelling.

NEWPORT, KY., Diocese of Covington.

Immaculate Conception Academy.

5 Volumes: Christian Doctrine, Church History, Map Drawing, Arithmetic, Grammar, Geography, Mental Arithmetic, Compositions, Remembered Reading, Spelling, Natural Philosophy, Zoology, Physiology, Drawing and Music.

PINE BLUFF, ARK., Diocese of Little Rock.

Annunciation Academy.

1 Volume Map and Freehand Drawing, 1 Volume Book-Keeping, 1 Volume Essays. 8 Volumes: Christian Doctrine, Orthography, Grammar, Geography, United States, Modern and Ancient History, Arithmetic, Book-Keeping, Algebra, Stenography, Typewriting, Natural History, Natural Philosophy, Geology, Chemistry, Mythology, Botany, Rhetoric, Logic, Astronomy. 22 Plain Drawings, 2 Crayon Drawings, 17 Oil Paintings, 1 Polish Painting, 3 Crystal Pearl Paintings, 1 Pastel, 39 Specimens of Embroidery, 1 Chart of Pine Bluff and Environs, 1 Catalogue of Academy, 5 Volumes Specimens of Botany.

PARISH SCHOOLS.

COVINGTON, KY., Diocese of Covington.

St. Mary's Cathedral School.

2 Volumes: Christian Doctrine, United States History, Grammar, Arithmetic, Letter Writing and Map Drawing.

St. Patrick's School.

3 Volumes: Map Drawing, Letter Writing, Geography, Compositions, Christian Doctrine, Penmanship.

FRANKFORT, KY., Diocese of Covington.

St. Joseph's and St. Aloysius' Schools.

14 Volumes: Christian Doctrine, Geography, Map Drawing, Grammar, Languages, Reading, United States History, Bible History, Algebra, Mathematics, Physical Geography, Astronomy, Latin and Rhetoric.

LEXINGTON, KY., Diocese of Covington.

St. Peter Claver's School (Colored).

2 Volumes: Map Drawing, Arithmetic, Grammar, Spelling, Catechism and Letters.

MEMPHIS, TENN., Diocese of Nashville.

St. Patrick's School.

10 Volumes: Christian Doctrine, Orthography, Arithmetic, Geography, Bible History, Grammar, United States History, Algebra, Ancient History, Rhetoric, Literature, Civil Government, Geometry, Mythology, Map Drawing; 3 Oil Paintings, Crayon Drawings (Figures and Ornaments).

NEWPORT, KY., Diocese of Covington.

Immaculate Conception School.

4 Volumes: Christian Doctrine, Map Drawing, Definitions, Spelling and Arithmetic.

PARIS, KY., Diocese of Covington.

St. Mary's School.

Catechism, Spelling, Dictation, Grammar, Arithmetic, Geography and Map Drawing.

PINE BLUFF, ARK., Diocese of Little Rock.

Colored Industrial School.

2 Volumes Arithmetic, 2 Volumes Geography, 2 Volumes Orthography, 1 Volume Map Drawing, 2 Volumes: United States History, Grammar and Popular Science, 4 Specimens of Knitted Work, Plain Sewing, Dressmaking, Specimens of Cotton and Cotton Bales.

Sisters of Christian Charity.

LE MARS, IOWA, Diocese of Dubuque.

St. Joseph's School.

3 Volumes: German, Geography, Christian Doctrine, Arithmetic, United States History, Map Drawing and 4 Plush Banners.

CHICAGO, ILL., Diocese of Chicago.

Josephinum Academy.

8 Volumes Class-Work, 27 Pieces Needle-Work, 8 Oil Paintings, 7 Crayons.

PARISH SCHOOLS.

CHICAGO, ILL., Diocese of Chicago.
St. Aloysius' School.

7 Volumes: Map Drawing, German, Grammar, Needle-Work (17 Pieces).

St. Teresa's School.

5 Volumes: Catechism, United States and Bible History, German Dictations, Arithmetic, Spelling, Geography, Translations, Map and Pencil Drawing. 2 Volumes: Drawing, Mending and Knitting, 1 Volume Plain Sewing, 1 Volume Articles cut and made ready for the machine, Fancy Articles of Embroidery.

Sisters of Mercy.

ALCOVES 56, 57 AND 59.

CONVENTS, ACADEMIES and SELECT SCHOOLS.

ALLEGHANY, PA., Diocese of Pittsburgh.
St. Ann's Academy.

1 Volume Christian Doctrine.

BEATTY, PA., Diocese of Pittsburgh.
St. Xavier's Academy.

17 Albums: Church History, Music, Geography, Stenography, Grammar, Essays, Literature, Freehand Drawing; 6 Charts Church History, 6 Folios Natural History (Illustrated), 1 Folio Botany (Illustrated), 1 Genealogical Chart of English and French Rulers, 1 Black Satin Screen (Embroidered).

BROOKLYN, N. Y., Diocese of Brooklyn.
St. Joseph's Academy.

2 Volumes: Christian Doctrine, Mechanical Drawing, Fancy Work, Arithmetic, Physiology, French, Music, Compositions and English Literature.

BRYN MAWR, PA., Diocese of Philadelphia.
Our Lady of Good Counsel School.

See Diocesan Exhibit.

BUFFALO, N. Y., Diocese of Buffalo.
St. Stephen's School.

1 Volume: Catechism, Arithmetic, Geography, Grammar, Letter Writing and Spelling.

CHICAGO, ILL., Diocese of Chicago.

Holy Angels' Academy.

1 Oil Painting of Pastor, Pastel Paintings, Ornamental and Figure Drawings (Crayon), Map Drawing, Penmanship, Ornamental Writing, Photographs of School and Pupils, Pen-Work Sketches.

St. Francis Xavier's Academy.

17 Volumes Examination Papers, 15 Specimens Ornamental Penmanship, 2 Volumes Essays, 2 Volumes Photographs, 1 Volume "The Echo," 4 Volumes Music, 44 Paintings, 1 Portfolio Drawings from Still-Life, 1 Portfolio Drawings from Cast, 2 Volumes Perspective Drawings and 1 Book from Medallions.

St. Patrick's Academy.

1 Volume each of Christian Doctrine, Algebra, History, Rhetoric, Science, Church History, Geometry, Trigonometry, Chemistry, Physics, Philosophy, Essays, French, German, Catalogues, Photographs, Academia, Maps, Poems, Gems from Geology, Literature, Herbarium; 3 Volumes Drawings, 2 Volumes Latin, 5 Volumes Thorough Base, 2 Volumes Original Music, 4 Volumes Kindergarten Work, 21 Paintings, 11 Pieces Needle-Work, Decorated China.

Mt. Carmel Academy.

14 Volumes: Catechism, Spelling, Language, Composition, Physiology, United States History, Bible History, Map Drawing, Physical Geography, Essays, Algebra, Literature, English History, Civil Government, Rhetoric, Zoology, French, Latin, German, Music and Drawing.

DEWITT, IOWA, Diocese of Dubuque.

St. Joseph's Academy.

1 Volume: Astronomy, Geometry, Physical Geography, Grammar and Church History.

EUREKA (HUMBOLDT CO.), CAL., Diocese of Sacramento.

St. Joseph's Convent.

8 Small Wall Maps, 1 Historical Map, 1 Model Drawing, 1 Crayon Drawing, 1 Painting (a few traces from MSS. of the Ancient Abbey of Cluney, France, founded A. D. 810 by St. Bruno and finally destroyed by the French Revolution. These MSS. were wrought by the hands of monks who were probably contemporaries of Columbus) and 2 Framed Maps.

GRASS VALLEY, CAL., Diocese of Sacramento.

Mt. St. Mary's Academy.

38 Albums: Christian Doctrine, Grammar, United States History, Orthography, Geography, Spelling, Book-Keeping, Compositions, Algebra, General History, Vocal Music, Freehand Drawing, Map Drawing, Oil Painting, Photographs, Pastels, Fancy Hair-Work, Embroidered Scarfs and Specimens of Botany.

GREENVILLE, MISS., Diocese of Natchez.

St. Rose of Lima's Academy.

3 Volumes: Christian Doctrine, History of the United States, Geography, Map Drawing, Arithmetic, Spelling, Physiology, Grammar, Music, Compositions, Ancient History, Mythology, Botany, Astronomy, Algebra, Physics, Physical Geography, Philosophical and Biographical Sketches.

LORETTO, PA., Diocese of Pittsburgh.
St. Aloysius' Academy.
7 Volumes: Algebra, Geometry, Physical Culture, Grammar, Essays on Sciences, Geography, Map Drawing; 1 Relief Map of South America, 1 Chart of American History, Sciences, Literature and Art. 1 Carved Easel, 1 Chart of Universal Biography.

MERIDIAN, MISS., Diocese of Natchez.
St. Aloysius' Academy.
2 Volumes: Catechism, Ancient and Modern History, Grammar, Mental Philosophy, Geometry, Algebra, Arithmetic, Natural Philosophy, Astronomy, Rhetoric, Book-Keeping. 1 Volume Original Essays (with Photographs of Writers).

NASHVILLE, TENN., Diocese of Nashville.
St. Bernard's Academy.
2 Volumes: Christian Doctrine, Orthography, United States History, Mensuration, Grammar, Natural Philosophy, Biography, Book-Keeping and Rhetoric.

OAKLAND, CAL., Archdiocese of San Francisco.
Academy of Our Lady of Lourdes.
1 Volume Christian Doctrine, 2 Volumes Mathematics, 2 Volumes Composition, 1 Volume: Grammar, Rhetoric, Word Analysis, Penmanship; 1 Volume Geography, 1 Volume History, 1 Volume: Astronomy, Philosophy, Botany and Physiology; 1 Volume Drawing, 1 Volume Music and 1 Album Photographs.

OTTAWA, ILL., Diocese of Peoria.
St. Francis Xavier's Academy.
4 Volumes: Christian Doctrine, Spelling, Arithmetic, Grammar, Geography, Object Lessons, Drawing, Physical Geography and Music.

PITTSBURGH, PA., Diocese of Pittsburgh.
St. Mary's Academy.
7 Volumes: Christian Doctrine, Arithmetic, Algebra, Geometry, Chemistry, Physical Geography, Physiology, Astronomy, Book-Keeping, Stenography, Typewriting, Latin, Greek, Compositions, American and European History, Maps. 1 Case Hand-Painted China and 4 Pieces Sewing and Embroidery.

RIO VISTA, CAL., Archdiocese of San Francisco.
St. Gertrude's Academy.
NORMAL DEPT.
Illuminated History of Academy, Photographs

STUDENTS' WORK.
25 Volumes: Arithmetic, Algebra, Spelling, Geometry, Grammar, Compositions, English Literature, Geography, Maps, Physical Geography, Ancient and Modern History, Rhetoric, Word-Analysis, Astronomy, Natural Philosophy, Music, Penmanship, Stenography, Typewriting, Christian Doctrine, Studies in Crayon and Oil.

SAN FRANCISCO, CAL., Archdiocese of San Francisco.

Our Lady of Mercy's Academy.

4 Volumes Religion, 4 Volumes Language, 6 Volumes Arithmetic, 1 Volume Book-Keeping, 4 Volumes Geography, 2 Volumes Spelling, 4 Volumes History, 1 Volume Literature, 1 Volume Science, 3 Volumes Oral Instruction, 6 Volumes Music, 6 Volumes Drawing and 1 School Album.

St. Peter's Convent.

7 Volumes Language, 4 Volumes Arithmetic, 3 Volumes Science, 2 Volumes Geography, 2 Volumes History, 1 Volume Penmanship, 4 Volumes Drawing and 1 Album Photographs.

VICKSBURG, MISS., Diocese of Natchez.

St. Francis Xavier's Academy.

7 Volumes: Christian Doctrine, Book-Keeping, Grammar, Geography, Arithmetic, Ancient and Modern History, Familiar Science, Philosophy, Drawing, Original Poem (Illustrated), Geology, Literature, Chemistry, Mythology; 1 Volume Photographic Views of Academy, Grounds and Buildings, 11 Oil Paintings, 3 Portfolios Studies in Oil, 3 Relief Maps and 1 Frame with 5 Pieces Painted China.

PARISH SCHOOLS.

BRADDOCK, PA., Diocese of Pittsburgh.

St. Thomas' School.

1 Volume: Christian Doctrine, Grammar, United States History, Geography and Physiology.

BUFFALO, N. Y., Diocese of Buffalo.

St. Bridget's School.

6 Albums: Penmanship, Grammar, Geography, Arithmetic, Compositions.

BILOXI, MISS., Diocese of Natchez.

Maris Stella School.

14 Volumes: Christian Doctrine, Grammar, Geography, Astronomy, Philosophy, History, Rhetoric, Arithmetic and 1 Volume Crayon Drawings.

BUTLER, PA., Diocese of Pittsburgh.

St. Paul's School.

3 Volumes: Book-Keeping, Grammar, Geography, Etymology, Maps, Arithmetic and Natural History.

St. Peter's School.

1 Historical Geographical Map.

CEDAR RAPIDS, IOWA, Diocese of Dubuque.

St. Joseph's School.

1 Table Cover (White Silk and Gold Spangles); Kindergarten Work.

CHICAGO, ILL., Diocese of Chicago.

All Saints' School.

43 Volumes: Bible History, Christian Doctrine, History, Mensuration, Compositions, Language, Geography, Maps, History, Pen Sketches, Photographs, Theory of Music; 25 Copy Books, 4 Portfolios of Drawing, 3 Framed Maps and 2 Pen Portraits.

Holy Angels' School.

17 Volumes: Arithmetic, United States and Bible History, Language, Spelling, Writing, Geography, Christian Doctrine; 1 Map of Illinois.

St. Agnes' School.

12 Volumes: Bible History, Catechism, United States History, Language, Geography, Compositions, Physiology, Spelling, Writing, Arithmetic, Map Drawing, Ornamental Writing; 9 Framed Maps; 1 Volume Work by Katie Forbes, a cripple born without hands.

St. Elizabeth's School.

31 Volumes: Christian Doctrine, Writing, Latin, Essays, Ancient History, Physical Geography, Algebra, Compositions, Language, Arithmetic. Physiology, Spelling, United States History, Bible History, Drawing; 19 Maps and Photographs.

St. Gabriel's School.

32 Volumes: Arithmetic, Language, Compositions, Catechism, Spelling, Geography, Physiology, History, Drawing, Map Drawing, Music; Map of the United States, Crayon Portrait and Map of War Campaign.

St. James' School.

20 Drawing Books, 5 Copy Books Writing, 14 Volumes Language Lessons, 4 Volumes Christian Doctrine, 6 Volumes Geography, 3 Volumes History, Geography, 9 Volumes Compositions, 1 Volume Map Drawing, 1 Relief Map, 6 Volumes Daily Work, 2 Volumes Mensuration, 1 Volume Bible History and Christian Doctrine, 1 Volume History Tests, 1 Volume Geometry, 2 Volumes Essays, 1 Volume Book Reviews, Poems and Themes, 1 Volume Physics and Zoology, 1 Volume Doctrinal Essays, 2 Volumes Algebra, 2 Volumes Latin, 1 Volume Zoology and Botany, 4 Portfolios of Maps, 6 Volumes History and Latin, 1 Volume Physiology, 2 Volumes United States History, 1 Volume Bible History, 24 Pen Sketches, 4 Charcoal Sketches, 8 Pastel Studies, 2 Charts English Literature, Relief Maps, Crayon, Sepia and Water-Color Drawings, Kindergarten.

St. Michael's School.

9 Volumes Class-Work, 4 Volumes Drawing, 2 Volumes Maps, 1 Volume Photographs and 8 Framed Maps and Drawings.

St. Patrick's School (South Chicago).

21 Volumes: Catechism, Spelling, Grammar, Arithmetic, Compositions, Language, Geography, History, Drawing, Physiology, Map Drawing and Pen-Work.

CONNELLSVILLE, PA., Diocese of Pittsburgh.

Immaculate Conception School.

6 Volumes: Church History, Etymology, Grammar, Arithmetic, Physiology, Rhetoric, Chronology; 2 Historical Geographical Maps.

DENVER, COL., Diocese of Denver.

St. Joseph's School.

> 1 Volume: Bible History, Grammar, Orthography, Arithmetic, United States History, Freehand Drawing and Photographs.

DURANGO, COL., Diocese of Denver.

St. Columba's School.

> 1 Volume: Christian Doctrine, Book-Keeping, Algebra, Arithmetic, Geography, Grammar, History, Orthography, Penmanship, Physiology, Botany, Natural Science, Natural Philosophy, Music and Photographs.

FT. DODGE, IOWA, Diocese of Dubuque.

Our Lady of Lourdes' School.

> 2 Volumes: Arithmetic, Grammar, Christian Doctrine, Astronomy, Geography and Map Drawing.

JACKSON, MISS., Diocese of Natchez.

St. Joseph's School.

> 1 Volume: Christian Doctrine, Church History, Geometry, Rhetoric, Philosophy, Algebra, Ancient History, Biography, Grammar, Mythology, Arithmetic, Geography and History.

JAMESTOWN, N. Y., Diocese of Buffalo.

Sts. Peter and Paul's School.

> 1 Album: Grammar, Arithmetic, Geography and Language.

JEANNERETTE, LA., Diocese of New Orleans.

St. Joseph's School.

> 1 Folio Drawing and 2 Folios Examination Papers.

KEENE, N. H., Diocese of Manchester.

St. Joseph's School.

> 3 Volumes: Christian Doctrine, Arithmetic, Language, Orthography, Bible History, United States History, Grammar, Geography and Composition.

LATROBE, PA., Diocese of Pittsburgh.

Holy Family School.

> 2 Volumes: Christian Doctrine, Grammar, Latin, English, Derivations, Composition, History, Stenography and Typewriting.

LOCKPORT, N. Y., Diocese of Buffalo.

St. John's School.

> 1 Volume: Christian Doctrine, Arithmetic, Geography, Grammar, Spelling, Mensuration and Drawing.

St. Patrick's School.

> 1 Volume: History, Arithmetic, Algebra, History of Columbus, Grammar, Analysis, Drawing, Kindergarten Work and Christian Doctrine.

MANCHESTER, N. H., Diocese of Manchester.

St. Agnes' School.

4 Volumes: Christian Doctrine, Church History, United States History, Arithmetic, Grammar, Letter Writing, Language and Geography.

St. Joseph's School.

6 Volumes: Christian Doctrine, Arithmetic, Geography, Orthography, United States History, Church and Bible History, Letter Writing, Composition, Penmanship and Grammar.

MANCHESTER, IOWA, Diocese of Dubuque.

St. Xavier's School.

1 Volume: Christian Doctrine, Arithmetic, Geography, Map and Mechanical Drawing and Letter Writing.

NASHUA, N. H., Diocese of Manchester.

Sacred Heart School.

5 Albums: Christian Doctrine, United States History, Bible History, Physiology, Physical Geography, Map Drawing, Grammar, Orthography, Composition, Arithmetic and Kindergarten Work.

NASHVILLE, TENN., Diocese of Nashville.

St. Joseph's School.

7 Volumes: Christian Doctrine, Orthography, Grammar, Arithmetic, Geography, Algebra, Modern History, Bible History and Penmanship.

St. Patrick's School.

49 Albums: Spelling, Grammar, Geography, Catechism, Arithmetic, History, Letter Writing, Map Drawing and Algebra.

NEW ORLEANS, LA., Diocese of New Orleans.

St. Alphonsus' High School.

1 Folio each: Pen-Work, Maps, Caligraphic Exercises, Examination Papers, Senior Class; Examination Papers, Second Year; Examination Papers, First Year; Original Compositions; 1 Framed Photograph of Pupils, 1 Framed Map of Cuba, Ocean Currents, Delta of Mississippi and The World.

St. Alphonsus' School.

1 Folio each: Examination Papers, First Grade; Drawing, First Grade; Drawings of Second Grade; Examination Papers, First to Fourth Grades and 2 Volumes Examination Papers, Second Grade.

Notre Dame de Bon Secours School.

3 Volumes: Christian Doctrine, Philosophy, Orthography, Reading, Geography, Grammar, United States History, Written Exercises, Penmanship, Drawing, Arithmetic, Translations, Astronomy, Rhetoric, Literature, Civil Government, Physical Geography, Compositions, Algebra, Ancient and Modern History, Physiology and Etiquette; 1 Volume Drawing and 1 Frame Photographs.

St. Michael's and St. Philippe's Schools.

1 Folio Maps, 4 Folios Examination Papers.

NIAGARA FALLS, N. Y., Diocese of Buffalo.

St. Mary's School.

Church History, Compositions, Rhetoric, Algebra, Physiology, Physical Geography, United States History, Book-Keeping, Civil Government, History of New York, Drawing and Christian Doctrine.

OLEAN, N. Y., Diocese of Buffalo.

St. Mary's School.

1 Volume: Christian Doctrine, Sacred History, Algebra, Geometry, Physiology, Geography, Grammar, Map Drawing, Natural Philosophy, Book-Keeping and Kindergarten Work.

OWEGO, N. Y., Diocese of Buffalo.

Sacred Heart School.

1 Album: Christian Doctrine, Grammar, Arithmetic.

PASS CHRISTIAN, MISS., Diocese of Natchez.

St. Joseph's School.

1 Volume: Christian Doctrine, Grammar, Spelling, Arithmetic, Geography, Philosophy, Church History and United States History.

PHILADELPHIA, PA., Diocese of Philadelphia.

St. Malachy's School.

Examination Papers.

PITTSBURGH, PA., Diocese of Pittsburgh.

St. Agnes' School.

1 Volume: Christian Doctrine, Algebra, Grammar, Geography, Map Drawing, United States History.

St. Benedict's School (Colored).

1 Volume: Christian Doctrine, Arithmetic, Spelling, Dictation and 4 Pieces Plain Sewing.

St. Bridget's School.

4 Volumes: Christian Doctrine, History, Grammar, Arithmetic, United States History and Map Drawing.

St. John the Baptist's School.

1 Volume: Christian Doctrine, United States History, Orthography, Geography and Grammar.

St. John's School.

1 Volume: Christian Doctrine, Language, Geography, Arithmetic, Grammar and Drawing.

St. Mary of Mercy School.

1 Volume: Christian Doctrine, Arithmetic, Grammar, Drawing, History and Geography.

St. Mary's School.

2 Volumes: Christian Doctrine, Book-Keeping, Literature, Grammar, Algebra, Arithmetic, Geometry and Stenography.

PITTSBURGH, PA., Diocese of Pittsburgh.—Continued.

St. Paul's School.

4 Volumes: Christian Doctrine, Arithmetic, Geography, Maps, Grammar, Dictation, Colored Maps, Composition; 3 Folios Freehand and Map Drawing and 2 Framed Maps.

St. Paul's School.

6 Volumes: Christian Doctrine, Arithmetic, Geography, History, Grammar, Dictation, Colored Maps, Composition; 3 Folios Freehand and Map Drawings.

St. Patrick's School.

2 Volumes: Christian Doctrine, United States History, Grammar, Arithmetic and Dictation.

PORTSMOUTH, N. H., Diocese of Manchester.

Immaculate Conception School.

1 Album: Christian Doctrine, Church History, Physiology, Physical Geography, Algebra, Typewriting, Orthography, Compositions, Arithmetic and Kindergarten Work.

ST. MARTINSVILLE, LA., Diocese of New Orleans.

St. Martin's School.

Folio of Examination Papers. 1 Framed Photograph of St. Alphonsus' Convent of Mercy. 1 Framed Photograph of St. Catherine's College (Annex to St. Alphonsus' Convent of Mercy).

TURTLE CREEK, PA., Diocese of Pittsburgh.

St. Coleman's School.

1 Volume: Christian Doctrine, Familiar Science, Arithmetic, History, Grammar and Geography.

TYRONE, PA., Diocese of Pittsburgh.

St. Matthew's School.

1 Volume: Arithmetic and Composition.

ORPHANAGES, INDUSTRIAL SCHOOLS AND KINDERGARTENS.

BROOKLYN, N. Y., Diocese of Brooklyn.

Industrial School of Mercy.

Samples of Silk Lace, Needle-Work, Crochet Jacket, 1 Pair Shoes, 12 Samples on Card, Crocheting and Buttonhole Making, Embroidery on Muslin, 1 Dressing Gown, 2 Baby Dresses (Embroidered), 3 Doilies and 2 Handkerchiefs.

GRASS VALLEY, CAL., Diocese of Sacramento.

St. Patrick's Orphan Asylum.

Spelling, Arithmetic, Letter Writing, Object Drawing, Photographs.

MANCHESTER, N. H., Diocese of Manchester.

St. Patrick's Orphanage.

1 Volume: Specimens Penmanship, Map and Freehand Drawing.

NEW YORK CITY, N. Y., Archdiocese of New York.

Institution of Mercy.

2 Pairs Crochet Lace Curtains, 1 Cotton Crochet Curtain, 1 Satin Cushion Cover (Crochet), 2 Satin Table Covers and 1 Bolster Cover.

OAKLAND, CAL., Diocese of San Francisco.

Our Lady of Lourdes Kindergarten.

3 Charts Kindergarten Work.

SAN FRANCISCO, CAL., Diocese of San Francisco.

St. Brendan's Kindergarten.

Sewing, Embossing and Weaving.

TUCKER, MISS., Diocese of Natchez.

Holy Rosary Indian School.

1 Volume: Spelling, Arithmetic, Christian Doctrine and Geography.

Sisters of Notre Dame (Cincinnati).

ALCOVE 4.

ACADEMIES.

BOSTON, MASS., Diocese of Boston.

Academy of Notre Dame.

5 Volumes: Drawing, Botany, Literature, Christian Doctrine and Specimens of Needle-Work.

LOWELL, MASS., Diocese of Boston.

St. Patrick's Academy.

2 Volumes Needle-Work, 1 Volume: Christian Doctrine, English Compositions, Spanish Translations, French Translations, German Poem, Latin Translations; 1 Volume: Geology, Botany, Chemistry, Mathematics, Geometry, Trigonometry and Commercial Forms.

PHILADELPHIA, PA., Diocese of Philadelphia.

Academy of Notre Dame.

3 Volumes Theory of Music, 1 Volume Musical Compositions, by Pupils, 1 Volume Music compiled and arranged by Sisters of Notre Dame.

ROXBURY, MASS., Diocese of Boston.

Notre Dame Academy.

1 Volume English and American Literature, 1 Volume: Zoology, Botany, Astronomy, Chemistry and Composition.

PAROCHIAL SCHOOLS.

BOSTON, MASS., Diocese of Boston.

St. Joseph's School.

1 Volume Specimens of Sewing, 1 Volume Drawing, 1 Volume: Grammar, United States History, Sacred History, Geography, Arithmetic, Compositions, Christian Doctrine, Literature and Penmanship.

St. Mary's School.

2 Volumes: History, Christian Doctrine, Business Letters, Grammar, Compositions, Geography, Penmanship, Literature, Botany, Sacred History, Algebra; 2 Volumes Specimens Drawing.

EAST BOSTON, MASS., Diocese of Boston.

Our Holy Redeemer High School.

1 Volume: Literature, Astronomy, Philosophy, Music, Book-Keeping, History, Algebra, Civil Government, Mineralogy and Botany.

Holy Redeemer School.
Assumption School.   } *United Work.*
Sacred Heart School.

2 Volumes: Christian Doctrine, Geography, Grammar, United States History, Compositions, Bible History, Language, Zoology, Botany, Book-Keeping; 1 Volume Specimens of Sewing.

LAWRENCE, MASS., Diocese of Boston.

St. Mary's School.

1 Volume: Examination Papers, Literature, United States History, Book-Keeping, Astronomy, Mathematics, Algebra, Philosophy, Penmanship, Poetry, Compositions, Geography, Grammar, Language, Catechism and Music.

LOWELL, MASS., Diocese of Boston.

St. Patrick's School.

4 Volumes Specimens of Needle-Work, 1 Volume: Compositions, Literature, Astronomy, History, Algebra, Geography, Arithmetic, Language and Grammar.

LYNN, MASS., Diocese of Boston.

St. Mary's School.

2 Volumes: Literature, Book-Keeping, Botany, Music, Algebra, Physiology, Conchology, Geology, Arithmetic, Compositions, 1 Volume: Drawing, United States History, Geography, Essays, Sacred History, Grammar, English History, Zoology.

SALEM, MASS., Diocese of Boston.

St. James' School.

1 Volume Methods in Teaching Geography, 1 Volume Topical Synopsis of Geography and 1 Volume Outline of Geography.

SOMMERVILLE, MASS., Diocese of Boston.

St. Joseph's School.

1 Volume Drawing, 2 Volumes: Christian Doctrine, Language, English Literature, Grammar, Geography, Algebra, Architecture, Arithmetic, Natural Science, Natural History, Book-Keeping and Music; 1 Volume Science (Work of Small Children).

SPRINGFIELD, MASS., Diocese of Springfield.

Sacred Heart School.

1 Volume Specimens Needle-Work, 1 Volume: Catechism, Geography, Grammar, Zoology, Astronomy, Botany, Arithmetic, Algebra, United States History, English History, Book-Keeping, Literature, Bible History and Spelling.

WALTHAM, MASS., Diocese of Boston.

St. Joseph's School.

1 Volume (High-School Grade): Essays, Grammar, United States History, English Literature, American Literature, Church History, Algebra, Book-Keeping, Astronomy, Natural Philosophy, Botany. 1 Volume (Grammar Grades): Grammar, Compositions, United States History, Arithmetic, Geography, Catechism, Bible History, Language and Spelling.

WORCESTER, MASS., Diocese of Springfield.

St. John's School.

1 Volume Drawing, 1 Volume: United States History, Geography, Grammar, Arithmetic, Language, Christian Doctrine and Compositions.

St. John's High School.

1 Volume: Church History, English History, Physical Geography, Astronomy, Algebra, Book-Keeping, United States History, Arithmetic, Map Drawing and Architectural Drawing.

Sisters of Notre Dame (Cleveland).

ACADEMIES.

CLEVELAND, OHIO, Diocese of Cleveland.

Notre Dame Academy.

3 Volumes: Christian Doctrine, Church History, Geography, Bible History, Spelling, Language, United States History, Definitions, Grammar, Compositions, Rhetoric, Literature, Algebra, Geometry, Trigonometry, Astronomy, Ancient History, Zoology, Physiology, Theory of Music, Book-Keeping and Drawing. 2 Oil Paintings, 1 Sepia Painting, Crayons and Landscapes; Leather Picture.

COVINGTON, KY., Diocese of Covington.

Notre Dame Academy.

2 Volumes: Christian Doctrine, Bible History, Arithmetic, Spelling, Dictation, Definition, Language, Compositions, Penmanship, Theory of Music, Hints on Letter Writing, United States History, Roman History, Astronomy, Rhetoric, Botany and Physics.

PARISH SCHOOLS.

AKRON, OHIO, Diocese of Cleveland.

St. Bernard's School.

1 Volume: Catechism, Bible History, Arithmetic, Grammar, Spelling, Compositions, United States History, Penmanship, Geography and Drawing.

St. Mary's School.

1 Volume: Arithmetic, Bible History, Spelling, Grammar, United States History, Geography and Penmanship.

St. Vincent's School.

1 Volume: Arithmetic, Christian Doctrine, Grammar, United States History, Geography and Penmanship.

ALEXANDRIA, KY., Diocese of Covington.

St. Mary's School.

Arithmetic, German Exercises, Compositions, Spelling and Penmanship.

BELLEVUE, KY., Diocese of Covington.

Sacred Heart School.

1 Volume: Arithmetic, German Exercises, Compositions, Spelling, Grammar, Penmanship.

CANTON, OHIO, Diocese of Cleveland.

St. John's School.

1 Volume: Christian Doctrine, Compositions, Geography, Grammar, Dictations and Spelling.

St. Peter's School.

1 Volume: Christian Doctrine, Grammar, Arithmetic, Compositions, Penmanship, Theory of Music, Astronomy, Physics, Book-Keeping. German Exercises: Christian Doctrine, Bible History, Grammar, Letter Writing, Compositions and Penmanship.

CARROLLTON, KY., Diocese of Covington.

St. John's School.

1 Volume: Catechism, Bible History, Arithmetic, Geography, United States History and Compositions.

CLEVELAND, OHIO, Diocese of Cleveland.

Our Lady of Lourdes' School.

1 Volume: Christian Doctrine, German, Grammar, United States History and Theory of Music.

St. Adalbert's School.

1 Volume: Christian Doctrine, Composition, Bible History, Penmanship and Letter Writing.

St. Francis' School.

1 Volume: Christian Doctrine, Grammar, Dictation, Compositions and Geography.

St. Michael's School.

1 Volume: German, Arithmetic, Grammar, Geography and United States History.

St. Peter's School.

2 Volumes: Bible History, Arithmetic, Spelling, Definitions, Grammar, Compositions, German Language Lessons, German Grammar, United States History, Theory of Music, Penmanship, Geography, Mechanical Drawing, Christian Doctrine, Dictations, English Compositions; Photographs of School and Church.

St. Stephen's School.

1 Volume: German Compositions, Grammar, Spelling, Dictations, Letters, Map Drawing and Penmanship.

COLD SPRINGS, KY., Diocese of Covington.

St. Joseph's School.

1 Volume: German Exercises, Religion, Penmanship and Composition.

COVINGTON, KY., Diocese of Covington.

Mother of God School.

3 Volumes: Arithmetic, Christian Doctrine, Spelling, German Exercises, Music, Penmanship and Map Drawing.

St. Augustine's School.

German, Arithmetic, Letter Writing, Map Drawing, Music, Compositions, United States History and German Exercises.

St. John's School.

1 Volume: Letter Writing, Compositions, Dictations, German Exercises and Map Drawing.

DELPHOS, OHIO, Diocese of Cleveland.

St. James' School.

1 Volume: Grammar, Drawing, Spelling, Christian Doctrine, United States History, Photographs.

St. John's School.

2 Volumes: Catechism, Bible History, Arithmetic, Algebra, Book-Keeping, Spelling, Grammar, Composition, Geography, United States History, German Composition, Penmanship; 1 Volume Drawing.

FREMONT, OHIO, Diocese of Cleveland.

St. Joseph's School.
1 Volume: Grammar, Drawing, Spelling, Christian Doctrine.

NAPOLEON, OHIO, Diocese of Cleveland.

St. Augustine's School.
1 Volume: Christian Doctrine, Grammar, United States History, Geography and Compositions.

NEWPORT, KY., Diocese of Covington.

St. Stephen's School.
3 Volumes. Penmanship, Letter Writing, Compositions, Dictations, German Exercises, Map Drawing, Phonography and Arithmetic.

NORWALK, OHIO, Diocese of Cleveland.

St. Paul's School.
1 Volume: Christian Doctrine, German Exercises, History, Grammar, Arithmetic, Geography, Dictation, Compositions, United States History and Penmanship.

TOLEDO, OHIO, Diocese of Cleveland.

St. Mary's School.
1 Volume: Christian Doctrine, Music, Drawing and Arts.

ORPHANAGE.

COLD SPRINGS, KY., Diocese of Covington.

St. Joseph's Orphanage.
1 Volume: Christian Doctrine, Compositions, Bible History, Arithmetic, Grammar, Spelling, Dictations and German Exercises.

Sisters of Notre Dame De Namur.

COLLEGES AND ACADEMIES.

MARYSVILLE, CAL., Diocese of San Francisco.

Notre Dame College.
Christian Doctrine, Bible History, Language, Orthography, Arithmetic, United States History, Grammar, Geography, Letter Writing, Rhetoric, Literature, General and Church History, Algebra, Geometry, Book-Keeping, Chemistry, Photographs, Needle-Work, Map Drawing, Tapestry Work.

SAN JOSE, CAL., Diocese of San Francisco.

Notre Dame College.

NORMAL DEPT.

Photographs, Chenille Work, Irish Point-Lace, Catalogues, Books Published by Former Students, Programmes and Addresses, Some Frontispieces, Selections from Herbaria, Cabinets, etc., Mounted on Transparent Celluloid, Diploma of College and History of the College.

STUDENTS' WORK.

Wild Flowers of California, Water Colors, Specimens of Needle-Work and Embroidery, 115 Volumes: History of Botany, Religion, Literature, Maps, Philology, Natural and Mental Science.

SAN FRANCISCO, CAL., Diocese of San Francisco.

Notre Dame College.

Photographs of College and Students, 1 Volume Essays, 17 Volumes Class-Work: History, Literature, Mathematics, Book-Keeping and Religion.

ALAMEDA, CAL., Diocese of San Francisco.

Academy of Notre Dame.

7 Volumes: Sacred History, Mathematics, Philosophy, Language, History and Geography.

SANTA CLARA, CAL., Diocese of San Francisco.

Academy of Our Lady of Angels.

5 Photographs, 16 Volumes Class-Work: Arithmetic, Geography, Drawing, Compositions, Christian Doctrine; 1 Box Needle-Work and Miscellaneous.

PARISH SCHOOLS.

REDWOOD CITY, CAL., Diocese of San Francisco.

Notre Dame School.

12 Volumes Class-Work: Orthography, Grammar, Rhetoric, Compositions, Literature, History, Arithmetic, Algebra, Geography, Maps, Object Lessons, Book-Keeping and Christian Doctrine.

SAN FRANCISCO, CAL., Diocese of San Francisco.

St. Francis' School.

6 Volumes Work of Preliminary and Grammar Classes: Catechism, Compositions, Arithmetic, Spelling, Dictations, Grammar, United States History, Civil Government, Physiology, Penmanship, Maps, Designs; 1 Volume Photographs.

SAN JOSE, CAL., Diocese of San Francisco.

St. Aloysius' School.

1 Volume Drawing.

St. Joseph's School.

26 Volumes Class-Work, of Preliminary, Preparatory and Grammar Classes: Arithmetic, Grammar, Language, English, Geography, United States History, Dictation, Botany, Hygiene, Ancient History, Compositions, Book-Keeping, Catechism and Bible History.

Sisters of St. Agnes.

COLUMBIA CITY, IND., Diocese of Ft. Wayne.

St. Joseph's School.

Christian Doctrine, Grammar, United States History, Church History, Freehand Drawing, Arithmetic, Geography and Compositions.

CROWN POINT, IND., Diocese of Ft. Wayne.

St. Mary's School.

Bible History, Arithmetic, Grammar, Geography and United States History.

DECATUR, IND., Diocese of Ft. Wayne.

St. Joseph's School.

Christian Doctrine, Arithmetic, Geography, United States History, Grammar, Algebra and Physiology.

MITCHELL, S. D., Diocese of Sioux Falls.

Holy Family School.

2 Volumes: Freehand Drawing, Grammar, Arithmetic, Book-Keeping, Algebra, Church History and United States History.

MUNCIE, IND., Diocese of Ft. Wayne.

St. Lawrence's School.

Orthography, Arithmetic, Language, Geography and Algebra.

NEW HAVEN, IND., Diocese of Ft. Wayne.

St. John the Baptist's School.

Christian Doctrine, Grammar, Arithmetic, History, Letter Writing, Business Forms, Book-Keeping, Geography and Map Drawing.

SHELDON, IND., Diocese of Ft. Wayne.

St. Aloysius' School.

Letter Writing, Grammar, Geography, Church History, Arithmetic.

TWO RIVERS, WIS., Diocese of Green Bay.

St. Luke's School.

1 Volume: Orthography, Christian Doctrine, Language, Letter Writing, Grammar, Arithmetic, Freehand Drawing, United States History, Penmanship and Book-Keeping.

Holy Angels' School.

2 Volumes: Christian Doctrine, Spelling, Arithmetic, Grammar, Geography, History, Freehand Drawing and Orthography.

WOODVILLE, WIS., Diocese of Green Bay.

St. John's School.

1 Volume: Christian Doctrine, Orthography, United States History, Geography, Arithmetic, Drawing, Civics, Physiology, Letter Writing and Penmanship.

Sisters of St. Francis (Joliet, Ill.).

JOLIET, ILL., Diocese of Chicago.

St. Francis' Academy.

9 Volumes Class-Work, 2 Volumes Drawing, 1 Volume Pen Drawing, 1 Volume Etiquette, 1 Volume Catalogue, Essays, Studies in Water Colors, 20 Drawings, 5 Photographs, 2 Pieces Tapestry, 41 Pieces Decorative and Fancy Needle-Work.

PARISH SCHOOLS.

CHICAGO, ILL., Diocese of Chicago.

St. Procopius' School.

English—1 Volume each: Grammar, Spelling, Arithmetic. Bohemian—1 Volume each: Catechism, Bible History and Grammar. 2 Volumes Class-Work, 3 Volumes Drawing and 7 Framed Drawings.

St. Francis of Assissi's School.

22 Volumes: Writing, Compositions, Arithmetic, Language, Spelling, Geography, Dictation, Grammar, Letters, Bible History, Translations, United States History, Business Forms, Map Drawing, Fancy Pen-Work and 17 Pieces Fancy Work.

St. Wenceslaus' School.

9 Volumes Class-Work, 2 Volumes Drawing, 1 Volume Knitting and Stitching, 1 Volume Crocheting, 1 Volume Fancy Penmanship, 27 Pieces Fancy Work.

AURORA, ILL., Diocese of Chicago.

St. Nicholas' School.

2 Writing Books, 1 Drawing Book, 2 Banners, Sewing and Kindergarten Work.

FREEPORT, ILL., Diocese of Chicago.

St. Joseph's School.

8 Volumes Class-Work and 1 Volume Needle-Work.

GALION, OHIO, Diocese of Cleveland.

St. Patrick's School.

1 Volume: Catechism, Bible History, Arithmetic, Geography, Dictation, Language, Penmanship, Grammar, Letters, Spelling, Compositions, United States History.

JOLIET, ILL., Diocese of Chicago.

St. John the Baptist's School.

6 Volumes Class-Work, 2 Volumes Pencil Drawing, 1 Volume Fancy Pen-Work, Map Drawing and 43 Specimens Needle-Work.

Sisters of St. Francis (Rochester, Minn.).

ASHLAND, KY., Diocese of Covington.
Holy Family School.
2 Volumes: Geography, Penmanship, Spelling, Language, Arithmetic, Bible History, Grammar, Composition, Physiology, Map and Mechanical Drawing.

Sisters of St. Francis (Greenburg, Pa.).

JOHNSTOWN, PA., Diocese of Pittsburgh.
St. Joseph's School.
4 Volumes: Christian Doctrine, German and English Compositions.

St. Mary's School.
4 Volumes: Christian Doctrine, Arithmetic, Dictation, History, Geography and Penmanship.

PITTSBURGH, PA., Diocese of Pittsburgh.
St. Augustine's School.
5 Volumes: Christian Doctrine, Arithmetic, Dictation, History, Geography and Penmanship.

St. George's School.
3 Volumes: Arithmetic, English and German Composition.

St. Peter's School.
5 Volumes: Arithmetic, Compositions, Penmanship, History, Geography, Dictations and Christian Doctrine.

St. Joseph's School.
5 Volumes: Arithmetic and English and German Compositions.

MILLVALE, PA., Diocese of Pittsburgh.
St. Anthony's School.
4 Volumes: Arithmetic, English and German Composition.

MT. OLIVER, PA., Diocese of Pittsburgh.
St. Joseph's School.
4 Volumes: Arithmetic and English and German Compositions.

SHARPSBURG, PA., Diocese of Pittsburgh.
St. Mary's School.
4 Volumes: Arithmetic, English Compositions, History and Dictation.

Sisters of St. Joseph.

ACADEMIES AND INSTITUTES.

BATON ROUGE, LA., Diocese of New Orleans.

St. Joseph's Academy.

36 Volumes: Geography, Grammar, Geometry, French Translations, Map Drawing, Physics, Compositions, History, Letters, Algebra, Astronomy, Book-Keeping, Arithmetic, Copy-Books; 2 Books of Maps.

BAY ST. LOUIS, MISS., Diocese of Natchez.

St. Joseph's Academy.

1 Volume: Christian Doctrine, Essays, Compositions, Botany, Grammar, Biographical Sketches, Arithmetic, Natural History, Map Drawing, Physiology, Astronomy and Physics.

BROOKLYN, N. Y., Diocese of Brooklyn.

St. Joseph's Academy (Flushing).

46 Mechanical Drawings and 12 Paintings; English, French, German and Spanish Essays, Photographs of St. Joseph's Academy.

St. Joseph's Novitiate (Flushing).

"Centennial Dream."

Nativity Academy.

3 Volumes: Map Drawing, Typewriting, Mechanical Drawing and Christian Doctrine.

Nativity Institute.

2 Volumes: Map Drawing, Algebra, Mechanical Drawing and Compositions.

Sacred Heart Institute.

Christian Doctrine, Arithmetic, Geography, Grammar, Map Drawing, Algebra, Orthography, United States History, Penmanship and Spelling.

St. Agnes' Seminary.

2 Volumes: Geography, Drawing, Letter Writing, Language, Arithmetic, Book-Keeping, General History, Autographies, Business Forms, French, Physiology, United States History and Christian Doctrine. 6 Oil Paintings, 1 Pastel, Essays, Plain and Ornamental Needle-Work and Photograph of St. Agnes' Seminary.

St. Teresa's Academy.

3 Volumes: Compositions, Grammar, Geography, Spelling, Arithmetic, Christian Doctrine, Mechanical Drawing, Book-Keeping, History and Algebra.

St. Thomas Aquinas' Academy.

2 Volumes: Christian Doctrine, Spelling, Map Drawing, Compositions, Definitions, Geography, Grammar, United States History, Civil Government, Natural Philosophy, Literature, Arithmetic, Algebra, German and French Translations.

BUFFALO, N. Y., Diocese of Buffalo.

Mt. St. Vincent's Academy.

1 Volume; History, Catechism, Geography, Dictation, Arithmetic, Orthography, German, Drawing, Fancy Work, Photographic Views; 1 Volume Maps.

CHARENTON, LA., Diocese of New Orleans.

St. Joseph's Convent.

19 Albums: Compositions, Letters, Analysis, Poetry, Maps, Dictations, Grammatical Exercises, Parsing, Notes, Geography, Zoology, Botany, Penmanship and Rhetoric.

KANSAS CITY, MO., Diocese of Kansas City.

St. Teresa's Academy.

3 Volumes: Christian Doctrine, Chemistry, Geometry, Logic, Botany, Book-Keeping, Geology, Physiology and Original Drafts of Quarterly Examinations.

LOS ANGELES, CAL., Diocese of Los Angeles.

St. Mary's Academy.

5 Mounted Maps.

NEW ORLEANS, LA., Diocese of New Orleans.

St. Joseph's Academy.

41 Albums: Language, Analysis, Punctuations, Epistolary Correspondence, Essays, Compositions, Arithmetic, Letters, Parsing, Exercises on Adjectives, Synonyms, Bills, Dictations, Algebra, United States History. Following in French: Grammar, Essays, Letters, Compositions; 6 Photographs and 38 Copy Books.

PEORIA, ILL., Diocese of Peoria.

Academy of Our Lady of the Sacred Heart.

3 Volumes: Grammar, Arithmetic, Geography, History, Catechism, Language, Philosophy, Rhetoric, Music, Literature, Algebra, Geology, Mythology, Zoology, Astronomy, Botany, Modern History, Stenography, Christian Doctrine, Memoirs and Book-Keeping.

PHILADELPHIA, PA., Diocese of Philadelphia.

St. Joseph's Academy (Chestnut Hill).

13 Volumes: Christian Doctrine, Latin, German, Astronomy, French Essays, English Literature, Church History, Zoology, Botany, Logic, Rhetoric, Book-Keeping, Philosophy, History, Civics, Arithmetic, Mythology, Stenography, Grammar, Geography, United States History, Bible History, Prospectus of the Academy; 1 Volume Photographs, 3 Volumes Music, 2 Volumes Examination Papers, 10 Copy Books Composition, 1 Album Original Designs (for Oil-Cloth), 1 Etching, 1 Pastel Crayon, 7 Albums Drawing, 2 Water-Color Designs (Original), Crayon Portrait of Most Rev. Archbishop Ryan, 1 Crayon Portrait of St. Joseph with list of schools, Specimens of Sewing, Embroidery and Lace-Work.

ST. LOUIS, MO., Diocese of St. Louis.

St. Joseph's Academy (Corondelet).

13 Volumes: Church History, Rhetoric, Stenography, Algebra, Latin, Geometry, Geology, Natural History, Physical Geography, Arithmetic, Christian Doctrine, Grammar, Zoology, Book-Keeping, Mythology, History, Natural Sciences, Language, Physiology, Map Drawing, Moral Philosophy; 1 Volume India-Ink Pictures, 1 Volume Literature, 4 Mounted Maps, 6 Pictures Illuminated Work, Lace Rochet and Alb, Drawn-Thread Table Cover, 5 Wash-Silk Embroidered Table Covers, 12 Embroidered Doilies, 2 Lace Doilies, 1 Silk-embroidered Handkerchief, 8 Tray Covers in Wash Silk, 3 Silk Picture Scarfs, 2 Photograph Holders, Embroidered Cushions, 3 Plaques, 1 Tambourine Bolten Cloth, 1 Table Mat, 1 Ciborium Cover, 1 Watch Pocket, 1 Table Cloth, 1 Lace Needle-Book, 3 Panels in Embroidery, 9 Oil Paintings, Sketch Book, Botanical Book and Album of Flowers from Nature.

ST. AUGUSTINE, FLA., Diocese of St. Augustine.

St. Joseph's Academy.

10 Albums Grammar, 10 Albums Arithmetic, 2 Albums Algebra, 8 Albums Book-Keeping, 13 Albums Maps, 6 Volumes Biographies, 1 Volume Poems, 1 Volume Compositions, 10 Junior Examination Papers, 36 Senior Examination Papers, 10 Examination Papers by Colored Pupils, 2 Pen-Drawing Books, 3 Copy Books, 43 Kindergarten Books, 54 Primary Books Needle-Work, 2 Yards Black Lace, $7\frac{1}{2}$ Yards Insertion, $2\frac{3}{4}$ Yards Alencon, $4\frac{3}{4}$ Yards Guipure, 3 Yards Duchesse, 3 Yards Torchon, 1 Yard White Guipure, 1 Lace Cushion, 3 Small Crayons, 2 Herbariums "Pascue Florida;" A Monthly edited by the Pupils. "The Glorification of Columbus," by a Sister of the Academy.

PARISH SCHOOLS.

ALDEN, N. Y., Diocese of Buffalo.

St. John the Baptist's School.

1 Volume: Arithmetic, Geography, Letters, Grammar, German.

BALTIMORE, MD., Diocese of Baltimore.

Star of the Sea School.

Examination Papers: Catechism, Literature, Civil Government, United States History, Book-Keeping, Arithmetic, Compositions, Ornamental Writing and Drawing.

BAY ST. LOUIS, MISS., Diocese of Natchez.

St. Rose's School (Colored).

1 Volume: Christian Doctrine, Penmanship, Geography, Grammar, Spelling, Arithmetic and Map Drawing.

BROOKLYN, N. Y., Diocese of Brooklyn.

Holy Cross School.

1 Volume: Christian Doctrine, Map Drawing, Letters, Arithmetic, Algebra, Grammar and History.

BROOKLYN, N. Y., Diocese of Brooklyn.—Continued.

Our Lady of Good Counsel School.

1 Volume: History, Christian Doctrine, Arithmetic, Geography, German and Mechanical Drawing.

Our Lady of Mercy School.

5 Volumes: Christian Doctrine, Spelling, Arithmetic, Book-Keeping, Geography, Map Drawing and Algebra.

Our Lady of Peace.

5 Volumes: Map Drawing, Geography, Christian Doctrine, Book-Keeping, Arithmetic and Spelling.

Our Lady Star of the Sea School.

5 Volumes: Christian Doctrine, Arithmetic, Geography, Spelling, United States History, Book-Keeping, Map Drawing, Compositions, Penmanship, Fancy Work and Mechanical Drawing.

St. Francis de Sales' School.

2 Volumes: Grammar, Catechism, Arithmetic, Geography, History, Civil Government, Spelling and Algebra.

St. John's School.

2 Volumes: Christian Doctrine, History, Physiology, Arithmetic, Church History, Geography and Grammar.

St. John the Evangelist's School.

10 Volumes: Catechism, Geography, Business Forms, Book-Keeping, Arithmetic, Grammar, History, Drawing, Spelling, Compositions, Algebra, Bible History and Civil Government.

St. Malachy's School.

3 Volumes: Christian Doctrine, Book-Keeping, Rhetoric, United States History, Penmanship and Spelling.

Sts. Peter and Paul's School.

4 Volumes: Christian Doctrine, Arithmetic, Grammar, United States History, Drawing, Spelling and Language.

BUFFALO, N. Y., Diocese of Buffalo.

St. Boniface's School.

1 Volume: Grammar, Geography, German, Arithmetic and Drawing.

Immaculate Conception School.

3 Volumes: Penmanship, Arithmetic, Spelling, Catechism, Geography, Analysis, Map Drawing, History, Music, Physics, Algebra, Physiology.

St. John the Baptist's School.

1 Volume: Spelling, Map Drawing, Arithmetic and Geography.

St. Louis' School.

6 Volumes: Penmanship, Drawing, Music, Arithmetic, Geography and Compositions.

BUFFALO, N. Y., Diocese of Buffalo.—CONTINUED.

St. Vincent's School.

1 Volume: Geography, Grammar, Arithmetic, Map Drawing, United States History, Spelling and Mechanical Drawing.

CHICAGO, ILL., Diocese of Chicago.

Nativity School.

20 Volumes Class-Work from First to Eighth Grade, 2 Volumes Drawing, 1 Volume Penmanship, 2 Volumes Map Drawing, Third to Eighth Grade; 1 Album Photographs, 18 Volumes Shorthand and Practical Music, Framed Photograph of School.

St. Stephen's School.

8 Volumes Class-Work, 1 Volume Map Drawing, 2 Volumes Drawing.

CLEVELAND, OHIO, Diocese of Cleveland.

St. Augustine's School.

4 Volumes: Physiology, Arithmetic, Christian Doctrine, Book-Keeping, Rhetoric, Map Drawing, History and Literature.

St. Coleman's School.

1 Volume: Drawing, Arithmetic, Language, Dictation, Christian Doctrine, Orthography, United States History and Bible History.

St. Procopius' School.

1 Volume: Christian Doctrine, Arithmetic and History.

CHARTIERS, PA., Diocese of Pittsburgh.

St. Francis de Sales' School.

1 Volume: Christian Doctrine, Arithmetic, Geography and Grammar.

CHARENTON, LA., Diocese of New Orleans.

St. Joseph's Convent.

19 Albums: Compositions, Letters, Analysis, Poetry, Parsing, Maps, Geography, Dictation, Grammatical Exercises, Notes, Zoology, Botany and Rhetoric.

DENVER, COL., Diocese of Denver.

St. Leo's School.

1 Volume: Geography, Christian Doctrine, Freehand Drawing, Object Drawing, Orthography, Penmanship, Arithmetic, Language Lessons, Map Drawing, Bible History, Grammar, United States History and Natural History.

St. Patrick's School.

1 Volume: Christian Doctrine, Freehand Drawing, Object Drawing, Language Lessons, Arithmetic, Grammar, Geography, Map Drawing, Letter Writing, United States History, Bible History and Natural History.

DUNKIRK, N. Y., Diocese of Buffalo.

St. Mary's School.

    5 Volumes: German, Penmanship, United States History, Christian Doctrine, Linear Drawing, Dictation and Map Drawing.

St. George's School.

    Map Drawing, Grammar, Geography, Penmanship, Translations.

EBENSBURGH, PA., Diocese of Pittsburgh.

Mt. Gallitzin's Academy.

    2 Volumes: Christian Doctrine, Arithmetic, Geography, Maps, History, Civil Government, Grammar, Spelling and Literature.

ELYRIA, OHIO, Diocese of Cleveland.

St. Mary's School.

    1 Volume: Christian Doctrine, Geography, Bible History, Spelling, Grammar, History, Music, Compositions, Map Drawing, Arithmetic and Book-Keeping.

GALLITZIN, PA., Diocese of Pittsburgh.

Borough School.

    4 Volumes: Book-Keeping, Literature, Spelling, Geography, History, Grammar, Biography, Civil Government, Arithmetic and Map Drawing.

GEORGETOWN, COL., Diocese of Denver.

School of Our Lady of Lourdes.

    1 Volume: Christian Doctrine, Arithmetic, Object Lessons, Geography, Grammar, United States History, Letter Writing, Algebra, Book-Keeping, Compositions and Physiology.

INDIANAPOLIS, IND., Diocese of Vincennes.

Sacred Heart School.

    3 Volumes: Grammar, Arithmetic, German, Botany and Geography.

JOHNSTOWN, PA., Diocese of Pittsburgh.

St. John's School.

    9 Volumes: Geography, Arithmetic, History, Civil Government, Spelling, Grammar, Algebra and Book-Keeping.

LEE, MASS., Diocese of Springfield.

St. Mary's School.

    14 Albums: Christian Doctrine, History, Arithmetic, Geography, Grammar, English Compositions, Sacred History, Practical Science, Map and Linear Drawing.

LONACOMING, MD., Diocese of Baltimore.

St. Mary's School.

    Examination Papers: Catechism, Bible History, Church History, Literature, Science, Rhetoric, Civil Government, United States History, Geography, Book-Keeping, Geometry, Algebra, Arithmetic and Compositions.

NEW OREGON, N. Y., Diocese of Buffalo.

St. Mary's School.

1 Volume: Spelling, Geography, Grammar, Penmanship, Letters, Arithmetic, Compositions, Drawing and Music.

NEW RICHMOND, WIS., Diocese of La Crosse.

Seat of Wisdom School.

2 Volumes: Christian Doctrine, Arithmetic, Geography, United States History, Physiology, Bible History, Spelling, Grammar, Compositions, Penmanship, Algebra and Rhetoric.

OAKLAND, CAL., Diocese of San Francisco.

St. Joseph's School.

15 Volumes Daily School-Work and Quarterly Examinations, including Language, Mathematics; 1 Volume Photographs.

OCONTO, WIS., Diocese of Green Bay.

St. Peter's School.

Christian Doctrine, Orthography, Arithmetic, Penmanship, Letter Writing, Grammar, United States History, German and English Translations, Album of Freehand Drawing.

ORANGE VALLEY, N. J., Diocese of Newark.

Our Lady of the Valley.

See Archdiocese of Philadelphia, Part I.

PEORIA, ILL., Diocese of Peoria.

St. Mary's School.

2 Volumes: Christian Doctrine, Language, Arithmetic, Geography, Grammar, Dictations and History.

PHILADELPHIA, PA., Diocese of Philadelphia.

Cathedral School.
See Philadelphia Diocese, Part I.

St. Ann's School.
See Philadelphia Diocese, Part I.

St. Bridget's School.
See Philadelphia Diocese, Part I.

Immaculate Conception School.
See Philadelphia Diocese, Part I.

St. Joseph's School.
See Philadelphia Diocese, Part I.

St. Joseph's School.
See Philadelphia Diocese, Part I.

St. Mary's School.
See Philadelphia Diocese, Part I.

St. Michael's School.
See Philadelphia Diocese, Part I.

PHILADELPHIA, PA., Diocese of Philadelphia.—Continued.

Nativity School.
See Philadelphia Diocese, Part I.

Our Mother of Consolation School.
See Philadelphia Diocese, Part I.

Our Mother of Sorrows School.
See Philadelphia Diocese, Part I.

St. Patrick's School.
See Philadelphia Diocese, Part I.

St. Philip de Neri's School.
See Philadelphia Diocese, Part I.

POTTSVILLE, PA., Diocese of Philadelphia.

St. Patrick's School.
See Philadelphia Diocese, Part I.

SHAWNO, WIS., Diocese of Green Bay.

Sacred Heart School.
1 Volume: Christian Doctrine, Arithmetic, Grammar, Geography, Bible History, Algebra, Botany, United States History, Civics, Compositions, Penmanship, Rhetoric, Geometry, Natural Philosophy, Physiology, Freehand Drawing and Map Drawing.

ST. JOSEPH, MO., Diocese of St. Joseph.

St. Francis de Sales' School.
1 Volume: Drawing, Physiology, Philosophy, Rhetoric, Algebra, Grammar, Map Drawing and Book-Keeping.

ST. LOUIS, MO., Diocese of St. Louis.

Holy Name School.
3 Volumes: Christian Doctrine, Arithmetic, Language, Geography, Mental Arithmetic, Practical Arithmetic, Orthography, Essays and Letter Writing.

St. Bridget's School.
7 Volumes: Christian Doctrine, Language, Bible History, Numbers, Geography, United States History, Grammar, Spelling, Practical Arithmetic, Mental Arithmetic, Philosophy, Rhetoric, Civil Government, Physics, Latin, Algebra, Penmanship, Physiology, Etiquette, Physical Geography, Zoology, Orthography, Poetry, English Literature and Book Keeping.

St. Aloysius' School.
10 Volumes: Language, Arithmetic, Christian Doctrine, Grammar, Geography, United States History, Bible History, Spelling, Physiology, Drawing and Writing.

St. Anthony's School.
1 Volume: Penmanship, Language, Arithmetic, Geography, Bible History, United States History, German, Reading, Grammar and Compositions.

ST. LOUIS, MO., Diocese of St. Louis.—Continued.

St. John's School.

1 Volume: Catechism, Notes, Algebra, Dictation, Letters, History, Vestments used at Mass, Spelling, Essays, Grammar, Civil Government, Literature, Physiology, Geography and Arithmetic.

St. Lawrence O'Tool's School.

3 Volumes: Christian Doctrine, Bible History, Spelling, Grammar, Essays, United States History and Arithmetic.

St. Francis' School.

1 Volume; Penmanship, Geography, History, Reading, Grammar, Compositions, German, Bible History, Catechism, United States History and 1 Volume Drawing.

St. Patrick's School.

3 Volumes: Geography, Grammar, Catechism, Book-Keeping, Arithmetic, Spelling, United States History, Definitions, Sacred History; 1 Volume Stenography and 1 Volume Music.

St. Vincent's School.

2 Volumes: Letter Writing, Grammar, Essays, Arithmetic, History, Book-Keeping, Christian Doctrine, Geography, Physiology and German Exercises.

SUSPENSION BRIDGE, N. Y., Diocese of Buffalo.

Sacred Heart School.

1 Volume: Map Drawing, Geography, Physiology and Catechism.

TUNNEL HILL, PA., Diocese of Pittsburgh.

Tunnel Hill School.

2 Volumes: Geography, Arithmetic, History, Civil Government, Spelling, Grammar, Book-Keeping and Physiology.

WEST SENECA, N. Y., Diocese of Buffalo.

Our Lady of Victory.

1 Volume: Arithmetic, Grammar, Geography, Maps, Mechanical Drawing and Spelling.

WHEELING, W. VA., Diocese of Wheeling.

Cathedral School.

1 Volume Maps.

SPECIAL SCHOOLS.

BUFFALO, N. Y., Diocese of Buffalo.

Le Couteulx St. Mary's Deaf Mute Institute.

7 Volumes: "Le Couteulx Leader." 2 Volumes: Arithmetic, History, Geography, Grammar, Map Drawing; 3 Photographic Views, 1 Oil Painting, 10 Water Colors, 1 Specimen Wood Carving and 1 Specimen Chair Caning.

DUNKIRK, N. Y., Diocese of Buffalo.

St. Mary's Orphan Asylum.

1 Volume: Grammar, Arithmetic, Geography, Needle-Work, Music, Map Drawing and Linear Drawing.

WEST SENECA, N. Y.

St. John's Protectory and Orphanage.—FEMALE DEPT.

4 Volumes: History, Arithmetic, Christian Doctrine, Essays, Grammar, Spelling, Geography and Specimens of Needle-Work.

KESHENA (Menominee Reservation), Diocese of Green Bay.

St. Joseph's Industrial School.

1 Volume: Geography, Letter Writing, Arithmetic, Spelling, Catechism, Bible History, Grammar; 1 Volume Map Drawing, Specimens of Needle-Work, Miniature Steam Engine made by an Indian Boy.

ST. LOUIS, MO., Diocese of St. Louis.

Mariæ Consilia Deaf Mute School.

1 Volume: Language, Catechism, History, Arithmetic and Geography.

CHICAGO, ILL., Diocese of Chicago.

St. Joseph's Orphan Asylum.

5 Volumes Class-Work, 1 Album Drawing, 1 Album Lace and Crochet Work, 1 Folio Kindergarten Work, Specimens Needle-Work, Embroidery, Knitting, Painting in Oil, Photographs.

St. Joseph's Providence Asylum.

1 Volume Class-Work, 2 Volumes Map Drawing, Frame Photographs.

Sisters of St. Mary.

ELMIRA, N. Y., Diocese of Buffalo.

St. John's School.

1 Volume: Spelling, Business Letters, Geography, Christian Doctrine, Arithmetic.

Sts. Peter and Paul's School.

2 Volumes: Arithmetic, History, Geography, Map Drawing, Analysis, Grammar and Letters.

St. Mary's School.

2 Volumes: Arithmetic, Christian Doctrine, Map Drawing, Compositions, Geography and Analysis.

LOCKPORT, N. Y., Diocese of Buffalo.

St. Joseph's Academy.

1 Book Essays, 1 Book Painting, 1 Hand-Painted Fire Screen, 1 Oil Painting, 1 Framed Photograph (St. Joseph's Academy), 2 Pieces of Hand-Made Lace, 2 Cushions (Raised Painting) and Specimens of Needle-Work.

Sisters of the Congregation de Notre Dame (Montreal).

ACADEMIES.

KANKAKEE, ILL., Diocese of Chicago.

St. Joseph's Seminary.

8 Volumes Class-Work, 1 Volume Music, 11 Volumes Drawing, 15 Paintings, 2 Pieces Hair-Work, 29 Pieces Needle-Work, Kindergarten and Photographs.

BOURBONNAIS, ILL., Diocese of Chicago.

Notre Dame Academy.

7 Volumes Class-Work, 1 Volume Photographs, 47 Drawings and 30 Pieces Needle-Work.

PARISH SCHOOLS.

CHICAGO, ILL., Diocese of Chicago.

Notre Dame de Chicago School.

1 Volume Superior French Course, 1 Volume Elementary French Course, 4 Volumes Superior English Course, 1 Volume French and English Course. 6 Volumes: Catechism, Bible History, Grammar, Spelling, Arithmetic; 7 Astronomical Charts, 7 Geographical Charts, 1 Chronological Chart. Series of Drawing Books, Series of Penmanship, Specimens of Plain and Fancy Sewing, Embroidery, Specimens of Mending and Darning.

St. Ann's School.

2 Volumes Class-Work, 13 Copy Books (Writing) and Needle-Work.

KANKAKEE, ILL., Diocese of Chicago.

St. Rose's School.

2 Volumes Class-Work, 4 Volumes Drawing, 1 Volume Kindergarten Work, 1 Volume Map Drawing, 1 Volume Photographs.

AURORA, ILL., Diocese of Chicago.

Sacred Heart School.

2 Volumes Class-Work and 2 Maps.

School Sisters of Notre Dame of Milwaukee and Baltimore.

LONGWOOD, ILL., Diocese of Chicago.
Institute of Our Lady of the Sacred Heart. (Omitted on Page 147.)

1 Volume Spelling, Etymology, Language; 1 Volume Grammar, Rhetoric; 2 Volumes Geography, Civil Government; 1 Volume Physiology, Natural History; 1 Volume Arithmetic, 1 Volume Algebra, Geometry, Orthography, Typewriting; 2 Volumes Compositions, 1 Volume Literature, 1 Volume Astronomy, History, Physics; 1 Volume Harmonic Exercises, 1 Volume Book-Keeping, 1 Folio Freehand Drawing, 1 Folio Maps, 2 Folios Charts, 1 Folio Ornamental Pen-Work, 1 Cabinet of Insects, 1 Chart of Currents and Rainfall, 16 Paintings, 7 Crayon Drawings, 1 Photograph of the Institute.

Sisters of the Good Shepherd.

CHICAGO, ILL., Diocese of Chicago.
Chicago Industrial School.
Specimens of Needle-Work.

House of the Good Shepherd.
Specimens of Needle-Work, Embroidery, Drawn-Work and Fancy Stitching.

Religious of the Sacred Heart.

CHICAGO, ILL., Diocese of Chicago.
Holy Name School.
9 Volumes Class-Work, Specimens of Needle-Work, Embroidery, Crochet-Work and Photographs.

Sacred Heart School.
6 Volumes Christian Doctrine, 5 Volumes Language, 4 Volumes Geography, 3 Volumes Physiology, 6 Volumes Arithmetic, 4 Volumes United States History, 1 Volume Algebra, 2 Volumes Book-Keeping, 1 Volume Maps and Fancy Work.

Sisters of the Holy Child Jesus.

SHARON HILL, PA., Diocese of Philadelphia.
Academy of the Holy Child.
See Archdiocese of Philadelphia, Part I.

PHILADELPHIA, PA., Diocese of Philadelphia.

  St. Agatha's School.
    See Archdiocese of Philadelphia, Part I.

  Assumption School.
    See Archdiocese of Philadelphia, Part I.

  St. Edward's School.
    See Archdiocese of Philadelphia, Part I.

  St. James' School.
    See Archdiocese of Philadelphia, Part I.

  Visitation School.
    See Archdiocese of Philadelphia, Part I.

CHESTER, PA., Diocese of Philadelphia.

  St. Michael's School.
    See Archdiocese of Philadelphia, Part I.

Sisters of the Holy Family.

SAN FRANCISCO, CAL., Diocese of San Francisco.

  Children's Day Home.
    Framed Pictures of Specimens of Kindergarten Work, 1 Framed Picture of Pope Leo XIII., 1 Specimen of Kindergarten Work.

Sisters of the Holy Names.

OAKLAND, CAL., Diocese of San Francisco.

  Convent of Our Lady of the Sacred Heart.

    NORMAL DEPT.
      2 Albums of Photographs collected by the Sisters, and used in teaching Art and History; Circular, Photographs of Students, etc.

    STUDENTS' WORK.
      13 Volumes: Arithmetic, Algebra, Geometry, Physics, Physiology, Astronomy, Botany, Compositions, Rhetoric, Literature, Map Drawing, Ancient History, History of Art, Christian Doctrine; 7 Booklets Penmanship, Juvenile Sewing Album, Painted Cushion, Table Scarf, Glove Case.

PARISH SCHOOLS.

SAN FRANCISCO, CAL., Diocese of San Francisco.

St. Joseph's School.

23 Volumes Class-Work: Grammar, Orthography, Dictation, Arithmetic, Geometry, Algebra, Compositions, United States and Church History, Literature, Physics, Astronomy, Geography, Drawing (Pencil and Colored Crayons), Christian Doctrine; 54 Booklets Class-Work: Maps, French and United States History, Literature, Grammar, Spelling, Dictation, Object Lessons, Bible History, Botany, Physics, Compositions; Drawing—First, Second and Third Grades; 1 Folio California Wild Flowers, 35 Exercise Books of Primary Grades, 1 Photo Album.

St. Rose's School.

11 Volumes: Arithmetic, Spelling, Grammar, Word Analysis, Compositions Dictations, Geography, United States History, Penmanship, Language, Letter Writing, Catechism; 3 Booklets of Drawing, 1 Booklet Doll's Outfit, 1 Booklet Picture Stories and 1 Album Photographs.

OAKLAND, CAL., Diocese of San Francisco.

St. Francis de Sales' School.

2 Volumes Christian Doctrine, 3 Volumes Composition, 2 Volumes Arithmetic, 1 Volume Algebra, 1 Volume Geometry, 1 Volume Astronomy, 1 Volume Spelling, 9 Volumes Class-Work.

St. Lawrence's School.

10 Volumes Class-Work: Physiology, Algebra, Arithmetic, Photographs, Christian Doctrine, Botany, Language, Literature, History, Geography.

St. Mary's School.

4 Volumes: Geography, Catechism, Grammar, Arithmetic, History, Analysis, Compositions, Algebra, Practical Philosophy, Astronomy, Geometry, Literary Analysis; 1 Volume Map and Freehand Drawings, 1 Volume of Photographs.

Sisters of the Humility of Mary.

NILES, OHIO, Diocese of Cleveland.

St. Stephen's School.

Arithmetic, Grammar, Compositions, Catechism, Map Drawing, Letter Writing and Mechanical Drawing.

VILLA MARIA, PA., Diocese of Cleveland.

NORMAL DEPT.

Hair Painting—Artistic Picture of the Landing of Columbus, made from the hair of Archbishops and Bishops of the United States. Specimens of Lace-Work.

Sisters of the Immaculate Heart of Mary.

ACADEMIES.

MONROE, MICH., Diocese of Detroit.

St. Mary's Academy.

12 Volumes: Christian Doctrine, Essays, Poems, Mathematics, History, Grammar, Geography, Mental Arithmetic, Language, Stenography, Typewriting, Herbarium; 1 Volume "History of St. Mary's Academy," 1 Volume Specimen Needle-Work, 4 Photographs and 1 Folio of 150 Art Studies. 1 Crayon Picture, 4 Water-Color Paintings, 2 Marine Monochromatic Crayons, 5 Oil Paintings, Antipendium (Painted on Bolting Silk), Chasuble, Ciborium Cover, Benediction Veil, 1 Pair Cream Lace Curtains and 20 Yards Silk Plush.

WEST CHESTER, PA.

Academy of the Immaculate Heart.

1 Embroidered Quilt and 1 Embroidered Throw.

PARISH SCHOOLS.

The Class-Work of the following Schools from the Archdiocese of Philadelphia, consists of a series of written examinations bound in large volumes, and include work from the twelve established grades. The examinations represent the following branches: Christian Doctrine, Church History, Spelling, Penmanship, Grammar, Letter Writing, Etymology, Homonyms, Bible History, Ancient and United States History, Geography, Compositions, Globe Studies, Mensuration, Arithmetic, Freehand, Crayon and Map Drawing, Algebra, Book-Keeping, Chemistry, Geometry, Trigonometry.

For further particulars, see the Diocesan Exhibit of Philadelphia, Part I.

PHILADELPHIA, PA.

Annunciation School.

St. Dominic's School.

St. Francis Xavier's School.

Gesu School.

St. Joachim's School.

St. John the Baptist's School.

St. Paul's School.

St. Teresa's School.

BRISTOL, PA.

St. Mark's School.

CHESTER, PA.

Immaculate Heart of Mary's School.

CONSHOHOCKEN, PA.
St. Gertrude's School.

KELLYVILLE, PA.
St. Charles Borromeo's School.

MAUCH CHUNK, PA.
Immaculate Conception School.

MORRISTOWN, PA.
St. Patrick's School.

PHŒNIXVILLE, PA.
St. Mary's School.

PORT CARBON, PA.
St. Stephen's School.

WEST CHESTER, PA.
St. Agnes' School.

Sisters of the Incarnate Word.

WEST DE PERE, WIS., Diocese of Green Bay.
St. Joseph's School.
3 Volumes: Christian Doctrine, Orthography, Arithmetic, Penmanship, Map Drawing, Language, Geography, Bible History, Grammar, United States History, Physics, Etymology, General History, Letter Writing, Physical Geography, Literature; Album of Music and Freehand Drawing.

The Poor Handmaids of Christ.

FT. WAYNE, IND., Diocese of Ft. Wayne.
St. Paul's School.
Christian Doctrine, Geography, Arithmetic, Orthography, Compositions, United States History and Grammar.

KOKOMO, IND., Diocese of Ft. Wayne.
St. Patrick's School.
Specimens of Letter Writing.

ORPHANAGE.

FT. WAYNE, IND., Diocese of Ft. Wayne.

St. Vincent's Orphanage.

Compositions, Grammar, Arithmetic, United States History and Bible History.

Ursuline Sisters.

ALCOVE 62.

COLLEGE AND ACADEMIES.

ARCADIA, MO., Diocese of St. Louis.

Arcadia College.

4 Volumes: Christian Doctrine, Grammar, Spelling, Etymology, Geography, United States History, Etiquette, Civil Government, Physical Geography, Arithmetic, Algebra, Elocution, Literature, Physiology, Rhetoric, Biography, Stenography, Typewriting, Book-Keeping, Natural Philosophy, Astronomy, Chemistry, Botany, Mythology, Modern and Ancient History, Trigonometry, Logic, Compositions, Music, Essays, Map Drawing, Pen Drawing, Colored Drawing.

FRONTENAC, MINN., Diocese of St. Paul.

Villa Maria Academy.

1 Volume: Printed Periodical, Photographs and Botanical Specimens.

GRAND FORKS, N. D., Diocese of Jamestown.

St. Bernard's Ursuline Convent.

4 Volumes: Diacritical Marking, Grammar, Rhetoric, Latin, German and French Exercises, Ancient and Modern History, Christian Doctrine, Algebra, Chemistry, Astronomy, Geology, Book-Keeping, Stenography, Typewriting; 2 Albums Photographs and Music.

SANTA ROSA, CAL., Diocese of San Francisco.

Sacred Heart Academy.

NORMAL DEPT.
1 Embroidered Benediction Veil, Photographs.

STUDENTS' WORK.
18 Volumes: Grammar, Compositions, Rhetoric, Algebra, Arithmetic, Geometry, Physics, Astronomy, Book-Keeping, Mythology, Word Analysis, Catechism, Music: Original Arrangements and 6 Charts.

ST. LOUIS, MO., Diocese of St. Louis.

Ursuline Academy.

5 Volumes: Language, Compositions, Grammar, Arithmetic, Orthography, Definitions, History, Familiar Science, Chemistry, Physiology, Natural Philosophy, Ethics, Civil Government, Astronomy, Literature, Mythology, Classical Biography, Mineralogy and Algebra.

NEW ORLEANS, LA., Diocese of New Orleans.

Ursuline Academy.

20 Volumes: English, Character Sketches, French Translations, Penmanship, Compositions, Arithmetic, Algebra, Miscellaneous Lessons, Drawing, Trigonometry, Book-Keeping; 2 Large Volumes "Studies in Black and White," 10 Volumes Book-Keeping, 1 Volume Drawing in Outline, 1 Volume Algebra, 1 Volume Geometry, 1 Piano Scarf and 1 Frame of Wax Flowers.

NEW YORK CITY, N. Y., Diocese of New York.

St. Jerome's Academy.

2 Volumes: Arithmetic, Grammar, Spelling, Christian Doctrine, Reading, Penmanship and Map Drawing.

PITTSBURGH, PA., Diocese of Pittsburgh.

Ursuline Convent.

5 Volumes: Book-Keeping, Arithmetic, Geography, Algebra, French, English and German Compositions, Universal History, Botany, Geometry, Mechanical Drawing; 9 Charts Church History, 11 Maps, 1 Water Color and 9 Pieces of Embroidery.

SIOUX FALLS, S. D., Diocese of Sioux Falls.

St. Rose's Academy.

5 Volumes: Bible History, Compositions, Geography, Grammar, Biographies, Music, Freehand Drawing, Arithmetic, Algebra, Geometry and Physiology.

TIFFIN, OHIO, Diocese of Cleveland.

Ursuline Academy.

6 Volumes: Christian Doctrine, Drawing, Rhetoric, Philosophy, Book-Keeping, Astronomy, Arithmetic, Mythology, Elocution, Trigonometry, Chemistry and Compositions; 4 Paintings on China, 1 Oil Painting, 4 Water Colors, 2 Sepia, 3 Pastels, 6 Crayons, 2 Charcoal and 2 Lead-Pencil Drawings, Chasuble, 2 Honiton Lace Handkerchiefs, 2 Honiton Lace Doilies, 2 Honiton Lace Borders and 1 Doilie (Drawn-Work).

TOLEDO, OHIO, Diocese of Cleveland.

Ursuline Convent of the Sacred Heart.

9 Volumes: Bible History, Catechism, Arithmetic, Grammar, Map and Mechanical Drawing, Essays, Astronomy, Book-Keeping, Algebra, Rhetoric; 1 Volume Photographs, 1 Oil Painting, 5 Kindergarten Charts, 2 Vases and 6 Pieces of Needle-Work.

NOTTINGHAM, OHIO, Diocese of Cleveland.

Ursuline Academy (Villa Angela).

8 Volumes: Christian Doctrine, Science, Botany, Arithmetic, Literature, Drawing, Painting, Etching; 1 Portfolio of Drawing, Botanical Specimens.

PARISH SCHOOLS.

ALTON, ILL., Diocese of Alton.

St. Patrick's School.

1 Volume: Catechism, Arithmetic, Compositions, Map Drawing, Geography, United States History, Grammar, Language, Spelling and Penmanship.

CLEVELAND, OHIO, Diocese of Cleveland.

Immaculate Conception School.

1 Volume: Christian Doctrine, Compositions, Physiology, Natural History, Geography, United States History, Music, Literature, General History and Church History.

St. John's Cathedral School.

3 Volumes: Christian Doctrine, Map Drawing, Arithmetic, Algebra, United States History, Literature, Physiology, General and Church History.

St. Joseph's School.

2 Volumes: Christian Doctrine, Grammar, German Translations, Letters, Language, German Dictation, English Dictation and United States History.

St. Malachy's School.

2 Volumes: Language, Arithmetic, Geography, Grammar, United States History, Catechism, Book-Keeping, Algebra, Physics and Drawing.

St. Mary's School.

1 Volume: Drawing, Composition, Dictation and Spelling. Lace-Work, Hair Picture.

DAYTON, OHIO, Diocese of Cincinnati.

St. Francis' School.

1 Volume: Christian Doctrine, German Exercises, Compositions and Arithmetic.

NEWPORT, KY., Diocese of Covington.

Corpus Christi School.

3 Volumes: Drawing, History, Arithmetic, German and Grammar.

NEW YORK CITY, N. Y., Diocese of New York.

St. Jerome's School.

8 Volumes: Spelling, Reading, Writing, Arithmetic, Geography, United States History and Christian Doctrine.

St. Teresa's School.

3 Volumes: Language, Arithmetic, Numbers, Catechism, Geography, United States History, English History, Grammar, Algebra and Map and Freehand Drawing.

ST. LOUIS, MO., Diocese of St. Louis.

Ursuline Day School.

4 Volumes: Compositions, Grammar, Christian Doctrine, Arithmetic, Rhetoric, Etymology, United States History, Civil Government, Book-Keeping, Logic, Physiology, Literature, Ancient History, Mythology, Botany, Chemistry, Physics, Astronomy, Mathematics; 4 Paintings, 1 Ciborium Cover, 1 Missal Cover, 1 Stand Cover, 2 Embroidered Handkerchiefs and 1 Cravat Case.

TIFFIN, OHIO, Diocese of Cleveland.

St. Mary's School.

1 Volume: Christian Doctrine, Grammar, Orthography, Arithmetic, United States History, Map Drawing and Mechanical Drawing.

TOLEDO, OHIO, Diocese of Cleveland.

St. Francis de Sales' School.

71 Volumes: Christian Doctrine, Penmanship, Spelling, Arithmetic, History, Grammar, Geography, Bible History, Compositions, Letter Writing, Music, Natural History, Literature, Physiology, Algebra; 1 Volume Kindergarten Work.

Visitation Sisters.

BROOKLYN, N. Y., Diocese of Brooklyn.

Visitation Convent.

4 Paintings.

Visitation Academy.

4 Volumes and 2 Albums: Christian Doctrine, Rhetoric, Penmanship, Compositions, Letters, Physiology, French, German, Latin, Music, Astronomy, Algebra, Physics, Literature; Large Album Painting and Drawing.

DUBUQUE, IOWA, Diocese of Dubuque.

Visitation Academy.

14 Pictures, 6 Pieces Plain Sewing, 10 Maps, 4 Volumes: Christian Doctrine, Arithmetic, Literature, Physiology and Rhetoric.

GEORGETOWN, D. C., Diocese of Baltimore.

Visitation Academy.

5 Historical Charts, 2 Genealogical Charts, 1 Chart Crown Heads of Europe in Family Groups, 4 Paintings and 1 Small Photo of Cotton Plant.

MOBILE, ALA., Diocese of Mobile.

Academy of the Visitation.

2 Volumes: Christian Doctrine, Sacred History, Arithmetic, Algebra, Geometry; 1 Volume United States History, Freehand Drawing, 1 Album Theory of Music, Water Crayon, Pastel Paintings, Photographs and Penmanship.

BIRMINGHAM, ALA., Diocese of Mobile.

Holy Angels' Academy.

3 Volumes: Christian Doctrine, Church History, Penmanship, Compositions, History, Arithmetic, Grammar, Business Forms, Chemistry, Astronomy, Dictation, Music, Language, United States History, Geography and Map Drawing.

PARISH SCHOOLS.

BROOKLYN, N. Y., Diocese of Brooklyn.

Visitation School.

6 Volumes: Christian Doctrine, Arithmetic, Geography, Spelling, United States History, Algebra, Civil Government, Compositions, Business Forms and Drawing.

Franciscan Sisters.

ALLEGHANY, N. Y., Diocese of Buffalo.

St. Elizabeth's Academy.

7 Volumes: Stenography, Mathematics, Drawing, Book Keeping, Penmanship, English Literature; 3 Oil Paintings, 1 Water-Color Painting, 1 Series of Object and Ornamental Drawing, 2 Needle-Work Pictures, 1 Veil Embroidered in Gold, 1 Preaching Stole and 1 Lace Alb.

BUFFALO, N. Y., Diocese of Buffalo.

Sacred Heart School.

4 Volumes Fancy Work, 11 Samples Drawing, 17 Paintings, 38 Volumes: Book-Keeping, Literature, History, Arithmetic, Rhetoric, Church History, Maps, Harmony, German Grammar, German Compositions, Elementary Drawing, Spelling and Kindergarten Work. Needle-Work: 1 Altar Lace in Filet, 1 Tidy, 1 Canvas Tidy, 1 Tray Cloth, 1 Night Gown, 1 Baby Dress, 1 Green Table Cover, 1 Neutral Tint, 2 Oil Paintings, 1 Map of New York, 1 Pair Silk Mittens, 1 Japanese Basket, 1 Lamp Shade, 1 Photograph Bag, 2 Fancy Wheels, 1 Fancy Toaster, 3 Watch Pockets and 2 Needle Cases.

ELMIRA, N. Y., Diocese of Buffalo.

Academy of Our Lady of Angels.

1 Book of Essays, 2 Volumes Class-Work, 1 Volume Drawing, 1 Pen Painting (Lyre Bird) and 5 Framed Drawings.

LEWISTON, IDAHO, Diocese of Idaho.

St. Aloysius' Academy.

Maps of the United States in Clay and Specimens of Clay Objects, Type-writing, Phonography, Photograph of Bishop Glorieux, Freehand Drawing and Embroidery.

MASON CITY, IOWA, Diocese of Dubuque.

St. Francis' Academy.

2 Maps of the United States.

PARISH SCHOOLS.

AHNAPEE, WIS., Diocese of Green Bay.

St. Mary's School.

1 Volume: School Regulations, Historical Account of School, Christian Doctrine, Arithmetic, Grammar, Geography, English and German Penmanship, Drawing, United States History, Letter Writing and Orthography.

ALTON, IOWA, Diocese of Dubuque.

St. Mary's School.

1 Volume: Arithmetic, Christian Doctrine, Language, Penmanship, History, Book-Keeping, Letter Writing and Music.

ANTIGO, WIS., Diocese of Green Bay.

St. John's School.

1 Volume: Drawing, Christian Doctrine, Spelling, Grammar, Compositions and Map Drawing.

AKRON, OHIO, Diocese of Cleveland.

Holy Trinity School.

2 Volumes: Christian Doctrine, Drawing, Arithmetic, German Exercises and Map Drawing.

BAY SETTLEMENT, WIS., Diocese of Green Bay.

Holy Cross and St. Francis' Schools.

1 Volume: Christian Doctrine, Orthography, Arithmetic, Grammar, Geography, United States History, Letter Writing, Map Drawing and Specimens of Kindergarten Work.

BELLEVUE, OHIO, Diocese of Cleveland.

St. Mary's School.

1 Volume: Arithmetic, Map Drawing, Grammar, Algebra, United States Constitution, Letters, Diagrams and Compositions.

BUFFALO, N. Y., Diocese of Buffalo.

St. Agnes' School.

2 Albums: Arithmetic, Grammar, Geography, Map Drawing and Penmanship.

St. Ann's School.

13 Volumes: Business Letters, Grammar, Geography, German, Verse changed to Prose, Spelling, History, Language, Arithmetic, Christian Doctrine, Analysis and Map Drawing.

St. Michael's School.

2 Volumes: Map Drawing, Arithmetic, Compositions, Grammar, Spelling and Penmanship.

Sacred Heart School.

5 Volumes: Penmanship, Business Forms, Drawing, Compositions, Geography, Map Drawing; 1 Picture—Reward of Merit, 1 Carved Ivory Cross.

Seven Dolors School.

Specimens Penmanship, 4 Volumes: Grammar, Arithmetic, Translations, Drawing, Geography, Map Drawing, Commercial and Business Forms; 1 Oil Painting (Peacock), 4 Crayon Drawings, 4 Silk Throws, 1 Silk Tidy, 2 Bobbinet Tidies, 22 Other Tidies, 3 Aprons, 2 Worsted Jackets, 1 Pair Worsted Boots, 1 Plush Box, 1 Glass Box, 1 Pair Silk Mittens, 1 Chatelaine Bag, 1 Japanese Basket, 1 Photograph Bag, 2 Fancy Bags, 4 Fancy Wheels, 1 Fancy Toaster, 1 Fancy Basket, 3 Watch Pockets and 2 Needle Cases.

CASIMIR, WIS., Diocese of Green Bay.

St. Casimir's School.

1 Volume: Christian Doctrine, Arithmetic, Geography, Orthography, Grammar, German and English Translations, United States History and Freehand Drawing.

CATO, WIS., Diocese of Green Bay.

St. Michael's School.

Christian Doctrine, Arithmetic, Grammar, Geography, Language Lessons.

CLARK'S MILLS, WIS., Diocese of Green Bay.

Immaculate Conception School.

Christian Doctrine, Arithmetic, Grammar, Geography, Language, German and English Translations.

CLEVELAND, OHIO, Diocese of Cleveland.

St. Stanislaus' School.

1 Volume: Christian Doctrine, Bible History, Arithmetic, Grammar, Geography and Compositions.

CLINTON, IOWA, Diocese of Dubuque.

St. Patrick's School.

1 Volume: Christian Doctrine, Letter Writing, Arithmetic, Photographs, Dictations, Geography and Grammar.

DECORAH, IOWA, Diocese of Dubuque.

Immaculate Conception School.

1 Volume: Map Drawing, Spelling, Mechanical Drawing, Kindergarten Work, Geography, Book-Keeping, Arithmetic and Christian Doctrine.

DUBUQUE, IOWA, Diocese of Dubuque.

Sacred Heart School.

10 Volumes: Christian Doctrine, History, Geography, Arithmetic, Compositions, Penmanship, Grammar and Catechism.

DYERSVILLE, IOWA, Diocese of Dubuque.

St. Francis Xavier's School.

4 Volumes: Kindergarten Work, Christian Doctrine, Geography, United States History and Map Drawing; Knitted Scarf, Paper Mat and Crochet Tidy.

EAST BUFFALO, N. Y., Diocese of Buffalo.

St. Agnes' School.

2 Volumes: Penmanship, Grammar, Geography, Arithmetic and Map Drawing.

EGE, IND., Diocese of Ft. Wayne.

St. Mary's School.

United States History, Geography, Grammar, Natural Philosophy.

FOWLER, IND., Diocese of Ft. Wayne.

School of St. John the Evangelist.

Christian Doctrine, Arithmetic, Penmanship, Grammar and Compositions.

GALION, OHIO, Diocese of Cleveland.
  St. Joseph's School.
    2 Volumes: Bible History, Geography, German Grammar, Arithmetic, Penmanship, Orthography and Map Drawing.

GARDENVILLE, N. Y., Diocese of Buffalo.
  14 Holy Helpers' School.
    2 Volumes: Letter Writing, Arithmetic, Grammar, Map Drawing and Geography.

HAMBURG, N. Y., Diocese of Buffalo.
  Sts. Peter and Paul's School.
    15 Volumes: Christian Doctrine, Map Drawing, Painting, Geography, Arithmetic, Grammar, Caligraphy, German Exercises, Mechanical Drawing, German Translations and Language.

HESSE CASSEL, IND., Diocese of Ft. Wayne.
  St. John's School.
    United States History, Geography and Lessons in Reading.

KENTLAND, IND., Diocese of Ft. Wayne.
  St. John's School.
    Geography, Arithmetic and Christian Doctrine.

KLAASVILLE, IND., Diocese of Ft. Wayne.
  St. Anthony's School.
    Letter Writing, Spelling, Geography and Arithmetic.

LAGRO, IND., Diocese of Ft. Wayne.
  St. Patrick's School.
    Grammar, United States History and Geography.

LUXEMBURG, WIS., Diocese of Green Bay.
  St. Mary's School.
    Arithmetic, Geography, Grammar, Penmanship, Orthography and Christian Doctrine.

NEW FRANKEN, WIS., Diocese of Green Bay.
  St. Kilian's School.
    Christian Doctrine, Arithmetic, Geography, Language, Orthography, Penmanship, Bible History, United States History.

NEW YORK CITY, N. Y., Diocese of New York.
  St. Francis Assissi's School.
    1 Volume: Christian Doctrine, Penmanship, Geography, Spelling, Arithmetic, History, Grammar, Map Drawing and German.

NORTH RIDGEVILLE, OHIO, Diocese of Cleveland.
  St. Peter's School.
    1 Volume: Bible History, Catechism, Grammar, United States History, Arithmetic, Geography, Dictation and Spelling.

OTIS, IND., Diocese of Ft. Wayne.

School of the Sacred Heart.

Letter Writing, Bible History, Geography, Arithmetic, Christian Doctrine, Translations, Polish and United States History.

REMSEN, IOWA, Diocese of Dubuque.

St. Mary's School.

1 Volume: Bible History, Christian Doctrine, Arithmetic, Kindergarten Work and German Exercises.

SOUTH KAUKAUNA, WIS., Diocese of Green Bay.

St. Mary's School.

2 Volumes: Christian Doctrine, Language, Arithmetic, Orthography, Geography, Penmanship, Grammar; 1 Album of Kindergarten Work.

VERPLANCK, N. Y., Diocese of New York.

St. Patrick's School.

1 Volume: Penmanship, Geography, Arithmetic, Grammar, Language, United States History and Spelling.

ORPHANAGE.

BUFFALO, N. Y., Diocese of Buffalo.

Roman Catholic Orphan Asylum.

5 Albums: Arithmetic, Geography, Map Drawing, Grammar, Translations, Drawing and Compositions. 3 Celluloid Whisk-Broom Holders, 2 Aprons. 1 each of the following: Picture, Painting on Doe-Skin, Oil Painting, Celluloid Paper Holder, Lavender Silk Throw, Bolting-Silk Cushion, Handkerchief Case, Silk Bonnet, Work Basket, Embroidered Shawl, Spider Duster, Paper Holder, Shopping Bag, Velvet Handkerchief Case, Bobbinet Throw, Pair of Mittens, Pink Dress, Towel Rack and Silk Throw.

Franciscan Sisters of Perpetual Adoration.

PARISH SCHOOLS.

ASHLAND, WIS., Diocese of La Crosse.

St. Agnes' School.

1 Volume Drawing, 3 Volumes: Christian Doctrine, Bible History, Spelling, Language, Grammar, Translations, Rhetoric, Literature, Compositions, Penmanship, Arithmetic, Algebra, Geometry, United States History, Physiology, Botany, Zoology and General History.

BALLTOWN, IOWA, Diocese of Dubuque.

St. Francis' School.

2 Volumes: Geography, Language, German, Grammar, Arithmetic, Christian Doctrine and Drawing.

BAYFIELD, WIS., Diocese of La Crosse.

Christ's School.

1 Volume Map Drawing, 2 Volumes: Penmanship, Compositions, Language, Arithmetic, Catechism, Grammar, Geography, United States History and Bible History.

BELLEVUE, IOWA, Diocese of Dubuque.

St. Joseph's School.

2 Volumes: Christian Doctrine, Arithmetic, Bible History, United States History, Business Forms, Compositions, Letter Writing, Hygiene and Physiology.

CARROLL, IOWA, Diocese of Dubuque.

St. Anthony's School.

2 Volumes: Christian Doctrine, Arithmetic, Geography, Commercial Exercises, Mechanical Drawing, United States History and Book-Keeping.

St. Joseph's School.

2 Volumes: Mechanical Drawing, Arithmetic, Christian Doctrine, Phonography, Geography, United States History and Epistolary Correspondence.

Sts. Peter and Paul's School.

2 Volumes: Christian Doctrine, Bible History, Grammar, Physiology, Compositions and Geography.

CASCADE, IOWA, Diocese of Dubuque.

St. Mary's School.

5 Volumes: History, Christian Doctrine, Compositions, Grammar, Book-Keeping, Penmanship, Arithmetic, United States History and Physiology. Crochet-Work, Drawn-Work on Handkerchief, 2 Splashers, 2 Wreaths of Paper Flowers, 1 Fascinator, 2 Lamp Mats, 8 Tidies, Patch-Work, Child's Apron, Crochet Hood, Table Covers, 2 Wall Pockets, Child's Cape, Crochet Tidy, Child's Dress, Baby Dress and Quilt.

FESTINA, IOWA, Diocese of Dubuque.

St. Mary's School.

2 Volumes: Christian Doctrine, German, Geography, History, Arithmetic, Paraphrasing, Compositions, Translations, United States History, Epistolary Correspondence, Book-Keeping and Grammar.

FT. MADISON, IOWA, Diocese of Davenport.

St. Mary's School.

1 Volume: Bible History, Penmanship, Language, Arithmetic, Geography, United States History, Catechism, German; 1 Center Piece.

FOUNTAIN CITY, WIS., Diocese of La Crosse.

St. Mary's School.

1 Volume Drawing. 2 Volumes: Arithmetic, Geography, Compositions, Grammar, Language, Christian Doctrine, United States History, Physiology, Civil Government, Book-Keeping, Bible History and Penmanship.

HAVERHILL, IOWA, Diocese of Dubuque.

Immaculate Conception School.

1 Volume: German Exercises, Geography, Mechanical Drawing, Arithmetic and Christian Doctrine.

KEY WEST, IOWA, Diocese of Dubuque.

St. Joseph's School.

1 Volume: Arithmetic, Geography, Grammar, Physiology, History and Christian Doctrine.

LA CROSSE, WIS., Diocese of La Crosse.

Holy Cross School.

1 Volume Drawing. 2 Volumes: Christian Doctrine, Bible History, Language, Grammar, Translations, Compositions, United States History, Geography, Physiology and Penmanship.

Holy Trinity School.

1 Volume Drawing. 2 Volumes: Christian Doctrine, Bible History, Grammar, Language, Compositions, Translations, Arithmetic, Penmanship, Geography and United States History.

St. James' School.

1 Volume: Christian Doctrine, Bible History, Grammar, Arithmetic, Language, Compositions, United States History, Physiology, Civil Government, Book-Keeping, Commercial Law and Algebra.

St. John's School.

1 Volume Drawing. 2 Volumes: Arithmetic, Book-Keeping, Civil Government, Commercial Law, Geography, Penmanship, Physiology, United States History, Bible History, Compositions and Translations.

St. Joseph's Cathedral School.

4 Volumes: Christian Doctrine, Language, Grammar, Compositions, Arithmetic, Writing, Geography and United States History.

St. Mary's School.

1 Volume Drawing, 2 Volumes: Christian Doctrine, Bible History, Spelling, Language, Grammar, Compositions, Arithmetic, Writing, Geography and United States History.

St. Wenceslaus' School.

3 Volumes: Christian Doctrine, Bible History, Spelling, Language, Grammar, Translations, Arithmetic, Geography, United States History, Penmanship, Compositions, German and Grammar; 1 Volume Drawing.

LANSING, IOWA, Diocese of Dubuque.

Immaculate Conception School.

3 Volumes: Christian Doctrine, Arithmetic, Sacred History, Essays, Phonography, Language, Paraphrasing, Epistolary Correspondence, Penmanship, Business Forms, Civil Government, Book-Keeping, United States History, Physiology, Map and Mechanical Drawing.

ST. LUCAS, IOWA, Diocese of Dubuque.

St. Lucas' School.

1 Volume: German Exercises, Compositions, Translations, Dictations and Geography.

LUXEMBURG, IOWA, Diocese of Dubuque.

Holy Trinity School.

2 Volumes: Christian Doctrine, Arithmetic, German Exercises, United States History and Church History.

MT. CARMEL, IOWA, Diocese of Dubuque.

Sacred Heart School.

2 Volumes: German Exercises, Christian Doctrine, Arithmetic, Geography, Grammar, Compositions, Paraphrasing, Penmanship, Drawing.

NEILSVILLE, WIS., Diocese of Green Bay.

St. Mary's School.

1 Volume Freehand Drawing, 2 Volumes: Catechism, Language, Grammar, Compositions, Arithmetic, Translations, Penmanship, Geography and United States History.

NEW VIENNA, WIS., Diocese of Dubuque.

St. Boniface's School.

1 Fascinator, 1 Apron, 1 Suit of Boy's Clothes, 2 Pairs Mittens, 3 Pairs Socks, 4 Volumes: Christian Doctrine, Arithmetic, Grammar, Spelling, Maps and United States History.

ROCK VALLEY, IOWA, Diocese of Dubuque.

Parochial School.

25 Albums: Arithmetic, Geography, History, Physiology and Compositions.

SAUK CITY, WIS., Diocese of La Crosse.

St. Aloysius' School.

1 Volume Drawing, 2 Volumes: Arithmetic, Geography, Grammar, Drawing, Spelling, United States History, Catechism, German and Bible History.

SHERRILL'S MOUND, IOWA, Diocese of Dubuque.

Sts. Peter and Paul's School.

3 Volumes: Letters, Christian Doctrine, Arithmetic, Geography, History, German Translations, Business Forms, Civil Government and Botany.

ST. MARY'S RIDGE, WIS., Diocese of La Crosse.

St. Mary's School.

1 Volume Drawing, 2 Volumes: Drawing, Book-Keeping, Bible History, Compositions, Translations, Arithmetic, United States History, Language, Grammar, Geography, Physiology and Penmanship.

TEMPLETON, IOWA, Diocese of Dubuque.

Sacred Heart School.

1 Volume: German Exercises, Drawing and Arithmetic.

WEST POINT, IOWA, Diocese of Davenport.

St. Mary's School.

2 Volumes: Christian Doctrine, Bible History, Orthography, Arithmetic, Language Lessons, Grammar, Geography, United States History, Letter Writing, Penmanship and English and German Translations.

WILLEY, IOWA, Diocese of Dubuque.

Immaculate Conception School.

1 Volume Christian Doctrine, Arithmetic, Geography, Essays, Translations, Paraphrasing, Penmanship and Mechanical Drawing.

INDEX.

	PAGE.
Preface	1

ARCHDIOCESES.

Baltimore	169
Boston	174
Chicago	6
Cincinnati	176
Dubuque	13
Milwaukee	19
New Orleans	21
New York	24
Philadelphia	34
San Francisco	41
Santa Fe	183
St. Louis	178
St. Paul	184

DIOCESES.

Albany	185
Alton	186
Belleville	187
Brooklyn	51
Buffalo	58
Burlington	187
Cleveland	64
Columbus	188
Covington	71
Dallas	190
Davenport	190
Denver	74
Detroit	76
Fort Wayne	77
Galveston	191
Grand Rapids	192
Green Bay	86
Harrisburg	193
Helena	193
Jamestown	193
Kansas City (Mo.)	194

	PAGE.
La Crosse	91
Lincoln	194
Little Rock	195
Louisville	195
Manchester	93
Marquette	196
Mobile	196
Monterey and Los Angeles	197
Nashville	198
Natchez	95
Natchitoches	200
Nesqually	200
Newark	201
Ogdensburg	202
Omaha	202
Peoria	202
Pittsburgh	97
Providence	204
Richmond	204
Sacramento	205
San Antonio	206
Savannah	206
Sioux Falls	102
Springfield	208
St. Augustine	208
St. Joseph	209
Syracuse	210
Vincennes	210
Wheeling	214
Winona	214

VICARIATES-APOSTOLIC.

Arizona	214
Idaho	215
North Carolina	215

INDIVIDUAL EXHIBITS.

American Catholic Historical Society	167
Ashe Art School	166
Brother Leobert	162

	PAGE
Brother Alexis	162
Brother Innocentinian	166
Brother Arille	167
Cahokia, Ill.	162
Catholic Total Abstinence Union	167
Catholic Historical Collections of America	48
Catholic University of America	162
Christian Brothers (Paris)	166
Columbian Library of Catholic Authors	163
Caldwell, Miss M. G.	166
De Paradis, Rev. A	163
Dawson, Rev. Æ. M.	166
League of the Sacred Heart	167
Mt. St. Mary's College	165
Notre Dame University	218
Noebisch, Rev. N. H.	166
Papal Josephinum College	163
Perin's Shorthand Institute	165
St. Joseph's Normal College, Amawalk, N. Y.	162
St. Jerome's T. A. Union	165
Ward, Miss M. W.	165

RELIGIOUS ORDERS.

	PAGE
Brothers of the Christian Schools	104
Brothers of Mary	127
Brothers of the Sacred Heart	132
Benedictine Fathers	217
Congregation of the Holy Cross	218
Congregation of St. Viateur	226
Fathers of the Holy Ghost	222
Franciscan Brothers	223
Jesuit Fathers	224
Lazarist Fathers	226
Sisters of Charity (Emmitsburg)	134
Sisters of Charity (B. V. M.)	240
Sisters of Charity (Greensburg)	243
Sisters of Charity (Mt. St. Vincent)	244
Sisters of Charity (Mt. St. Joseph, Ohio)	247
Sisters of Charity (Leavenworth)	248

	PAGE
Sisters of Charity (Nazareth)	249
Sisters of Christian Charity	250
Congregation of Notre Dame (Montreal)	260
Sisters of Divine Providence	137
Franciscan Sisters	290
Sisters of the Good Shepherd	281
Gray Nuns	237
Sisters of the Holy Cross	237
Sisters of the Holy Family	282
Sisters of the Holy Names	282
Sisters of the Holy Child Jesus	281
Sisters of the Humility of Mary	283
Sisters of the Immaculate Heart of Mary	284
Sisters of the Incarnate Word	285
Sisters of Loretto	142
Ladies of the Sacred Heart	281, 239
Ladies of the Sacred Heart of Mary	238
Sisters of Mercy	251
Sisters of Notre Dame de Namur	265
Sisters of Notre Dame (Cleveland)	262
Sisters of Notre Dame (Cincinnati)	260
Sisters of the Precious Blood	155
Sisters of Providence (Vigo Co.)	157
Polish Felician Sisters of Detroit	235
Presentation Nuns	239
School Sisters of Notre Dame of Milwaukee and Baltimore	146
Sisters of St. Agnes	267
Sisters of St. Benedict	226
Sisters of St. Dominic	228
Sisters of St. Francis (Greensburg)	269
Sisters of St. Francis (Joliet)	268
Sisters of St. Francis (Oldenburg)	140
Sisters of St. Francis (Rochester, Minn.)	269
Sisters of St. Francis of P. A.	294
Sisters of St. Joseph	270
Sisters of St. Mary	279
The Poor Handmaids of Christ	285
Ursuline Nuns	286
Visitation Nuns	289

SAINT MARY'S COLLEGE

Brothers of the Christian Schools.

A BOARDING SCHOOL

For Young Men and
Boys Over Fourteen Years of Age.

FOUNDED AT
SAN FRANCISCO, 1863.

TRANSFERRED TO
OAKLAND, CAL., 1889.

. . TERMS . .

(PAYMENTS IN ADVANCE.)

Tuition, Board, Medical Attendance, Books, Stationery, Washing and Mending per term of five months, $160.00.

REV. BROTHER MICHAEL
Director.

REV. BROTHER BETTELIN,
President.

REV. BROTHER WALTER,
Secretary.

REV. BROTHER SABINIAN,
Treasurer.

ST. JOSEPH'S SOCIETY FOR THE NEGRO MISSIONS

ST. JOSEPH'S SEMINARY, BALTIMORE, MD.
EPIPHANY APOSTOLIC COLLEGE, HIGHLAND PARK, BALTIMORE, MD.

EIGHT MILLIONS OF THE AFRICAN RACE Are in this country, less than two hundred thousand of whom are members of the True Church. More than half do not profess any sort of Christianity, and of those who do, a great proportion follow but low and superstitious forms of the more vulgar Protestant sects. Yet the colored people are naturally intelligent, have admirable moral qualities, and are remarkably gifted by nature with the religious sense, being fond of participating in public worship, easily lead to accept the truths of revelation, and have a bright perception of the beauties of a moral and religious life.

THE HARVEST IS GREAT In one word, there is a ripe harvest of converts ready at our very door. A whole race of men, newly elevated to the dignity of American citizenship, whose career in the world is barely beginning, are willing to hear the Word of Life, and whose future depends on Holy Church's success among them.

The Epiphany Apostolic College.

Into this college youths are received for their college course, getting a good classical and scientific education. It is called apostolic to express its purpose of fostering the missionary spirit among its students.

THE CONDITIONS FOR ADMISSION.

1st. A decided inclination for the colored mission.
2d. Recommendation from a priest.
3d. A sound preparatory course in a good school.
4th. Good health and not less than fifteen years of age.
5th. Love of study and discipline, together with a docile and cheerful disposition.
6th. Besides supplying their own clothing and books, students are expected to pay as much as possible toward the expenses of tuition. The annual pension is fixed at $150, which will be modified as circumstances demand.

All these students are in preparation for

St. Joseph's Seminary

Which provides the aspirants for the negro missions with their course of divinity. Its students attend the lectures in philosophy, theology, natural sciences, liturgy, canon law, and Sacred Scriptures at St. Mary's Seminary, Baltimore, receiving, together with the diocesan clergy, the superior training imparted by the Sulpician Fathers, who are specially devoted to the training of priests. At St. Mary's, our young men are thrown in contact with the future pastors of a great part of the land. Friendships will be formed which are sure to tend, in one way or another, to the evangelization of the negroes and spread of the missionary spirit.

RULES OF ADMISSION.

1st. Students on entering become postulants for membership in St. Joseph's Society, as members of which they intend to devote their lives to the salvation of the negroes.
2d. Previous novicship or profession in any religious order or congregation, or dismissal from any missionary society, prevents admission.
3d. They must be fit to enter upon the study of philosophy, at least, and be able to follow the lectures at St. Mary's Seminary.
4th. Every postulant, if able, shall pay an entrance fee, and also provide himself with clothing, books and stationary until he becomes a full member of the society.

St. Joseph's Society is also composed of Laity.

"All persons contributing prayers and an annual alms, or giving substantial aid for the education of the missionaries, or for their work upon the mission, are affiliated members of St. Joseph's Society, and participate in all its merits and good works." The laity become members of St. Joseph's Society by means of our annual paper, "THE COLORED HARVEST." It is issued every October, at 25 cents yearly subscription. All of its subscribers are affiliated members of St. Joseph's Society, and thus, besides the special favors offered for themselves, are in touch with the whole missionary work of the society.

REV. J. R. SLATTERY,
ST. JOSEPH'S SEMINARY,
BALTIMORE, MD.

REV. D. MANLEY,
EPIPHANY APOSTOLIC COLLEGE,
HIGHLAND PARK, BALTIMORE, MD.

ST. JOSEPH'S ACADEMY, EMMITSBURG, MARYLAND.

ST. JOSEPH'S ACADEMY, EMMITSBURG, MD.

This Institution, for the education of young ladies, was established in 1809 and incorporated by the Legislature of Maryland in 1816. It is directed by the Sisters of Charity of St. Vincent de Paul. St. Joseph's is situated at the base of the Blue Ridge, in a valley noted for the picturesque beauty of its scenery and for the salubrity of its climate.

The buildings, spacious and commodious, are provided with all modern improvements—steam, gas, and an abundant supply of water. The lawns of the extensive and well-shaded play-ground are provided with croquet and tennis sets. Calisthenics and games of various sorts afford opportunity for physical training within doors. The spacious play-room presents a most attractive appearance, a prominent feature being an excellent piano, affording inexhaustible amusement.

The Sisters who conduct the establishment consider themselves conscientiously obliged to respond to the confidence which parents and guardians place in them, by giving their pupils a Christian and virtuous education; attending strictly to their intellectual improvement; cultivating that refinement of manners which will fit them for society, and giving them the physical care which they would receive under the parental roof.

The plan of instruction embraces a thorough and complete course in English. The modern languages are also taught. The pupils have at their command a library; an observatory, with telescope; chemical and philosophical apparatus, with the advantage of monthly lectures and experiments by an able professor. Special attention is paid to music, both vocal and instrumental; also to the art department. Letters of inquiry must be addressed to the

SUPERIORESS, ST. JOSEPH'S ACADEMY, EMMITSBURG, MD.

MT. ST. JOSEPH YOUNG LADIES' ACADEMY.

This institution is under the care of the Sisters of St. Joseph. The Course of Studies includes all the branches of a useful and Christian education.

Terms, Regulations as to Uniforms, etc., are given in full in Catalogue, for which apply **to**

MOTHER SUPERIOR,

Mt. St. Joseph, Chestnut Hill, Philadelphia.

URSULINE ACADEMY,

12th St. between Russell and Ann Aves.,

ST. LOUIS, MO.

THIS INSTITUTION, opened in 1849, is conducted by members of the Ursuline Order, one of the oldest of the Religious Orders founded for the education of youth; an Order, which, since its foundation in the early part of the sixteenth century, has devoted itself solely and unceasingly to the noble work marked out by its venerated foundress.

The plan of education combines every advantage for both intellectual and moral culture.

TERMS.

Board, with Tuition in English and German, and in all kinds of Plain and Ornamental Needle-Work,	per annum, $150.00
Use of Bedding,	" " 12.00
Laundry,	" " 24.00
Drawing and Painting,	" " 20.00
Tuition on Harp,	" " 80.00
Tuition on Piano, and use of instrument,	" " 48.00
Tuition on the various other instruments in vogue, each,	" " 40.00
Private Lessons in Vocal Music,	" " 24.00
Tuition in French,	" " 20.00
Use of Library,	" " 2.00
School Books, etc., at current prices.	
Graduating Fee,	" " 10.00

Wax Work, Hair Flowers, etc., form extra charges. Those who wish, are given lessons in the Culinary Department.

GENERAL REGULATIONS.

The Scholastic Year begins on the First of September, and ends the latter part of June. For convenience, it is divided into four terms or quarters, commencing, respectively, September 1st, November 15th, February 1st and April 15th.

Payments for each session are to be made in advance. Pupils are received at any time, charges counting from date of entrance. No deduction is made for temporary absence from the Academy, except in case of protracted illness.

All written communications to and from the Academy are subject to inspection.

A black uniform is worn on Sundays and Thursdays (visiting days); hence, in addition to the neat, seasonable wardrobe with which every good housewife keeps her children furnished, each pupil must be provided with a black dress; no particular make or material is designated. They are also required to have a white and a black bobbinet veil, and a furnished toilet-box. For table use: Napkins, a knife, fork, goblet, table and teaspoon.

None of these articles will be furnished by the Institution, unless special arrangements have been made, and money sufficient for the purpose deposited with the Treasurer; nor will expenditures be made for dress, or cash advanced to pupils at any time, except on the foregoing conditions.

Difference of religion is no obstacle to the admission of pupils, provided that for the maintenance of order, they are willing to conform exteriorly to the established routine.

BROTHERS of the CHRISTIAN SCHOOLS

THE AIMS, THE NEEDS, AND THE CREDENTIALS OF THE INSTITUTE.

In response to a query as to the immediate aims of the Brothers throughout the world, the following will suffice:

WE—the Brothers of the Christian Schools—are preparing young men to cooperate heartily with the Reverend Clergy in giving a thoroughly practical Christian education to boys, wherever we have schools. For this purpose we receive good boys of fair talent, and of fourteen to seventeen years of age; we give them a five years' training of study and prayer. At the end of the course they are expected to take certificates for elementary teaching. They are then appointed assistant teachers in the parish schools of which we have charge, and so continue until their experience enables them to act as principals. We also receive zealous young men of liberal education, who are anxious to consecrate their lives to the Christian education of others. These, after the ordinary trials, are classed according to their ability. The work will be extended just in proportion as we get fitting subjects. All qualified are heartily invited to come.

What are our credentials? First, the HOLY FATHER, BENEDICT XIII., in his Bull of Approbation, says:—

"We, by Apostolic Authority, approve and confirm the said Institute of the Brothers of the Christian Schools, and the said Rules. . . . The Brothers shall imbue the minds of their pupils with the Gospel and Christian precepts; and, for this purpose, they shall teach Catechism for half an hour daily, they shall teach the Commandments of God and of the Church, and all things necessary for salvation."

The Gloriously Reigning Pontiff, His Holiness Leo XIII., desires "that this most advantageous work of the Novitiates should flourish more and more; and being moved by the earnest requests that have been made on behalf of this work," His Holiness grants special spiritual benefits to those who encourage this most excellent object. Moreover, His Holiness renews "all the spiritual favors" accorded by His Holiness, Pius IX., of blessed memory.

We could multiply letters from bishops in every part of the Christian world; but the fact that we have schools in nearly all Christian countries, and that we can not enter any diocese unless invited by the Ordinary, shows how we stand with the Hierarchy in all countries. Our life demands devotedness and self-sacrifice. We rise early, and are engaged in prayer, meditation, and the Holy Mass until breakfast. After breakfast, until school opens, we study. After school, until nine o'clock, we resume prayer and study, except an hour and a half for supper and recreation. On the weekly holiday, half the day is devoted to out-door exercise. Any youths or young men who may wish to join our organization for building up a new generation of zealous Catholics can make application to

BROTHER JUSTIN, VISITOR,
Manhattan College, New York City.
Or to De La Salle Institute, 108 West 59th St., New York City.

BROTHER PAULIAN, VISITOR,
Christian Brothers' College, St. Louis, Mo.

BROTHER ROMUALD, VISITOR,
Ammendale, Md.

BROTHER BETTELIN, VISITOR,
St. Mary's College, Oakland, Cal.

TEXT-BOOKS AND EDUCATIONAL WORKS

PUBLISHED BY THE

Brothers of the Christian Schools.

Reading—Primer, Easy Steps, Introductory Reader, Elementary Reader, Intermediate Reader, Advanced Reader, Christian Duty.

Spelling—Elementary Speller, Pronouncing Speller, Etymology.

Arithmetic—Primary Arithmetic, Elementary Arithmetic, Commercial Arithmetic, Complete Arithmetic. Key to same.

Grammar—First Lessons in English Grammar, Principles of English Grammar. Key to same.

Book-Keeping—Questions on Book-Keeping, Students' Manual of Book-Keeping. Key to same.

Writing—Complete Course in Nine Books.

Drawing—Freehand Drawing, Complete in Ten Books; Linear Drawing, Complete in Seven Books. Teacher's part to same.

History and Geography—In course of preparation.

Literature—Books and Reading, Development of Old English Thought, Phases of Thought and Criticism, Philosophy of English Literature.

Algebra and Geometry—In course of preparation.

Philosophy—Christian Philosophy, Aristotle and the Christian Church.

Teaching—Notes on Teaching; Managing of Christian Schools or Manual for Organizing, Managing and Teaching School; Exercises of Piety for Class; Reflections, or Points on which to advise Pupils; The Blessed De La Salle and His Educational Methods.

Devotional—Scholar's Manual of the Sacred Heart; Series of Meditation Books for every day of the week, in Nine Volumes; Life of the Blessed De La Salle.

N. B.—For Price List or further information, address:

F. S. C. PROCURE,

50 Second Street, NEW YORK CITY, N. Y.

www.ingramcontent.com/pod-product-compliance
Lightning Source LLC
Chambersburg PA
CBHW022020240426
43667CB00042B/994